Parody
and
Decadence

Parody and Decadence

Laforgue's
*Moralités
légendaires*

Michele Hannoosh

Ohio State University Press
COLUMBUS

Copyright © 1989 by the Ohio State University Press.
All rights reserved.

Library of Congress Cataloging-in-Publication Data

Hannoosh, Michele, 1954–
    Parody and decadence : Laforgue's Moralités légendaires / Michele Hannoosh.
    p.   cm.
    Bibliography: p.
    Includes index.
    ISBN 0-8142-0480-5 (alk. paper)
    ISBN 978-0-8142-5323-6

    1. Laforgue, Jules, 1860–1887. Moralités légendaires.
2. Decadence (Literary movement)—France. 3. Parody.
I. Title.
PQ2323.L8M634   1989
843'.8—dc19   89-2996
                                                       CIP

The paper in this book meets the guidelines for permanence and durability of the Committee on Production Guidelines for Book Longevity of the Council on Library Resources.

9 8 7 6 5 4 3 2 1

For my parents

Contents

	Acknowledgments	ix
1	The *Moralités légendaires* and a Theory of Parody	1
	Introduction 1	
	History and Theory 9	
	Features of Parodic Narrative 26	
2	Decadence and Parody	31
	Aspects of Decadence 38	
	The Other Side of Decadence. Parody in the Late Nineteenth Century 61	
3	*Hamlet, ou les suites de la piété filiale*	74
4	*Le Miracle des Roses*	104
5	*Lohengrin, fils de Parsifal*	128
6	*Salomé*	148
7	*Persée et Andromède, ou le plus heureux des trois*	170
8	*Pan et la Syrinx, ou l'invention de la flûte à sept tuyaux*	194
	Conclusion	216
	Notes	223
	Bibliography	257
	Index	267

Acknowledgments

This book was written during my tenure as a Mellon Fellow in the Society of Fellows in the Humanities at Columbia University. To the Society I am indebted not only for the provision of free time, so necessary for the research and composition of a book, but also for three years of inspiring, productive, and thoroughly enjoyable exchange with others committed to the study of the humanities. I would like to thank all those, too numerous to mention by name, who listened patiently to the early versions of this work at the Society's seminars and contributed by their questions and comments to its elaboration.

I am grateful as well to the many individuals who offered information, advice, and encouragement at different states of the project, and indeed in my work on Laforgue overall. James Hiddleston and Steven Winspur read the manuscript in its entirety, and Claude Bernard portions of it. My husband, Richard, provided detailed comments on chapter one, and countless discussions with him helped me to refine the theory of parody developed therein. J.-L. Debauve graciously answered my many questions on Laforgue's life and work. David Arkell did likewise, and his ongoing interest in my work on Laforgue is greatly appreciated. To R. G. Cohn, too, go thanks for his continued help and encouragement. Finally, an anonymous reviewer for the Ohio State University Press made some penetrating comments on the whole and saved me from at least a few ludicrous mistakes.

I would like to thank the National Endowment for the Humanities for twice providing funds for travel to Paris to consult the collections of the Bibliothèque Nationale, the Bibliothèque littéraire Jacques Doucet, and the Musée Gustave Moreau, which together furnished the material for chapter two. An early version of chapter six appeared previously in the *Romanic Review* and has been substantially revised; a portion of chapter seven was published in *Laforgue aujourd'hui* (Paris, José Corti, 1988).

With customary humility and self-mockery, Laforgue informed his friend Teodor de Wyzewa of his intention to dedicate to him, *faute de mieux,* his volume of *Moralités,* "cette chose falote," in thanks. The dedication of this book is made in the same spirit.

I

The Moralités légendaires *and a Theory of Parody*

Introduction

In June of 1886, Jules Laforgue wrote to his friend, Gustave Kahn: "Mon volume de nouvelles, tu en connais le principe: de vieux canevas brodés d'âmes à la mode."[1] In these terms, he described his only collection of stories, the *Moralités légendaires,* one of the two great products of his last years, and one of the most ingenious prose creations of the late nineteenth century. In particular, he here identifies the controlling principle of the tales—introducing a modern spirit into established stories of literary tradition, a major device of parody. Indeed, the *Moralités* are parodies that freely modernize major stories of literary history, giving them new meaning according to the spirit, tastes, and characteristics of contemporary life. They take as their model a specific work, myth, legend, or group of works, and refashion it in accordance with the preoccupations of the time, particularly those that Laforgue associated with Decadence in its 1880s sense, the avant-garde movement of which he felt himself a part. There has never been a study of the *Moralités,* yet they offer at once a brilliant analysis, critique, and example of Decadent writing which can enhance our conception of that movement. (I shall discuss the characteristics of 1880s Decadence in chapter two.) Moreover, they have considerable implications for our understanding of parody itself in both theory and practice. In reworking and modernizing well-known stories in this way, the

Moralités realize the anachronistic and intertextual principle of parody: they contain the essential elements of the genre, employ its characteristic devices and narrative techniques, and perform its distinctive critical and self-reflexive functions.

Much work has been done in recent years to elaborate a theory of parody adequate to the history of the term's usage and the variety of particular examples.[2] These studies have usefully concentrated on parody as a metafictional form, that is, containing a commentary on fiction from within a fiction, exposing the processes of artistic creation as it realizes them. However, in probing the question, they also raise problems which a study of the *Moralités* as parodies can help to resolve. Laforgue's stories shed light on such issues as the nature of the parody's target, the role of humor, the relation of the parody to the work parodied, the function of parody in the avant-garde, the relation between it and an aesthetic of originality and genius, the self-sufficiency of a form customarily considered dependent, and the reflexive action of the parody upon itself. Even more importantly, they bring to light features of the genre that have not previously been identified or formulated, such as the creative implications of parody, its self-critical aspects and its intelligibility in the absence of the original. They thus provide a solid basis for investigating the procedures of parody and for developing a theory sufficiently general and flexible to account for the diversity of its forms over time, but precise enough to have useful meaning in defining a single genre.

Any genuine theory is an abstraction from practical usage. The one presented here comes from a study of many parodies but derives particularly from the *Moralités,* which offer some unusual and illuminating features; in them, Laforgue exploits the creative implications of the genre to the full. Some aspects of the theory manifest themselves conspicuously in Laforgue's volume and are formulated here for the first time; nevertheless, in retrospect we can see them at work in other parodies, as I shall indicate accordingly. Implied by the genre's definition, consistent with its inner logic, and realized in its practice, they legitimately take their place as features of the genre, to be drawn upon or not, according to the parodist's purposes. Thus the theory that follows applies to parody overall, not merely to its Laforguian, or even Decadent, variety. As will become clear, it is radical in several respects. But while theory, being an abstraction, is usually radical, by the same token it necessarily benefits from a certain indulgence: it need not, indeed cannot, describe works of art in their complexity but only articulates general rules and their implications, which the individual artist inherits in choosing a particular form. These allow a certain choice: not every potential aspect of parody, for instance, will appear in a given example. From the highly innovative and creative parody of the *Moralités,* we can derive a theory that revises and enhances our understanding of the genre and is valid for parody as a whole.

With respect to method, my analysis of parody refers frequently to an intertextual, and specifically Riffaterrean, model of literary theory.[3] This does not simply reflect a critical ideology but is proposed by the nature of the subject itself: parody is overtly and, by its very definition, necessarily intertextual. Like any literary theory, this one can be adequately demonstrated and tested only in the context of a complete (or at least extended) work, not merely, as is frequently the case, applied to the idea behind the work or to particular moments in it.[4] The *Moralités* suit this task especially well because a parodic structure fully informs each of the stories and is responsible for its sense. Laforgue's tales are disconnected, allusive, and difficult to interpret (or even, sometimes, to follow). In analyzing them, I present them in a perhaps deceptively coherent narrative in order to bring out the relations of significance, but try to preserve his deliberate narrative structure as well. Thus I proceed according to the plot whenever possible and reconstruct it when necessary for comprehension. Every page of his volume contains some element relevant to the parody—a pun, an incongruity, an anachronism; it is impossible and unnecessary to include them all. Instead I concentrate on those aspects which are particularly important for the working of parody in the story and the sense deriving from it, and for our understanding of the features and possibilities of parody in general.

Before I proceed to the theory proper, the place of parody in Laforgue's *oeuvre* as a whole deserves some consideration. Although he frequently described the *Moralités* as a modern rewriting of old and familiar stories,[5] he never once referred to them as parodies but consistently called them *nouvelles*. This neglect is significant, because it suggests to what extent the idea of modernization governing the *Moralités* dominates his art and his aesthetic thought overall. For Laforgue, modernization applies not exclusively to parody, but to literature and art in general. It motivates his work from the very beginning and is one of the most central and persistent concerns of his imagination: the relation of a past tradition to a modern, original creation. Moreover, the formula of reworking art of the past according to the present articulates the conception of modern art put forward in his essays on aesthetics. This has not received adequate attention, for his emphasis on the new and the original would seem rather to discredit works of the tradition and place all aesthetic value in a negation of the past. I have argued elsewhere, however, that such a view is erroneous; his poetic and critical works provide ample evidence to disprove it.[6] The important concept in his aesthetics is not revolution but *evolution,* which the philosophical readings of his twentieth year had firmly implanted in his mind. The idea and the term itself recur constantly in his criticism, notes, and private journals, most notably in the theory and defense of modern art contained in his essay on Impressionism and *L'Art moderne en Allemagne*. Only one other concept is as prevalent as evolution and far from being a rival it is on the contrary its necessary companion—originality. Indeed, Laforgue defines originality within the context of an evolving history of art in which certain received and sometimes inescapable conventions are variously maintained, neglected, subverted, or, most often, transformed. He emphasizes the important role played by works of the past in the development of man's aesthetic sensibility and thus their significance in the ongoing process of artistic creation.

Laforgue's belief in the *necessity* of this process, however, removes from evolution any sense of ameliorative progress. In refuting the notion of a fixed standard of beauty and a scale of artistic value over the ages, he insists, in his aesthetic essays, on the variety of forms and manners, all necessary and valuable, that constitute the history of art.[7] Modern forms could not have arisen without what preceded them, and thus the more recent should not be regarded as superior to the past; the new is merely the most appropriate creation for the contemporary world.[8] Even Laforgue's most formally radical poetic work, the free verse *Derniers Vers*, must be read against a background of existing lyric poetry, from specific allusions to Heine and Baudelaire to more general Romantic conventions, which Laforgue revises to serve his particular purpose: to make the *Derniers Vers* a truly modern love poem, expressing the problems, and the few pleasures, of love in the pessimistic world of the 1880s.

The anachronistic principle of modernization informs Laforgue's work from the beginning. For example, his earliest surviving composition, the two-act play *Tessa* (1877), transports stereotypical concerns of the late nineteenth century, notably Schopenhauerian pessimism and misogyny, into the Italian Renaissance. The allusions are explicit and, in a manner typical of the later *Moralités*, freely drawn from a variety of sources of different periods, including Dante, *Le Barbier de Séville*, and Schopenhauer.[9] Using a more orthodox method of parody, the trivialization of heroic figures, a prose piece of 1879 entitled "Chronique stygianopolitaine"[10] depicts everyday life in the underworld among the greats of history and legend, in the manner of Lucian's *Dialogues of the Dead*, and, like *Tessa*, anachronistically refers to the contemporary world. Proserpine, Pluto, Isocrates, Cicero, Aeneas, Mohammed, François Ier, Napoleon, Madame de Pompadour, Baudelaire, and others live side by side; the 1879 war between England and Zululand is reenacted in Charon's boat as he transports a cargo of quarreling Englishmen and Zulus across the river into the underworld; Proserpine reads the novels of the popular nineteenth-century sentimental novelist Xavier de Montépin; and all is recounted in the colloquial schoolboy language of 1879.

Even in Laforgue's less explicitly anachronistic works, the principle of modernization plays a significant role. For instance, however little the *Complaintes* resemble medieval *complaintes*, as a volume they are based on the union of an old poetic form (and its connotations) and specifically modern themes. The title of his collection of poems, *L'Imitation de Notre-Dame la Lune* presents a new *Imitation de Notre Seigneur Jésus-Christ;* moreover it ironically transforms one chaste lady into another, the Virgin Mary into Diana the moon, and substitutes a cult of the moon and a religion of Decadence for Christianity. Similarly, *Des Fleurs de Bonne Volonté* plays on *Les Fleurs du mal* and the biblical "hommes de bonne volonté," with a quiet reminder of the most famous, though hardly good, *Volonté* of the nineteenth century, Schopenhauer's Will. This title too is ironic (*some* flowers rather than Baudelaire's general *les*), specifically regarding the indecisive and irresolute speaker of the poems, whose good will is called into question by the pessimistic Schopenhauerian sense of the term. The speaker's *volonté* may in fact produce a few flowers, but in matters of love it definitely cannot bring him the peace that men of good will are supposed to deserve.[11]

Laforgue's long-held taste for using the device of modernization in his poems, and his theoretical defense of an evolutionary history of art, help to explain why, after many unsuccessful attempts to write prose throughout his career, he produced his tales in the form of parodies.[12] The *Moralités* are the logical outcome of two of his oldest aesthetic concerns: the relation between a received tradition and an aesthetic of originality, and the role of modern art within the entire, ongoing history of art. Parody incorporates the evolution and modernization that he sought in all artistic creation, as well as the ironic humor characteristic of his work generally; by writing parodies, Laforgue fulfilled his stated objective of creating a set of distinctively modern stories. The title itself, while not playing on a specific work, directly conveys the idea of legendary stories retold according to the modern sensibility, for both of its terms reflect the importance of the past to the present.[13] It calls attention to the "moralité," or general moral lesson, to be derived from them, and thus to their universal, timeless applicability, including their relevance to the contemporary world—an idea implicit in *légendaires* itself. Since it is also a medieval theatrical form, *moralité* is anachronistic in the title of a modern work and suggests the anachronism on which the parodies will depend. More specifically, the title topically plays on the pervasive use, and abuse, of legendary subjects in the arts of this period; thus it contains a veiled allusion to the parody's target, Decadence.[14]

The *Moralités légendaires* and a Theory of Parody

It is significant in this context that two of the stories (*Persée et Andromède* and *Pan et la Syrinx*) take as their original a work renowned for its parody, Ovid's *Metamorphoses,* which like them freely reenacts famous legends of antiquity with humor and irony, gives them a new interpretation, places them in a different context, and highlights the theme of love. Laforgue alludes to Ovid's poem elsewhere in the *Moralités* as well, thus paying direct tribute to a great predecessor in the genre and suggesting the relation of his own work to it. Moreover, the *Moralités* frequently refer to the *opéra-comique* (Persée is an "opéra-comique" hero, a "phare d'opéra-comique" lights up the sea in *Salomé*, the town of *Le Miracle des Roses* has an "opéra-comique" atmosphere, etc.), thereby evoking specifically the modern retelling of legend, as in the works of Offenbach, and more generally the parodic status of the *opéra-comique* with respect to the *opéra*.

The relevance of parody for Laforgue's aesthetic of the modern raises two points important for a theory of the genre. First, it undermines the claim that parody, when applied to contemporary works or conventions, is inherently conservative, criticizing its modern object and seeking thereby to return to more traditional norms and values.[15] The *Moralités* provide an effective counter to this, for Laforgue, in mocking the modern artistic sensibility and its conventions of expression, cannot in any way be seen as advocating a return to earlier ones; rather, his parody makes fun of contemporary art in order to advance it beyond itself to even newer forms. Significantly, the most frequent object of his parody is also that which he considered the newest of creations, namely his own work. In Laforgue's hands, parody becomes a vehicle for the most forward avant-garde and takes its place at the very head of the creative line. This function of parody is implied by its essential self-reflexivity, which I shall discuss more fully later; in mocking a target, contemporary or otherwise, parody must also mock itself, and in proposing something different, it must, by the logic of its own structure, allow for the reworking, reinterpretation, or even parody, of what it has itself proposed. Parody lets nothing rest secure, including what it seems to endorse, and thus is theoretically inconsistent with conservatism.

Second, Laforgue's aesthetic demonstrates that parody is fully compatible with a "Romantic" aesthetic of genius and originality, despite assertions to the contrary.[16] His evolutionary theory of art sought to justify genius and originality precisely in terms of a continuous but everchanging process, realized and represented in the history of art. According to this view, genius is a manifestation in the individual of the law that governs all aspects of the universe, including the evolution of artistic forms and manners; the artist of genius is the one who is original, reveals something new within this process, and thereby takes a step forward in the aesthetic evolution of man. There is no conflict in Laforgue between parody and originality; both entail a reusage and transformation of existing art and a redefinition of the conventions established by it. It is not surprising that the great originality of his own parodies was recognized in all contemporary accounts of the book.

Originality was in fact one of Laforgue's most urgent concerns in writing the *Moralités*, as many of his letters attest.[17] He resolved to make the tales different from those of the two major short-story writers of the period, Villiers and Maupassant.[18] The *nouvelle*, conducive in its brevity to a poetic prose and an aesthetic of the ephemeral,[19] suited his formal needs well. The principle of modernization and the comic element necessary for parody allowed him to realize his customary humor and self-irony in a thoroughly novel form, in keeping with his philosophy of artistic creation, and to produce a prose work consistent with his theory of the modern. The *Moralités* represent Laforgue's latest—and, as history determined, final—response to the aesthetic and formal challenge posed by his own theory of modern art.[20]

The order of the stories has provoked some discussion because Edouard Dujardin, who brought out the first edition shortly after Laforgue's death, reversed the last two, placing *Pan et la Syrinx* before *Persée et Andromède*. Why he did this is unknown; modern editors have rightly restored Laforgue's original order. This follows exactly the order of composition, except that *Salomé,* the first one written, is placed fourth, a detail explained by the fact that Laforgue revised it considerably in 1886, between *Lohengrin* and *Persée et Andromède,* precisely in the place it now occupies. Thus the "architecture" of the *Moralités* seems to follow the rather prosaic plan of chronology.[21]

The stories are written in an unusually complicated prose, marked by allusions, puns, anachronism, syntactical obscurities, sound play, hermetic imagery, incongruous juxtapositions, a consistently bewildering association of ideas, unexpected authorial asides, an uncertain point of view, and an inconsistent time scheme—hence their difficulty but also their brilliance. Laforgue creates a subjective narrative which communicates the characters' thoughts and attitudes through an ostensibly objective, third-person one, but he interrupts it constantly with authorial asides, apostrophes, and ironic commentary. Reading the tales in terms of the features of parody will explain many of these difficulties and help us to understand them not only as parodies of other works, but also as coherent and significant works in themselves which exploit other texts for their own creative ends. It will emerge that these apparent eccentricities are far from gratuitous and are actually vital sources of the parody and its effects—its humor, its criticism, and its self-criticism. They belong among the special devices of the genre and function as signals, warning the reader that the work in general, or a particular moment in it, should be read as parody. This approach will also account for one of the main themes of the *Moralités*, inherent in their form as parodies: the intrusion of illusion into reality, or art into life.

History and Theory

The long and protean history of parody complicates the effort to define it adequately, to embrace the many works exemplifying it and yet describe a single, distinct phenomenon. The divergent conclusions of those studies which have attempted this, and the contradictions which they contain, bear witness to the problem. Various solutions have been proposed from the history of parody, but none provides a comprehensive formula: transposition of a serious text into a low style, application of a noble style to a low subject, application of a serious text, either verbatim or transformed, to a low subject, imitation of a text's general thought and style with exaggeration of its characteristics, and quotation or imitation of any text, but applied to a new context which gives it a different meaning.[22] Even the status of parody as a genre has been challenged, and "mode" preferred instead. T. Shlonsky, for example, argues that parody is in one sense generically neutral, since, as an imitation, it takes its generic characteristics from the genre of its object; and that it is in another sense antigeneric, in so far as it distorts its object and thereby aims to "disrealize" the norms which the original tries to realize.[23] While I would agree with this, it does not account for parodies that use a different genre from their original, a frequent phenomenon in the modern period especially; "genre" would include such cases. This study will retain "genre," understood as designating a literary category that has identifiable characteristics and follows given rules of operation.[24]

In addition, the profusion of terms commonly associated and indeed confused with parody—travesty, pastiche, burlesque, caricature, satire, even forgery—further crowds the picture and complicates the theorist's task. The distinctions among these have elicited much commentary, for usage is inconsistent; the terms derive from different traditions and periods, and in casual contexts are often used interchangeably. G. Genette, for example, proposes a schema of categories based on the function of the new text (playful, satirical, serious) and the relation of the new text to the old (transformation or imitation), but these break down when he applies them to existing works; L. Hutcheon distinguishes travesty and burlesque from parody by their element of ridicule, but parody can surely contain ridicule also, as we shall see; M. Rose points out where the terms overlap.[25] The problems are real and extremely difficult to resolve, especially since the methods of one form may legitimately be applied to the purposes of another: for example, parody may be used in pastiche or satire, and vice versa. To differentiate all of these rigorously would overextend this study, although I shall discuss satire below since it has particular significance for the theory of parody.[26] I shall use the term parody to denote the comical reworking and transformation of another text by distortion of its characteristic features.[27] The *Moralités* in particular belong to the type described earlier which involve the modernization of well-known stories. Their comic aspect derives from the disjunction between the seriousness of the original and the highly exaggerated contemporary context into which it is reworked.

Although the early history of the word should not necessarily carry final authority in the dispute over what parody is, it can nevertheless indicate some basic features of its practice. The connotations ascribed in antiquity to parody as a generic term can provide a useful point of departure from which to trace its various later applications. Ancient usage is only sparsely documented but suggests that parody meant, literally, an imitative song, and, functionally, mock-heroic poetry. Aristotle uses *parodia* in this latter sense at *Poetics* 2.1448a13, where he cites Hegemon of Thasos as the first parodist. With Hegemon he pairs Nicochares, author of a mock-epic poem, the *Deiliad*, an *Iliad* of cowards. There Aristotle makes parody one of the forms of mimesis and distinguishes it with respect to the object that it represents; parody, like comedy, represents men as worse than those we know in life,[28] whereas epic, like tragedy, represents them as better. Parody would thus belong, for him, in the realm of the comic.

This point is significant, for it provides strong evidence against the view that *parodia* did not originally imply a comic element. To maintain that the word had no comic implications until the scholiasts of later antiquity gave it one, as has been suggested, is to ignore the relation between parody and comedy signalled here, by the first literary theorist, at the earliest appearance of the term.[29] Athenaeus' use of *parodia* supports Aristotle's.[30] Originally, then, the term designated a mock epic, a poem in hexameter verse, employing epic diction and style but comically applied to a trivial subject or set of circumstances, as in the Hellenistic *Battle of the Frogs and Mice*.[31] Although the etymology of a term is often misleading or meaningless in defining the genre that it denotes, the components of *parodia* convey to some degree its practical sense, as others have observed, that is, something sung in imitation but with a difference: from *ode*, singing, and *para*, meaning, on the one hand, nearness, consonance, derivation, imitation, and resemblance, and, on the other, transgression, opposition, and difference.[32]

Even more significantly, *parodia* may have originated as a parodic transformation of the word designating the epic performance itself, *rhapsodia*.[33] Genette proposes that, because of its formulaic style, epic necessarily leaves itself open to parody and contains inherently the possibility and materials of self-parody, which occurs if the poet involuntarily causes laughter; formulaic composition operates according to the same principle as parody, that is, reusage and repetition, or one text applied to different objects, contexts, or intentions. "En vérité, le style épique . . . est constamment en instance, voire en position d'autopastiche et d'autoparodie involontaires. Le pastiche et la parodie sont inscrits dans le texte même de l'épopée".[34] But this view is highly questionable. Formulaic epic such as Homer's certainly lends itself to parody, since the mechanization of its style is, as it were, already provided by the repetition of formulae.[35] However, parody is not "toujours déjà présente et vivante"[36] in it any more than in any other work of art; the repetition of epic formulae does not in itself have a comic element, voluntary or involuntary, for it is the *normal* (and thus expected) means of composition. Repetition is only remarkable, and ludicrous, in a text where it is not a generic convention.[37] A formulaic text may be easily parodied by others but is no more susceptible to involuntary self-parody than any other work of art.

The association of *parodia* with mock-epic—the comic imitation and distortion of epic style by its application to a low subject—suggests that parody, in its earliest use, already possessed the characteristics now considered essential to it: imitation, transformation or distortion, and a comic element.[38] Although this last was not included in the etymology of the word, it nevertheless belonged to it in its Aristotelian use as mock-epic, and, as others have noted, was later emphasized by the Romans.[39] In his section on wit, Quintilian cites parody specifically as a comic procedure ("verses resembling well-known lines, called *parody*").[40] Cicero, following Demetrius, makes the insertion of verses and proverbs, as they are or slightly changed, a device of wit, though he does not call this parody.[41] In the *Rhetoric*, Aristotle had described the alteration of verses as a device of wit and given as an example a parody of an epic hexameter.[42] The comic element did not necessarily imply criticism, although parody could act as a form of criticism through its humor or be used for satirical purposes, as sometimes in the plays of Aristophanes. In sum, a basic definition of parody, consistent with ancient and modern usage, includes the imitation and distortion, or transformation, of a well-known work with comic effect and critical purposes of some kind, even if only self-critical ones. (I shall discuss the critical purposes of parody in some detail shortly.) For now, let it suffice to say that the criticism need not aim at the work parodied but may rather target the distortion itself. The object of the parody can be one text, a school, a manner, a genre, a group of works on the same theme, an author's entire corpus, and so on. So, although in the following discussion I shall refer, for the sake of convenience, to one work only as the object of the parody, it is frequently less definite than this practice would imply.

As essential features of the genre, parodic imitation and its comic element deserve clarification, particularly in view of the position recently adopted by Hutcheon, who challenges the comic element and criticizes the notion of parody as a kind of quotation.[43] Parody imitates, "quotes," or alludes to another work to such an extent as to raise expectations in the reader, but by its distortion it disappoints those expectations, usually quite pointedly, and thereby produces a comic effect. The "quotation" is clearly not *verbatim,* nor the imitation exact, due to the essential transformation involved in parody—distortion of stylistic traits, inversion of values, transposition into a new, incongruous, and frequently trivial, context, and so on. Moreover this difference between the original work and the parody, between the expectations raised for a work and the disappointment of those expectations, ensures the presence of a comic element, which may imply satire, derision, or simply humor, for which the deception of expectations has always been, as Aristotle formulated it, a basic rhetorical device.[44]

The *Moralités* confirm this aspect of the theory. Some form of the comic, from playfulness to ridicule, is a necessary element of all parody and is implied by its basic structure of *contra exspectationem*. Hutcheon has challenged the "stubborn retention of . . . ridicule or of the comic" as elements in the definition of parody, in favor of a more neutral irony which she considers less "restrictive" and more appropriate to the relation of twentieth-century art forms to their models.[45] But this argument seems to me to contain serious flaws. First, irony is a form of the comic, a species within a larger genus, and does not alone suffice to describe the range and effects of parody. Second, it is equally misleading to equate the comic with ridicule and derision, which are, rather, varieties of it;[46] the comic understood broadly includes also the neutrally playful attitude that she does allow for parody, the "zero degree of aggressivity," the "lightest of mockeries."[47] Parody need not ridicule either its model or its target, and in fact frequently does not, as a survey of examples reveals, but it must have a comic component.[48] The *Moralités,* as we shall see, provide a clear example of parodies that display no aggression toward either the works parodied or their more contemporary Decadent target but rather treat them with humor and irony. Here Bakhtin's analysis of the various forms of "carnivalesque literature" is especially useful, for he attributes a wide range to the comic, from the harsher "retentissant" to the attenuated "résorbé," with humor and irony belonging to the latter.[49] A definition of parody as simply the remodeling of familiar forms to say something serious, that is, emptied of its comic element, as Hutcheon holds,[50] is inconsistent with the origin and history of both the term and the genre. Moreover, it allows parody to apply to inappropriate forms, such as purely deferential or reverential homage. The comic element of parody usually involves a certain sympathy, in keeping, as we shall see, with the parodist's ambivalent attitude toward the parodied work, implied by the form itself; it need not contain any cynicism or envy at all. As D. Baguley notes, the degree of "comic incongruity" ranges "from flagrant travesty to effects of debased recontextualization," the latter bordering on neutral intertextuality.[51] Its comic effect depends on our recognition of the distortion or transformation, and our pleasure in it on our perception of the relative justice of the mockery toward its object.[52]

The nature of the comic element is important, for it clarifies the status of the parody's target. Although the target has normally been equated with the work parodied, some theorists have suggested otherwise. F. Lelièvre, for example, points out that many outstanding parodies take as their target something other than the work parodied, notably something contemporary; H. Marckiewicz documents the seventeenth-century practice of recasting a serious work in order to ridicule contemporary customs or politics; Hutcheon remarks that Pope's *Dunciad* does not mock the *Iliad*, nor does the mock-epic usually target the epic at all; J. Priestman traces an eighteenth-century tradition, following Pope, of parody with no derision implied toward the parodied work.[53] In such cases, the parody actually has a tripartite structure, involving three texts—the parody itself, the original and the target—or else two texts and a nonliterary target (when the parody is used for satirical purposes). The target is thus deflected: the parodist distorts the original in order to mock something closer to home, frequently the distortion itself.

The *Moralités* illustrate this triple structure perfectly, for they do not target the originals on which they are based but on the contrary attest a reverence for these (Shakespeare's *Hamlet*, Flaubert's *Hérodias*, Wagner's *Lohengrin*), while distorting them playfully. Laforgue's mockery acts rather upon the distortion, the modern Decadent heroes and heroines into which the originals have been transformed—with their metaphysical concerns and their confusion about love—and the forms of expression proper to them. Both the original (or model) and the target are parodied, though in different ways, the originals by the alterations they undergo, the target by the exaggeration of its features. Cervantes does likewise in *Don Quixote,* in parodying romances of chivalry; he aims not at the "authentic" ones, but at the popular ones of his own period in which the conventions of romance became clichés and were mechanized in the Formalist sense. *Amadis of Gaul* is thus saved from the pyre during the book-burning episode of I,6 for being "the best of all the books of its kind ever written," despite the fact that, as the first of its kind in Spain, it gave birth to all the subsequent, pernicious books of chivalry.[54] In Laforgue's case, targeting the distortion—contemporary Decadence—means targeting his own work as well, which uses Decadent forms, themes, and images to an extreme, albeit with irony; the mockery becomes blatant self-mockery.

Although using an older work to target something contemporary might suggest a conservative ideology behind the parody, as Hutcheon maintains, this need not be so.[55] In fact, as I argued earlier, parody is *theoretically* inconsistent with conservatism. The charge of conservatism may apply in cases where the original is held up as an ideal form from which the target has degenerated and which the parodist wishes to revive. However, a deflected target does not always use the original in this way but frequently, rather, as a vehicle for the parody, an authorized and intelligible form against which to read the distortion. Once again, the *Moralités* furnish enlightening examples: Laforgue's *Hamlet* does not propose a return to Shakespeare; this would be no less anachronistic than the parody, and indeed no less comical. But the Decadent Hamlet is mocked by his contrast with the earlier one, and with him the specific problems of the 1880s literary sensibility, above all those of the Laforguian persona itself.

Because the parodist conspicuously uses another work, and is obliged by the nature of his art to do so, he holds the position not only of author (of the parody) but also of reader (of the original). Rose has described him specifically as a critical reader who from his "reading" creates his own revisionary work.[56] The parodist does not accept the original unquestioningly by adopting its methods, subject-matter, style, or ideology; instead he distorts it comically, rewrites it, interprets it for a new age, sensibility, and readership. This critical function of parody was described and analyzed in the Formalist theory of its metalinguistic character, one text's commentary on another within one and the same work. The parodist's dual status as reader and writer accounts for his essentially ambivalent attitude toward the parodied work, which is an object of his comical transformation, or, in the case of the target, his mockery, yet is also the material of his own creation. More than any other author, he is dependent upon the text that he undermines, because it provides him with the fundamental elements of his parody. With respect to the parodied work, he is necessarily both irreverent and admiring, daring to alter an established text and revising it so as to serve his purposes; the parody must both play with it and reaffirm it, "destroy" it in its original form and renew and revitalize it in another one. Tynjanov's radical concept of destruction—"une filiation littéraire . . . est avant tout combat, *destruction* de l'ensemble ancien et nouvelle construction des anciens éléments"[57]—might be tempered so as to fit parody in its many forms; it should be understood neutrally, both because the destruction which parody effects cannot be total (for parody depends on the materials and even structure of the original), and also because it may consist simply of a comic reworking of material.[58]

I insist on this point because it constitutes a major distinction between parody and satire. The parodied work is indeed an object of play, mockery, or criticism, but by providing the parodist with his materials it is also a model and constituent of the parody itself. Satire displays no such ambivalence; it merely criticizes its object without transforming it. It is an object of attack only, whereas that of parody is an object of mockery *and* admiration, becoming the material and model for the parody itself. Parody is potentially both destructive and creative, critical and constructive; although it operates directly upon a work of art or specialized language, its critical function, as Rose has argued, can extend as far as that of the most biting social satire, to the attitudes and values that the work may represent and the public to which it may have appealed.[59] Unlike satire, it also contributes to the ongoing history and tradition of literature by reworking the original into a new form. In this respect, it may be usefully compared to Bakhtin's concept of genre,[60] which conserves the past precisely by renewing itself, making itself contemporary, and being reborn in each new work which uses it; the past, or "archaism," thus preserved in genre is eternally alive and capable of renewal. Like genre as Bakhtin describes it, parody is a present reminder of the past; it possesses the memory of literature and thus guarantees both the unity and the continuity of the process of literary history.

Although parody may, by its comic element, criticize the parodied work, it differs from satire by the self-criticism implied in its definition. In studying parody as a metafictional form, Rose has argued, rightly, that parody possesses inherently a self-reflexive quality due to the dual function of the parodist as reader and author.[61] By showing the parodist's interpretation and use of other material, literally of his reading, parody gives us as readers a model by which to interpret itself. The analogy between the parodist as a reader and the reader of the parody ensures that the parody's effect will turn upon itself; the parodist's relation to the parodied work is transferred to ourselves reading the parody. Its very form presents us with an example of a critical reading and thereby suggests a similar reading of itself.

The self-reflexivity described by Rose, however, has more significant implications than even her analysis allows, implications which are in fact borne out by the *Moralités*.[62] The parody does not merely provide for a critical reading of itself as a fixed work by demonstrating the mechanics of art; rather, parodic reflexivity becomes a more direct form of self-criticism. In comically reworking another text, the parody leaves itself, as a text, open to the same playful or critical action that it performs on the original and thus suggests its own potential to be altered, or even parodied, in its turn. Parody's basic definition as a comical rewriting of another work prevents it from proposing itself as definitive. Implicating itself in its challenge to the parodied work, it suggests its own potential as a target or model text. From a theoretical perspective, it suffers from no self-delusion but rather flaunts the fact that it is as vulnerable and tenuous as the parodied work. It necessarily provides for a critique of itself and does not, as Barthes charged, neglect to call itself into question.[63]

The *Moralités* are especially useful for examining this self-critical aspect of parody, which, though inherent in the logic of the genre, has hitherto passed unnoticed. They provide excellent and explicit examples of three important self-critical techniques. First, the parody may overtly discredit its own story, as in the epilogue to *Persée et Andromède*, in which one of the speakers challenges the veracity of the parodic version just told; or the final line of *Hamlet*, which mocks the preceding story as arbitrary and unimportant. Second, the parody may openly evoke other existing or future versions of the same story (most of the *Moralités* do this) and even, as we shall see in *Hamlet*, propose ways in which the alternative ones might differ.

In these first two cases, a theoretical point implied by the definition of parody and conspicuously realized in the *Moralités* can, with

The *Moralités légendaires* and a Theory of Parody 19

hindsight, be found in other examples and should be admitted as a prominent feature of the genre. Cervantes, for example, exploits both techniques at the end of part 2. Having completed his narrative, the Arab Cide Hamete Benengeli defends his account as the only genuine one and puts a curse on anyone who might be tempted to revive Don Quixote's story. By doing so, however, he in fact suggests that this may happen: "For myself alone was Don Quixote born, and I for him; he knew how to act and I to write; we two alone are one, despite that false Tordesillescan writer *who has dared, and may dare again,* to write with his coarse and ill-trimmed ostrich quill of the exploits of my valorous knight" (emphasis mine).[64] In this way, Cervantes ironically makes Cide Hamete's claims to absolute authority the vehicle of parodic relativism, calling his own version into question by acknowledging other, competing ones. As elsewhere, Cervantes here brilliantly integrates his direct attack upon Avellaneda's apocryphal *Don Quixote,* part 2, into the parody; thus Cide Hamete alludes not only to Avellaneda's existing version but also to a possible future one.[65] Cervantes makes Cide Hamete's claims all the more questionable because the historian is an Arab, and we are told repeatedly in the story that Arabs are untrustworthy and unreliable; the other version, or the future one, may actually be the more authentic. Thus parody provides a new version of an old story but, as it always involves self-parody to some extent, it cannot propose itself as the true one. It follows from this that the parody does not claim for itself higher authority or value than either the parodied work or the target.[66] It is different, and new, but it carries within itself the seeds of its *own* destruction as well as of its regeneration in yet a new form.

A third self-critical technique, the most revolutionary of the three, consists of challenging the very message of parody, the scepticism that it develops in the reader by transforming allegedly fixed works and exposing the methods of art. Parody not only makes us beware of taking works of art as true, real, or definitive, but also, in a radical self-reflexive move, can make us doubt the warning itself. This is logically implied by the definition and structure of parody but is not often realized overtly. However, as we shall see in detail in chapter seven, Laforgue's *Persée et Andromède* provides a rare and enlightening example which allows us to examine and describe this feature at work for the first time: the epilogue undermines the very moral of parody as stated openly by the narrator. Parody may teach us that stories are merely fictions, but that message must be questioned too.

The definition of parody as a comical rewriting of another work makes it especially relevant to the theory of intertextuality, which considers texts an absorption and transformation of other ones.[67] Parody is deliberately intertextual, conspicuously referring to another work as it distorts and transforms it, recalling the original and-or target precisely in altering it. Thus M. Riffaterre sees parody as an example of intratextual intertextuality, where the intertext is partly encoded within the text but conflicts with it: "... la trace, bien qu'elle appartienne à l'intertexte, se trouve insérée ou enkystée dans le texte—corps étranger dont l'assimilation signalera le remplacement du sens par la signifiance."[68] Parody signals to the reader that it refers to some other work located ostensibly outside itself, whose traces remain within it. The particular sense of the parody derives from the difference between it and the parodied work, a difference defined and communicated by the distortion.

The intertextual nature of parody raises two points particularly important for a theory of the genre. First, in relating the principle of parody to that of literary creation generally, it suggests how a parody may be understood as a creative work with literary meaning, rather than as merely a critical commentary on another work or its values. It provides a method of reading parody as a literary form. Traditional notions of parody as parasitic must be revised in the light of intertextual theory, according to which *all* works are understood in terms of other ones and the conventions established and realized in them. Second, intertextuality suggests an answer to a problem raised in almost every discussion of parody, that of the reader's competence: to what extent is prior knowledge of the original necessary for the reader's perception of the parody? This has been a considerable stumbling block for theorists, for if knowledge of the original is required parody becomes subject to charges of elitism and narrowness; only the reader whose background allows him to grasp the allusions will be capable of perceiving the parody. Parody is derivative and secondary since, if the original disappears or is unidentified, the parody cannot be understood, and so on.[69] This view seems at first reasonable; if the meaning and effect of the parody derive from the difference between itself, as a distortion, and the original, how could a work *without* a perceptible original be seen and interpreted as a parody? Even Formalist and Structuralist theorists have evoked the problem: in Tynjanov's terms, if the parodied work is forgotten, the parody will be perceived only on a single rather than a double plane, that is, as an ordinary work.[70]

But here the theory of intertextuality as referred to above offers a ready solution, in the vestiges of the intertext present within the text. Parody by nature preserves the original in itself and is therefore self-sufficient, capable of being understood even when the details of the parodied work (original or target, when these are distinct) are lost or unknown. In practical terms, identification of the model may certainly clarify aspects of the parody and enhance our appreciation of the distortion, but is not essential to an understanding of it. By certain noticeable devices, usually those of humor, we are made to see that the text is transforming another[71] and to identify the objects of its transformation. Therefore in theory we do not need to know the original in order to understand the parody, which retains of the original what is relevant to itself. This raises two points which demand clarification. First, the self-sufficiency of parody does not mean that we can (or should) reconstruct the original from the parody's distortion, but merely that we can discern from it those aspects of the original which are mocked by the parody. Second, it does not follow that knowledge of the original is useless; on the contrary, this may facilitate understanding, especially of details, as experience attests. But this point in no way contradicts the theory; the parody may be understood as a parody, and its object perceived, without knowledge of the original. One does not need to be familiar with the contemporary romances of chivalry which Cervantes parodies in *Don Quixote* in order to grasp either *that* the novel is a parody, or *what* it parodies. The text provides what we need, notably the formulas and clichés of romance, and signals them by a variety of means, such as conspicuous archaism, level of diction, and repetition.[72]

On this point the *Moralités* are particularly illuminating. *Le Mi-*

racle des Roses provides an excellent example, for the original on which it is based has never been recognized and has usually been presumed not to exist, while the story was thought to be otherwise consistent with the rest. As I will show in detail in chapter 4, *Le Miracle des Roses* confirms that the original, even if lost or unknown, will be contained within the parody itself as the basis of its essential distortion, and can be grasped by the reader as such from the parodic signals offered in the text. Thus when I succeeded in identifying the original (a piece of music), this knowledge did not substantially alter my understanding of the parody; significantly, it did explain certain of the story's problematic aspects which had thus functioned as clues. It is in the nature of parody to set the reader on a quest for the original, only to reveal, once found, that he did not really need it anyway. This does not mean that it has nothing to do with the parody; on the contrary, the parody is a retelling and, in the process, a telling too. In a sense, it creates the original in the reader's mind, constructing it in the very act of transforming it. This aspect of parody suggests yet another way in which it differs from satire, which does not preserve its object within itself and thus cannot be properly understood without reference to the exterior object or situation satirized.

As others have remarked,[73] the importance of imitation in the structure of parody (as a rewriting, or imitation with a difference) is reflected in its prominence as a major *theme* of the genre. *Don Quixote* provides the standard model for this observation, since the theme informs the entire novel. It constitutes the hero's famous problem, a slavish and unproductive notion of imitation: he imitates to the letter the romances of chivalry, seeking in doing so to prove the reality of the fictions he has read. In fact he confuses the two, taking his readings as real, and reality, which impertinently asserts itself at every turn, as the fictional creation of some sage enchanter.[74] The parody challenges this view of imitation in two ways: first, through its form (in particular, having the characters in part 2 read about themselves, i.e., what we have experienced as part 1, and to criticize the published account as inaccurate) and, second, through its comical treatment of the theme—the ridiculous misfortunes into which imitation leads the hero, and his ultimate recognition of failure.

The *Moralités légendaires* and a Theory of Parody 23

The theme of imitation is particularly relevant to the main target of the *Moralités,* Decadence. In mocking the confusion of art and life, and working against it, parody well suits a movement dedicated to leading a life of art, a movement in which everything—nature, society, human psychology—is seen and presented as theater.[75] Laforgue's characters try to live in the fictional world of their imagination; having read and dreamt too much, they are incapable of functioning within the prosaic world of men, or—as is usually the case—women. The Decadent's emphasis on artifice, symbol, dream, and a rejection of the world makes him, in the words of one critic, an "être de fiction,"[76] defined by his refusal to live otherwise than in fictions and fantasies, and by his desire to make the world a book and substitute art for life. Hamlet, Ruth, Lohengrin, Salomé, Andromède, and Pan all try to lead their lives according to an artificial ideal, and either fail utterly or are saved in the nick of time by another character's good sense. They seek to make reality conform to their dreams and are tormented by their constant failure to do so. Laforgue saw this desire and its frustration as a basic aspect of Decadence, a consequence of the effort to introduce art into life and the pessimistic conviction that the effort was futile.

From a formal perspective too, parody poses a challenge to imitation. In exposing the methods, effects, presuppositions, and processes of art (including its own), it leads the reader to take fictions not as realities, or even as images of reality, but rather as interpretations of it. As Shlonsky has argued, it exposes the illusory nature of literature, reveals its conventions and devices, and prevents the reader from taking it as true or real.[77] Parody proposes a radical view of art as interpretation rather than as imitation in the strict sense, as Rose has observed; it holds a mirror not up to life, in the traditional formula, but up to art, and the mirror is a distorting one.[78] By conspicuously signalling the distortion, it also calls attention to the circumstances (frequently contemporary ones) that affect the interpretation it offers. Parody is imitation that transforms and ultimately reveals. Cervantes dramatized this in the Prologue to part 1, by applying to his parodic hero a deformed version of a standard chivalric cliché, "flower and mirror": Don Quixote is, rather, the "light and mirror of knight errantry," a mirror that also illuminates, at once reflecting and exposing knight errantry, revealing to us his self-deception and the possibility of our own.[79]

While parody's emphasis on interpretation has been noted, the important implications of this have not been fully appreciated. It suggests a relativist ideology, which accords with the self-critical aspect of parody described earlier. In uncovering the methods—and dangers—of works of art, and revising artistic imitation to mean interpretation, parody implies the possibility of other interpretations, other results, and other stories, depending on more or less different conditions. An interpretation may always be challenged, and even superseded, by another. In moral terms such pluralism could, by questioning the truth of the "image," be disturbing; in aesthetic terms it is reassuring, since it provides for the continuation of art. The parody calls into question the original and the target by playing with them but simultaneously revives them for further use. Laforgue's Salomé does not kill her biblical ancestor, or Flaubert's, or even the contemporary creations of Huysmans and Gustave Moreau, but rather perpetuates their tradition in a radically new form. Moreover, in rebounding upon itself, leaving room for subsequent versions or even suggesting the forms these might take (as I discussed earlier), parody ensures that the tradition which it revises will continue even beyond itself.

This last point reveals an important aspect of parody, first elaborated systematically in Formalist theory: the development of new literary forms. Parody operates especially when the procedures of a tradition become mechanized;[80] although by mocking the tradition, parody brings it to an end, it also regenerates it, altering its course rather than terminating it altogether. The *Moralités* confirm this and in addition suggest that neither the parodied work nor the target need be in decline. Indeed, the parody itself frequently *fixes* the conventions that it targets, precisely by exaggerating them. Such is the case, for example, with the *Déliquescences d'Adoré Floupette* of 1885, which defined the clichés of Decadence in the very act of ridiculing them. Parody thus may flourish at the height of a formal tradition and confer upon it a unified and consistent identity; it is a storehouse for the conventions of a genre, which, abstracted and exaggerated, become recognizable as they are transformed. The *Moralités* are an outstanding example of this, but it is true of other parodies as well; the conventions of the gothic novel are apparent from *Northanger Abbey,* those of the chivalric romances from *Don Quixote,* those of Roman love elegy from Ovid's *Amores.* The analogy between parody and periods of historical decadence has often been made; research into the latter has suggested that decadence coincides not with the decline of a civilization, but rather with the forms that it acquires at its culmination.[81] This same principle applies to parody too, which frequently brings to its height the tradition that it parodies, while redirecting it toward the future.

Although other functions of parody have been identified and described, notably by Rose,[82] these are not, like literary evolution, inherent in the genre itself, and they may even contradict its implications. For example, parody may be used as a way around censorship, but many other forms have been employed for this purpose, such as satire, allegory, and the *roman à clef.* Those parodies which criticize a past work may be the expression of a present overburdened by the past, but this contradicts parody's essential ambivalence toward its object—mocking and admiring, destructive and regenerative. Parody implies a desire not to annihilate the past but to revise it into an appropriate creation for the contemporary world; hence the Formalist conception of parody as a motor for the evolution of literary forms, altering, but therein renewing, a tradition that it helps to mechanize.[83] *Don Quixote* is again the standard example, transforming the romance into the "modern" novel of realism;[84] Rose argues that *Tristram Shandy* transformed the Cervantic novel into the eighteenth-century novel of idealism in which the imagination becomes the principle that structures meaning;[85] Priestman suggests that Fielding's *Shamela,* parodying Richardson's *Pamela,* assisted the development from the sentimental to the realist novel, notably, as Baguley argues, *Joseph Andrews.*[86] While such neat patterns (indeed the categories too) leave themselves open to challenge, it is undeniable that the dual capacity of parody to close and renew a tradition or form ensures for it a catalytic function. The *Moralités* constitute a fine example, giving their originals a new and special significance in modern literature and aiding the passage of Decadence into modernism.

Features of Parodic Narrative

Parody has a number of characteristic ways of signalling that it is a comic rewriting of another work. For the most part, these can be arranged into three groups, corresponding to three major aspects of the genre: the comic element, imitation and transformation, and the analogy between the parody and the experience of the reader.[87] Since the comic is essential to parody, the narrative relies on the numerous devices of humor, many of which effect some kind of distortion and deception of expectations (e.g., substitution, exaggeration, incongruity and anachronism, condensation, displacement, puns, sound play, repetition, cataloguing, neologism, periphrasis, and allusion). Laforgue relies particularly on anachronism and incongruity, freely recycling and mingling stories from various periods and traditions in a single work, and modernizing the characters. The most obvious anachronism lies in his language: in every story, regardless of the original, the characters speak the same 1880s language and use the clichés and formulas associated with Decadence. This not only identifies the target but, by its consistency over the six stories, reflects the principle of modernization which governs them all. Laforgue's parodies immediately identify themselves as such because they use a recognizably personal style for subjects ostensibly taken from a variety of sources distant in time. We expect a distinct form, genre, style, or vocabulary for each story, and we get only the same one, six times over. His prose also relies heavily on word and sound play, and his repetition serves humorous and ironic purposes rather than the allegedly poetic ones being introduced at the time. As Riffaterre has shown about intertextual humor in general, humor that is not initially obvious will be signalled by a seeming gratuitousness which arrests the reader's attention on the vehicle of the humor until he recognizes the joke or the allusion.[88] The *Moralités* contain instances of all these devices, on levels ranging from individual words and expressions to whole portions of the plot. I shall call attention to them in my discussion of the individual stories to follow.

The *Moralités légendaires* and a Theory of Parody 27

The theme of imitation inherent in the structure of parody accounts for its many reflexive devices, which work to persuade the reader that it is an imitation of something else and, more precisely, a retelling of an earlier story. The most direct means of accomplishing this consists of providing an interpretative situation within the parody which functions as a model for reading the larger story, much like a play within a play. Attention has been drawn to these by Rose.[89] Although such reflexive devices should not be equated with parodic signals, they frequently function as such. Clearly a parody within the parody achieves this end most efficiently; if we recognize a parody within the text, we are encouraged to read the text itself as one. The *Moralités* present several instances of this, such as the recitation of Salomé, Hamlet's play, and the bullfight and procession of *Le Miracle des Roses,* all of which reflect comically on the larger story. Any interpretative situation, parodic or not, will call attention to the status of the text as an imitation and will usually offer us another reader in the story itself with whom we can identify; but it will specifically indicate parody only if it meets the other criteria of the genre, notably the comic element.

Making writing or interpretation an explicit issue in the story also highlights the theme of imitation. With the hero's literary concerns and anxieties over producing an original work, Laforgue's *Hamlet* provides a splendid illustration of this, but the other *Moralités* contain allusions to it as well. Nearly every story includes an artist of some kind; the ending of *Persée et Andromède* openly addresses the issue of interpretation, and at some length; the theme of artistic creation dominates *Pan et la Syrinx.* The intervention of the parodist in the narrative constitutes a third model for the parody; it provides a commentary on the text from within and, when ironic, is particularly appropriate. Laforgue constantly breaks his narrative with parenthetical asides, direct commentary, apostrophe, suspension points, and etceteras. Switching from subjective narration to authorial intervention and back, the narrative focuses attention on its artifice and prevents us from taking it as true, in accordance with the purposes of parody. Finally, a pretension to displaced authorship, creating the illusion that the story is told at a number of removes, operates on a larger scale like a story within the story, furnishing within the work a retelling (and possibly an inaccurate one) like the parody's. *Don Quixote* is celebrated for its three removes: the Arab historian Cide Hamete Benengeli, the Moor who translated his text, and the author who edits it. In Laforgue, the epilogue to *Persée et Andromède* and the flashback structure of *Lohengrin* and *Le Miracle des Roses* are examples of this device.

The analogy between the parody, as a reading and interpretation, and the experience of the reader himself accounts for a number of typical devices. As Borges notes with respect to *Don Quixote*,[90] these implicate the reader in the parody by confusing the fictional with the real and challenging the distinction between them. For example, the narrator's intervention, so frequent in parody, allegedly distances him from the text but, by allying us with him, it actually incorporates us into the narrative. Moreover, in commenting openly on the story from within, such intervention reflects the metalinguistic character of the parody itself, as I have said above. In Laforgue, the narrator's recurrent intrusions make him simultaneously part of the fiction and part of our own world, whereby we are led to question the status of our reading. Incorporating one of the parodist's own works into the parody, either merely in quotation or, more importantly, as a target text, likewise breaks down the barrier between fiction and reality by placing the author—someone whom we thought to be outside the narrative—inside the fiction; having considered ourselves safely outside it with him, we are consequently led to see that we may be implicated too, as he is. When the author's own work is included as a parodied text, we reason by analogy that the parody itself may at some time receive the same treatment. In *Don Quixote*, for example, Cervantes makes his own *Galatea* one of the books happily saved from the pyre (1, 6). In all the *Moralités*, Laforgue exploits this feature by including verses from his own poems, easily recognizable by their distinctive Laforguian character (as embodied in the stories themselves) and, in the case of *Pan et la Syrinx*, their free verse.

By the extreme freedom of their adaptations, the *Moralités* provide an outstanding case for an analysis and defense of parody as a creative form in the fullest sense. The metaphor of the parasite, which with its negative connotations has so often been applied to this genre, is decidedly inapposite, for although parody requires an original text, it does not merely feed on it at the original's expense; rather, in taking the original as its own material, it actually renews it in a different form, perpetuating it instead of depriving it of life. Moreover, in leaving room for, and sometimes even suggesting, subsequent versions within itself, parody directly ensures the continuation of art. It may be preferable to think of it in terms of the old cliché of the book as a child, as did Cervantes in the Prologue to his own great parody. Modifying the cliché, he described his book not as the traditional "child of his brain," but more precisely as his stepchild, and himself, the editor and parodist, as its stepfather, a father at one remove. To modify this comparison in its turn, we could call parody the child not of an author at all but of a book; we would thus consider the original text a parent and the parody its spirited child, who, in altering and revising the parent's values according to the sensibility of its own generation, nevertheless perpetuates them in a new form, thereby assuring the vitality and viability of a family, or literary, tradition.

The epigraph to the *Moralités légendaires* as a whole bears witness to the function of parody as revising and renewing such a tradition, for it comes from *La Tentation de Saint Antoine* of Flaubert:

La reine de Saba à Saint Antoine:
— Ris donc, bel ermite! Ris donc, je suis très gaie, tu verras! Je pince de la lyre, je danse comme une abeille et je sais une foule d'histoires toutes à raconter plus divertissantes les unes que les autres.

Gustave Flaubert

An epigraph is particularly appropriate to parody, for it functions in a similar way; it too quotes another work in a different context and gives to the quotation a new meaning, one relevant to the story that it introduces. Separated from the text, and singled out conspicuously at the very beginning, an epigraph signals the incongruity between the literary authority cited and the work to follow, while it simultaneously implies a relation between them, just as the parody does with respect to the parodied work. Moreover, an epigraph calls attention to the reusability of a work for purposes other than its original ones, the very principle on which parody depends. And, as with parody, the particular sense of the quotation as an epigraph derives from its relation to the new context.[91]

By its privileged position, an epigraph carries considerable authority and claims to have special importance for the work to follow.[92] In the epigraph that introduces the *Moralités*, the obvious allusions to art and, in particular, to storytelling make the Queen of Sheba a figure for the parodist who, literally like her, "knows a host of stories each one more amusing than the other." Her reference to laughter carries the likeness further, as the parodist too will elicit laughter from the reader. But the significance of the epigraph for the volume lies in the fact that, in its new context, it is an inversion of the original situation and is thus ironic; the Queen of Sheba is the arch-temptress and a favorite Decadent image of the Eternal Feminine, to whom the heroes of the *Moralités* can never reconcile themselves. Laforgue thus uses the standard Decadent figure of the *femme fatale*, luring the resistant man to his doom, to represent the parodist in his relation to the reader: art is deception, and storytelling the poet's equivalent to the much-berated deception of the Eternal Feminine.[93] In using the figure parodically, Laforgue makes the epigraph a model for the stories that follow.

Furthermore, since *La Tentation de Saint Antoine* is one of the sacred works of the Decadent canon, Laforgue reveals pointedly both the target of the parody and the parodic process by which it will be transformed. In relating himself to the Queen of Sheba, in particular, the parodist travesties himself according to one of the oldest of comic devices, putting himself in a woman's dress, and thus signals the self-parody that dominates the volume. Finally, this self-parody communicates an essential, unrelenting self-mockery, as Laforgue hereby suggests that he may have no more success with winning the reader, or even entertaining him, than the Queen of Sheba had with her notoriously unresponsive hermit. The epigraph demonstrates some of the most important aspects of parody, and so provides a guide to reading the entire volume.

2

Decadence and Parody

On 6 August 1885, Laforgue remarked in a letter to Kahn, "Le *Temps* d'aujourd'hui a un grand article de Paul Bourde sur les *Décadents*, je n'y suis même pas nommé—il a cependant mon volume."[1] Bourde's article, "Les Poètes décadents," was prompted by the second edition of the famous spoof on Decadence, *Les Déliquescences d'Adoré Floupette,* and constituted the first serious, though hardly generous, study of the new school of poetry to appear in a major French periodical.[2] Laforgue's disappointment at being left out of such an unsympathetic survey, which discussed only a half dozen poets anyway, suggests how much he considered himself part of the Decadent movement.[3] The reviews that he wrote clandestinely for his own *Complaintes,* and also his personal letters, testify to his conviction that his work reflected in both form and ideas the principles of Decadence, considered as the main contemporary trend in poetry, and in turn made a contribution to them.[4] Other reviews confirmed Laforgue's sentiment and placed him consistently among those writers to whom the term was applied: Verlaine, Mallarmé, Corbière, Rimbaud, Huysmans, Moréas, and Villiers. In his preface to *A Rebours,* written twenty years after the publication of the novel, Huysmans added Laforgue to des Esseintes' pantheon of contemporary authors, Corbière, Mallarmé, and Verlaine: "Arthur Rimbaud et Jules Laforgue eussent mérité de figurer dans le florilège de des Esseintes, mais ils n'avaient rien imprimé à cette époque-là."[5]

Laforgue's commitment to Decadence, however, did not prevent a characteristic raillery at its expense, and one all the more mordant for being directed toward himself. Making fun of the very attitudes and forms to which he subscribes is the single most distinctive feature of his work from the very beginning, with the exception of some of the philosophical poems of 1881. This self-irony is particularly suited to parody, for it ensures the ambivalent attitude necessary to it, as described in chapter one. Indeed, the *Moralités* are stories in the best Decadent tradition which use a canonical model to mock the very Decadence on which they draw. Laforgue takes a foundation of the Decadent sensibility, excessive self-consciousness, and turns it back upon itself, paradoxically making of it a source of relief—the sympathetic mockery that is humor—from the intolerable dilemma that it otherwise causes. Self-consciousness becomes self-detachment, and this otherwise unattainable ideal of Decadence is thus achieved.[6] In both realizing and denying the goals of Decadence in this way, humor makes it overcome the limitations inherent in it. Decadence must die out, by the law of its own development, or revert to moderation, being thus defeated; humor takes it beyond itself, precisely by not taking it altogether seriously. Indeed, Laforgue deemed the humor of the *Complaintes* a source of their modernity and originality:

> Ajoutons que *l'humour* qui circule dans ce volume nous conduirait volontiers à croire que l'auteur n'y est pas toujours dupe du sérieux de ses tours de force et de ses jongleries et s'amuse simplement à jeter ses gourmes. Cela et les originales qualités de langue et d'observation . . . nous sont un sûr garant que lorsque la nouvelle école prendra sa place au soleil . . . M. Jules Laforgue y aura contribué par de nouvelles poésies d'une tenue moins décadente et d'un idéal plus sérieusement moderne. (Debauve, 194f.)

Humor makes the work surpass the poetic school in which it participates and achieve a modern rather than simply Decadent ideal. The type of parody exemplified by the *Moralités* fits Laforgue's scheme well. Indeed Wyzewa, in his review of the *Moralités* in 1887, saw them as a further stage in the evolution of the movement, a step beyond Decadence for those seeking something new: "Ces oeuvres seront le plus sûr refuge des prochains des Esseintes contre la banalité des chefs d'oeuvres quotidiens."[7]

Decadence and Parody

The theory of parody presented in the previous chapter maintains that if Decadence is the principal target of Laforgue's stories, it is also necessarily the material of which they are composed; indeed, the *Moralités* employ the typical features of Decadent writing as they play with them. Laforgue parodies the clichés of the movement and covers a whole range of authors, including, most of all, himself. This chapter seeks to define and clarify specifically the conception of Decadence in the 1880s, to describe its language, from particular words, images, expressions, and stylistic devices to its general themes and ideological assumptions. While, as I have argued earlier, the parody can ultimately be understood without reference to an exterior model because it preserves the original (and the target) within itself, knowledge of these may nevertheless legitimately facilitate interpretation by making more evident the character of the distortion. Identifying the common elements of Decadence locates specifically the language with which the *Moralités* play and consequently transform. Reciprocally, Laforgue's parodies contribute to our understanding of Decadence by their treatment of its stock conventions as such, which, thus mechanized, may be isolated and identified. The movement that was itself a conscious work of art, a pose, offers itself not only as an excellent target for parody, but also as an object for formalistic analysis.

A careful examination of Decadence imposes itself all the more in a study of the *Moralités,* because both the term and the group that it designated have been greatly misunderstood. The extent of the misunderstanding and the abundance of material that undermines it have together motivated the presence and scope of this chapter. Decadence has been defined almost wholly in terms of a single type, exemplified by the peculiar hero of Huysmans's *A Rebours,* des Esseintes. The role of des Esseintes himself in the self-identity of Decadence is important; however, his poor relations—the heroes and heroines of Péladan, Rachilde, Lombard, and others who exploit Huysmans's themes of corrupt aristocratic blood, perversion, vice, and artificiality—have inspired a very limited, even erroneous, impression of the movement.[8] Neurotic recluses with a fascination for the exotic and the unhealthy, an erotic imagination modeled on the Marquis de Sade's, a taste for abusing body and mind with intoxicants, sexual experiments, and self-imposed tortures, and a ferocious and unscrupulous revolt against nature: to such a portrait have the Decadents been reduced. To persist in these misconceptions, however, not only does a severe disservice to an interesting, varied, and important movement but also ignores some rather obvious and persuasive evidence. Decadence in France was principally an 1880s phenomenon and, when studied as such, produces rather a different picture from the accepted one. The semipornographic, licentious works of those mentioned above are only infrequently acknowledged during the period as belonging to the Decadent school, even the most well-known of them, Péladan's *Etudes passionnelles de décadence. Le Vice suprême* (1884), despite its title and an introduction by the venerable Barbey D'Aurevilly. Contemporary sources make clear that these works were not considered at the time a very important part of the movement, or even in many cases taken seriously.[9]

Huysmans' *A Rebours,* on the other hand, was cited as the "bréviaire de la décadence" (Richard, *Mouvement décadent,* 250), the supreme example of the attitudes and style that characterized the new literary trend. But if this novel is quintessentially Decadent, it is precisely because it is the *ne plus ultra* of Decadence, the implications of Decadence taken to their outrageous conclusion; it exaggerates the characteristics of the group, deliberately taking them to the extreme in order ultimately to demonstrate their failure and impossibility. Exaggeration is, nevertheless, the distortion of a reality, and the reality of literary Decadence is that it was a serious and distinctly modern response to metaphysical, ethical, and aesthetic questions of the late nineteenth century.[10] It was consistent with the philosophy of history prevalent after the Revolution, the pattern of growth-maturity-decline applied to the development of civilizations.[11] It consisted principally not of now-forgotten *fumistes,* aesthetes, and libertines, but of some of the major writers of the second half of the century. Baudelaire was its father, with Verlaine and Mallarmé his most important sons,[12] a genealogy attested in most contemporary articles on the movement.[13] The others consistently named are Rimbaud, Huysmans, Moréas, Laforgue, and Villiers.[14] Decadence thus designated all the Symbolist poets before this label existed; it served as the general term for modernity in poetry from at least as early as Gautier's preface to the 1868 edition of Baudelaire's *Fleurs du mal*, and in literature overall throughout the 1880s. It was considered the poetic equivalent of the major modern movements in the other arts, Impressionism in painting and Wagnerism in music.

Histories of Decadence have not taken sufficient account of the prominence of the term and the attitudes that it represented, nor have they adequately identified these; our understanding of the movement has thus been unfortunately deficient. One of the shortcomings of Michaud's influential *Message poétique du symbolisme* was his emphasis on Decadence as a transitional, short-lived period between Naturalism and Symbolism, an early lyrical phase of a movement of which Symbolism was the mature, more intellectual phase; Decadence merely prepared the way for the great poetic revolution of Symbolism.[15] This view has in general prevailed. Its inadequacy, however, has been demonstrated by Jean Pierrot's important study, *L'Imaginaire décadent*, which alone begins to indicate the significant and substantial evidence that disproves and overturns it.[16] As his work reveals, Decadence was a varied and significant phenomenon of literary history, describing distinct attitudes to nature, art, aesthetic forms, tradition, sexuality, women, the unconscious, religion, and metaphysics, and involving many artists whose importance has continued to grow with time. An examination of contemporary source material bears this out and presents a fuller, more diverse picture. This revised notion of Decadence matters for evaluating the *Moralités* and their achievement, because in treating the materials of Decadence parodically, Laforgue takes on not a frivolous and insignificant *cénacle* with only topical interest, but rather the modernist movement in its early phase. In exaggerating it, mocking it, parodying it in the fullest sense, the *Moralités* dismantle the Decadent edifice from within and lay the foundation, on the same spot and with the more resistant of its materials, for a new modern structure. The *Moralités*, in short, suggest the transformation of Decadence into twentieth-century modernism.

A few points of clarification regarding the term "Decadence" should be made from the start. First, the advent of Symbolism around 1886 was far less perceptible then than has since been thought; this term was merely a euphemism suggested by Moréas in 1885 to replace the more loaded word *décadence*, which had historically negative overtones. At this point, Symbolism was no more than Moréas's effort at public relations, a less controversial name for the trend designated universally by *décadence*. In his essay entitled, significantly, "Les Décadents," Moréas used *décadent* and its cognates throughout, except for one casual aside toward the end: "Les poètes décadents—la critique, puisque sa manie d'étiquetage est incurable, pourrait les appeler plus justement des *symboliques*."[17] The following year he entitled his famous manifesto "Le Symbolisme," and more aggressively championed the new name: "Nous avons déjà proposé la dénomination de *Symbolisme* comme la seule capable de désigner raisonnablement la tendance actuelle de l'esprit créateur en art. Cette dénomination peut être maintenue."[18] Moréas makes it clear that his proposal is inspired by a desire to avoid the negative connotations of *décadence*, which render the term irrelevant to the new school; the contemporary trend is, rather, a renaissance, and *décadence* "une inexplicable antinomie" to be abandoned (Pakenham, 30). Introducing the manifesto, nevertheless, the editor of *Le Figaro* persists in using the old, and by that point well-established, *décadence*. Clearly, no distinction existed between the two terms, both denoting merely "la nouvelle manifestation d'art" (Pakenham, 29, 31).[19] Even after the manifesto had appeared in September 1886, they continued to be used interchangeably for several years, particularly in the press.[20] "Décadent" was always applied to Laforgue before "symboliste" (or "symbolique," more frequent at the time) came into use; after September 1886, both terms served.[21]

Second, theories of symbolism that attempted to detach themselves from Decadence by evolving a theory of the symbol did so on the basis of a specific metaphysical and aesthetic doctrine deriving mainly from the work of Mallarmé, such as the early Moréas, René Ghil, Stuart Merrill, and Gustave Kahn. This distinction, however, has little importance for a definition of Symbolism, because it omits most of the important poets whom literary history has rightly or wrongly included in it: Baudelaire, Verlaine, Mallarmé himself, Rimbaud, and Laforgue. These theories provide valuable material for understanding the diverse features of late nineteenth-century poetics but do not reflect the thought or practice of the major writers. Third, the actual differences between Decadent and Symbolist poetry are negligible among the minor writers, who would adhere more closely to the doctrines of a "school" than would the more original and independent ones. The same themes and methods appear in both groups: pessimism, ennui, dream, the unconscious, mysticism, artifice, musicality, free verse, synaesthesia, and a common body of late-Romantic, Baudelairean imagery of gems, flowers, perfumes, the moon, the city, autumn, and twilight.

Fourth, Decadence had extremely close relations with the major avant-garde movements of the period in other genres. Although considered a reaction against Naturalism, Decadence was not wholly antithetical to it and shared with it a common pessimistic view of life, themes of depravity, heredity, and the nerves, and an aesthetic of the sickly. In a youthful defense of Naturalism in 1877, Laforgue quoted Zola in this context: "Mon goût, si l'on veut, est dépravé; j'aime ... les oeuvres de décadence où une sensibilité maladive remplace la santé plantureuse des époques classiques."[22] More commonly, Decadence is linked explicitly with Impressionist painting and Wagnerian music in the critical vocabulary of the period: the *écriture artiste* of the Goncourts is at once impressionist and "décadente" (Bourget, 402); Wyzewa speaks of Laforgue and Mallarmé in terms of "littérature wagnérienne" and the Impressionist and Symbolist painters in terms of "peinture wagnérienne";[23] the Decadents are the "impressionnistes de la littérature."[24] Paul Adam directly compares the stylistic features of the new poetry to "le ton multitonique de Wagner et la dernière technique des Impressionnistes."[25] The Polish writer Antoni Lange likened the climate in which Decadence developed to that which gave rise to Impressionist *plein-air* painting and Wagnerism.[26] Laforgue himself perceived a connection between Impressionism and the new style in poetry; *impressionnisme* is one of the four terms by which he sums up the ideal and processes of Decadence in his own review of the *Complaintes;* and in his essay on Impressionism, he remarks that the principle of Impressionist technique "a été non systématiquement, mais par génie appliqué dans la poésie et le roman chez nous".[27]

Despite such confusion, a relatively precise understanding of the notion of Decadence in the 1880s may be had by examining two kinds of source: first, the writings of contemporary theorists, historians, and critics of the movement, and second, literary works thought to belong to it. Although I will sometimes rely on the latter, I have elected not to compile a set of characteristics to be called "Decadent" from so varied a group of writers, but rather have abdicated that task to critics contemporary with them and cited their works only as illustrations. This chapter concentrates on the many essays and articles of the period which formulate some aspect of Decadence as Laforgue would have encountered it. This is the Decadence of the *Moralités,* the target and substance of their parody; later commentary provides only an incomplete description which must be revised. In spite of considerable diversity, a number of qualities common to the majority of examples studied emerge to form a relatively consistent and coherent picture. Two works stand out in this survey as major expressions of the Decadent sensibility: Gautier's important "Notice" to the 1868 edition of Baudelaire's *Fleurs du mal,* and Bourget's *Essais de psychologie contemporaine.*

Aspects of Decadence

Gautier's preface constitutes the first major statement of specifically late-nineteenth-century Decadence. Although histories of the idea frequently begin earlier than this date, with Barbey d'Aurevilly, the Romantics, D. Nisard's influential *Etudes de moeurs et de critique sur les poètes latins de la décadence,* the Marquis de Sade, or even ancient Decadence, Gautier's preface provides a starting point more appropriate to this study. It had tremendous influence on the generation of poets that emerged about ten years after Baudelaire's death in 1867 and sought to follow his example. It also had extraordinary exposure, for the edition which it introduced remained the only one available for the following fifty years. Thus the preface largely determined the late-nineteenth century's perception of Baudelaire, and the *décadence* that Gautier considered one of his main characteristics.[28] It definitely affected Laforgue, for he read it and took careful notes on it in preparing his own essay on Baudelaire in 1885.

Gautier's article was not the first to associate Baudelaire with Decadence; reviews of the *Fleurs du mal* had done so from the beginning.[29] This view was consistent with Baudelaire's defense of the Decadence of Poe in the famous opening to his "Notes Nouvelles sur Edgar Poe" (1857). While rejecting the term "littérature de décadence" (levelled against Poe) for implying a scale of value, Baudelaire nevertheless consecrates it by applying to it a favorite metaphor, the setting sun. Decadence is the splendid setting sun of Romanticism: "Dans les jeux de ce soleil agonisant, certains esprits poétiques trouveront de délices nouvelles; . . . une splendeur triste, la volupté du regret, toutes les magies du rêve, tous les souvenirs de l'opium".[30] But Gautier's essay actually defines Decadence in terms of Baudelaire's vision and method, and equates it with modern art. His article by itself identifies most of the themes and issues that would in fact characterize the movement later in the century: dandyism, dilettantism, sensuality, Orientalism, a depravity conscious of itself, an intense spirituality with strong mystical associations, artifice, ennui, neurosis, the Eternal Feminine, and a taste for the bizarre and unnatural.

Gautier prepares the way for the Decadent hero by presenting Baudelaire as a dandy, with "ce culte de soi-même qui caractérise l'homme imbu des principes de Brummel" (Gautier, 273). He describes the exoticism of Baudelaire's Nature, with its strange plants, exotic flowers, warm tones, and heady odors, a vision apparently inspired by the famous truncated journey to India: "cette magnifique et gigantesque végétation aux parfums pénétrants, ces pagodes élégamment bizarres, ces figures brunes aux blanches draperies, toute cette nature exotique si chaude, si puissante et si colorée" (Gautier, 282). He accordingly insists on Baudelaire's extraordinary, "oriental" sensuality, especially regarding jewels and fragrances (Gautier, 296). He presents Baudelaire's taste for the artificial, and his aesthetic of the bizarre and the monstrous, as a Decadent revolt against the tyranny of nature, an assertion of human will against an otherwise uncontrollable power: "ce goût excessif, baroque, presque toujours contraire au beau classique, était pour lui un signe de la volonté humaine corrigeant à son gré les formes et les couleurs fournies par la matière. . . . La *dépravation*, c'est-à-dire l'écart du type normal, est impossible à la bête, fatalement conduite par l'instinct immuable" (Gautier, 296).

He traces this emphasis on artifice to the influence of Poe and sees in it an opposition to "bourgeois" ideals of democracy, materialism, and progress. Baudelairean art, rather, reflects the ideals of an aging civilisation, "l'art arrivé à ce point de maturité extrême que déterminent à leurs soleils obliques les civilisations qui vieillissent" (Gautier, 286)—and accordingly portrays its human subject as neurotic, ill, "pâle, crispé, tordu, convulsé par les passions factices et le réel ennui moderne" (Gautier, 290). Depravity and perversity constitute for Gautier important themes of the *Fleurs du mal*, "ce livre consacré à la peinture des dépravations et des perversités modernes," which paradoxically reflect Baudelaire's spirituality and morality (Gautier, 301). He cites other aspects of the poet's spirituality, notably his Swedenborgian belief in the capacity to perceive synaesthetic *correspondances*, invisible relations among disparate phenomena, universal analogies, all mysteries accessible to the elected *poète-voyant* (Gautier, 300f.).

Gautier distinguishes in Baudelaire's work two principal types of women: the ideal one, beauty incarnate, never attained, like the heroines of Poe or the Seraphita-Seraphitus of Balzac's Swedenborgian novel; and the Eternal Feminine, either an unknowing creature of instinct ("prostitution inconsciente et presque bestiale"), or a viciously destructive, perfidiously cruel demon, a Delilah incapable of love and taking pleasure in crushing the hearts of men (Gautier, 305f.). This last distinction is crucial and yet frequently overlooked; the chief female type of Decadence, the Eternal Feminine, indeed separates into the two natures here described, the instinctual, animal, and unspiritual on the one hand, and the more cruel and evil *femme fatale* on the other.

Perhaps most importantly, Gautier relates Baudelaire's style to that of the late empire and the Byzantine school, thereby establishing the main terms of Decadent poetics:

> style ingénieux, compliqué, savant, plein de nuances et de recherches, reculant toujours les bornes de la langue, empruntant à tous les vo-

cabulaires techniques, prenant des couleurs à toutes les palettes, des notes à tous les claviers, s'efforçant à rendre la pensée dans ce qu'elle a de plus ineffable, et la forme en ses contours les plus vagues et les plus fuyants, écoutant pour les traduire les confidences subtiles de la névrose, les aveux de la passion vieillissante qui se déprave et les hallucinations bizarres de l'idée fixe tournant à la folie. Ce style de décadence est le dernier mot du Verbe sommé et poussé à l'extrême outrance. On peut rappeler, à propos de lui, la langue marbrée déjà des verdeurs de la décomposition et faisandée du bas-empire romain et les raffinements compliqués de l'école byzantine, dernière forme de l'art grec tombé en déliquescence. (Gautier, 286)

These in fact constitute the clichés of Decadent style: complication, nuance, rare words, vocabulary drawn from a variety of specialized sources, ineffability; the expression of neurosis, hallucination, depraved passion, obsession; *outrance, déliquescence,* refinement; connections between the late Roman and Byzantine empires and the late nineteenth century; decomposition and corruption, *faisandé* becoming a key adjective for style and language in the 1880s; and, most importantly, freer, less rigid forms. Des Esseintes later adopts Baudelaire's preference for the late Latin writers like Apuleius, Petronius, Juvenal, Augustine, and Tertullian, over Virgil and Cicero, and his taste for the free forms of the prose poem (Gautier, 336ff.).[31]

Of all the major aspects of Decadence attested in other sources, only two are entirely absent from Gautier's initial essay, the unconscious and pessimism. That it lacks the first is understandable, for the unconscious is not an explicit theme in Baudelaire's work, except in so far as it applies to the *Paradis artificiels,* and these Gautier treats in terms of the poet's mysticism. His omission of pessimism is more puzzling, and although he does discuss Baudelairean ennui and spleen, he does not relate these specifically to a conviction that life inherently involves suffering. This is an interesting lacuna in Gautier's otherwise complete description, for nearly all subsequent accounts acknowledge pessimism as the primary cause and feature of Decadence. In emphasizing this, Bourget, notably, made one of the most important contributions to the history and evolution of the movement.

Bourget's *Essais de psychologie contemporaine* study ten major writers of the Second Empire whose work most reflected and influenced the modern sensibility of the 1880s. They appeared in the *Nouvelle Revue* between 1881 and 1885, and every historian of Decadence has since confirmed their importance in formulating the presuppositions, characteristics, even goals of the emerging movement. Bourget's influence was especially great in Laforgue's case because of their close personal relations in the early years of Laforgue's career. He read virtually everything that Bourget ever wrote and consistently recommended his work to his own less appreciative friends; he met weekly with Bourget during 1881; his letters testify to his respect for the *Essais,* each of which he read with interest and admiration.[32] He found the Preface to the collected edition of the *Essais* (1885), on pessimism, particularly compelling and maintained that it had not been fully appreciated.[33] In the draft of his own article on Bourget (1882),[34] he suggests those areas in which Bourget might have influenced him: a profound belief in pessimism, an interest in Buddhism and mysticism, a taste for modernity and the personal in art, dilettantism, and most importantly, the Decadence associated with Baudelaire.

In his Preface, Bourget explicitly states the importance of pessimism to the volume and, accordingly, the authors examined in it:

> Le résultat de cette minutieuse et longue enquête est mélancolique. Il m'a semblé que de toutes les oeuvres passées en revue au cours de ces dix essais une même influence se dégageait, douloureuse et, pour tout dire d'un mot, profondément, continûment pessimiste. (Bourget, xvi)

He describes this as a late version of the Romantic *mal du siècle,* in modern dress and a Parisian setting: absolute discouragement, misanthropy, ennui, "une mortelle fatigue de vivre, une morne perception de la vanité de tout effort," an overwhelming feeling of "à quoi bon" (Bourget, xvii). The theme is firmly established in the first essay in a section entitled "Le Pessimisme de Baudelaire." For Bourget, contemporary European society perceives pessimism as the inescapable universal law, inspiring in modern man a sense of *taedium vitae,* ennui, spleen, melancholy, "une nausée universelle devant les insuffisances du monde"; it manifests itself among the Slavic peoples as nihilism, the Germanic as pessimism, the Latin as "solitaires et bizarres névroses," or Decadence (Bourget, 10).

Baudelaire represents the modern Parisian pessimist who has an absolute horror of 'being', and an equally powerful desire for 'nothingness' and the Buddhist state of beatitude, nirvana. In his attitude to love, Baudelaire combines the mystic, libertine, and *analyseur*, that is, spirituality, sensuality, and a critical intelligence. Bourget cites as an example of the concurrence of these three tendencies the poet's unorthodox use of liturgical imagery in a highly erotic, and frequently ironic, context. This convention of Decadence would be exploited also by Verlaine, Huysmans, and Mallarmé, and both employed and mocked by Laforgue, notably in *Lohengrin*.[35]

Bourget's theory of Decadence derives principally from that of his mentor, Taine, who attributes it to an unnatural imbalance: the disruption of organic unity by the excessive development of one part to the detriment of the rest.[36] Bourget applies this principle in the famous "Théorie de la décadence" section of the Baudelaire essay, describing Decadence in terms of the egoism and individualism characteristic of societies in decline: "Par le mot de décadence, on désigne volontiers l'état d'une société qui produit un trop petit nombre d'individus propres aux travaux de la vie commune . . . L'individu est la cellule sociale" (Bourget, 15). Both heredity and acquired well-being contribute to this development and exaggerate the importance of individual, at the expense of collective, life. This may have serious social consequences, as the Roman decadence attests: "l'entente savante du plaisir, le scepticisme délicat, l'énervement des sensations, l'inconstance du dilettantisme, ont été les plaies sociales de l'empire romain" (Bourget, 16). But Bourget maintains that these "social evils" can hold an aesthetic and psychological benefit:

> Si les citoyens d'une décadence sont inférieurs comme ouvriers de la grandeur du pays, ne sont-ils pas très supérieurs comme artistes de l'intérieur de leur âme? (Bourget, 16)

Laforgue quoted this sentence approvingly in defending modern art against the rigid classical system of Taine, with its hierarchy of aesthetic value ordered according to the degree of moral and formal harmony.[37] In particular, he uses Bourget's argument to counter Taine's assessment of Decadence, which ranks low on the scale, its perverted inspiration, and notably its individualism, being disproportionate with and insufficient to its technical capabilities. Bourget's portrait of the "concitoyens d'une décadence" justifies them on precisely those grounds condemned by Taine's system: ill-suited for public or private action, they nevertheless excel at solitary thought; uninterested in producing offspring, they have become, by their delicate sensations and exquisite, rare sentiments, the sterile but refined virtuosos of pleasure and pain; incapable of faith, they have rid themselves of prejudice and reached a "supreme equity," which admits and tolerates a variety of doctrines (Bourget, 17).

In literary terms, Bourget sees in Decadence an analogously individual style, in which "l'unité du livre se décompose pour laisser la place à l'indépendance de la page, où la page se décompose pour laisser la place à l'indépendance de la phrase, et la phrase pour laisser la place à l'indépendance du mot" (Bourget, 16). Like the social evils that contain and permit a psychological good, the individualism of Decadent literary style holds an aesthetic advantage. To the objection that such literature would not survive because its subtleties would render it unintelligible to future generations, Bourget responds with a resounding "Qu'importe? Le but de l'écrivain est-il de se poser en perpétuel candidat devant le suffrage universel des siècles? Nous nous délectons dans ce que vous appelez nos corruptions de style, et nous délectons avec nous les raffinés de notre race et de notre heure" (Bourget, 17). The political metaphor plays on a favorite cliché of the nineteenth century—notably following Baudelaire on Poe, and Gautier on Baudelaire—the hatred of democracy. The Decadent exception is really an aesthetic aristocracy and the rest, including an uncomprehending future, merely an ignorant crowd.

Bourget carries out this polemic, however, wholly through the lips of others. A hypothetical "psychologue pur," a student of moral life like the author, is introduced to bring out the positive value of Decadence. And Baudelaire himself speaks through the poetry, favoring morbidity and artificiality over simplicity; odors over all other sensations; late autumn with its melancholy charm over the other seasons; thin, adolescent women, or ravaged aging ones over all other forms of female beauty; languishing music, strange furnishings, and the evening hours. Baudelaire's Decadence permitted the *Fleurs du mal*, and despite Bourget's contrived objectivity the essay is clearly an apologia, setting forth and endorsing the aesthetic and morality of Decadence for an age to which it offered a relevant, even necessary, approach to life and art.

Bourget's remaining *Essais* (on Renan, Flaubert, Taine, Stendhal, Dumas *fils*, Leconte de Lisle, the Goncourts, Turgenev, and Amiel) develop the ideas and themes of the article on Baudelaire but also introduce some new ones which contribute to the idea of Decadence. Pessimism is extended to include such issues as dilettantism, nihilism, the overly analytic spirit, the inability to love, and the lack of will. The essay on Renan, which Laforgue called "étonnant" and "merveilleux,"[38] concentrates on the modern problem of dilettantism. As P. Moreau notes, this favorite concern of Decadence testifies to the close relation between this movement and the visual arts, from which it borrows the term to apply to its own aesthetic interest in the self.[39] Bourget defines it as the disposition to embrace all forms of life without committing oneself to any, a lack of *parti-pris* that may ultimately paralyse and lead to "une anémie de la conscience morale" (Bourget, 51). In the essay on Flaubert, he sees this attitude as destructive of human will (Bourget, 119), and in the one on Taine links it to the collapse of religious and metaphysical doctrine in modern life, where disparate hypotheses proliferate without there being a credible, integral one to reconcile them. Contemporary moral life is characterized by an extreme and anarchic scepticism with debilitating consequences: "cette disposition à douter même de son doute entraîne avec elle un cortège d'infirmités que nous connaissons trop: vacillation de la volonté, compromis sophistiques de la conscience, dilettantisme à demi détaché et toujours indifférent" (Bourget, 163). The theme recurs frequently in the *Essais*, with respect to Stendhal, the Goncourts, and Dumas (Bourget, 226, 307, 396), and is applied to more contemporary examples, such as Huysmans, Paul Alexis, and Maupassant. Although scepticism may bring pleasure to the true dilettante (as in Renan), it is more often a source of nihilism, the conviction that life is not worth living, which Bourget finds in Flaubert, Dumas, and Leconte de Lisle. The spirit of Spinoza hovers over all the

Essais, and Bourget refers to him frequently as a model for the pessimist's view: nature is all-powerful and has no purpose but itself; free will is thus a total illusion.

The essay on Dumas *fils* sets forth the principal Decadent view of love and women. Consistent with Bourget's pessimism, the attitude described here derives from the tradition of Schopenhauer, whom he presents as a philosophical parallel to Dumas. The female type for both is the "Eternel Féminin" who, in the Schopenhauerian formula, lures men into submitting themselves to the loathsome procreative purposes of the universal life force, the Will. Thinking that they will find the Ideal, or even pure pleasure ("volupté"), men in fact become instruments of the Will in its effort to perpetuate itself and, as a result, prolong the misery of life. Love is a trap set by the Will to ensure the continuation of the species, and women are its chief accomplices. Bourget sums it up thus: "il y a dans le mirage de l'amour quelque chose de décevant, une duperie mystérieuse qui conduit ceux qui s'y laissent prendre au pire malheur, à travers l'espérance du plus grand bonheur." Or, in Dumas's words to a new father from *Homme-Femme:* "le féminin . . . s'est servi de toi pour l'oeuvre qu'il a à faire" (Bourget, 296). Laforgue conveys this attitude more concisely in a favorite ironic rhyme, *dupe/jupe;*[40] he makes fun of it in *Hamlet*, where the hero rails constantly against the treachery of women while falling desperately in love with each one who crosses his path; and he parodies it directly in *Lohengrin*.

In several of the essays (Baudelaire, Renan, Flaubert, Dumas), Bourget exploits the notion of an aging civilization, with its Decadent models (Nero, Heliogabalus, Caesar, Alcibiades) and the symptoms of its physical and psychological degeneracy—neuroses, diminished energy, frailty, impoverished blood, strange excesses, and vice. He also raises the relatively new issue of the unconscious, which he regards as a further complication in the effort to understand the self, and thus to restore a human order (emotional or rational) in the face of the disorder of nature: "Hélas! où donc prendre cet ordre du coeur, où cet ordre de l'esprit . . . si notre *moi* nous échappe presqu'à nous-mêmes, sans cesse envahi par les ténèbres de l'inconscience?" (Bourget, 183). He mentions this only with respect to Taine's positivist theory of the self as a series of phenomena and nowhere discusses either the new experimental psychology of the French school or the metaphysical psychology of Hartmann, which had such an effect on him and the Decadent imagination in general. It is, however, the first mention of the unconscious in an important study of Decadence; the relation between the two would grow as the Unconscious became a major subject and source of imagery.

Like Gautier, Bourget discusses Decadent style in terms of complication and specifically sees the *écriture artiste* of the Goncourts as a model of it, with inversions, unusual combinations, repetition, impressionistic notation, syntactical difficulties, and neologisms. But in his view its dominant quality is the individualism described in the essay on Baudelaire, the shrinking of the literary and aesthetic unit from book to page to sentence to word, like the movement from community to the individual in social life. The *Moralités* confirm (and mock) the Decadent interest in language in itself; Laforgue freely mixes neologisms with archaisms, and colloquial with poetic language, uses assonance and interior rhyme to an exaggerated extent, and exploits the effects of rhythm in a prose work.

The picture of Decadence that emerges from Gautier and Bourget may be completed by the many articles and reviews published in the contemporary press. These begin to appear after Bourget's first essays of 1881–82; they proliferate after the publication of Verlaine's *Poétes maudits* in 1883, Huysmans' *A Rebours* in 1884, and the *Déliquescences* parody of the movement in 1885. The Decadent controversy of 1885–86 was inspired by this last event and, in its turn, provoked more discussion. They articulate the central aesthetic and moral issues understood by the term, i.e. the assumptions and formal conventions of the movement.

One of the most prominent features of Decadence mentioned is (following Bourget) pessimism, particularly its Schopenhauerian variety. Articles acclaim him as the father of Decadence, and cognate forms of his name occur with remarkable frequency: Decadence is "schopenhauérisme à outrance," born of the "surblaséisme d'une civilisation schopenhaueresque"; one even finds the verbal form "schopenhaueriser."[41] "Schopenhauerisme" is part of Laforgue's own definition of Decadence in 1885 (see above, n. 27). Moréas remarked that "toute revue qui se respecte est tenue de publier son petit article sur l'inventeur de la fameuse volonté," and himself wrote such articles.[42] His "Notes sur Schopenhauer" insist on the pessimistic assumption of "cette affreuse existence, qui n'est que tourments, aspirations impuissantes, ennui monotone et perpétuelle désillusion," and paraphrase closely Schopenhauer's chapters on love, that "malheur de l'individu pour le bien de l'espèce."[43] Reviews of *A Rebours* explicitly call attention to des Esseintes' espousal of Schopenhauer's ideas in chapter seven of the novel.[44] A simplified picture of Schopenhauer's pessimism was drawn and offered to the French public in a well-known and highly influential interview published by P. Challemel-Lacour in 1870: "Un Bouddhiste contemporain en Allemagne".[45] Several other studies appeared subsequently and likewise had a large readership: Ribot's *Philosophie de Schopenhauer* (1874), Janet's articles in the *Revue des deux mondes* (April–June 1877), and Caro's *Pessimisme au XIXè siècle* (1878).[46] These constituted an important source—often the only one—of information on Schopenhauer's thought, for although French translations of his books began to come out in 1877, his main work was not available until 1886.[47]

These studies bring out a few salient traits of Schopenhauer's system. First, the notion of a universal force governing all of life, the omnipotent Will, whose sole aim is self-perpetuation: it works for the continuation of the species and tricks human beings into contributing to its effort. Second, the fundamental disappointment and suffering of human existence: man's aspirations and sense of free will are illusions, merely the means by which the Will uses him to realize its own ends. Third, a "metaphysics of love", by which man is deceived against his will into procreation, thereby extending the suffering of life, precisely that which, in loving, he seeks to escape. As Bourget puts it in the essay on Dumas, man loves in order to reach the Ideal but then discovers that he has been duped into serving the Will. In Schopenhauer's words, "Les hommes ne sont mus ni par des convoitises dépravées, ni par un attrait divin, ils travaillent pour le Génie de l'espèce sans le savoir, ils sont tout à la fois ses courtiers, ses instruments, et ses dupes."[48] Fourth, two means of overcoming the Will, namely, art and asceticism: aesthetic emotion provides only a momentary escape from the Will's domination, but asceticism and renunciation a more permanent one, for they suppress desire, the emotion by means of which the Will accomplishes its purpose. In the supreme state of Buddhist nirvana, the intellect frees itself from the Will and achieves the tranquillity of detachment.

The variety of pessimism presented by Eduard von Hartmann in his *Philosophy of the Unconscious* (1868)[49] was also linked to the Decadents: "Un système récent de philosophie leur a fourni une solution précisément appropriée à leur tempérament.... Rappelons seulement que M. de Hartmann veut voir dans les mouvements réflexes ou instinctifs la révélation d'une substance éternelle qu'il appelle l'inconscient."[50] Hartmann modifies Schopenhauer's views in a few important ways. First, he replaces the notion of a blind and evil Will with the Unconscious, an intelligent, teleological power governing all of life, phenomenal, conscious, and unconscious. Unlike the Will, the Unconscious is infallible and omniscient and has a plan that actualizes itself in history as it progressively moves toward its goal of full consciousness, the dispelling of illusion, the perfection of the species, and the elimination of human misery. Because Hartmann attributes intelligence and purpose to the Unconscious, he sees pessimism as a means toward its end, specifically by laying bare the illusions of happiness. Pessimism will ultimately bring man to that degree of perfection where he rejects these and loses all desire, that manifestation of the life-affirming Will so disturbing to Schopenhauer. Hence pessimism, despite the suffering that it entails, leads to the state of tranquillity to which all human effort has ever aspired; it provides a modern faith similar to fatalism, which reconciles inevitable pessimistic convictions with belief in a larger metaphysical plan.

Second, although Hartmann's views on the relation between the sexes resemble Schopenhauer's and use the same metaphors—love is an avid demon constantly claiming new victims, and women are agents in the deception—this is part of the plan of the Unconscious to redeem humanity from its enslavement to nature. The suffering caused by women and love is thus justified by the positive goal of the Unconscious toward which they work. This had particular significance for Decadent notions of women, which, as Pierrot remarks, took two main forms, following Gautier's analysis of Baudelaire:[51] first, that of the destructive *femme fatale* like Salome, Herodias, the Queen of Sheba, Delilah, the Sphinx, Circe, and Astarte, ruthlessly drawing men to their ruin; second, the milder form of the creature of instinct, an unwitting agent of the life process, bound to the physical, animal side of existence and closed to the spiritual. Baudelaire's description of women in *Mon Coeur mis à nu* and *Le Peintre de la vie moderne*—governed by their instincts, contemptible because close to nature, and devoid of spirituality—is an especially harsh example of this view.[52] Laforgue qualifies the traditional pessimistic line, however, by portraying women as victims of the same natural law that they are obliged to serve and whose purposes they must work to realize: "O femme, mammifère à chignon, ô fétiche, / On t'absout; c'est un Dieu qui par tes yeux nous triche."[53] This view figures prominently in his notes and constitutes a persistent theme of his work, especially after 1881; women are "pauvres pions sociaux," "victimes," "martyres," and "historiques esclaves," fulfilling a function accorded by nature and sanctioned by culture for which they are not themselves responsible.[54]

Third, Hartmann views both mysticism and aesthetic pleasure as direct and spontaneous manifestations of the Unconscious. They are immediate intuitions, instincts that have not reached full consciousness, in which the self is dissolved and united with the Absolute and the goal of the unconscious momentarily glimpsed. Hartmann's argument provided an impetus for aesthetic exploitation of the psychological Unconscious, through whose communications an ideal could be attained and transmitted. The ideas of Schopenhauer and Hartmann greatly influenced Laforgue's thought, notably his belief in an infallible yet unintelligible universal law in perpetual evolution, his notion of love as an illusory and ultimately disappointing quest for the Ideal, and his qualified pessimism, all themes treated with irony and compassion in the *Moralités*.

Articles on Decadence insist on its characteristic pessimism, the Romantic *mal du siècle* taken to an extreme:

Aujourd'hui René n'est plus mélancolique; il est morne et il est âprement pessimiste. Il ne doute plus, il nie ou même ne se soucie plus de la vérité. Il ne sent plus d'inégalité entre son désir et son effort, car sa volonté est morte. Il ne se réfugie plus dans la rêverie ou dans quelque amour emphatique, mais dans les raffinements littéraires ou dans la recherche pédantesque des sensations rares. René avait du "vague à l'âme"; à présent "il s'embête à crever". René n'était malade que d'esprit; à présent il est névropathe.[55]

Similarly, in a pair of articles devoted to pessimism in literature,[56] E. Hennequin associates it with ennui, inertia, a fundamental sense of the uselessness of life and the futility of human effort, a weakening of the will, and an overdeveloped and hypertrophic sensibility. In a review of *A Rebours,* he characterizes Decadence in terms of excessive self-analysis, irresolution, hypochondria, and a state of sluggish "atonie."

De leur impuissance volitionnelle, on peut déduire leur incapacité de vivre dans la société, leur aspiration . . . vers une existence monacale, solitaire et récluse, enfin leur absolu pessimisme, leur misanthropie acerbe, leur dégoût de toute vie active.[57]

Other articles repeat the same themes. The paralysing effect of doubt and self-analysis is mentioned frequently, following Bourget's "nous sommes malades d'un excès de pensée critique" (Bourget, 307). For example, Charles Morice qualifies the Decadents as "êtres de réflexion à qui trop de science enseigne une défiance prudente et paralysante";[58] and a review of the *Déliquescences* describes the target of their parody as "affamés d'analyse; malades de psychologie."[59] The weakening of the will attendant on this accounts for a favorite Decadent condition designated by a variety of terms: hypochondria, abulia, atony, anemia (considered the illness of the Roman empire),[60] even hamletism; Hennequin, for example, sees Hamlet as the type of the contemporary writer suffering from a paralysing "atonie de la volonté."[61] But consistent with Bourget's essay on Baudelaire, the most frequent one is neurosis. "Notre maladie à tous," neurosis constitutes the Decadent syndrome *par excellence,* and the *névropathe* a model for the Decadent hero.[62] Laforgue parodies this openly in *Le Miracle des Roses*.

The desire for evasion cited by Hennequin and realized by des

Esseintes is frequently named as a Decadent attribute, especially vis-à-vis Verlaine, Mallarmé, and Flaubert: "Tous ces écrivains byzantins ont en commun . . . un profond mépris pour les suffrages de la foule, dérivant de cette conviction que le véritable artiste ne doit pas s'adresser à une foule mais à quelques esprits élus."[63] Bourde cites evasion as a chief trait in his sarcastic portrait of the "parfait Décadent": "aversion déclarée pour la foule, considérée comme souverainement stupide et plate" (Pakenham, 11). This attitude comically torments Laforgue's Hamlet and Lohengrin and, predictably, brings about their downfall.

The important theme of artifice and those related to it—perversity, depravity, sensuality, exoticism—are generally traced to Baudelaire and ascribed to either the tensions of contemporary society or the hereditary corruption of a dying line. They are perceived to express an inversion of conventional values, and thus attitudes of subversion and revolt, the individual's desperate or cynical protest against the mockery of nature or society. The abnormal, unhealthy, artificial, and monstrous characterize not only Decadent art, but art itself in its relation to reality, and the poet with respect to the normal man: "les poètes, monstrueux parmi les ordinaires, malades parmi les sains, détraqués parmi les raisonnables. Ceux-là seront toujours la proie des révoltes et des nostalgies. Et cela nécessairement, parce que la maladie est l'essence même de toute nature supérieure."[64] They account for the peculiar sexuality of Decadent art: des Esseintes' complicated experiments; a Baudelairean preference for the sterile woman; Lord Edwards' love for a mechanical model in Villiers' *Eve future;* homosexuality in the work of Verlaine, Jean Lorrain, and others; and incestuous love in Elémir Bourges' *Crépuscule des dieux* (1884) and Moréas's *La Faënza* (1883).[65]

Exotic images accordingly proliferate: flowers, plants, perfumes, and gems, following Baudelaire; a vogue for orientalism, following Baudelaire and Flaubert; and a preoccupation with the rare, the bizarre, the exquisite, and the refined, mentioned in nearly all articles on Decadence. In the minor writers, especially, this becomes ludicrous in its intensity: "Car, tu [Désespérance] me crées d'artificiels jardins où croissent, bizarres et contournées, sinistres aussi, les plantes tropicales, aux senteurs âcres, aux parfums empoisonnés. Avec délices, je respire leur atmosphère lourde et vénéneuse, et la pourpre enflammée de leurs fleurs me comble d'une délicate et précieuse volupté."[66] More importantly, Bourde uses the strange flower as a metaphor for Decadence itself: "le romantisme épuisé a donné cette dernière petite fleur, une fleur de fin de saison, maladive et bizarre" (Pakenham, 21). Consistent with this, the Decadent season is by all accounts autumn, with its pale suns and its hints of oncoming winter; in Huysmans, it functions directly as a metaphor for the Decadent sensibility, "l'esprit qui a atteint l'octobre de ses sensations."[67] Gautier, Bourget, and Laforgue all call attention to this in their studies of Baudelaire, and it is amply attested in the literature of the period as well, in Mallarmé, Verlaine, Huysmans, and Laforgue, to name only a few. Such an aesthetic applied to the day makes the most beautiful hour twilight: "M. Paul Verlaine a, comme Baudelaire, l'amour des heures crépusculaires."[68]

The association of late-nineteenth-century Decadence with that of the late Empire or Byzantium, as in Gautier's essay on Baudelaire, informs many works of the period (e.g., Mallarmé's "Plainte d'automne," with its "poésie agonisante des derniers moments de Rome," Huysmans's *A Rebours*, Verlaine's famous "Langueur," the parodic *Déliquescences* published in "Byzance"), as well as articles on the movement: "notre époque . . . nous est l'image fidèle de l'ère des derniers Césars."[69] It provided a stock of ancient models for the Decadent hero: Nero, especially, but also Heliogabalus, Sardanapalus, Alcibiades, and Caesar—these latter two in particular types of the dandy.[70] "Néron, le plus débauché, le plus ignoble de tous les hommes, était un artiste":[71] depraved, debauched, deranged, the artist of *qualis artifex pereo* furnished an appropriately corrupt example for the Decadent. Laforgue alludes to Nero on many occasions, and notably in *Hamlet*, where the maniacally aesthetic hero dies with the emperor's words on his lips.[72] The physical characteristics of the Decadent hero conformed to the idea of these ancient predecessors: pale, thin, anemic, frail, and feminine, but dressed in the Baudelairean black suit.

The mysticism that Gautier and Bourget discuss in their essays on Baudelaire becomes a commonplace of Decadence. It is linked to a loss of conventional religious faith, replaced by a less sectarian belief in a spiritual realm beyond the physical world with which the human soul aspires to be united. The Romantic origins of Decadent mysticism are acknowledged from the beginning: Gautier mentions Swedenborg's influence on Baudelaire's spirituality and theory of correspondences; Villiers's spiritist hero of *Claire Lenoir* reads Swedenborg; Balzac's *Séraphita* was considered a forerunner of Symbolism; Flaubert's *Tentation de Saint-Antoine* was one of the most important books of the period, along with the *Imitation de Jésus-Christ*, both favorites of des Esseintes.[73] Nearly all articles on the movement call attention to its mystical strain: the Decadents are "religieux de mysticisme" and characterized by "un curieux mélange de positivisme et de mysticisme"; Verlaine combines a "mysticité catholique" with refined *libertinage;* V. Pica cites the mélange of "misticismo catolico e pessimismo alemanno; and Laforgue himself includes "mysticisme" in his definition of Decadence.[74]

Bourget saw the tendency to mysticism as one response to the torturing problem of the age, the conflict between a desire for a stable, unified self and world, on the one hand, and the unsettling results of scientific and psychological analysis, on the other. Mysticism reflects the thirst of the nihilist for an ideal, as with Baudelaire, "assoiffé d'un infini perdu," and Flaubert, "nihiliste affamé d'absolu" (Bourget, 13, 127). In his review of *A Rebours*, Barbey makes a similar observation about des Esseintes, "une âme malade d'infini dans une société qui ne croit plus qu'aux choses finies."[75] But des Esseintes's love for medieval mystics and all the mystical works in his library do not save him from the defeat of the ending, when he is forced, in a choice between suicide and returning to society, to give in to the powers of conformity. The hero's failure points up the shortcomings of mysticism, the ultimate impossibility of a Schopenhauerian union of the self with the absolute. This ideal of Decadence was thus undermined by a basic Decadent conviction, an irony exploited constantly by Laforgue.

Mysticism provided a large stock of imagery: metaphors of dissolution, emanation, expansion, and metamorphosis, as in the

Spinozian pantheistic finale to *La Tentation de Saint-Antoine,* and the parodic title of the *Déliquescences;* underwater, lunar, and liturgical imagery, the latter usually in an erotic context.[76] Bourget had noted this last phenomenon, which derives from a long tradition relating Christian texts to eroticism, in Baudelaire, but it occurs also in other major writers of the period: Verlaine, Laforgue, Mallarmé, and Viélé-Griffin.[77] It is parodied in the *Déliquescences,*[78] and mocked by Bourde in the article cited above: "Les oeuvres de l'école font briller plus d'ostensoirs et resplendir plus d'or sur les chapes, allument plus de cierges, ouvrent plus de missels et fournissent plus de décors de basilique que la rue Saint-Sulpice tout entière n'en pourrait fournir" (Pakenham, 14). Laforgue uses the liturgical metaphor ironically throughout his work, especially in the *Complaintes,*[79] and parodies it explicitly in *Lohengrin.*

Bourget had noted the Decadent insistence on individualism and the importance of the self, with respect to both the subject of modern literature and its form; Decadence results when the individual, be it self or word, becomes exaggerated at the expense of the whole, society or text. In the period of the *Essais,* he saw this as a source of aesthetic and psychological interest, even pleasure, despite (or perhaps, because of) the crises that it involved; later he would depart from this position.[80] For Bourget, the self is a complex, variable entity formed by heredity and environment; it has an unconscious domain to which we have limited access; it may be studied, if not—in its variability—securely known; and such self-study reveals the source of an individual's reality: "Chacun de nous aperçoit non pas l'univers, mais son univers; non pas la réalité, mais de cette réalité, ce que son tempérament lui permet de s'approprier" (Bourget, 98). Bourget emphasized the personal as the sole valid access to the real and the principal source of aesthetic emotion. His subjective idealism was not extreme, however, for he maintained that art had the capacity to communicate the artist's vision to others by its power of suggestion. To cultivate, examine, and protect the self for the purposes of artistic creation was a cliché of 1880s Decadence: "Les personnages doivent vivre en dedans et y construire le monde intérieur";[81] "repousser toute réalité de la matière et n'admet[tre] le monde que comme représentation."[82] Villiers, for whom the individual consciousness constitutes the only reality, is the extreme figure in the solipsistic trend; cultivating the self allows one to create a reality for oneself, as in *L'Eve future* and, of course, *Axël*. Huysmans illustrates this view in *A Rebours* and proclaims its failure. Egoism, individualism, narcissism, subjective idealism: the terms are used loosely and interchangeably to designate the importance of the self and self-analysis as the basis of an approach to life. Moreover, as Moreau has noted, the self, particularly the unconscious, is repeatedly treated in metaphors of theater and spectacle as a drama to be interpreted, consistent with the ideology of Decadence itself.[83] All life, including the intimate life of the unconscious mind, is a work of art.

Decadent style and form constitute the single most important theme in discussions of the movement during this period. Nearly every article devotes some attention to the technical novelty of Decadent writing and tries to describe it, particularly in terms of decomposition or fragmentation, as Bourget had suggested. Floupette humorously called it "une attaque de nerfs sur du papier" (Richard, *Symbolisme*, 310), with which judgment certain readers of Laforgue's *Complaintes* seemed to agree, as we shall see shortly. But everyone acknowledged that the Decadents had realized the revolution in poetic language and form begun by the Romantics. Although Bourde was sarcastic about the subjects of Decadent art, he nevertheless paid tribute to its language as an original contribution to the history of poetry:

> Mais autant ils mettent de vanité à rechercher des sensations inédites, autant ils apportent de soins à les exprimer dans des rythmes rares et dans une langue renouvelée. ... Les essais que font ces poètes sur la langue sont plus nouveaux en notre pays que leurs sentiments et leurs opinions. (Pakenham, 15f., 21)

Characteristic features cited repeatedly include a neglect of the caesura and of the rule of alternating masculine-feminine rhymes; innovative language, neologisms, rare words, variable rhythms, heavy assonance and alliteration, novel metaphors, synaesthesia, discontinuity, the use of adjectives as substantives, a mixture of popular and *savant* vocabulary, and an emphasis on suggestion.[84] Complication is a major theme, with the questionable justification

Decadence and Parody

that a complicated style is necessary for the expression of complicated sensations, ideas, and the Idea itself.[85] Accordingly, incoherence, imprecision, and unintelligibility form the principal objections of critics: "c'est l'école du *flou* . . . Les mots, entre leurs mains, sont . . . des instruments destinés à volatiliser les impressions, et à les rendre encore plus fuyantes et vaporeuses qu'elles ne le sont dans la réalité. Ils ont l'amour du vague à la phrase"; and more sarcastically, "avec quelque peu de bonne volonté, tirant les mots au sort dans un dictionnaire, et comptant sur ses doigts le nombre de syllabes nécessaires pour former un vers, on a la grande chance d'atteindre la perfection dans le genre et de devenir un très brillant poète décadent."[86]

Laforgue's first published collection, the *Complaintes,* appeared precisely at the time when the Decadent controversy, touched off by the publication of the *Déliquescences,* was becoming prominent in the press.[87] For better or worse, his volume was involved in the popularization of the Decadent debate; there were accordingly more than four times as many reviews of the *Complaintes* as of his subsequent collections. This coincidence had significant consequences, for his poems were read entirely in the light of the "new school," and nearly all reviews discuss him in these terms. The most important feature to emerge from these articles is his wholly unconventional and original style: his irregular meter, novel and broken rhythms, neglect of the caesura, ellipses, use of a spoken idiom, neologisms, humor, incongruous juxtapositions, a mixture of popular and learned language, and his rhyme for the ear rather than the eye. Charges of unintelligibility abound, and some critics describe his verse as gibberish, delirium, or the random utterances of an *halluciné*. One of the first readers of the *Complaintes* predicted of the Laforguian trend: "Si ça continue, il suffira dans six ans: 1. de n'avoir rien à dire; 2. de le dire en mauvais vers et en vers faux; 3. d'écrire comme un javanais: pour être un poète de génie" (Debauve, 198). Even L. Trézenik, who appreciated Laforgue's innovative form to some extent, noted the incomprehensibility of some of the poems: "M. Laforgue se complaît à siéger dans une bouteille à encre de la plus indéniable opacité . . . bon nombre de complaintes sont totalement indéchiffrables. M. Laforgue est un

Sphinx . . . pour les énigmes duquel peu d'Oedipes sont nés encore."[88] Others put it more directly: "Le livre de M. Laforgue demeure parfaitement inintelligible";[89] its fragmented phrases "paraissent avoir été tirés au sort et assemblés au hasard."[90] The *Complaintes* were even compared to the *Déliquescences* as a parody of Decadent writing: "à certaines pages, on se croirait en face d'une parodie plus loin poussée que la brochure des *Déliquescences*."[91]

Significantly, however, all those who objected to Laforgue's technical innovation acknowledged that it was both original and deliberate. Trézenik admits that his "indépendence prosodique . . . n'est pas le résultat de l'impuissance. C'est voulu" (Debauve, 199). Amédée Pigeon notes the "négligeances très voulues de son style" and places him in the rhetorical family of Rimbaud, Mallarmé, Verlaine, and Corbière.[92] F. Nautet likens Laforgue's prosody to the techniques of Wagner, and Wyzewa counts him among the writers of "littérature wagnérienne," particularly for his rhythms.[93] The master of Decadence himself, Huysmans, praises their "langue si avancée": "ce livre des Complaintes m'a très insidieusement requis, avec ses horizons fuyant dans les brumes, ses épithètes suggestives ouvrant des échappées sur lesquelles on rêve, ses verbes fabriqués curieusement, ses vers bizarrement rimés où les pluriels baisent le singulier . . . Ça a été un fin régal pour des Esseintes: quelle singulière chose, pourtant!"[94]

Laforgue's own reviews of the *Complaintes* reveal that he considered his formal originality one of the two most notable features of the volume. He acknowledges his debt to Decadent style, which he defines as "une langue enfilant au petit bonheur des consonances imprévues et sans syntaxe presque, les images les plus criardes et les mots les plus exotiques qu'on puisse glaner dans les troisièmes dessous du *Dictionnaire* de Littré."[95] Of his own, he noted the "originales qualités de langue" and his novel rhymes and meter, meant to impart subtle nuances and create special effects, as well as his neologisms and unusual metaphors (Debauve, 195).

The discontinuity of the *Moralités*' prose is consistent with the Decadence that they both mock and affirm. It relies, like his poetry, on puns, sound play, peculiar metaphors, a rapid and wide-ranging association of ideas, repetition, substantivized adjectives, incongruous allusions, clichés, a variety of specialized vocabularies, autoquotation, neologisms, suspension points, exclamations, apostrophe, and levels of diction ranging from the most poetic to the most colloquial.[96] As noted in chapter one, the point of view changes frequently from the most personal interior monologue to a disconcerting narratorial intervention; problems of interpretation, and sometimes mere intelligibility, arise frequently. His descriptions of nature are highly stylized, as Moreau has remarked,[97] and one of the most common aspects of Decadent writing, synaesthesia, is applied brilliantly: a hush is compared to a sweep-net unfolding on the water in *Salomé* (221); in *Pan*, water and breezes are compared to fabrics (306), a fountain to a fan (306), and a melody to a garland unwinding round a statue's pedestal (307). Sounds are likened to shades of a watercolor, and a scene to a seventeenth-century tapestry in *Hamlet* (11); the countryside is described as a color print in *Le Miracle des Roses* (59). But Laforgue does not mock Decadence merely by exaggerating its favorite stylistic features; his language is more sophisticated and radical, now exaggerating them, now ironically deflating them, now employing them masterfully to communicate his point. It provides an especially good example of how Decadence may parody itself in the fullest sense, creating a new language as it mocks itself. Reviews of the tales consistently praise their stylistic virtuosity: their "imprévues abracadabrances d'images," their "multicolores et inusités vêtements de phrases," the "sauts de carpe" of their dialogues, their distinctive "style inouï, bariolé de science, de transcendance, de blague, de calembours, de folie et de raison, un style insoupçonné," with the suppleness of an acrobat and a clown, and the sleight of hand of a magician.[98] Their unusual images and strange combinations disconcert ("tour à tour science, art, folie, rêve sont évoqués. Les mots s'emmêlent en un tout bizarre"), but make for a "richesse d'expression" largely responsible for the incomparable originality of the stories.[99]

It is interesting that, except for Laforgue, critics of the period did not identify humor as an aspect of Decadence, save by an occasional allusion to the *Déliquescences*, Corbière, or Laforgue himself. This omission is understandable, given the utterly, ponderously humorless quality of many Decadent works; on the other hand, the wry, caricatural humor of *A Rebours* is undeniable.[100] A movement that produced, in addition, the *Déliquescences,* the *Moralités,* and a host of more minor works of *fumisterie* and *blague,* and led to the comic works of Jarry after 1893, ought to be examined for its relation to humor. One of its chief features—exaggeration—is indeed one of the oldest devices of humor. This other side of Decadence has been generally ignored. Pierrot's study, the most complete, never mentions it, and others have merely pointed it out. For example, M. Décaudin considers "l'esprit de blague" an important counterweight to the neurotic element of Decadence.[101] P. Stephan remarks its "parodying, *pince sans rire* side" and states that "parodies of decadence seem almost as typical of the movement as more serious poetic expression."[102] R. Thornton observes that "the Decadent is grotesque, a caricature from the start," and "the central figure of Decadence . . . a parody. This self-mocking note of Decadence . . . is a fundamental characteristic, uniting aspects of Lionel Johnson, Max Beerbohm, and Aubrey Beardsley, not to mention *Punch* and Adoré Floupette."[103] And in his edition of the *Moralités,* P. Pia cites the importance of parody in the nineteenth century, especially parodies of theater and poetry, notably of Hugo.[104]

These remarks depend on varied and free senses of "parody," somewhat less precise than the one formulated in the preceding chapter; however, they all suggest that Decadence involves, inherently or simply in practice, a comic element—humor, mockery, and self-mockery. While I would not maintain that Decadence ultimately demands parody, according to my view of it, a relation between them certainly exists. The relation has been studied somewhat with respect to the Aesthetic movement in England, which not only offered perfect targets for parody but also was to some extent a product of parody, the aesthete's conscious pose, an image deliberately exaggerated to mock middle-class values and the realist art associated with them.[105] Exaggeration, self-consciousness, artifice, the spirit of novelty, self-reflexive art: these features of Decadence leave the movement easily open to the comic and to parody, whose distortion is, as it were, already provided.

The Other Side of Decadence. Parody in the Late Nineteenth Century

An examination of the numerous and often short-lived literary reviews of the late-nineteenth century reveals a climate remarkably conducive to the production of parody.[106] Some of the most important periodicals representing the multiple new poetic currents of the anonymous "jeunes" depended upon the comic in their effort to offer an alternative to established values, institutions, writers, critics, and literary works; it assisted the aesthetic of novelty, originality, and modernity which motivated the new poetry. *Le Chat noir* (1882–1894), *Lutèce* (1883–1886), *L'Hydropathe* (1879–1880), and *Le Scapin* (1885–1886), to name some of the more notable *feuilles humoristiques,* used parody, satire, and pastiche to promulgate a specifically modern art and formulate its relation to past, or even contemporary, standards. Humor provided a means of achieving, in particular, the aesthetic freedom (ideological and technical) that was by all accounts, contemporary and later, a chief characteristic of early modernism.

Some of this was directed toward political targets; certain journals were devoted to it, and other, more literary ones frequently contained a section of political satire. I have not included these examples in the present study, however, for two reasons. First, they are not distinctive to the period, as France has a long and rich tradition of political satire and caricature; on this basis, the period would not be more favorable to parody than any other. Humor applied consistently to the arts distinguishes the early 1880s and creates an atmosphere in which parody might develop. Second, political satire does not present a useful parallel to literary parody, for the theoretical reasons given in chapter one: it does not preserve the target within itself, and the satirist does not share the parodist's ambivalence toward his object. Forms of the comic became an essential feature, rather, of the *literary* avant-garde and the aesthetic of the new that it consciously sought to promote. The growing importance of humor in areas other than the political is reflected in the gradual abandonment by some small literary journals of their political component, as in the passage of the *Nouvelle Rive Gauche* to its more purely artistic successor, *Lutèce*.

Although examples of parody are frequent in the nineteenth century in both published works and scores of periodicals, none reflects the particular procedures or achieves the level of artistry of the *Moralités*. Most are mediocre efforts, in Pia's terms "petites drôleries,"[107] which have no reputation today, and suffer from standard flaws: they are often too brief to put the humor in the service of a new aesthetic; the distortion is crude and turns easily into allegory; the humor is doubtful—highly topical or consisting only in the discrepancy between speech and setting. However, by their prominence they deserve some attention, for they reveal a context, as yet unexplored, in which to place the *Moralités*. They indeed exploit many of the same parodic techniques: anachronism, particularly modern speech, dress, and ideas attributed to an older subject; the deformation of a familiar story, or its continuation beyond the traditional ending; all the conventional devices of humor; quotations from the original in a different context; some acknowledgement from within the work of the reader's world outside. They thus provide a contemporary background against which to appreciate the ingenuity and creativity of Laforgue's comic imagination.

Canonical texts of French culture, such as *La Marseillaise* and the Lord's Prayer, frequently function as objects or vehicles of parody in the manner of the schoolboy joke: one finds a "Marseillaise des Infirmes," a "Marseillaise des locataires," a "Notre père Zola, qui êtes à Médan, que vos romans soient payés très cher."[108] Well-known folk tales are also exploited freely. For instance, the story of Red Riding Hood is reversed in an issue of *La Parodie*, with the villain of the original the hero of the parody, and the title accordingly altered from the "Le Petit Chaperon Rouge" to "Le Loup"; the wolf, who has already read Perrault's tale, is figuratively devoured by Chaperon Rouge, a true Eternal Feminine who toys with his love and destroys his heart.[109]

Another common form of parody involves using a famous writer as a character in a new scenario, contrived to foster citations out of context. For example, an issue of *Le Chat noir* features "Les

Decadence and Parody

Poètes, boulevard Rochechouart," depicting the nocturnal encounters of celebrated poets with the street walkers of the boulevard Rochechouart, location of the Chat Noir literary club:[110]

RONSARD: Mignonne, allons voir si la rose, qui, ce matin, av . . .
LA FILLE: —Eh, zut! J'ai pas de rose chez moi! Viens-y plutôt.
VILLON: Viens dans notre bourdeau où tenons notre estat.
LA FILLE: Va donc parler argot à tes marmites, sale marlou!
BOILEAU: Ce que l'on conçoit bien s'énonce clairement,
Et les mots, pour le dire, arrivent aisément.

The give and take continues with artists from Racine to the present, including the journal's editor, Emile Goudeau. The humor derives from the anachronism and the disjunction of poetic and vulgar language; from the citation taken out of context, spoken by its author, and applied to an incongruous but ironically apt situation; and from the self-reference of *Le Chat noir* (through the presence of its editor and the location of the club). Another spoof, on Félicien Champsaur's novel, *Dinah Samuel,* uses a similar type of parody. In an extension of the *Inferno,* Victor Hugo, dressed as Dante, appears to the sleeping Champsaur in a dream and tells him to go to Paris, a modern Inferno ("enfer des vertus provinciales"), to join the Hydropathes, one of the first literary clubs of the period: "Félicien tu rêves . . . la bouche d'ombre me l'a dit." Hugo literally applies his own poem, "Ce que dit la bouche d'ombre," to an ironically pertinent context, whose distance from the proper one provokes the humor. As the piece continues, the two enter the second circle, that of Montmartre (home of the Chat Noir), and watch Champsaur's lover, Dinah Samuel, run off with a banker, "parodiant à la moderne l'antique Francesca di Rimini."[111] Again, the journal refers to itself; and more explicitly, the text signals itself as a modern version of Dante's celebrated story of the adulteress Francesca, thus exposing its own parodic methods.

The specific parodic device of retelling and distorting a well-known story occurs relatively infrequently during this early period, except in the popular theater where parodies of Flaubert, Zola, and Wagner, in particular, were performed regularly.[112] Most literary "rewritings," particularly those involving modernization, come well after the *Moralités*.[113] This is surprising, for the technique had been used extensively, and sometimes masterfully, during the Second Empire in the *opéra-comique*. Retelling a familiar story in a comical way is the principle of Offenbach's works, notably *Orphée aux enfers* and *La Belle Hélène,* which have the additional parodic feature of using a distant story to make fun of something closer to the aesthetic world of the author and audience. Thus *Orphée* parodies Gluck's *Orfeo ed Eurydice* and the clichés of Italian opera as it trivializes the story, and *Hélène* parodies the singing contest in Wagner's *Tannhaüser*.[114] In conception, this type of *opéra-comique* resembles the *Moralités,* and Laforgue exploited the likeness by alluding frequently to the *opéra-comique* in the stories. In purpose and result, however, the two differ considerably. Offenbach's works are *principally* satires (and brilliant ones at that) on Second-Empire Parisian life, which use parodic methods for satirical purposes; Laforgue's have an occasional satirical component (as in the ridiculous bourgeois parade of *Le Miracle des Roses*), but are essentially parodies of Decadent art. Moreover he puts his humor in the service of a larger and more important effort of modernization, ultimately making the stories *moralités* for modern life; his mockery of Decadence takes the movement beyond its obvious limitations and offers, according to his wishes for the *Complaintes*, a more seriously modern ideal. The connection between the *Moralités* and the *opéra-comique* was made early on, but was criticized by one reviewer: "Il en est qui ne voient dans le livre de Jules Laforgue que des bouffonneries très réussies venant après Offenbach . . . Ce sont là des jugements corticaux. Les *Moralités légendaires* ont toutes plus haute et décisive portée. . . . voici de la profonde psychologie et de la philosophie nette."[115]

Examples of parodic rewriting that come after the *Moralités* include such works as *Les Aventures du roi Pausole* of Pierre Louÿs (1900), a story based on the *roi d'Yvetot* that lampoons contemporary figures, notably Gide. Georges Fourest's *Négresse blonde* (1909) is a series of poems that transposes the subjects of Racine and Corneille into the contemporary world, particularly in speech, dress, and décor: Bérénice rides in a sleeping car and plays golf; Hippolyte is "un jeune homme d'élite"; Pyrrhus wears a frock coat and white gloves. Fourest accordingly mixes grand descriptive alexandrines with the rhythms of popular verse. In another example, Paul-Jean Toulet extends and transforms the story of Don Quixote in "Le Mariage de Don Quichotte" (*Mon Amie Nane*, 1904): the hero, having recovered his reason, becomes an ultrapositivist who seeks to convince the world of the value of science and rationalism. And the work of the established drama critic Jules Lemaître consistently uses this device. Lemaître owned a copy of the first edition of the *Moralités*, and it is possible that they influenced his own work.[116] As the title of his tales suggests, the *Contes en marge des vieux livres* (1905) follow parodic principles, lowering gods and heroes to human level, bringing a secondary character to the fore, taking the story to a conclusion implied but not realized by the original narrative itself. The volume contains stories inspired by a variety of genres and periods: the *Iliad*, the *Odyssey*, the *Aeneid*, the Gospels, the *chansons de geste*, and so on. His procedure consists principally in spinning off a story from a traditional one; the model is clearly identified by the title and usually by a quotation from it in the new version. Thus, "Thersite" makes the most lowly and unheroic character of the *Iliad* the main character of a story of his own, which begins with Homer's line itself: "C'était l'homme le plus laid qui fût venu devant Ilion."[117]

Lemaître's stories, however, differ markedly from the *Moralités*. First, they are highly moralistic in the most literal sense of the term, and not in the ironic way that Laforgue uses his title; they have a serious, and usually very simple, moral lesson to tell, which considerably reduces the humor. Second, Lemaître's modernization consists principally of having the characters use modern speech; his purpose lay, by his own admission, in the past, "rêver dans le passé." Third, his stories are not parodies, properly speaking, for they do not include the comic element necessary to the genre. Laforgue's, in contrast, depend on this element as the main mechanism for realizing his aesthetic of modernity, calling even the present into question.

In the 1890s, the "esprit de blague" attained a certain authority and a wide following by its association with the foremost Symbolist journal of the decade, the *Revue blanche*. In *Le Chasseur de Chevelures*, its humorous monthly supplement, one finds various forms of parody, notably by Tristan Bernard, "informateur du possible," and Pierre Veber, "déformateur du réel." These usually have a topical and often satirical interest. For example, Baudelaire's "Harmonie du soir" is altered to make fun of the crisis in Parisian theaters:

> Voici venir le temps où perdant leur prestige
> Les pauvres directeurs sont tous au désespoir;
> Plus personne aux fauteuils, hélas! ne vient s'asseoir,
> Abandon lamentable et néfaste prodige![118]

In another, famous poetic lines of nineteenth-century poets are transformed into advertisements for merchandise: Musset, Hugo, Baudelaire, and Verlaine are all integrated into the world of the marketplace.[119] Poetry may indeed be applicable to life; or, more likely, the bourgeois world, confident and simple-minded in its spirit of utility, is open enough to embrace even the mysterious world of art. Other parodies include a dramatic fragment written in the manner of Maeterlinck, featuring a reunion of Parisian critics in the basement of the Bouffes during the intermission of *Pelléas;* a Gospel according to St. Judas Iscariot, in which, for example, the story of Mary and Martha has Martha telling Jesus off and refusing him dinner; and a Robinson Crusoe who takes his Eternally Feminine bride to a desert island to keep himself from being cuckolded and ends up losing her to a baboon.[120]

The contributions of Bernard, Veber, and Roman Coolus made the *Revue blanche* known for this type of parody. Veber's, in particular, reflect the Laforguian manner of infusing a familiar story with the characteristics of modern life. "Alceste régénéré" uses Molière's *Misanthrope* to parody the late nineteenth-century literary hero.[121] Alceste is still a misanthrope, but of a distinctly Decadent variety, a frustrated poet, who has quarrelled with Célimène and is thus angry at the world. Using a typical device of parody, Veber makes a comical allusion to the original text and its genre: "[Alceste donne] un solide, *misanthropique* coup de pied ... Après avoir accompli cet acte un peu *théâtral,* Alceste regagne son carrosse" (emphasis mine). Laforgue does similarly in *Hamlet,* by making the hero count "si tragiquement" on the players to carry out his plan. Typically, Alceste wishes to flee an unappreciative world: "Ils n'ont pas soupçonné mes intentions; ils n'ont pas eu la curiosité de soulever mes métaphores pour voir ce qui se trouvait derrière." He blames his disappointments and failures on a notion of heredity worthy of Laforgue's hero:

> J'ai été singulièrement déçu dans mes aspirations. . . . Il n'y a qu'à regarder mes portraits d'ancêtres; une jolie collection de moroses et de figés-dans-l'Attitude; évidemment ils ont déterminé ma manière d'être. On m'a fait légataire universel d'une tristesse capitalisée par les grands parents.

But heredity is not all; the formula calls also for *milieu*, and thus he rails against the false teachings of his youth, which deceived him about the relativism and uncertainty of all things. With a characteristic pun, he remarks, "On ne panse pas les plaies morales avec des antisceptiques."

Like Laforgue's Hamlet, Alceste is concerned for his posthumous reputation: his disgust with life makes him want to throw himself into the water, but he hesitates each time at the thought that his suicide would be attributed to something as prosaic and unphilosophical as disappointed love. With the sobering remark that "quand on est mort, c'est pour longtemps," he decides in a parodic turn to renounce renunciation, defy the world, meet its "saleté générale" with his own, and adopt the cult of the ego. He is only momentarily disconcerted when, trying out his new self on a passerby whom he attempts to rob, the victim turns out to be M. Jourdain. Inserting a character from another of Molière's plays exploits the common feature of parody described in chapter one, by which the reader, supposedly outside the parody along with *Le Bourgeois Gentilhomme,* finds himself implicated in it. The tale ends when the hero, having lived the life of a total scoundrel, admits that the world contains some good after all. A moral closes it ironically: "Plaise à Dieu que nous parvenions à un âge avancé, après avoir, ainsi qu'Alceste, trouvé le sens de l'existence." Clearly the answer to modern ennui lies elsewhere than in the despairing philosophy of poets. Moreover, the wish that we may follow in Alceste's path suggests, in the manner of parody, that we may turn his story inside out, as he, in this parody, did to the original Alceste's; as I argued in chapter one, parody provides for a revision of itself.

Veber wrote other stories of this type: for example, a modernized version of *Barbe-Bleue*, where the hero, Max Bluebeard, is a young English lord with monocle and polished shoes, an "imagination de serre-chaude," and a Decadent taste for "livres méconnus et ignorés."[122]

Pastiche and its more extreme form of *mystification* were extremely common during the 1880s. Trézenik's *Lutèce* published pastiches of Decadent poetry, such as "Les Fleurs blêmes," complete with flowers, morbidity, verbal play, and a blank epigraph from Verlaine signalling the joke and its object:

> Rose arrose d'argyrose
> La morose rose rose!
> Oh! l'hymen d'un cyclamen
> Amène un amène amen.
>
> (Richard, *Symbolisme*, 171)

Anatole Baju's journal, *Le Décadent*, was notorious for such games and published a number of apocrypha as jokes, including some fake Rimbaud poems.[123] One of these carried a note that pushed to extreme the characteristics of Decadent writing, aiming particularly at the contorted style of Mallarmé with its ellipses, disrupted syntax, neologisms, and use of capital letters:

> D'aucuns messages épistolaires du Ponant et de l'Orient advenues en les bureaux de la Décadente Ecriture, interrogent—dubitatifs—la foi de notre du Plessys touchant l'authentique des Poèmes—combien trop rares!—par nos soins pieux colligés—du paradisiaque Rimbaud.
> (Richard, *Mouvement décadent*, 203)

The real authors, Laurent Tailhade and Georges Fourest, responded to accusations of forgery, not by revealing their identities, but by creating a straw man forger with the caricatural name of Mitrophane (reminiscent of "Aristophane" and "shot") Crapoussin, who then went on to have a brilliant career in *Le Décadent* for the next few months. *Le Décadent* printed other such jokes: sonnets supposedly written by the nationalist opposition leader General Boulanger and Louis II of Bavaria, and a fake letter from Sarcey, the venomous conservative critic of *Le XIXè Siècle*, announcing his conversion to Decadence and his collaboration on *Le Décadent*.[124] Some of these were subsequently twisted ironically and parodied again by *La Plume* in its special issue on the Decadents (34, 15 September 1890), where Sarcey, for example, transfers his allegiance (and services) to the rival *Chat noir*.

The parodic work that received the most publicity during this period, however, was the *Déliquescences d'Adoré Floupette*, a spoof on the new tendencies in poetry, a Decadent version of the earlier one on the Parnassian movement, *Le Parnassiculet contemporain*. It was written by two minor poets, Gabriel Vicaire and Henri Beauclair, and parodied not only the principal figures of Decadence, Verlaine and Mallarmé, but especially, as Richard remarks, the cult that had grown up around them among the young poets.[125] It appeared in May of 1885, ostensibly published by "Lion Vanné" in "Byzance": Vanier's name is metamorphosed into a favorite Decadent adjective of lassitude,[126] and the place of publication the model city of those "écrivains byzantins" themselves. Even the title implies a parody of the techniques and practices of the Decadent group, so often referred to as the "école du flou" for its vagueness and impressionism.[127] The idea of liquefaction conveyed by "Déliquescences" supports the blurriness of "flou" in a metaphor dear to Decadent writing, and in a term having old and authoritative Decadent origins, Gautier's preface to the *Fleurs du mal*. It also has the advantage of verbal echoes relevant to the Decadent aesthetic—"délicat" and "essence"—a pun that signals the parody. The preciosity of "Adoré" and the comicality of the ending "pette" renders the name appropriately ridiculous.

The *Déliquescences* parody most of the major themes of Decadence: pessimism and the Baudelairean *horreur de l'être,* morbidity, the mixture of mysticism and sensuality, the use of liturgical imagery in a context of *libertinage,* perfumes, exotic flowers, and gems. It also employs *à outrance* some of the common stylistic devices of the new poetry: repetition, neologisms, unusual vocabulary, syntactical obscurities, capital letters, incongruity, oxymoron, the *impair,* and synaesthesia. The poems play now with individual writers, now with the general features of Decadence; for example, "Pour avoir péché" parodies Mallarmé's "Prose pour des Esseintes," while others are more vaguely reminiscent of his manner, and are, more properly speaking, pastiches employing the techniques of parody. Although the *Déliquescences* thus differ greatly from Laforguian parody, they nevertheless provide a useful example of a work that, like the *Moralités*, mocks and targets the conventions of Decadence.

The work appeared at a time when the Decadent aesthetic was being formulated, following Verlaine's *Poètes maudits* (1883) and Huysmans' *A Rebours* (1884). By its exaggeration of the features of the new poetry, it contributed to the elaboration of the Decadent myth. Trézenik went so far as to maintain, wrongly, that Decadence itself was wholly a creation of Floupette.[128] It had actually been understood as a term and an ideology for several years (Trézenik himself had used it in his essay on Laforgue of the previous week), and Floupette's comical imitation and distortion of Decadent conventions reveal the extent to which these were identifiable. However, Trézenik's statement confirms the suggestion made in chapter one that parody may fix the conventions of its target as it exaggerates them, mocks them, neutralises and ultimately even reforms them. It is significant in this respect that the poems of the *Déliquescences* first appeared in one of the mainstays of the Decadent movement, *Lutèce*.

Even more blatantly than the poems, the preface that introduced the second edition (June 1885) parodies the conventions of Decadence. Like the preface to the earlier *Parnassiculet*, this one consists of a long introduction on the life of the Adoré Floupette by his friend Marius Tapora (an anagrammatical pun on the familiar term for his profession, "potard," pharmacist.) It comically portrays the Decadent hero's progress from *un jeune homme de province* to a full-fledged member of the 1880s Parisian literary *cénacles*, and the parallel evolution of his taste from Racinian classicism, through all the nineteenth-century movements to Decadence. In recounting the experiences of Tapora and Floupette among the poets at the *Panier fleuri* literary cafe, it uses the standard devices of parody: puns, quotation out of context, exaggeration of Decadent style, themes, and terms, imitating the *Parnassiculet* and parodying the theme of literary initiation, introducing elements of the real world into the parody (as in Mallarmé's "Mort de la pénultième"), and parodies-within-the-parody. It even includes a certain self-mockery, when

Decadence and Parody

at the end the text suggests that, like a good Decadent poem, it may have only a "sens affreusement obscène." Particular contemporary poets are caricatured (the names of Verlaine and Mallarmé become Bleucoton and Arsenal), and poems parodied:

> Je voudrais être un gaga
> Et que mon coeur naviguât
> Sur la fleur du seringa.

This plays not only with a line from Verlaine's *Sagesse* ("Qu'il faudrait que mon coeur en panne naviguât," I, X), but also with a favorite poetic issue of the Decadents: a ludicrous discussion of the "t" in *naviguât* targets the *rime pour l'oeil / rime pour l'oreille* controversy of the period.

The preface also presents the clichés of Decadent aesthetics: an insistence on nuance, dream, expressing the inexpressible, the *poète-voyant*; neologisms, archaisms, popular and erudite vocabulary; exotic flowers, gems, and perfumes; incestuous or perverse love; the pessimistic conviction that all is vain and existence an illusion; mysticism; the use of drugs; opposition to nature and health; the beauty of evil; the religion of Satanism; and the most parodic and parodied of all, perversion, "De la perversité, mon vieux Tapora. Soyons pervers" (Richard, 308).

Laforgue recognized the place of the *Déliquescences* in the evolution of Decadence as a necessary stage in the coming of age of the new movement, as the *Parnassiculet* had been for the now-accepted Parnasse; the parody consecrated it as the movement of the future. In his review of the *Complaintes*, he sketched the pattern thus:

> On se souvient qu'en pleine ferveur du cénacle parnassien deux sceptiques anonymes lancèrent, sous le titre de *Parnassiculet,* une élégante plaquette de vers dont chaque pièce était un pastiche réussi de la manière d'un des coryphées de cette école dite des Impassibles . . . L'excentrique cénacle d'alors est aujourd'hui arrivé: Sully Prudhomme et Coppée sont de l'Académie, Leconte de Lisle y va succéder à Hugo, Paul Bourget vient d'être décoré, les autres suivent et le Parnassiculet est recherché comme une curiosité par les bibliophiles. Or il faut croire que le nouveau cénacle atteint à son tour le paroxysme de la crise littéraire qu'il traverse, car il vient d'avoir aussi son *Parnassiculet.* . . . Les *Déliquescences,* c'est-à-dire de la décadence au dernier degré de la décomposition, de la décadence qui coule, sont datées significativement non de *Paris*

mais de *Byzance,* et l'on y trouve d'assez heureuses caricatures de l'idéal et des procédés qui passionnent les alentours de l'Odéon. . . .

Au moment où les Déliquescences raillaient le cénacle, celui-ci donnait son *ut* avec les *Complaintes* de M. Jules Laforgue. (Debauve, 193f.)

This last remark suggests that, as I have argued in chapter one, a parody need not come at the end or decline of a tradition, but on the contrary, may work most effectively at its height. The tradition must be established to some extent, in order for the exaggeration of the parody to be performed and perceived, but it may be flourishing rather than languishing, as it undergoes the criticism and mockery of the parody. In such cases, the parody defines the conventions of the genre and thereby leaves room for their reusage, revision, and even redefinition; in the best of cases, this latter process takes place within the parody itself. One might reasonably argue that the *Déliquescences* perform the first but not the second of these functions, that is, they identify and exaggerate the distinctive characteristics of Decadence but do not carry out the important transformative function of parody. They employ its devices and methods but do not use the distortion for any purpose other than mockery. This sets them apart from the *Moralités,* whose playing with the conventions of Decadence under the guise of an old story elaborates both a particular conception of modern art and a lesson for what Laforgue considered the moral quandary of modern man.

The importance of parody in the literary world of this period, roughly from the late 1870s to the early 1890s, makes the later phenomenon of Jarry's works, with their persistent use of parodic methods, less isolated and more understandable. The title of *Ubu Roi* of course parodies Sophocles' *Oedipus;* its plot takes up that of Shakespeare's *Macbeth,* which the famous "hoscha la poire" of the epigraph makes evident; and certain of its lines deform ones from Racine, Molière, and others. Although in general the Ubu plays do not fit the definition that I have given, the devices of parody are frequently responsible for their humor. If these works may be placed at the beginning of twentieth-century theater, they represent also the culmination of a strong comic tradition which had been a mainstay of the avant-garde since the late 1870s. The *Moralités* are a very different sort of work, in both form and spirit, from Jarry's theater, but the comic tradition that Laforgue so masterfully exploited also served Jarry's creations and should be restored to its position as one of the dominant forces of early modernism.

3

Hamlet, ou les suites de la piété filiale

Laforgue's story is inspired by the most illustrious of the predecessors suggested by the title, Shakespeare's *Hamlet*. As with the other *Moralités,* Laforgue alters the title, in this case by adding a qualifying subtitle, in order simultaneously to identify the story as modelled upon another one and to differentiate it from the other.[1] The subtitle here is ironic for, although "the consequences of filial piety" might well describe the character and actions of Shakespeare's hero, it does not in its most obvious sense fit Laforgue's, who is motivated relatively little by devotion to his father. We might rather take the phrase literally, to mean what happens when the question of filial piety is followed, even superseded, by another one far dearer to the hero's heart: writing a play, becoming an artist, and making a mark on the world. Hamlet himself confirms this sense in a monologue early on: his original intention in writing the play—to spur his vengeance against his father's murderers—got lost in his enthusiasm for writing it and his excessive attention to its aesthetic qualities. For Laforgue's hero, filial piety is only a starting point, a rallying point, perhaps even a pretext, for confronting the matters that really bother, and interest, him: art, women, fame, freedom, and death. In a manner typical of parody, the subtitle comically deforms the original title and therein provides a clue to the parodic hero's character. This one has the additional significance of reflecting the status of the parody vis-à-vis the original, for Laforgue's story is, in some of its details, a *suite*, a sequel, to Shakespeare's, with Ophelia and Polonius already dead and Hamlet already courting a new lady.

Laforgue extends the figure of Hamlet, so important to the nineteenth century, into the 1880s, consistent with the *hamlétisme* of the period.[2] The famous concerns of Shakespeare's hero—indecision, excessive self-analysis, misogyny, an obsession with death, madness, the question of being, a taste for acting and playwriting—are here exaggerated and given a Decadent cast. The "glass of fashion and mould of form" (III,i,153) becomes an 1880s dandy, with an ever-present taste for the elegant, the refined, and the aesthetic. He is at what Laforgue, in his prose sketch on the Hamlet theme, called the "psychological" age of thirty,[3] a trait common not only to the original Hamlet but also to the stock Romantic and Decadent hero, including des Esseintes. Like Huysmans' hero, Hamlet is a "noctambule," subject to regular bouts of insomnia, anemically pale and frail, with delicate, almost female features. Like the original Hamlet, with his "nighted color," "inky cloak," and "customary suits of solemn black," Laforgue's dresses entirely in black, but ludicrously extends his somber attire to his hat, a sombrero, keeping his face and thoughts ever dark and shadowy. And like Laforgue's transcendental lunar dandy, Pierrot, he wears an Egyptian scarab ring, a play on the Decadent taste for ancient religions.[4]

While calling himself a man of action, Hamlet spends most of his time gazing into a stagnant pool beneath the window of his *tour d'ivoire* (11), stock seat of the superior individual contemplating life, and the rest of it trying to decide what to do, a parodic victim of the late nineteenth-century paralysis of will described earlier.[5] Laforgue explicitly portrays him as all too willing to waste time, particularly when it comes to dreaming about his future glory: "Hamlet, homme d'action, perd cinq minutes à rêver devant son drame maintenant en bonnes mains" (18); or when he suspects that an encounter with Laertes would be inopportune, such as after the deaths of Ophelia and Polonius: "Hamlet, homme d'action, ne quitte sa cachette qu'assuré, bien entendu, que cette brute de Laërtes a filé avec toute l'honorable compagnie" (34).

Hamlet is imbued with nineteenth-century notions of heredity, environment, relativism, and the Hartmannian Unconscious. "J'ai mangé du fruit de l'Inconscience" (10): in a parodic reversal of the fall of man, this forbidden fruit has lost him to normal life and enslaved him to a world and an ideal beyond the senses. He wishes to replace the "Impératif Catégorique" of Romantic metaphysics with a more relative and arbitrary "Impératif Climatérique" (10).[6] He is moody, introspective, narcissistic, morbidly melancholic, and obsessed with the idea of death, although unlike the original or even his Romantic predecessor, he has an uncharacteristically dilettante attachment to life, especially when it resembles art. He suffers from the most standard form of ennui, as the transience of things makes him reluctant to bother doing anything: "Ah! que je fusse seulement poussé à m'en donner la peine!" (9). At the same time, however, he is tormented by the Infinite ("mais ce sixième sens, ce sens de l'Infini!," 19f.) and, more prosaically, an infinity of things to do, as a parodic "J'ai de l'infini sur la planche" (34) succinctly expresses. He can never find enough time to accomplish his many projects or even think through his thoughts: "Où trouver le temps pour se révolter contre tout cela?" (32); "La mort! Ah! est-ce qu'on a le temps d'y penser, si bien doué que l'on soit?" (30). "Had I but time . . .": this troubles Laforgue's Hamlet throughout his life, not simply when faced with death.

Laforgue includes in his hero suggestions of the nervous disease and madness to which the Decadent temperament was usually attributed, and follows the late nineteenth-century convention of making this the inheritance of a tainted ancestry: Hamlet will parodically discover in the graveyard scene that his father, the King, was a *bon vivant,* and his mother not the Queen but a travelling gypsy, mother also of the court fool, Yorick. He has nihilistic tendencies but as a cynic and dilettante cannot take them very seriously. He is given to rather perverse acts of violence, an example of typical Decadent depravity rendered comical by his constant childlike efforts to excuse them, and by the nagging moral conscience that these suggest. He has the Decadent's stock contempt for the majority, a sentiment reflected in his cynicism on social questions and in his attitude toward women; these he regards in typical Decadent fashion as domesticators who aim to deceive him

Hamlet, ou les suites de la piété filiale

into relinquishing his freedom and leading a life of bourgeois conformity. He talks chastity and sterility, the Decadent's rebellion against the rule of vulgar Nature, but hardly practices what he preaches, instead falling in love with every new *jeune fille* that comes his way, notably the actress Kate. Using a typical device of comedy, Laforgue makes his hero an outrageous egotist, who imagines himself at the heart of a conspiratorial intrigue ("Ah! ils sont tous contre moi!," 18), when in fact no one in Elsinore pays him the slightest attention ("Hamlet, dont nul jamais ne s'inquiète," 41) or even recognizes him ("On ne reconnaît guère le prince Hamlet à Elseneur," 23). He wishes to flee the world, "s'évader" being one of his favorite terms, but, unlike des Esseintes, Hamlet the artist and egotist seeks in his escape not seclusion but glory and fame, imagining himself, according to another stock formula, as making a sensation in the literary and theatrical circles of Paris.

The paralyzing conflict in the original hero between his despair and his duty becomes in Laforgue's a conflict between his pessimistic beliefs and his irrepressibly optimistic hopes for the future. Hamlet loves life too much to play his Decadent role very consistently, and thus he vacillates between indolent ennui and visions of artistic celebrity, a sense of utter futility and an all-encompassing exuberance, a belief in fatality and a passion for freedom; he chooses whatever attitude fits his mood or purpose of the moment. But both his Decadent beliefs and his visions of the future derive from a single problem, his essential inability to accept life as it is, whence the ceaseless effort of his imagination to see or make it otherwise. This Hamlet definitely wants "to be," but only if this means to be a star. Strengthened by his lovely new *amour* and confident in his artistic future, he renounces his pessimism, nihilism, misogyny, and cynicism, and resolves to live; but his image of life on the Paris stage with Kate is yet another act, fit more for his plays than for the world, and as destined to failure as the parody implies *they* are. Hamlet's Decadence ultimately gets the better of him and ironically reminds him of his responsibility to his role. He, of all people, should have known that Decadent heroes never reach stardom; they either die, or return, ill and broken, to the normal world. Des Esseintes may do the latter, but a Decadent hero based on Shakespeare's Hamlet can only reasonably do the former, and Laforgue's accordingly expires. But although he dies, the parody, taking its cue from Shakespeare's original, remains to "tell his story"; a story, or even a literary movement, which risks being killed off may just as easily regenerate itself, through the parody, and ensure for itself a literary succession.

The Epigraph

Hamlet originally carried two epigraphs, which Laforgue later replaced with a single, different one.[7] The earlier epigraphs deserve attention, however, for they shed special light on the story. Since *Hamlet* itself changed very little from the early version to the later, the original epigraphs apply as well to the one as to the other.

> If thou didst ever hold me [in] thy heart,
> Absent [thee] from felicity awhile,
> And in this harsh world draw thy breath in pain,
> To tell my story.
>
> Hamlet

> In vera nescis nullum fore morte alium te,
> Qui possit vivus te lugere peremptum,
> Stansque jacentem?
>
> Lucrèce[8]

Both epigraphs involve a concern for immortality, for someone to mourn the hero and tell his story after his death. They thus reflect Hamlet's desire for literary fame, literary immortality, and suggest that he can attain his goal only in death. They also imply that the parody to follow performs this function, immortalizing the original by retelling its story in a new way.

The first epigraph, consisting of Hamlet's dying words to Horatio, is particularly appropriate to the parody, since it comes from the parodied work itself and expresses a theme central to both. Its relation to Laforgue's *Hamlet*, however, is ironic in two ways. First, during one of his monologues, Hamlet parodically paraphrases this epigraph, lamenting the fact that he has no friend to tell his story for him: "Je n'ai pas un ami qui pourrait raconter

Hamlet, ou les suites de la piété filiale 79

mon histoire, un ami qui me précéderait partout pour m'éviter les explications qui me tuent" (19). Confronting the original text (in the epigraph) with the hero's parodic version of it would have structurally mirrored the parody directly from within the story. The original Hamlet asks Horatio to tell his story after his death; Laforgue's, in keeping with his egotistical interest in celebrity, wants his story to precede him, so that the ladies might weep over his "divin coeur" as over the body of Adonis (19). Despite his obsessive passion for writing and his desire for literary recognition, however, he cannot be bothered with doing it himself; his literary ambition aims higher than the mere writing of memoirs (19).

Second, the epigraph is ironic in that there is no Horatio in Laforgue's version. Hamlet has no friend to tell his story, or to do anything else, for that matter. He is almost universally disliked, and the inhabitants of Elsinore, when they think about him at all, consider him either mad or wilfully dangerous; a voice from the crowd at Polonius's funeral expresses the opinion of Hamlet's subjects: "Hé! Quand on a un fou à la maison on l'enferme!" (25). In fact, the epigraph subtly attributes Horatio's role to the parodist himself; Shakespeare's Hamlet authorizes the parodist to tell his story, as it were. The epigraph thus refers directly to the parody; the story of Hamlet evoked by the original hero at the end of the play may be interpreted parodically to produce the one at hand.

The second, more pessimistic epigraph comes from Lucretius's great meditation on death, *De Rerum Natura* III. Laforgue, however, has altered the original text, which reads:

> hinc indignatur se mortalem esse creatum
> nec videt in vera nullum fore morte alium se
> qui possit vivus sibi se lugere peremptum
> stansque jacentem [se] lacerari urive dolere.[9]

Arguing that death is a relief from suffering and thus contains nothing to fear, Lucretius belittles the man who troubles about what will become of his body afterward, since he will be unable to feel anything. For Lucretius, such a man only worries because, when he sees a corpse being harmed or mangled, he associates himself, a living, feeling being, with it. He does not realize that, after death, he will have no living self to look on and feel his pain, no living self to mourn the dead one.

There is some evidence that Laforgue saw his own age as a descendant, at least in the scientific and philosophical domains, of the materialistic Epicurean one described by Lucretius. In a note, he called him "ce fils sacré de l'Inconscient."[10] Lucretius's belief (following Epicurus) in an integrated and self-regulating Nature, his attempt to explain all experience and phenomena in terms of it, his doctrine of acceptance, and his ideas on death in Book III and on love and sex in Book IV—these reminded Laforgue of Hartmann's *Philosophie de l'Inconscient*, which accounted for all phenomena by recourse to an unintelligible universal principle, the Unconscious. It is significant, however, that for the epigraph Laforgue changed the third person to the second, and the declarative statement to a negative question. Where Lucretius considers it a truth that death is a finality in which we will feel nothing at all, nor be able to mourn ourselves, Laforgue prefers the less certain negative-interrogative form, and specifically poses the question to the reader. Hamlet cannot mourn himself, but a self may actually remain after death, a parodic Hamlet like Laforgue's. The epigraph realizes what I have argued in chapter 1, that parody implies and ensures the "other self" left even after death, a *Hamlet, ou les suites de la piété filiale*, which keeps the original *Hamlet* from "truly" dying.

The definitive version of Laforgue's tale carries a terser and more enigmatic epigraph whose relation to the story is less clear: "c'est plus fort que moi." He uses the same phrase in *A propos de Hamlet* when the narrator tells Shakespeare's hero about his modern Parisian descendants, Bourget, Rimbaud, and himself:

> . . . il y a moi qui vous prends en gaieté, Altesse, à la Yorick, "un garçon de beaucoup d'enjouement, d'une très excellente imagination", qui vous prends en gaieté parce que c'est plus fort que moi. (336f.)

The narrator quotes Hamlet's line (translated) from the "Alas, poor Yorick" speech of Shakespeare's original ("a fellow of infinite jest, of most excellent fancy," V,i,173)[11] and in this way reinforces his acknowledged relation to the jester Yorick. This is a parodic Hamlet, a Hamlet "à la Yorick," whose humor is inevitable; in the *Moralité* he quite literally turns out to be Yorick's half brother.

This gloss, however, is provided only by *A Propos de Hamlet*, to which the *Moralité* may be easily compared in title and theme. Standing alone as an epigraph, "c'est plus fort que moi" can refer only to something much less definite. What is ultimately at issue in this expression, taken in its common usage, is the weakness of the will, that Hamletic problem *par excellence*. But Laforgue evokes this stock trait only to revise it through the parody, suggesting its peculiar manifestation in his own hero: Hamlet's exasperating moral indifference and his outrageous ability to justify his actions, however perverse. Indeed, Hamlet cannot help anything. He uses the excuse repeatedly to account for his actions, blaming them on heredity, environment, the times, the nature of things, anything, as long as it lies outside his realm of responsibility: "si les temps étaient moins tristes" (13), "si les temps étaient plus propres" (17), "je ne l'ai pas fait exprès" (20), "Et par mon frère et ma mère et tout, j'étais damné d'avance" (32), "Le sort est jeté" (40), and so on. Significantly, "c'est plus fort que moi" also leads him to his death as, "piqué d'on ne sait quelle tarentule" (44), he is powerless to resist the attraction of Ophelia's tomb, where he is stabbed by an avenging Laertes. Laforgue thus sends us back to the epigraph and reminds us that Hamlet's problem is ultimately one of the will: the Decadent's overpowering conviction that he is not master of his destiny and the dilettante's unsatisfactory (and in this case fatal) response to the problem. His final defense—or escape—is his hyperactive imagination and his faith in art, but even these desert him as, in a last unsuccessful imaginative effort, he dies uttering the famous *qualis artifex pereo* of Nero.

The Story

In a manner typical of parody, many of the original's scenes do not take place here, because Laforgue either omits them altogether or makes them happen before the time of the narrative. In this case, we are informed of them in another context, usually in Hamlet's monologues and frequently in parenthetical asides (e.g., the suicide of Ophelia), as though they hardly mattered, a device typical of parodic inversion and trivialization. Most of what the play communicates through dialogue here figures instead in Hamlet's rambling monologues, which dominate the narrative. Indeed, this reflects a major distortion consistent with the late nineteenth-century context: Laforgue's story concentrates on the peculiar, egotistical psychology of the hero. The Ghost, Horatio, Ophelia, and Polonius are all suppressed, the latter two having died just prior to the beginning of the story; and most of Shakespeare's minor characters are omitted as well. Besides the hero, there remain only two players, two clowns, Laertes, and the King and Queen (who themselves appear merely in the scene of the play). Laforgue has arranged his story to reflect the exaggerated self-centeredness of its hero and stacked the cast of characters with players and clowns, reflections of that chief actor and clown, Hamlet himself.

The story retains some of the plot, major scenes, and famous monologues of the original, which are clearly discernible through the distortion, such as the cemetery scene with its Decadent version of "Alas poor Yorick." Laforgue quotes from the original in a different context, making Hamlet's famous "words, words, words" the very motto of his ultraliterary hero. He reduces the genre of the original to yet another of the hero's moods: "ces comédiens . . . sur lesquels il compte si *tragiquement*" (10, emphasis mine). Similarly, at the end of the long, meandering first monologue, the narrative ironically remarks that "le prince Hamlet en a comme ça long sur le coeur, plus long qu'il n'en tient en cinq actes" (10). Laforgue converts the form of the original into a joke about Hamlet's anxieties and thus signals the parody: this Hamlet is exaggerated and parodic, with more on his mind than could possibly be told in the five acts of the original. Laforgue also retains some of the language and imagery of the original, which he recasts in metaphors or puns relevant to the parody, as we shall see in several instances. By these methods, typical of all the *Moralités*, the work identifies itself as a parody from within and calls attention to both the model which it transforms and the target which it mocks.

Laforgue makes the parody clear in the opening paragraph:

> De sa fenêtre préférée, si chevrotante à s'ouvrir avec ses grêles vitres jaunes losangées de mailles de plomb, Hamlet, personnage étrange, pouvait, quand ça le prenait, faire des ronds dans l'eau, dans l'eau, autant dire dans le ciel. Voilà quel fut le point de départ de ses méditations et de ses aberrations. (6)

Hamlet's favorite activity—making ripples in the water[12]—and the explicit link between water and sky mark him clearly as a dreamer, and one somewhat subject to his whims and impulses ("quand ça le prenait"). Significantly, we are told that *this* was the beginning of his "meditations and aberrations"; not until the following paragraph do we learn of the death of his father. The opening lines thus attribute the odd behavior of this parodic Hamlet not to a vision of a ghost, nor even to grief over the death of his father, but rather to the advantageous position of the window for brooding. Hamlet suffers less from grief than from *ennui*. In suppressing the famous Ghost scene which opens the original, Laforgue provokes the obvious question about Hamlet's motive for revenge: how does he know the truth about his father's "irregular" death (mentioned in the following line) if he has not heard it from the Ghost? The emphasis on his meditations here suggests rather disturbingly, and comically, that he may have dreamt the whole thing up. From the beginning, we have a clear sense of Hamlet's overly active imagination.

The lengthy description of the tower, where the hero "s'est décidément arrangé pour vivre" since his father's death, reinforces this impression of its melancholy and aberrant inhabitant. The repeated formula, with its noticeable "décidément," comically calls attention to the legendary Hamletic problem, indecision: the parodic Hamlet is decisive about at least one thing, secluding himself in the lonely, sickly tower. The first piece of information given about the place is a curious and somewhat puzzling comparison of it to a "lépreuse sentinelle oubliée" (6). In a story based on Shakespeare's *Hamlet*, this reference directly recalls the famous opening scene, here suppressed, where the sentinels recount to Horatio their vision of the King's Ghost. Laforgue transforms the scene into a metaphor, which preserves the original and reminds the reader of the parody's deviation from it. In fact, there is no need for a Ghost scene in this *Hamlet*, since the milieu which the tower oversees suffices to motivate the hero's melancholia. "The very place puts toys of desperation, / Without more motive, into every brain / That looks so many fathoms to the sea" (I,iv,75–77). Laforgue parodically develops Shakespeare's suggestion into the nineteenth-century law of milieu: Hamlet's temperament, as he himself asserts repeatedly, is a product of his environment.

The tower, like the hero, is a "paria" (7), shaken and battered by the inclement effects of, if not a physical, at least a psychological, autumn: "Pauvre chambre tiraillée ainsi au sein d'un inguérissable, d'un insolvable automne! Même en juillet, comme aujourd'hui" (7). It has two yellow-paned windows providing a literally jaundiced view of the world. It stands isolated on a typically Decadent stagnant inlet[13] at one end of the royal park, an insalubrious dump ("cloaque," 6), where bouquets of withered flowers discarded by *jeunes filles* after the evening ball remind the hero constantly of the ephemeral nature of things, parodic Decadent testimony to the original's famous "Tis brief, my lord—As woman's love."

Hamlet's temperament is reflected everywhere in his surroundings and communicated by a comically subjective narrative. The "pauvre anse" (6, 7), with mucky depths, strange underwater plants in "floraisons inconscientes" (7), and chorus of catarrhal frogs, is described as having a skin disease, thus reflecting the aspect of the sickly, leprous tower itself, and the unconscious mind, like the physical image, of the hero: "C'est pourquoi (sauf orages) ce coin d'eau est bien le miroir de l'infortuné prince Hamlet" (7). The waves of the "pauvre Sund" are likened by apposition to the hero's nostalgic meditations: "flots abrutis par les autans inconstants, nostalgies bornées par les bureaux très quotidiens du Fortimbras d'en face" (7), an ironic reminder of Fortimbras' invasion at the end of the original. Laforgue's Fortimbras, however, is "indigent et positif" (6), the very antithesis of our indolent, introspective, aristocratic, pessimistic Hamlet brooding at his window. One understands why the gravediggers are converting their small savings into Norwegian bonds, as we are told later; Hamlet the Decadent and dilettante hardly inspires faith in the future of his country, economic or otherwise.

The first blatant anachronism to signal the parody concerns the date of the action: "C'est aujourd'hui le 14 juillet 1601, un samedi; et c'est demain dimanche, dans le monde entier les jeunes filles iront ingénument à la messe" (7). Laforgue in fact combines the most famous day of the French Revolution with the year of the first performance of Shakespeare's *Hamlet*. This reflects on the parody in two ways. First, the parody is set in the year that the original was performed, as a nonparodic work might be set in the year of the event recounted; the date identifies the parody as a retelling of a literary text (or, here, a dramatic performance). Second, the fourteenth of July has connotations relevant to the parody, which revolutionizes the original and contains a literal revolution of its own, as everything returns to normal at the end. In this context, the anachronistic and emblematically Laforguian image of young girls en route to church, symbol of bourgeois routine and stability, seems gratuitous, but actually prefigures the outcome of the story, as, after Hamlet's death, "tout rentra dans l'ordre" (47). This, the penultimate sentence of the parody, qualifies the nature of Hamlet's parodic "revolution," his unorthodox attempt to gain freedom and literary fame, which in fact changes nothing at all, except, through the parody, the history of literature.

The décor of the tower's interior enhances the portrait of Hamlet as a dandy, dilettante, and Decadent: pictures of his native Jutland, that image of gray skies and bleak landscapes; an etcher's laboratory with the artistic products of his idle hours;[14] books for one who reads too much; a full-length mirror to satisfy his narcissism; and, at the back of the *alcôve*, a mysterious "appareil à douches, hélas!" (8), with compromising implications for Hamlet's alleged chastity. A painting of the hero "en dandy" comes as no surprise, but a portrait of his father, King Horwendill, with an "oeil coquin et faunesque" is slightly more disquieting. The godlike father in Shakespeare's play, who was to the usurper Claudius like "Hyperion to a satyr" (I,ii,140), here parodically includes something of the satyr. Laforgue does not explain this peculiarity until the graveyard scene, but it is the first indication of the deceased king's numerous *aventures galantes*, and a subtle hint at Hamlet's shady parentage. His penchant for falling in love is a trait inherited, in good nineteenth-century fashion, from his rogue of a father, a vice present in his family line and reflected in his own portrait, with its "sourire attirant" (8) coming mysteriously out of a shadowy background. The most conspicuous furnishing is a wrought-iron gothic aedicule, a small temple holding two wax statuettes of Gerutha his mother and her new husband Fengo stuck through the heart with needles, that familiar image of evil and ill fortune. Hamlet turns the needles once a day as a votive ritual to his betrayed father and a reminder of his own pressing duty.

The names of Hamlet's parents are all three surprising to the reader, who expects King Hamlet, Claudius, and Gertrude, and instead finds Horwendill, Fengo, and Gerutha. Others have observed that Laforgue goes back to the pre-Shakespearean version of Saxo Grammaticus for these details.[15] This specifically serves the parody, extending its target to other Hamlets, to the origin of the whole tradition, and also providing a model of the parody from within. Incorporating Shakespeare's original into a story ostensibly *based* on Shakespeare, confronting the alleged original with the one that inspired it, urges the reader to see the story at hand as based upon an earlier one too. Moreover, by analogy this implies that the current version may in its turn inspire another, as I have argued of parody in chapter 1. (Laforgue develops this suggestion more fully at the end.) A similar play with names occurs in the scene with the actors, William and Kate. Both carry obvious Shakespearean associations, William the bard himself, and Kate the heroine of *The Taming of the Shrew*. The original author becomes not only a character in a story based on his own work, as in other examples of parody, but an actor in the play within it. Participation implies consent; in the role of William, Shakespeare consecrates Laforgue's *Hamlet* as the proper sequel to his own, and also provides a model for the parodist himself, who may do likewise in a future parody of his own work.

Kate presents a more complex case, since at first she gives her name as Ophelia.[16] In a parenthesis, Hamlet perceives the danger of her extraordinary beauty and sulky smile ("Oh! mon Dieu, comme elle est belle! Encore des histoires! . . . ," 14), and can only cover up his agitation by railing about her name:

> Comment! Encore une Ophélia dans ma potion! Oh! cette usurière manie qu'ont les parents de coiffer leurs enfants de noms de théâtre! Car Ophélia, ce n'est pas de la vie, ça! Mais de pures histoires de planches et de centièmes! Ophélia, Cordélia, Lélia, Coppélia, Camélia! Pour moi, qui ne suis qu'un paria, n'auriez-vous pas un autre nom de baptême (de Baptême, entendez-vous!) pour l'amour de moi? (14)

Hamlet's diatribe against theatrical names conveniently reflects on the parody: the "usurière manie" of parents who appropriate names from literary works for their children represents the parodist's similar literary recycling, and, as we will see in his play,

Hamlet's practice too. The diatribe is especially absurd, considering his own name (which comes from the same source as Ophelia's) and the theatrical quality of his life. The ludicrous outburst actually betrays the real source of his anguish: "encore une Ophélia dans ma potion." Kate, alias Ophelia, is a second Ophelia, and will accordingly succeed her in Hamlet's affections. Ironically, the "paria" by which he means to mark his distance from the theatrical names in fact draws him all the closer by its rhyme; he does not realize just how like them he is. He also fails to realize that the name which he considers normal (Kate) is as theatrical as the others and appropriately Shakespearean, evoking an image of woman that he would not like but might well, in his misogyny, believe: the shrew.

Hamlet launches into his first monologue with a characteristic pun: "Ah! me la couler douce et large comme ces flots, soupire Hamlet. Ah! de la mer aux nuées, des nuées à la mer! et laisser faire le reste . . ." (9). In a manner typical of Laforguian parody, the play on "me la couler douce" exploits the literal sense of this normally metaphorical phrase—to take life easy—both senses comically suiting the context. However, Laforgue makes the joke fit the parody specifically, by deriving it from the famous opening lines of Hamlet's first monologue in the original (I,ii). "O that this too too solid flesh would melt, / Thaw, and resolve itself into a dew" becomes, in Laforgue's parodic and Decadent hero, a plea to dissolve rather into the sea, "l'heureux panorama inconscient" (9), symbol of the mystical bliss of the unconscious. The *ennui* of Laforgue's Hamlet, however, derives less from a conviction of worldly corruption than from a Decadent preoccupation with the passing of time and the transience of things. Laforgue makes the relation between the original and the parody explicit by deforming Hamlet's celebrated "Frailty, thy name is woman!", aimed particularly at Gertrude, to address a more typically Decadent concern: "Stabilité! ton nom est femme" (9). Such an alteration of Shakespeare's celebrated formula not only produces the humor of surprise, but also reflects a change in the theme of women itself, diverting the issue from female infidelity to the female instinct for domesticity and routine.

With the simple adjustment of one word, Laforgue thus gives the theme of women a Decadent cast: destined, by their biological role, to the propagation of the species and, by their social one, to the maintenance of the family, they threaten the liberty, creativity, and individuality so dear to Hamlet, ever in search of the rare, unique, and original. The substitution is also vital to the story, for it shifts the target of Hamlet's anguished vituperations from the Queen to Ophelia, who, like all "real" women, represents a well-being and comfort that the hero finds repugnant: "Un Hamlet confortable! Ah, malheur!" (10f.). In fact, the Queen figures rarely in his thoughts and turns out not to be his mother at all. But Laforgue does not dismiss so fertile a theme as Hamlet's psychological relationship with his mother, which remains, as in the original, the cause of his condition. Laforgue alters the relationship from a temporary state, caused by the knowledge of her adultery and betrayal, to a chronic one: product of an artist, gypsy mother, and a gadabout rogue of a father, and nurtured in a climate of nineteenth-century pessimism, Hamlet turns out a tormented Yorick, the artist at only one remove from his half brother, the clown.

Hamlet's legendary misogyny actually comes not from his contempt for his adulterous mother, but rather from what his readings lead him to think about Ophelia:

> Elle ne m'eût d'ailleurs jamais compris. Quand j'y songe! Elle avait beau être adorable et fort mortellement sensitive, en grattant bien on retrouvait l'anglaise imbue de naissance de la philosophie égoïste de Hobbes. "Rien n'est plus agréable dans la possession de nos biens propres que de penser qu'ils sont supérieurs à ceux des autres," dit Hobbes. C'est ainsi qu'Ophélie m'eût aimé, comme son "bien", et parce que j'étais socialement et moralement supérieur aux "biens" de ses petites amies. (10)

Hamlet has no other reason for associating Ophelia with the despotic materialism of Hobbes, except that she is English. But this argument does not hold, for Ophelia is only English as a character in the most famous of English plays; and in that case, the hero is as English, and as potentially Hobbesian, as she is. The absurdity uncovers the truth; in a typical move, he finds in his readings a neat argument by which to hide his *real* reason for treating her so nas-

Hamlet, ou les suites de la piété filiale

tily, revealed only in an afterthought ("elle ne m'eût d'ailleurs jamais compris"). Hamlet the misunderstood artist wants more than anything to be understood, goal of all his creative efforts.

The only woman capable of satisfying his requirements is, predictably, a literary one, and not from this play, but from another:

> Ah! s'il me venait par un soir pareil, dans ma tour d'ivoire, une soeur, mais cadette, de cette Hélène de Narbonne qui sut aller conquérir à Florence son adoré Bertrand, comte de Roussillon, bien que connaissant son mépris pour elle! (11)

Laforgue thus inserts into the parody another Shakespearean model, *All's Well that Ends Well*. This is especially ironic, and apt, in view of Hamlet's repeated "tout est bien qui n'a pas [de] fin" (24, 30), a parodic version of the French title of that play, "Tout est bien qui finit bien." The allusion reminds us directly of the parody by placing one of the original author's own works within it, in a manner typical of the genre. It also bears significantly on our interpretation of the parodic hero, first, because his ideal woman is imaginary, outside the world of the original play on which his own story is based, impossibly unreal, merely a figure in another fiction; and second, because in the play, Helen of Narbonne comes off exceedingly well at the expense of the foolish and vain Bertrand. Hamlet does not realize how much his wish works against him. Ophelia, too, will have the upper hand in the outcome of this story: it is *her* grave that draws him to his death.

Hamlet's other major concern in the first monologue is the famous question of being. Laforgue parodically alters this, according to his hero's literary ambitions, from "to be, or not to be" to "to be, or to be a hero": "Un héros! Ou simplement vivre" (10). Hamlet's conception of heroism is a literary one, having less to do with avenging his father and conserving the throne than escaping and making a name for himself, keeping himself from being "anonymous" (19), producing quotable formulas, and leaving his life story as an example to the philistine bourgeois (18f.). Hence the quintessential importance of his play: for Hamlet, the play is indeed the thing, as the abundance of his creative efforts attests, not just "The Mousetrap," but also dramas, poems, metaphysical treatises, and fantasies (39).

Indeed, Hamlet's passion for art specifically gets in the way of his filial duty. An excessive involvement in his play has distracted him from the purpose which it was meant to serve, avenging his father's murder:

> Voilà, pourtant! Mon sentiment premier était de me remettre l'horrible, horrible, horrible événement, pour m'exalter la piété filiale, me rendre la chose dans toute l'irrécusabilité du verbe artiste, faire crier son dernier cri au sang de mon père, me réchauffer le plat de la vengeance! Et voilà (ὦ Πόθος τού εἶναι!) je pris goût à l'oeuvre, moi! J'oubliai peu à peu qu'il s'agissait de mon père assassiné, volé de ce qu'il lui restait à vivre dans ce monde précieux (pauvre homme, pauvre homme!), de ma mère prostituée (vision qui m'a saccagé la Femme et m'a poussé à faire mourir de honte et de détérioration la céleste Ophélie!), de mon trône enfin! Je m'en allais bras-dessus, bras-dessous avec les fictions d'un beau sujet. Car c'est un beau sujet! Je refis la chose en vers iambiques; j'intercalai des hors d'oeuvres profanes; je cueillis une sublime épigraphe dans mon cher Philoctète. Oui, je fouillais mes personnages plus profond que nature! Je forçais les documents! Je plaidais du même génie pour le bon héros et le vilain traître! Et le soir, quand j'avais rivé sa dernière rime à quelque tirade de résistance, je m'endormais la conscience toute rosière, souriant à des chimères domestiques, comme un bon littérateur qui, du travail de sa plume, sait soutenir une nombreuse famille! Je m'endormais, sans songer à faire mes dévotions aux deux statuettes de cire et leur retourner leur aiguille dans le coeur! (11f.)

Hamlet's frequent "horrible, horrible, horrible" comes directly from Shakespeare's original, in which it is uttered by the Ghost. Since Laforgue omits the Ghost, it is reasonable that he should give the line to his confidant, Hamlet himself; this supports the earlier suggestion that Hamlet's "Ghost", or source of information, may be nothing other than his own imagination, ever ready to provide him with a "beau sujet." Parodically forgetting everything at stake in favor of his fiction is Hamlet's answer to the question of being, and being a hero; he literally finds himself, creates a self, in writing his plays and creating fictions. Significantly, this is the sole moment in the story where he imagines himself with an untroubled conscience, leading a "normal" life. But Laforgue also hints that Hamlet is self-deluded, perhaps even a fraud: in the parenthetical Greek phrase he tries to justify his absorption in his work by likening his Decadent egoism to the long philosophical tradition of the

Hamlet, ou les suites de la piété filiale

"désir de l'être." But the strategy backfires; the high tradition and the language of literary and philosophical authority reveal his own effort to be merely a parody of them. And the portrait, at the end of the monologue, of the self-satisfied bourgeois man-of-letters supporting a large family by his pen differs hardly at all from the idea of a "comfortable Hamlet" that had so disgusted him earlier. With this highly ironic image, Laforgue implies that Hamlet's heroic ideal is ultimately as "stable" and unoriginal as he accuses Ophelia's of being.

As this passage makes clear, the hero's submission to the lure of his work at the expense of his purpose keeps him also from being a good writer. The play sounds like somewhat of a salad; to preserve his own metaphor, his "immaculate conception" (15) is a bastard: it is written in iambic lines, Hamlet's parodic attempt to imitate Shakespeare; the epigraph from Sophocles' *Philoctetes,* one of Hamlet's favorites, would evoke the hero's longing for death, as intense as his alleged own; his zeal for showing his talent makes it difficult to decide between the hero and the villain. Too episodic, with too many flights of fancy and too many unintelligible and gratuitous literary allusions, the play reflects Hamlet's larger inability to focus attention on a single theme, keep to one topic. An example of this tendency in one of his own monologues occurs in a familiar complaint about women; citing Michelangelo, he blames "ce temps de *danno* et *vergogna*" (9), but cannot help taking the opportunity to express an irrelevant opinion on the superiority of Michelangelo to the Danish neoclassical sculptor, Thorvaldsen. The anachronistic comparison calls attention to the parody, all the more comically for the appropriateness of Thorvaldsen's nationality; but Laforgue uses it to convey the hero's cluttered and broken train of thought. He cannot be bothered to develop the comparison of Michelangelo's "age of injury and shame" to the present situation, and instead, like a bad parodist, he leaves the literary reference lying in his haste to include yet another one.[17]

The play's incoherence is confirmed objectively when Hamlet reads portions of it aloud to the actors. Even he acknowledges later during the performance that he got carried away and should have made further cuts in it (42). The play is so free a fantasy that the King and Queen do not seem to understand a word of it until the garden scene, the bit fortunately retained from Shakespeare's more reliable and effective original. It has less to do with treachery than with Hamlet's favorite topics—love, art, and the nature and socialization of women, indeed, the themes of the *Moralité* itself. Hamlet's play is in fact a parody, albeit an unwitting one, with the same Decadent target as the larger story; as always, such a parody-within-the-parody urges us to interpret the story likewise. Many of the excised verses which Hamlet insists on reading aloud come from Laforgue's own work. Such autocitation provides a blatant example of reusing literary texts and also insists on the self-parodic nature of the genre.[18] It is particularly significant that the suppressed portions are (with one exception) all we actually have of the play; for all we know, it may consist only of bits and pieces of other works, like a bad parody. Hamlet's parody provides a model against which to measure Laforgue's, but, by the parallel with it, suggests the self-criticism that is a basic element of the genre. Perhaps *Hamlet, ou les suites de la piété filiale* should be revised, cut, and eventually abandoned, like the hero's own creation.

Laforgue further suggests the parodic nature of Hamlet's play by one major detail. Although, as in Shakespeare's "Mousetrap," the king is called Gonzago and the queen Baptista, the treacherous murderer here is not the King's nephew Lucianus, but his own brother Claudius. Laforgue constructs the plot of the play-within-the-parody according to the plot of the original play itself, in which Hamlet's father is indeed killed by his brother Claudius. Like putting Shakespeare within the play, this has the effect of conflating the fictional and the real, a frequent device of parody, but here considered from within the fiction: the "real", or at least authentic, Claudius is inserted into the "fictional" play-within-the-parody. The irony consists in the fact that neither is real at all, but merely one fiction within another, consistent with the structure of parody itself.

Hamlet will not take responsibility for the flaws in his play, blaming them instead on the same causes as his failure to be a hero: the gloomy times, his equally gloomy surroundings and vulgar company, the damp castle, "cet antre à chacals et à grossiers personnages" (13), his "répugnantes préoccupations domestiques" (39), and a certain knavery inherited from his father. "D'ailleurs, tout est hérédité" (13): once again, he cannot help it. Laforgue's insistence on the poor quality of the play ironically suggests why Hamlet later instructs the director not to identify him as its author (39); the original Hamlet may have feared for his life, but this one fears for his reputation, and with reason. Laforgue drives the point home by ironically transferring the famous "horrible, horrible, most horrible" from the crime to Hamlet's horrible play: "cet horrible, horrible, horrible drame" and "l'horrible, l'horrible, l'horrible pièce" (42).

Another example of a parody-within-the-parody occurs when, taking leave of Hamlet, William comments on the situation by parodying Malherbe:

> La démence est partout; et, sans cérémonie
> Frappe l'humble marchand ou l'acteur de génie,
> Et la garde qui veille aux portes du palais
> N'en défend pas Hamlet. (18)[19]

As before, this commentary exposes the methods of the parody itself and provides a model by which to read it. But William's example also illustrates another aspect of this device: by alluding to the "acteur de génie," it reflects back upon himself as well as on its more obvious object, the mad Hamlet. As I argued in chapter 1, the parodist sees himself and his own creation as implicated by the parody. Moreover William's deformation bears significantly upon the larger story, for the unstated subject of the *consolatio*, death (which he replaces with "démence"), relates ironically to Hamlet's situation: nothing can defend him from death any more than from madness, however "overflowing with life" (31) he later proclaims himself to be.

Laforgue parodically trivializes the whole Polonius episode by making it one of Hamlet's many pretexts for self-exoneration. Hamlet initially admits killing Polonius as practice for the killing of Fengo (18): as in the original, Polonius had been spying on him behind the famous arras, here parodically (and prophetically) depicting a "Massacre of the Innocents." He is informed of the burial but refuses to cancel the evening's performance of his own masterwork; he even comes up with an irreverent pun on the conflict of events: "Eh bien! En voilà des considérations! Les uns jouent, tandis que les autres rentrent dans la coulisse, voilà tout" (13f.). Hamlet's joke, however, in fact predicts his own future: he will himself be the next player then on stage to be metaphorically retired to the wings in this way and, ironically, after the very show that he here insists must go on. When he actually sees the funeral cortege, however, he seems to realize it for the first time: "Alors là, Hamlet, qui, en conscience et malgré son âme si lettrée, ne s'en était pas encore avisé, sent qu'il a décidément tué un homme, supprimé une vie . . ." (26). Though this be madness, yet there is method in't: something is rotten in Denmark, and it has to do with the hero's "âme si lettrée." Either he really did not grasp the significance of his deed, in which case his powers of interpretation are exceedingly dull, or he chose simply to ignore it and now conveniently forgets that it ever happened, a characteristic trick that he tries again later, unsuccessfully, on Laertes. Hamlet finds himself, for once, at a total loss for words and thus falls back on "*Words! words! words!* entendez-vous! des mots, des mots, des mots!" (26)—ironically, what the original Hamlet says to none other than Polonius himself (II,ii,191).

Laforgue parodies the Decadent vogue for violent and lurid scenes precipitated by the hero's depravity (itself a product of his worn-out senses and his tainted bloodline) in two episodes illustrating Hamlet's sadistic, gratuitous brutality, examples of the "étranges impulsions destructives" (21) that have gripped him since his father's death. In the first, he wrings the neck of the gatekeeper's canary and throws it into the lap of a young girl at work crocheting.[20] Although his first instinct is to flee, he as usual has second thoughts and, throwing himself at her feet, asks to be punished in expiation:

> Oh! pardon, pardon! Je ne l'ai pas fait exprès! Ordonne-moi toutes les expiations. Mais je suis si bon! J'ai un coeur d'or comme on n'en fait plus! Tu me comprends, n'est-ce pas Toi? (21)

To his dismay, however, the young lady, who by that capital "T" is unmistakably a stock *jeune fille,* is more than willing to pardon him, and in fact bursts into declarations of love. Hamlet's disgust at

Hamlet, ou les suites de la piété filiale

thus finding her a potential daughter of Eve ("'Encore une!' pense-t-il," 21), stifles his remorse and, as in the case of Polonius, permits him to rationalize his behavior in the name of practice: "'C'est encore pour me faire la main que j'ai tué cet oiseau,' pense-t-il" (21).

This peculiar scene recalls and distorts two from the original, Hamlet's interviews with Ophelia. In the first (II,i), he visits her as she is sewing in her closet, like the girl crocheting here; and in the second (III,i) delivers the famous "get thee to a nunnery," in which his sarcastic remarks resemble the parodic Hamlet's here (e.g., "Where's your father" becomes "Est-ce que ton père est malade?," 21). To drive home the allusion and lead the reader to understand it, Laforgue makes the connection between the canary scene of the parody and the Ophelia scenes of the original explicit:

> C'est fort commode; et si Hamlet n'en est pas encore à songer qu'il n'a guère autrement apprécié la triste Ophélie (oh! guère autrement pauvre oiseau!) son Ange Gardien n'en pense pas moins. (23)

Hamlet's murder of the "petit oiseau" (22) reflects his treatment of that other "pauvre oiseau" that he drives to death, Ophelia—a fact which may escape the hero's consciousness but, as the parenthesis indicates, certainly not his Unconscious, his Hartmannian "Ange Gardien." Hamlet's Unconscious recognizes this so well, in fact, that it will take its revenge and in the form of yet another "strange destructive impulse"—this time self-destructive—send him fatally to Ophelia's tomb at the end.

In the second episode, Hamlet, while out hunting, gleefully does violence to the insects and animals of the forest, sticking pins through beetles, plucking the wings from butterflies, cutting the hind legs off frogs, sprinkling saltpeter on an ant hill and setting fire to it, gathering up birds' nests and distributing them along the next stream, and so on, following the model of Flaubert's Saint Julien. Later, acting upon another "impulsion destructive," he gouges out the eyes of his victims and greases his hands with them ("il s'en lava les mains, il s'en graissa les phalanges," 22). Hamlet's sadism is related to his cynicism and moral relativism, his conviction that reality contains no inherent morality, which he expresses in the stock nineteenth-century formula of the nihilist, "tout est permis":

> Ah! c'était LE DEMON DE LA REALITE. L'allégresse de constater que la justice n'était qu'un mot, que tout est permis—et pour cause, Nom de Dieu!—contre les êtres bornes et muets. (22)

Hamlet deforms the "démon de la Perversité" of Poe (cited by des Esseintes as the source of his own "impulsions irrésistibles")[21] and blames reality for his perverse impulses and unmotivated crimes: a parody reflecting both the methods and the target of the larger one. And although he pays for his escapade by a night of cold sweats and terrifying dreams of gouged-out eyes bathed in tears, he rationalizes his brutality in the name of reality, notably past atrocities: "Et les guerres! Et les tournées d'abattoir des siècles du monde antique, et tout!" (22). Hamlet can always find a precedent by which to excuse his cruelty, except in that most "irréparable" (22) of murders, Ophelia's. Laforgue explicitly relates the two by having Hamlet later remark that he should have put out Ophelia's pure, heavenly eyes and "m'y laver les mains" (33), a scenario directly reminiscent of the night hunt. Ophelia is a victim of the same "impulsion destructive" that made him put out the eyes of the creatures of the forest and wash his hands with them.

Hamlet tries out his peculiarly Decadent brand of nihilism on some proletarians returning from their daily drudgery:

> Mettez tout à feu et à sang! Ecrasez comme punaises d'insomnies les castes, les religions, les idées, les langues! Refaites-nous une enfance fraternelle sur la Terre, notre mère à tous, qu'on irait pâturer dans les pays chauds.
>
> *Dans les Jardins*
> *De nos instincts,*
> *Allons cueillir*
> *De quoi guérir.* (24)

These verses on the primacy of instinct (yet another Laforguian autocitation) suggest Hamlet's idea of social revolution:[22] to give oneself over to the Unconscious. He is a lapsed revolutionary, or more precisely a reformed one, whose pessimism has changed his earlier "folie d'apôtre" from social to psychological and eventually replaced it altogether with Decadent resignation and cynicism. He cheerfully admits to being a feudal parasite, but justifies himself by

Hamlet, ou les suites de la piété filiale

parodying a cliché to make it fit his own situation and reflect his own moral relativism: "Ne soyons pas plus prolétaire que le prolétaire. Et toi, Justice humaine, ne soyons pas plus forte que Nature" (25). The workers represent nothing more advanced than the famous bourgeois slogan of Guizot, "enrichissez-vous," here parodically ascribed to Polonius; they are "pas assez esthétiques" and "trop lâches devant l'Infini" (25), clearly not Hamlet's type. His position on social inequality differentiates him radically from Laertes, who has taken up the question of workers' housing and gained the popularity of the people; the revolution of this fourteenth of July does not promise to go in Hamlet's favor.

The cemetery scene serves the important function of informing Hamlet of his parentage and his relation to the court fool, Yorick. Hamlet sees in his own caesarian section birth a first sign of his Decadent's reluctance to live in the world, although the reader takes it as a humorously corrupt borrowing from *Macbeth,* and thus a reminder of the parody. He does not grasp the resemblance of his parents' story to his own, however: the beautiful travelling gypsy is not very different from the beautiful travelling actress, Kate; the king is here described as having a "coeur d'or" (27), as Hamlet has already said of himself (21); and when Hamlet proclaims, in the Yorick monologue that follows, "Je comprends tout, j'adore tout et veux tout féconder," we see in the son the literal legacy of the *coureur* (27) father.

Laforgue deforms the "Alas, poor Yorick" speech to explore the newly discovered fraternal relation between Yorick and the hero. As in the original, the speech is a meditation on death, but here it includes concerns typical of the parodic Hamlet: a desire for escape, a sense of moral relativism, Hartmannian ideas of cosmic evolution, and most of all, himself. Indeed, Hamlet effortlessly passes from Yorick to the first person and considers the obsessive questions of being and death: "Mais ne plus être, ne plus y être, ne plus en être!" (30). Hamlet's new "to be or not to be" parodically produces three unhappy "not to be"s; he does not want to die, but to be famous. He must find a way of justifying this parodic desire, however, and characteristically turns to "words, words, words," simply talking himself into the value of living and persuading himself, by a ridiculous line of reasoning, that he is overflowing with life:

> Voyons: quand j'ai faim, j'ai la vision intense des comestibles; quand j'ai soif, j'ai la sensation nette des liquides; quand je me sens le coeur tout célibataire, j'ai à sangloter le sentiment des yeux chéris et des épidermes de grâce; donc si l'idée de la mort me reste si lointaine, c'est que je déborde de vie, c'est que la vie me tient, c'est que la vie me veut quelque chose! (31)

However, the first thing that this reinvigorated Hamlet encounters is a troublesome and prophetic image of death, Ophelia's funeral train; just as at the end, here his assertion of life is thwarted by the reality of her death.

The sight of the procession brings out Hamlet's ambivalent feelings about Ophelia and provides the occasion for a parody of Decadent attitudes to women in general. On the one hand, he congratulates himself for having saved her from a sordid fate, such as becoming the mistress of Fortimbras, dying of shame, and leaving behind her the scandalous reputation of a Belle-Hélène. This reminder of Offenbach's famous operetta reinforces the parody, not only by alluding to another one which uses the same methods, but also by pointing directly to Hamlet as a parodic hero: he may have saved Ophelia from becoming a parodic heroine by killing her off before the story, but the obvious implication is that he could not do likewise for himself. On the other hand, the hero feels remorse, remembering her "grands regards bleus," her thinness, her modesty, and her eyes. Only pat Hamletic excuses can ease his conscience this time: the proverbial call of art ("l'art est si long et la vie si courte!"), the force of heredity, a newfound one for which he is grateful ("oui, il y a de ça"), and his old standby, fatality ("Je l'ai aidée à se faner, la Fatalité a fait le reste," 34). Hamlet once again deludes himself into believing that he has no cause for guilt, that, in the formula of the epigraph, he cannot help it:

> Que puis-je à tout cela, maintenant? Allons, je donne dix ans de ma vie pour la ressusciter! Dieu ne dit mot! Adjugé! C'est donc qu'il n'y a pas de Dieu, ou bien que c'est moi qui n'ai même pas dix ans à vivre. La première hypothèse me semble la plus viable, et pour cause. (34)

But that last "cause" remains in question, and the reader realizes that it consists of nothing more than "words, words, words," the doubtful rhetoric by which Hamlet, in the parallel instance above, convinced himself that he was overflowing with life. Once again, the specious argument gives away the truth; indeed he does not have ten years left to his life, not even the rest of this one revolutionary day.

Hamlet's love scene with Kate gives the impression of enacting the untold story of his relations with Ophelia. When he encounters her, she is "éplorée comme une Madeleine . . . prostrée dans la supériorité de ses larmes, de son enfance retrouvée" (35f.), a direct reminder of his previous image of Ophelia bathed in tears, "cette source rajaillie de l'enfance, de la créature primitive incapable de mal" (35). Kate, alias Ophelia, is, as we have seen, another Ophelia, a point to which Laforgue calls explicit attention: she sheds tears on Hamlet's waistcoat "où Ophélie en a déjà pas mal versé le mois passé" (36); he instinctively calls her "Ophélia," the name to which he had earlier objected with such vehemence for being too theatrical. And he himself makes the connection: "'[Ophélie] avait (comme cette actrice de Kate, avouons-le) deux fins yeux'" (33); "'[Kate] a, comme Ophélie, cet air collet-monté'" (42). As a "sequel" to Shakespeare's play, the parody deals with Hamlet's second love; but some things never change, notably our hero's relation to women. Indeed, he immediately loses all interest in his play and its "moralité," his throne, his father's death, and Kate's other lovers (40); renounces his Decadent past, his "jeunesse stérile et mal nourrie" (41); and resolves to elope to Paris with her after the performance.

As the play gets underway, Hamlet becomes totally absorbed, anticipating in it the glory that he will find in Paris: "Le cliché 'public houleux' lui vient aux lèvres" (41). He becomes so involved as to respond to Kate's lines himself, even feeling his views about women change as a result of his own play, the quixotic—and parodic—problem translated into the egoism of decadence. At last, the garden scene has its desired—and traditional—effect: the King and Queen understand its message, and the performance is duly interrupted. However just when, for once, Hamlet carries through a plan, and therefore might make his final decisive move, he parodically decides not to bother. Concluding on the spot that the play has been punishment enough for them, he flees without taking vengeance and, anxious to avoid being poisoned "comme un rat, un sale rat" (43), goes off to join Kate. Here Laforgue uses Hamlet's paranoiac fear of being poisoned, mentioned earlier in a parenthetical aside (8), as a pretext for alluding to the killing of Polonius, like "a rat," in the original Shakespeare (IV,i,10). This reminder of the parodied work does not augur well for the hero, however, who is soon to be stabbed by Polonius' son, as the original Polonius was by Hamlet himself.

Laforgue transfers the details of Ophelia's burial in the original (V,i), where Hamlet and Laertes struggle with one another in the newly-dug grave, to the death scene of Hamlet himself. The escape occurs initially without difficulty, but a parenthetical aside, like Hamlet's nagging moral conscience, warns that misfortune lies ahead: "(Non, non! Ce n'est pas possible! Cela s'est fait trop vite!)" (43). Indeed, drawn by a force greater than himself, "piqué d'on ne sait quelle tarentule . . . il va droit à la tombe d'Ophélie, de la déjà si mystérieuse et légendaire Ophélie" (44). The narrative's allusion to itself, in "légendaire," signals Hamlet's fate: his best chance of becoming legendary lies not in writing plays, but in following in the footsteps of "la déjà si mystérieuse et légendaire Ophélie," dying, and becoming the hero of a parody.

The hero's last decisive move (the emblematic "décidément" reappears) is therefore to goad Laertes with an infuriating moral indifference ("O Laërtes, tout m'est égal," 45). Ever the progressive positivist, Laertes would excuse him on the grounds of insanity ("un pauvre dément, irrésponsable selon les derniers progrès de la science," 45), but cannot reconcile himself to such an "absence de sens moral" (45). Hamlet's offer to take his views into consideration and his attempt to question the reality of the killings ("Alors, vous croyez que c'est arrivé?" 45), as he had done earlier in the same setting vis-à-vis Polonius, here drive Laertes into a fury:

— Allons! Hors d'ici, fou, ou je m'oublie! Quand on finit par la folie, c'est qu'on a commencé par le cabotinage.
— Et ta soeur!
— Oh!

A ce moment, on entend dans la nuit toute spectralement claire l'aboi si surhumainement seul d'un chien de ferme à la lune, que le coeur de cet excellent Laërtes (qui aurait plutôt mérité, j'y songe, hélas! trop tard, d'être le héros de cette narration) déborde, déborde de l'inexplicable anonymat de sa destinée de trente ans! C'en est trop! Et saisissant d'une main Hamlet à la gorge, de l'autre il lui plante au coeur un poignard vrai. (45)

As usual, Hamlet has a ready pun, a vulgar formula of provocation (and a very nineteenth-century one) which, for all its flippancy, nevertheless calls Laertes' assertion cleverly into question by pointing to the literal example of his sister. If Ophelia was not a ham actor who ended up mad, perhaps Hamlet is not one either. Indeed, Laertes gets the formula wrong; Hamlet is not mad, merely a ham actor, in everything.

But the dagger is, even for Hamlet, unquestionably real ("vrai") and, falling to his knees in a grotesque death agony, he has just enough strength to utter a relevant cliché, the dying words of Nero, the famous *Qualis . . . artifex . . . pereo!* Hamlet's appeal to the quintessential artist also bears an ironic relation to the original play, for Shakespeare's hero had likewise called upon Nero in the scene with Gertrude (III,ii,378–79): "Let not ever / The soul of Nero enter this firm bosom." Laforgue's hero is, on the contrary, full of the soul of Nero throughout, not in the original sense of his mother's murderer, but as the exemplar of nineteenth-century Decadence.

With Hamlet thus given his longed-for place in history ("O soir historique, après tout!" 47), the story ends with everything returning to the way it was, a literal, full-circle revolution on this fourteenth of July. Kate goes back to being William's mistress, although not without being punished for having tried to abandon him in favor of Hamlet, a misfortune on which the narrative comments with a simple but highly resonant digression: "Et cependant elle était si belle, Kate, qu'en d'autres temps, la Grèce lui eût élevé des autels" (47). This Greek goddess has fallen parodically low, perhaps even to the level of a Belle-Hélène, such as Hamlet had earlier predicted for Ophelia. The second Ophelia fulfills Hamlet's fears for the first; he was not able to save her, however, by driving her to suicide.

Even more importantly, in the final sentence, the return to normal occasions a comment on the highly abnormal story, the parody itself: "Un Hamlet de moins; la race n'en est pas perdue, qu'on se le dise!" (47). It illustrates perfectly the self-reflexive feature of parody described in chapter 1, that is, the expressed anticipation within the parody of other versions of the story. "One Hamlet less" implies that there are others in the line; and "la race" ambiguously (and punningly) refers either to the human race or, more particularly, to the race of Hamlets. The parody thus suggests that its version of the story is not the only one, or the definitive one, or even, ironically, an important one ("la race n'en est pas perdue"), but rather one among many, past and future. Accordingly, in another line, Laforgue had already called his version directly into question by hinting at the unreliability of the parodist and thus at the inaccuracy of his story. When William punishes Kate ("Ah! . . . c'est comme ça qu'on voulait lâcher Bibi?" 47), the narrative comments parenthetically, "(Bibi est une abréviation de Billy, diminutif de William)." The narrator's gloss is incorrect, and comically so, for "Bibi" is a popular childish term for "myself." The parodist is suspect, and so the story may be too.

Moreover, Laforgue actually suggests how the story might have differed. In the passage from Hamlet's death scene quoted above, the narrator realizes, in the parenthetical aside inserted at the moment of the stabbing, that Laertes could have been the hero: "(qui aurait plutôt mérité, j'y songe, hélas! trop tard, d'être le héros de cette narration)" (45). Laforgue calls attention to the many narrative possibilities by citing one, and also to the unpredictable element of chance that determines which one will find expression. The text gives the distinct impression that Laertes would have dominated this *Hamlet* if the parodist had merely thought of the possibility earlier. In fact, he even prepares Laertes to take over the hero's role by making him resemble Hamlet. Laertes goes mad from the deed; the narrative suggests that he may become a monk, again recalling Hamlet, earlier described as resembling a monk more than a crown prince of Denmark (23); and like Hamlet, a thirty-year-old potential hero spurred by the thought of his anonymity ("déborde de l'inexplicable anonymat de sa destinée de trente ans," 45), Laertes here takes the revenge that Hamlet could

Hamlet, ou les suites de la piété filiale

not. In this way, Laforgue proposes an alternative to his story from within the story, itself already an alternative one; the parody leaves room for, and sometimes suggests explicitly, another version of itself. This "one Hamlet less" actually adds one more Hamlet to the corpus and proposes yet another one, still to be realized, with Laertes as hero. Hamlet himself sets us an example when, after the love scene with Kate, he scornfully rejects his play and its *moralité* ("je me moque de cette représentation et de sa moralité," 40); perhaps this *Moralité* should ultimately be rejected, too, revised and rewritten according to the spirit of a future age. As the final line implies, the race will indeed not be lost, but rather continued, and extended, for it.

4

Le Miracle des Roses

Le Miracle des Roses occupies a unique place in the *Moralités légendaires* as a whole, for while the titles of the other tales clearly identify the originals with which they play, here the model is not immediately apparent, and from the beginning has been thought not to exist.[1] Laforgue's friend, Teodor de Wyzewa, to whom he dedicated the *Moralités*, recognized the modernizing principle behind the stories but ignored *Le Miracle des Roses* altogether.[2] In a review of the volume in 1903, Lanson did likewise, describing the method as "reprendre les sujets des maîtres," but naming only the other five stories as examples.[3] *Le Miracle des Roses* thus constitutes a particular case in this discussion of the *Moralités* as parodies and presents a number of problems which the theory of parody, as I have formulated it in chapter 1, must address for it to apply usefully to the whole volume. If the story does not seem to be, in Laforgue's words, "de vieux canevas," that is, does not appear to have a model, by what criteria do we call it a parody? How does it signal itself as one if we have no original with which to compare it? Finally, if the meaning of the parody depends upon distortion, the difference between itself and the original, how may a work *without* a perceptible original be understood as a parody? *Le Miracle des Roses* thus represents a special instance not just of Laforgue's stories but of parody in general, and provides a rare example by which to test the theoretical point argued in chapter 1: the parody's intelligibility in the absence of the original, and its "construction" of the original through parodic transformation.

Nevertheless, although it is always considered an exception to the rule of the volume, the story is in fact based on an earlier model. Even before my own discovery of the original, however, a number of factors indicated that there was one. First, for exterior evidence, Laforgue himself implied as much, although he never identified it. Describing the volume in a letter to Kahn, he singled out two stories for not being "de vieux canevas," neither of which was *Le Miracle des Roses*.[4] Moreover, independently of this letter, features of the story itself suggest that it follows the pattern of the rest. First, it contains the same type of parodic signals, including not only devices of humor (which of course need not be limited to parody) but also indications that it modernizes an older story: anachronism, allusions to the work as a staging and restaging of a drama, and the quotation and transformation of other works, such as Shakespeare's *Macbeth* and Flaubert's *Un Coeur simple*. Second, the disjunction between the miracle story and the otherwise modern late nineteenth-century atmosphere of a *station d'eaux* suggests a parody consistent with the others. Third, the main episode involves a comical disappointment of expectations, for the miracle is a bogus one, a mistaken perception on the part of the heroine; one would expect such an anti-miracle story to be parodic, based on a more conventional miracle story.

Le Miracle des Roses has a rather bizarre plot, involving a young heroine, Ruth, an invalid, consumptive, neurotic *hallucinée* who, attended by her brother Patrick, passes what appear to be her last days at a fashionable 1880s-style spa which Laforgue compares, throughout part 1, to the setting and spirit of an *opéra-comique* by Offenbach. Although Ruth had long been plagued with tuberculosis, her illness had been only recently complicated by hallucinations, after she witnessed the enigmatic suicide of an unhappy male admirer. On her breast she wears a strange enamel plaque, mysteriously tossed at her feet one day by an unidentified "pauvre diable" (77), who ordered her never to part with it, lest he lose, or take, his life as a result: an enormous medallion representing the most Decadent of images, a peacock-feather eye set under a human eyelid and surrounded by colorless polished stones. Most importantly, she has since that time left suicide in her wake, the details of which we are given in several flashback episodes. Finally, during the Corpus Christi Day parade, Ruth watches the Holy Sacrament pass by and is reminded of the first *suicidé* who had died for love of her. Hallucinating that she sees his blood on the lawn, she falls in a faint, while a little girl from the procession scatters rose petals from her basket all around her. Upon awakening, Ruth sees the roses and proclaims the "miracle": blood changed into rose petals, the suicide's blood at last redeemed.

Although the parodied work has never been identified, the parody clearly turns on the miracle of the roses that occurs at the end, the alleged transformation of blood into roses, which, emphasized by the title, focuses our search for the model: the original would also have involved a miracle by which a transformation into roses takes place. Laforgue actually took the idea for his story from the rather unlikely source of the medieval legend of Saint Elizabeth of Hungary. Elizabeth, known for her great acts of charity, was forbidden by her husband to give extravagant gifts to the poor. When he unexpectedly meets her carrying a bundle of provisions and questions her about her activities, she tells him that she has been gathering roses. Indeed, when she opens her bundle, the provisions have been miraculously changed into roses. Laforgue has altered the heroine's name from Elizabeth to Ruth, which in an English context has connotations of calamity and ruin consistent with her effect on others. The English connection is in fact justified, for he blatantly associates her with a formidable heroine of English literature, thereby calling her alleged innocence in the suicides sharply into question: the bizarre refrain that she sings when hallucinating is a line of Lady Macbeth's. Ruth is actually a parodic saint, a deformation, or even perversion, of the original heroine, for she causes doom and destruction rather than salvation; she is a demon, and the peacock medallion on her breast is a symbol not of the Christian resurrection but, following another tradition, of the evil eye, with all the sinister properties attributed to it.[5]

Although not universally known, the story of Saint Elizabeth was by no means wholly unfamiliar in the nineteenth century. In 1836 Montalembert wrote his *Histoire de Sainte Elisabeth de Hongrie*, and a number of paintings of the period (by G. Moreau, F. Over-

Le Miracle des Roses

beck, E. Dubufe, and Moritz von Schwind, for example) illustrate the miracle of the roses episode. Nevertheless, Laforgue does not appear to have had any contact with these, and the life of Saint Elizabeth could hardly be considered a major story of Western literary history. As with *Lohengrin* and *Salomé*, we must look to a more contemporary version which would have called his attention to it, and also made it recognizable enough to be used effectively in his parody. The 1883 *Agenda* obligingly carries the following note for Wednesday, 4 April: "St[e] Elisabeth de Listz [sic]—Philharmonie, Bergenburger Strasse."[6] Liszt's oratorio on the Legend of Saint Elizabeth, which Laforgue thus saw performed in Berlin, contains six sections, of which the second is indeed "The Miracle of the Roses."[7] Laforgue's parody is clearly inspired by this work. Significantly, in May of the same year, he watched a Corpus Christi Day parade in front of the Hôtel d'Angleterre in Baden-Baden, which provided the material for part 3;[8] and in August he attended a bull fight in San Sébastien, which, as scholars have long been aware, he transformed into the *corrida* of part 2.[9] Although this *Moralité* dates from 1885–1886, the discovery of its model confirms the thesis that much of its material comes from 1883.[10]

Two points important for the theory of parody emerge from this discovery. First, knowledge of the original, beyond what is provided in the parody itself, adds relatively little to our understanding of Laforgue's free adaptation, either as a parody or otherwise; and second, in retrospect the text can be seen to contain numerous clues that point to the identity of the original. These points support the contention made in chapter 1 that we do not necessarily have to know the original in order to grasp the sense of the parody, which theoretically maintains within itself enough of the original for us to perceive the distortion, and in this way "creates" the parodied work, that is, those aspects of the original that are relevant to the parody. This has been confirmed empirically by the fact that the model for *Le Miracle des Roses* was unknown and its existence doubted for a century, while the story itself was otherwise considered to have the same method, purpose, and effect as the other *Moralités*. In fact those elements which allude to the original operate normally as guides to the parody. Dropping hints as to the identity of the parodied work is a device of the genre to signal the distortion or the transformation, and therefore to guide the reader through it to the sense of the parody itself.

A few devices by which Laforgue communicates the original as a backdrop for his own parodic version deserve mention from the start. The most outstanding one occurs early in part 2, where the narrative describes the altar decorations of the little town's two rival hotels, which annually compete to mount the most impressive "reposoir." This year, the Hôtel d'Angleterre has once again triumphed over the Hôtel de France; but the text here adds a prophetic aside, meant to redeem the France from its defeat:

> Tandis que le reposoir de l'hôtel de France, sans vouloir discuter l'àpropos de ses charmantes corbeilles de lys (qui ne filent pas), allait être le théâtre d'une seconde édition plus esthétique du Miracle des Roses! Oui, le légendaire Miracle des Roses! (67)

This passage conspicuously signals the parody, particularly the modernizing variety of the *Moralités,* by referring to the story as a *second* edition of the Miracle of the Roses, thus based on a first edition, or model. The capital letters specifically indicate a title, a work of art, thereby suggesting that the second edition is a parody, a new version or rewriting of an existing work.

The passage also provides some clues to the first edition itself. First, the curious aside about the appropriateness of the hotel's "charmantes corbeilles de lys" makes sense only with respect to a story in which baskets of flowers (if not lilies) are relevant to a miracle of roses. This fits Liszt's version specifically, which features a basket in contrast to the iconographically traditional bundle (usually the saint's apron). The narrative looks ahead and gives a bit of the secret away: the baskets of lilies that here adorn the Hôtel de France are connected to the miracle that will take place there at the end, although the "sans vouloir discuter" playfully leaves in question whether the relation is actually one of suitability or unsuitability, appropriateness or inappropriateness. This comment contains a second clue, in the peculiar and comically unexpected reference to the lilies of the field: the allusion to the Biblical miracle of the lilies of the field, arrayed more beautifully than Solomon in all his glory, suggests another of the same kind, a religious miracle story involving flowers. What appears merely a device of humor—the automatic, association of lilies with "nor do they spin" in an incongruous context—actually indicates subtly the character of the original story.

Third, the mention of the "legendary" Miracle of the Roses, in the line set apart, points directly to the world of legend for the original of this *Moralité légendaire,* and further, provides part of the original's title, *Die Legende von der heiligen Elisabeth*. In retrospect, Laforgue's title may be seen, as in all the *Moralités,* to reflect the status of the parody as a deformation of the original. In this case, there is no qualifying subtitle (as in *Hamlet, Persée et Andromède,* and *Pan et la Syrinx*), or addition to the title (*Lohengrin*), but rather a name related, though not identical, to the original one: "Le Miracle des Roses" constitutes one part (scene 2) of a larger work of a different title.[11] Finally, the specific reference to the story as a "more aesthetic" version of the original suggests the actual target; the parody "aestheticizes" the medieval legend by transforming it according to the most aesthetic of literary movements, Decadence.

Another feature of the narrative that hints at the character of the original is the remarkable predominance, especially in part 1, of musical motifs. In the first six pages alone, we find over a dozen: the prominent *opéra-comique,* English waltzes, concerts in the Casino, Don Giovanni, ballads of Chopin, arpeggi played on the harmonica, tunes from Offenbach, the local band, a little harpist, the march from *Aïda*. The musical theme serves primarily to reflect the romanesque, operetta-like character of the town: the artificial, Romantic world of elegant young men and lovely young ladies waltzing in the Casino, the well-off, precious, and dangerously fragile world of the resort, the loss of which the narrator regrets with melancholy and nostalgia ("Ah! que tout n'est-il opéra-comique! . . ." 53). But by insisting on the musical theme, Laforgue calls attention subtly to the specific nature of the model, a piece of music. *Le Miracle des Roses* preserves the parodied work in its musical imagery, transposing the genre of the original into one of the parody's conspicuously dominant metaphors, which then takes on a crucial role of its own: to illustrate the late-Romantic nostalgia which is a quality, even a major source, of Decadence, and the real target of the parody. This technique reflects a major principle of parody, which transforms the original into a new work, or in the case of the *Moralités légendaires*, adapts an old story to the issues of the modern, specifically Decadent, imagination. The motif of the *opéra-comique*, present in several of the *Moralités*, has particular significance for this one: Laforgue comically suggests that *Le Miracle des Roses* is an *opéra-comique* version, a parody, of Liszt's original oratorio.

The late-nineteenth-century theme of illness described in chapter 2 informs the whole story, including the miracle on which it turns. Laforgue's spa harbors those two sickly heroic types of the Decadent imagination, the neurotics ("névropathes, enfants d'un siècle trop brillant") and the consumptives ("phtisiques, race à pas lents mais chère au dilettante," 55).[12] Ruth, with her chronic consumption and her recently acquired hallucinations, combines the two types and thus makes a perfect Decadent heroine, a "typique créature trop tôt enlevée ... au dilettantisme de ses amis" (67, 69). Predictably, she is also a mystic and esoteric, thoroughly detached from life, "déjà retirée des conflits de ce bas monde sanguin" (73), with her "regards déjà réinitiés aux altitudes originelles d'au-delà la vie" (69) and her bizarre medallion "qui semble cadenasser d'*ésotérisme* sa poitrine sans sexe" (77, emphasis mine). Laforgue associates her and her brother with the North, easy symbol of Romantic mysticism. In addition to the northern connotations of Patrick's name, a simile likens him to "un vert sapin de son pays" (71); Ruth is covered with tartan blankets; he plays pieces by the nineteenth-century Norwegian composer Kjerulf on the piano and reads Balzac's Swedenborgian novel *Séraphita* aloud to her. Significantly, as we shall see later in more detail, this Romantic work is not extreme enough for the Decadent Ruth, who contemptuously labels it "de la basse confiserie séraphique" (77). One wonders, however, if this judgment might better apply to her own story, with its exaggerated romanesque: a *poésie de confiseur* in the most pejorative sense, a parody of the seraphic industry, with its own parodic *vision séraphique*, the final hallucination that constitutes the spurious miracle.

The Epigraph

Laforgue introduces the parody with a quotation, translated into French, from the first chapter of Darwin's *The Power of Movement in Plants* of 1880:

> L'autre semis de Sensitives se comporta d'une manière un peu différente, car les cotylédons s'abaissèrent dans la matinée jusqu'à 11 heures 30, puis s'élevèrent; mais après midi 10, ils tombèrent de nouveau. Et le grand mouvement ascensionnel de la soirée ne commença qu'à 1 heure 22.
>
> Darwin[13]

This curious passage appears to have little relation to the story, except for the rather superficial one of the flower motif common to both. To base an important relation on an apparently unimportant one is a procedure of the epigraph generally, as Riffaterre observes,[14] and one that applies to parody too. Indeed, with a play on words and on the cliché of the woman as an exotic flower, "sensitives" allude not only to sensitive plants, but also to the hypersensitive, indeed neurotic heroine, herself a sensitive plant, perhaps even a *mimosa pudica* of the type described in the Darwin passage, whose leaves droop at the slightest touch. The epigraph warns us at the beginning that this is a story of a most sensitive flower who shrinks from all contact, notably from men, as the suicides of her potential *prétendants* attest; it thus provides a clue to the unexplained curse.

But this does not sufficiently explain the epigraph, which concentrates on the behavior of the "sensitives," the cyclical fall and rise of the cotyledons twice daily. Applied to the story's "sensitive," this dual cycle reflects the two turns of Ruth's life—her consumption redressed by a period of cures at fashionable resorts, and her later hallucinations. The story indeed follows the epigraph by ending on a "grand mouvement ascensionnel de la soirée," as her hallucinations are cured by the spurious miracle of the roses. But it is significantly a rise "de la soirée"; for Ruth, this "être de crépuscule" (67), actually moves in her evening rise toward death. Part 1 accordingly takes place long after she has died. Ruth's story follows the pattern of the rest of life, including the plants, although like the cycle of the special "sensitives" of the epigraph hers differs from the norm ("d'une manière un peu différente") and is a parody.

The Story

The story has a rather contrived temporal structure consisting of five frames: a present (part 1), a past recounted in flashback (parts 2 and 3), and three flashbacks, all to different moments, within that (part 2). Part 1 introduces the little resort town with its *opéra-comique* atmosphere, about which the narrator reminisces in preparation for the tale to follow.[15] The insistence on the *opéra-comique*, from the very first sentence, signals the parodic relation of the story to its original model. Moreover, as I have mentioned, Laforgue makes this a metaphor for the elegant, bygone heyday of a late-Romantic era:

> Jamais, jamais, jamais cette petite ville d'eaux ne s'en douta, avec son inculte Conseil municipal délégué par des montagnards rapaces et nullement opéra-comique malgré leur costume.
>
> Ah! que tout n'est-il opéra-comique! . . . Que tout n'évolue-t-il en mesure sur cette valse anglaise, *Myosotis,* qu'on entendait cette année-là (moi navré dans les coins, comme on pense) au Casino, valse si décemment mélancolique, si irréparablement derniers, derniers beaux jours! . . . (Cette valse, oh! si je pouvais vous en inoculer d'un mot le sentiment avant de vous laisser entrer en cette histoire!) (53)

The spirit of the *opéra-comique* is identified with the "époques brillantes et irresponsables" (55) which the speaker so regrets, embodied in the English waltz, "Mysotis." The name of the waltz is significant, not only for the floral theme that it playfully extends (from the parody's title and the epigraph), but also for the unstated popular name of this flower, the forget-me-not, the *ne m'oubliez pas*. Like its title, the waltz itself is a nostalgic reminder of the past and of a bygone, probably illusory, happiness.[16] It evokes a melancholy sense of the passing of time, the atmosphere of late summer days soon to end. Here, it specifically recalls the last days of the "romanesque" before its decline into something less aesthetic, reflected in the "montagnards rapaces" and the uncouth municipal council, who never even suspected the miracle (introduced accordingly in

Le Miracle des Roses

the mysterious "en" of the first line). *Myosotis* is ultimately ironic, for, as the past tenses overwhelmingly remind us, the time which it symbolizes was as fleeting as a summer night's waltz, and the happiness that it represented likewise. Moreover, as the final parenthetical aside suggests, *Myosotis* is crucial for understanding the parody, itself a forget-me-not too, but with enough of a difference to sustain the story beyond the time destined for it.

The central symbol of that Romantic world and its decline is the Casino, its ballrooms no longer the scene of a "brillant et mélancolique va-et-vient de ces existences" (53), its gaming rooms now "bien tristes" and "bien désertées" (55), its piano stored away under an appropriate "draperie à fleurs fanées" (57) and no longer intoning the "ballades incurablement romanesques de Chopin" (57). Only the speaker's nostalgic imagination continues to produce such poignant music, as he seems to hear, in the evening air passing through the crystal branches of the chandelier, harmonica-like tones that remind him of its past glory: "mais les courants d'air des belles soirées hasardent d'étranges arpèges d'harmonica dans les stalactites de cristal de ce lustre qui éclaira tant d'épaules bien nourries dansant sur les airs coupables d'Offenbach" (57). But an irony informs this stock Romantic topos: as we shall see more clearly later, when the speaker's nostalgia creates a music even more "étrange," the parody itself.

From these elegant "épaules bien nourries," the casino's clientele has degenerated into the *névropathes,* ironically described in a negative comparison with the waltzers: "les bons névropathes, traînant une jambe qui ne valsera plus même sur l'air fragile et compassé de Myosotis" (55). The "va-et-vient" of *these* "existences" is hardly "brillant et mélancolique" (53): their "étranges bruits de déglutition automatique" (55, 57) disrupt concerts or make one flee the reading room of the Casino; with their choking and twitching, the over-sensitive *névropathes* are "enfants d'un siècle trop brillant" (55). The emphasis might fall on "trop": they represent the extreme, ludicrous state into which the former Romantic brilliance has naturally and inevitably evolved, the grotesque condition at which Decadence, following the logic and implications of its own system of values, ultimately arrives.

The resort thus presents a Romantic world in its last days, a decaying elegance reflected in the "sourires aigus et pâles" (61) of the evening strollers; a place artificially preserved, as though all the "malades de romanesque et de passé" (like the nostalgic narrator) had been placed there in a "prison de luxe," far from the industrious and energetic urban "capitales sérieuses où s'élabore le Progrès" (61). Only parodic reminders of the royal families that used to frequent it now remain, like the "reine catholique déchue" (59), who spends her time sulking, attracts no followers, and yet persists in believing that her presence provides the town with business; or worse still, the disappearing line of Stourdza princes, unceremoniously relegated to the basement of the local Greek chapel for their eternal repose (59).[17] Instead, a new generation of young people, models of health, vigor, and responsibility, replaces these ludicrous representatives of a disappearing age:

> Ah! mais aussi, de la terrasse du coupable casino d'antan, on a vue sur une saine et drue pelouse verte de *lawn-tennis,* où toute une jeunesse en vérité moderne, musclée, douchée et responsable de l'Histoire, donne cours à ses *animal spirits,* les bras nus, le torse altier et responsable devant des Jeunes Filles instruites et libres qui vont, boitant élégamment avec leurs chaussures plates, tenant tête au grand air et à l'Homme (au lieu de cultiver leur âme immortelle et de songer à la mort, ce qui, avec la maladie, est l'état naturel des chrétiens). (57–59)

The contrast between the "guilty" casino, with those plump shoulders dancing to the guilty tunes of Offenbach, and the lithe young people playing the recently imported game of lawn tennis reflects the difference between the old world and the new.[18] The "époques irresponsables" (55) have given way to a "jeunesse . . . responsable de l'Histoire"; the dancers, with their "épaules bien nourries" (57), have become a "jeunesse musclée"; the "malades" have been replaced by an active, athletic youth of *animal spirits;* the free, self-respecting attitude of the modern young girls replaces the "mélancolie" (53) and self-pity (57) of the *jeune fille* at the piano; an obsession with death and the immortality of the soul no longer concerns them. The parenthetical remark seems comically gratuitous but, in a manner typical of parody, actually signals the distortion. Illness, morbidity, and the cult of the soul may not really be "the natural state of

Le Miracle des Roses

Christians" but are perhaps that of a certain kind of Christian, a saint, and notably a parodic one like Ruth. The aside hints at the model on which the heroine is based.

From the start, the text calls attention to the first-person narrator by providing three blatant examples of first-person narration in the opening page alone. He is never identified but clearly knows the town well enough to reminisce on what used to happen there. Indeed, a parenthetical remark indicates that he was among the people listening to the "Myosotis" waltz in the Casino "cette année-là (moi, navré dans les coins, comme on pense)" (53), and thus makes him a character in the parody itself. He has allegedly returned to the town long after the events of the story to follow took place. This sets up a metafictional structure consistent with that of parody generally, for he retells (in the flashback to come) the parodic miracle story from within the parody. For the reader, this has the effect of confusing the fictional with the real and casting doubt on the reliability of the narrator's account.

But as the point of view abruptly changes to the third person at the start of part 2, the obvious question poses itself: who is the mysterious narrator who knows the story of the miracle so well, particularly when, as the first sentence conspicuously announces, no one else suspected what happened? The paragraph that closes part one provides an important clue. While it seems merely to restate the speaker's sentimental attachment to the town, it in fact introduces for the first time two puzzling details: an unnamed, now-deceased "Elle" and the speaker's unexplained relation to her.

> O petite ville, vous avez été mes seules amours, mais en voilà assez. Depuis qu'elle (Élle) est décédée, je n'y reviens guère, je ne m'y frotte guère; ce n'est pas sentimentalité (bien que la sentimentalité ne soit pas ce qu'un vain peuple pense), mais un je ne sais quoi qui n'a de nom dans aucune langue, de même que la voix du sang. (63)

The lady materializes unexpectedly and mysteriously, but the text hints at her identity in the curious final phrase: "la voix du sang" alludes, literally and playfully, to that *obsédée de sang* whom we will soon encounter, Ruth. It thus points to the subject of the story and the character of the miracle.

This phrase, however, does not here apply directly, or even syntactically, to Ruth; it serves rather as a comparison by which the speaker expresses the nameless emotion (in contrast to "sentimentalité") that keeps him from frequenting the town any longer. Taken figuratively, "la voix du sang" means familial instinct, kinship; the text thus suggests subtly that the unidentified speaker may be none other than Ruth's brother and companion, Patrick. If, like the indescribable quality of the evenings themselves, the speaker's "je ne sais quoi" feeling toward the town cannot be expressed by any word ("sentimentalité" is inadequate) or in any language (Laforgue comically applies to it Bossuet's famous phrase for the inexpressible, originally denoting a corpse), perhaps it may be expressed obliquely in a comparison ("de même que"), or better still, in a pun, and his mysterious identity indicated likewise. The narrator may be not only a character in the parody, as Laforgue suggested earlier, but a privileged witness of the parodic event, notably one of its two principal characters.

The abrupt sentence that opens part 2 announces the time of the main action: "Ce fut le jour de la Fête-Dieu" (63).[19] The feast of Corpus Christi celebrates the Holy Sacrament and the presence of Christ in the eucharist and is relevant to the parody in three ways. First, it explains Ruth's curious reaction, in part 3, to the appearance of the Holy Sacrament in the parade: she is reminded of, literally confronted with, her first *suicidé*, who died "par trop d'amour" (95), like Christ for love of man. There is no other reason for her to think of his blood at this time, for unlike the other episodes that provoke her bloody hallucinations, this one has no actual blood to inspire them. The nature of the holiday itself ensures her reaction and prepares the parodic "resurrection," the miracle by which she is cured. Second, the *Fête-Dieu* procession traditionally features the scattering of rose petals, and in this way provides an appropriate setting for a new, parodic miracle of the roses. This aspect of the parade figures prominently in what I take to be the third motivation for Laforgue's choice, a significant literary precedent in which a *Fête-Dieu* procession brings about the mystical fulfillment of a delirious heroine, Flaubert's *Un Coeur simple*. The parallels between the two accounts are striking, and Laforgue, in following and distorting Flaubert, suggests that Ruth's resurrec-

Le Miracle des Roses

tion is no less a hallucination than Félicité's dying vision of her parakeet, enlarged to gigantic proportions and hovering over her head: a colorful and parodic Holy Ghost.[20]

The scene is set in the square before the two hotels, the Angleterre and the France, which "réveillaient les pénibles rivalités de Waterloo et du Grand Prix dans la mise en scène de leurs reposoirs" (65). The competition between the two is presented as a reenactment of the legendary rivalry between France and England, already realized in two celebrated, and comically incongruous, events, the Battle of Waterloo and the Grand Prix. A parody-within-the-parody, this reflects the "reenactment" of the parody itself. But just as parody departs from the pattern of the original, so this story will differ from the usual: although, as in the past, the Angleterre has again won the prize, the France will in fact be the figurative winner as the scene of the miracle. The narrative remarks mysteriously that the Angleterre's victory "sera payée cher, plus tard, dans un monde meilleur" (67), more precisely, later in the *story*, when the France becomes the chosen site for the miracle of apparent redemption.

The altar decorations reflect this parodic reversal and to some extent prepare the outcome of the story. The France has only its customary "orgies de fleurs" (65), appropriate to the miracle that will occur there. In contrast, the victorious Angleterre features a conspicuous statue of Saint Theresa, patron saint of the place, that has a singularly unhealthy effect: "dont l'hystérique rococo polychromé tirait malsainement l'oeil" (65). The description of the statue not only reminds us of the absent "patron saint" of the original, Elizabeth of Hungary, but also prefigures the heroine of the parody. Ruth's hallucinations liken her to the hysterical, visionary Saint Theresa of the statue; she will imagine the blood of her *suicidé* on the lawn, like Theresa's famous visions of the crucified Christ; and the showy ("clinquant," 67) polychrome rococo with its unhealthy properties resembles an equally extravagant and unhealthy attention-grabber, Ruth's prominently displayed medallion with the peacock-feather eye. As the text indicates, the Angleterre will pay for its cheap victory, and so, ultimately, will Ruth: she is momentarily saved, but part 1 confirms that she in fact died thereafter.

Indeed from early on, the narrative calls into question the reality of the miracle ironically by attributing it solely to the heroine's imagination ("Du moins aux yeux de celle qui en fut l'héroïne," 67). Laforgue underlines this by an extended theatrical metaphor, as though it were merely an act. The Hôtel de France is the scene ("théâtre") of a second edition of the Miracle of the Roses, and Ruth its "héroïne" (67); her arrival in the sunny square is truly an *entrée en scène* ("voici entrer en scène un être de crépuscule," 67), and her handkerchief, sweets box, fan, and phial of musk are props for her role ("ces tristes accessoires du rôle de sa soeur," 69). Emphasizing the theatricality of the miracle story calls attention to Ruth's association with Decadence, for which life *is* theater, and also to the status of the story as a parody, a "restaging" of the original.

As in the theater, Ruth's "props" have particular significance for her part, for they are described synaesthetically in terms of a favorite Decadent metaphor, the scent; short-lived and fleeting, the scent represents the heroine herself, "trop tôt enlevée" (67). Her filmy handkerchief is "diaphane comme un parfum"; her sweets are flavored with "cachou à l'orange," known specifically for its scent; her odorous phial of musk is ironic, for although it is "le dernier réconfort des mourants" (and is later put to work when she faints during the parade, 95), it symbolizes by its perfume her death. The perfume metaphor also looks ahead to the phrase by which she repeatedly refers to herself, "faible comme un sachet éventé" (71), itself playing on the Baudelairean metaphor of the woman as a sachet, in "Hymne" (cf. "Le Parfum"). Ruth is no "sachet toujours frais qui parfume / L'atmosphère," however, for she is fading continually, a sachet losing its scent on contact with the air. It is also consistent with the perfume theme of her Lady Macbeth "refrain," uttered later during her hallucinations: "tous les parfums de l'Arabie" (85, 95).

This fading *sensitive* has also lost her color, like the pale yellow tea roses which she carries in preference to the more suggestive "roses rouges couleur de sang," or the "cabochons exsangues" of her medallion: Ruth's blood has passed rather into her hallucinations, leaving her with a waxen complexion that we are told will probably never color with the red glow of a lover's jealousy. This

Le Miracle des Roses

detail, given casually in an aside, actually suggests our heroine's unexplained problem, her inability to love. The suicides that follow so mysteriously in her path take place for this reason, "par trop d'amour" (95) for one who cannot, or will not, love in return:

> Trop pure, en effet, pour vivre, trop nerveuse pour vivoter, mais aussi trop de diamant pour se laisser entamer par l'existence, l'inviolable Ruth, tel un sachet, s'évente peu à peu, de stations d'hiver en stations d'hiver, vers le soleil ami des cimetières, des décompositions et des poupées de cire vierge. (73)

The comically puzzling epithet applied to the sun (and repeated from earlier, 55) is ironic, for the warm sun would actually hasten decomposition, cause wax dolls to melt, make the cemetery exhale—as in Baudelaire's "Le Tir et le Cimetière"—the "ardents parfums de la mort," and disturb the souls of its inhabitants in their eternal rest. But the epithet relates significantly to Ruth, whose "teint de cire" (71) associates her directly with the wax dolls and their unfortunate future, an ominous prediction for her sojourn in the sunny town and specifically in the sun-filled square. Moreover, although "vierge" applies syntactically to the wax, it nonetheless reminds us of the heroine who has never been married or engaged, despite a wedding band on her ring finger (to which the text calls attention by a comically parenthetical "Encore quelque mystère," 69). "Pure," "inviolable," "diamant," Ruth refuses to love and thus places a curse on the young men who come into contact with her. The medallion with the peacock-feather eye, "qui semble cadenasser d'ésotérisme sa poitrine sans sexe" (77), is the symbol of her detachment from life, an evil eye causing death; but it is ironically so, for the frightening sexuality usually associated with it exists here only in the symbol and nowhere in the heroine's reality. Ruth's medallion imparts a curse of frustration; it is a reminder of her inviolability, a sexuality unfulfilled and unobtainable, reflected in her "poitrine sans sexe" and the "inapprivoisable" (71, 75) quality of her eyes.

Of Patrick, we learn, first, that he is Ruth's adolescent younger brother by a "very different" (71) mother (playing with ironic understatement on the Decadent convention of heredity) and, second, that this period of his life constitutes only an interlude:

> Allons, ainsi qu'en un rêve qui interrompt, pour une saison ou deux, ses voyages personnels et son développment de héros, le bon Patrick suit d'un oeil fataliste, les mourantes mourantes aurores des taches hectiques aux pommettes de sa soeur et les lunules de sang à ses mouchoirs. (75)

The simile suggests that the period of the story is itself a kind of dream, interrupting a larger narrative of Patrick's "heroic development." If, as we have been told, Ruth is the heroine of *this* drama, Patrick may be the hero of another one; as implied earlier in the "voix du sang" pun, he may even be the narrator himself, hero of the first section. The story thus realizes the feature of parody described in chapter 1: pointing beyond itself from within, to a different story having another hero, who at present plays merely a secondary role. The future story is that of Patrick's interrupted "voyages personnels," which we have already glimpsed in part 1. The flashback structure allows the parody to exploit its self-reflexive and creative implications: it suggests a future story and even provides a portion of it within itself.

The suggestion that Patrick may be the narrator is reinforced when he reads aloud from Balzac's esoteric novel, *Séraphita,* and is interrupted by a vehement objection from Ruth:

> C'est facile â décrire! dit Ruth; non, c'est décidément de la basse confiserie séraphique, cette étude; cela sent Genève où ça a été composé. Et ce messager de lumière qui a une épée et un casque! Pauvre, pauvre Séraphita! non, ce Balzac au cou de taureau ne pouvait pas être ton frère. (77)

Ruth takes the work to be a silly, unartistic rendering of a subject for which she has obvious sympathy and with whose heroine she clearly identifies ("pauvre, pauvre Séraphita"). She pities her for being relegated to such a cheap version, a perversion of her true, or potential, story. As I have suggested earlier, this self-conscious allusion to parody reminds us of the one at hand and urges us to take it as a "basse confiserie séraphique" too. But it also identifies the narrator and parodist. Ruth's remark about Balzac seems to refer to his unspirituality, his inability to understand and portray his extraordinary heroine properly, but it actually suggests her own relation to Patrick. Unlike Balzac, Patrick is the heroine's brother and therefore will one day be a better Balzac, a better teller of his sister's

Le Miracle des Roses

story, ironically, in a parody. Significantly, the passage quoted from *Séraphita* describes the assumption of the heroine's spirit into the heavens, a subject omitted in Patrick's biography of Ruth but implied in the pretext for recounting it: the decease of the "Elle" mentioned at the end of part one.

The first important episode of Ruth's past, a flashback-within-the-flashback, is told to explain her hallucinations, which had begun the previous year during her stay in Darjeeling, site of the famous sanatorium. There, in a moonlit garden, she had involuntarily inspired and witnessed a suicide:

> ... un étrange suicide dont elle (déjà pourtant retirée des conflits de ce bas-monde sanguin) s'est trouvée improvisée par une nuit de lune, au fond d'un jardin, l'inspiratrice involontaire et l'unique témoin. Et depuis cette nuit-là, dans le fin sang de poitrinaire qu'elle crache elle croit toujours voir le sang rouge et passionné, le sang même de l'énigmatique suicidé, et elle délire à ce sang si radicalement répandu des choses concises et poignantes. (73)

The suicide remains strange throughout the story, its cause never given explicitly. However, the parenthetical remark suggests that it was inspired by Ruth's detachment from life and love, the "inviolability" and unattainable quality described earlier, even before she began to wear the medallion. The emblematic peacock-feather eye merely represents a permanent condition of her character.

The second episode involves another *étrangeté*, the medallion itself:

> Etrange, étrange, en effet, cette plaque d'émail qu'elle caresse sur sa poitrine sans sexe! Approchons-nous, de grâce; c'est un émail champlevé, d'un goût barbare et futur, un énorme et splendide oeil de queue de paon sous une paupière humaine, le tout encadré de cabochons exsangues. (77)

This image, reminiscent of the Redon paintings in des Esseintes' collection,[21] rapidly works on the first of the victims whom Ruth, "par une insondable fatalité" (79), mysteriously claims: he asks for her medallion, she refuses, and he takes his life. But this is not as "insondable" as it appears. The proscription of the medallion's anonymous donor ("le jour où vous la quitteriez, je me soustrairais à la vie," 77) binds her forever to him and to her chastity, as in the mystical marriages of nonparodic saints to Christ—thus the "mystère" of her wedding band. Ruth turns the fearsome emblem of her sexuality, and of her jealously guarded solitude, on anyone who attempts to transgress it.

The second suicide takes place near Biarritz, the spa where Ruth "opérait" (79) before coming to plague ("attrister," 79) the present one. In "opérer," Laforgue ironically likens Ruth's effect on others to a more obviously criminal offense, thus suggesting her real guilt in the suicides. Indeed, in this episode we see a rather less innocent heroine: despite her professed "horreur du sang" (79), she expressly wishes to attend a bull fight, quivers ("vibrait," 79) with the excitement of anticipation, and exults in the bloody procession of gored creatures. A guest of the governor, she urges him to ignore the calls of the crowd for ending the massacre and begs him to let it continue ("— Oh! pas encore, signor presidente, un engagement encore, c'est le plus beau . . . ," 83). If, as the narrative suggests, Ruth delights in the bloody spectacle because it "supplantait celui de son cauchemar normal" (81), we must wonder how she feels about the more immediate massacres in her life, the suicides. The parallel between them makes it clear that she actually takes pleasure in her fatal powers, delighting in the torment which her inviolability causes to her admirers, just as she exults in the gory scene before her. Ruth is a *femme fatale* in the guise of an innocent "inspiratrice involontaire" (73), the Decadent notion of women carried to an outrageous and parodic extreme. Each of her victims is accordingly a noble, suffering, poetic soul: a "pauvre âme d'amateur de choses artificielles" (79), a "lasse et étrange âme" (87), and a "jeune homme radieux et crispé" (95).

The long description of the bullfight plays a crucial role in the story as a whole because, first, it directly implicates Ruth in the suicides and, second, it prepares us to interpret the miracle episode of part three. It centers on the figure of the "pauvre taureau" (83) who, despite his wounds, refuses to be riled by the bandillero's taunting; instead he sniffs solicitously at the two maimed and agonizing horses, sits down in front of them "en sentinelle fraternelle, et comme cherchant à comprendre" (83), and meditates on the absurdity of his situation: "tout hébété de ce champ clos aux clameurs multicolores où il n'éventrait que des rosses aux yeux bandés ou de rouges flottantes loques" (85). But when a capador throws a goatskin bottle in his face, a minor miracle occurs:

> Et alors, voilà que soudain, devant ces vingt mille éventails palpitant dans un grand silence d'attente à splendide ciel ouvert, cette bête s'était mise, le col ostensiblement tendu vers Ruth, comme si seule elle était cause de toutes ces vilaines choses, à pousser au loin des pacages natals un meuglement si surhumainement infortuné (si génial, pour tout dire), qu'il y eut une minute de saisissement général, une de ces minutes où se fondent les religions nouvelles, tandis qu'on emportait, évanouie et délirante, qui?—la belle et cruelle dame de la loge présidentielle. (85)

In the great silence of the audience's expectation, the beast, his neck "ostensiblement" stretched toward Ruth, seems to point directly at her as the cause of "toutes ces vilaines choses." His unhappy bellowing seems the cry of a genius, an exile far from his native pastures in a cruel and unjust world that he does not understand. The moment of general "saisissement" has a transcendent quality ("où se fondent des religions nouvelles"), and the unconscious, delirious Ruth must be carried out, raving her refrain from that most responsible and red-handed of heroines, Lady Macbeth: "Le sang, le sang . . . là, sur le gazon. Tous les parfums de l'Arabie . . ." (85).

"Here's the smell of the blood still: all the perfumes of Arabia will not sweeten this little hand" (V,i,51); Shakespeare's heroine speaks this line during the famous sleepwalking scene, in which she unconsciously reveals her guilt to the doctor looking on. Ruth's secret, her responsibility in the suicides, is likewise discharged in her delirium, but only by means of the parodically disguised quotation. In addition, "more needs she the divine than the physician" applies similarly to her, whose cure will be effected by the Holy Sacrament in the scene to come. The supposedly innocent, "sexless" (77) heroine is as guilty as the more famous one who, to strengthen her murderous resolve, had pleaded with heaven, "unsex me here" (I,v,42); and the series of suicides is actually a series of murders, like hers. Ruth, the "belle et cruelle dame," the Decadent *femme fatale,* pays for her massacre of innocents with her hallucinations, like Lady Macbeth's sleepwalking; but whereas Shakespeare's heroine takes her own life, Laforgue's parodically exploits her punishment and hallucinates her guilt away.

The "procession de la Fête-Dieu" to which the narrative returns for part 3 recalls Flaubert's account of the same provincial parade at the end of *Un Coeur simple,* as the delirious heroine, Félicité, listens to it pass by. It includes Flaubert's "gamins" surveyed by their schoolmaster; the nun watching over her little girls, three of whom, "frisées comme des anges," scatter rose petals as they march; the censers announcing the dais which contains the priest and the "grand soleil d'or" of the Holy Sacrament; and the footsteps of the marchers, dulled and softened by the flowers strewn about, making the sound of "un troupeau sur le gazon."[22] Laforgue draws out his account considerably, however, and parodically emphasizes the ludicrous, bourgeois character of the procession. His "gamins" (89) are dressed "comme de petits bouts de bourgeois influents," and are likened more directly to a herd of beasts ("dans un piétinement de troupeau"). Flaubert's angelic little girls here become sugar candy cherubs ("angelots en sucre d'orge," 91); both are "frisées" and carry baskets of flower petals, but Laforgue's wear the emblematic white dress of his own poems.[23] To their ranks he adds a line of equally typical Laforguian communicants with lowered eyes and folded hands who murmur "des choses apprises par coeur," the meaninglessness of which he mocks with a parenthetical pun on the cliché, "Ah! quand le coeur y est . . ." (91). A parody of a band, with its dented brasses, "clarinettes de Jocrisse," and bruised bass drum, brutally dismembers ("équarissaient," 91) the wedding march from Mendelssohn's *Midsummer Night's Dream,* an appropriate prelude to the miracle (itself merely a dream) to follow. Four little girls "avec leurs corbeilles pleines de pétales de roses à semer" (93) precede the dais carrying the priest and the "soleil légendaire du Très-Saint-Sacrement," like Flaubert's "grand soleil d'or."

Laforgue, moreover, makes his procession and the miracle scene not only parody Flaubert, but also ironically reflect the bullfight, thus providing another parody-within-the-parody. They repeat exactly the major features of the earlier episode: the silence of the crowd in the sunshine of the outdoor theater, the procession, the central figure's gesture to Ruth, cries of superhuman suffering, a moment of general shock, and her fainting and delirium. Moreover, the narrator alludes to the parade as the "procession de Celui qui règne dans les cieux," echoing the line from part 2 that brought the *corrida* episode to a close ("Et qui les conçut jamais, sinon Celui qui règne dans les cieux?" 87). The procession of animals preceding the bull's entry is here matched, with high irony, by the parade of bourgeois marchers, especially the thundering herd of schoolboys. Even the bell rung at the offertory recalls the previous scene:

> Mais pour Ruth, l'infortunée et typique héroïne que j'ai assumée! Ce silence fascinant à crier, cette sonnette grêle et implacable comme au Jugement Dernier, n'est-ce pas l'appareil des désolations de désolation des injustes vallées d'outre-tombe où erre l'autre, le Suicidé, le Suicidé par trop d'amour, le Suicidé sans phrases, avec son trou au front? (93–95)

The bells, which for Ruth evoke the Last Judgment and the unhappy world beyond the grave where the Suicide wanders unsaved and unredeemed, echo the lonely, sad bellowing of the bull, "un meuglement si surhumainement infortuné" (85) which had earlier sent her into hallucinations. Now, the sound has exactly the same effect (she raves and faints) and elicits the same refrain ("Le sang, le sang, là, sur les gazons! . . . Tous les parfums de l'Arabie," 95). The text here hints at the source of her Lady Macbeth refrain by mentioning the "limbes *somnambulesques*" into which she has fallen; the Decadent catchword playfully refers to the sleepwalking scene from which the refrain derives. Even the bull's earlier gesture, his "col ostensiblement tendu" (85) in her direction, is mirrored here: first in a verbal echo (the repeated "ostensoir," 93), and then in the position of the priest, who "se tourne *ostensiblement* un instant vers la jeune riche malade" (95, emphasis mine), this time in a gesture not of implication (as with the bull), but of blessing. But if the earlier scene in fact prefigures the later one, the "blessing" here may also be an indictment, and Ruth's salvation parodically false.

Flaubert's Félicité likewise reacts violently to the announcement of the Sacrament, but her trembling and foaming at the mouth represent the first stages of her death agony, with its final vision of the giant parakeet. The traces of Flaubert's account here remind the reader of the falsity of Ruth's alleged miracle, fit, perhaps, for a hallucination like Félicité's, but not for reality. Indeed, Laforgue insists on the parodic spuriousness of the miracle by commenting, just after the little girl scatters her rose petals around the unconscious heroine: "Il y a dans la vie des minutes absolument déchirantes pour toutes les classes de la société. Celle-ci n'en fut pas, mais il en est; et l'exception ne saurait que confirmer la règle" (95–97). This comical and seemingly gratuitous remark specifically parodies the bullfight's "minute de saisissement général, une de ces minutes où se fondent des religions nouvelles" (85): the later "minute déchirante," the miracle, is not one at all, except in the heroine's mind. Thus we understand that the townspeople never suspected it, not because it was too subtle for their unrefined sensibilities, as suggested in the first line, but more ironically because it never happened.

Ruth awakens and exults at the blood supposedly changed into roses: "Vois, des roses à la place! Plus de sang, mais des roses d'un sang passé et désormais racheté!" (99). That this is only another hallucination, however, is stressed by Patrick's automatic and mindless agreement, "sans y penser, d'instinct tendre et tout à sa soeur" (99), as though her reaction were wholly predictable. Laforgue also reminds us that if the "miracle" exorcises her hallucinations and frees her from her obsession with the original suicide, it nevertheless changes nothing at all. The narrative tells us what she does not know, that in keeping with the pattern of the bullfight, the little girl's brother, like the governor, "se suicidait à son adresse, dans une chambre d'hôtel, sans autre témoin de l'état de son pauvre coeur que Celui qui règne dans les cieux" (101). The unfortunate story continues, for the miracle was not one, and nothing was redeemed.

Laforgue leaves us with a picture of Ruth cheerfully devoting herself "sans partage au seul et pur travail de sa tuberculose, dont elle reprit le journal" (101). Such an obvious literary reference reflects on the work at hand: if *Le Miracle des Roses* has told the story of her hallucinations, perhaps we can expect another one, the story of her consumption, recorded already in a first version in her pri-

Le Miracle des Roses

vate journal. As earlier, the parody here suggests the possibility of another work, a sequel to this one, perhaps just preceding the story of Patrick's "développement de héros" to which we have already been introduced. Laforgue thus realizes, in a slightly different way from that in *Hamlet,* the multiple creative possibilities in the open-ended quality of parody.

The final line similarly sheds light on one of the theoretical issues of the genre. Although the curse and the suicides continue, Laforgue nevertheless defends the validity of the miracle: "Mais le Miracle des Roses était accompli dans toute sa gloire de sang et de rose. Alléluia!" (101). The Miracle of the Roses was indeed accomplished, at least according to the parodic principle formulated just previously: "l'exception ne saurait que confirmer la règle" (97). If the exception confirms the rule, then the rule stands, and the spurious miracle confirms the miracle. Such a self-conscious statement applies to the parody itself, that exception which indeed confirms, affirms, and preserves the rule, or parodied work. Laforgue's cliché states a basic feature of this genre as described in chapter 1, the parody's capacity to preserve and recreate the original in transforming it, as the parodic *Miracle des Roses* does its Lisztean, and hitherto unrecognized, model.

5

Lohengrin, fils de Parsifal

Laforgue's *Lohengrin*, written during the height of *wagnérisme* in 1886, leaves no doubt as to the work on which it is based: Wagner's opera of the same name.[1] The title contains the first parodic deformation, a qualifying epithet, which both undermines and affirms the relation of the story to the parodied work. This identifies the original, while simultaneously distinguishing the parody from it, and also indicates the Wagnerian source by the spelling of "Parsifal".[2] Moreover, "fils de Parsifal" defines Lohengrin with respect to his famous father and thus reminds us directly that this parody, and parody in general, is a generation of "sons," or at least a second generation, deriving its identity from its relation to an established authority whose traits are preserved within it. Laforgue plays on this analogy, however, for *Lohengrin, fils de Parsifal* is actually the "son" not of Wagner's *Parsifal* but of his *Lohengrin*. Finally, as we shall see, "fils de Parsifal" has an important and ironic role in the parody, for it provides the hero with an escape: when the parodic Lohengrin fails to live up to his role and carry through his mission, he conveniently remembers his epithet and passes the burden on to his more effective and reliable father.

Wagner's *Lohengrin* was not produced in Paris until May of 1887, only three months before Laforgue's death. Despite the French cult of Wagner at this time, therefore, the work was less well-known than the parody might suggest.[3] As his letters and notebooks attest, however, Laforgue had seen numerous productions of Wagnerian opera, including *Lohengrin,* during his years in Germany, and allusions to the story appear in his poetry from 1885 onward.[4] More importantly, the controversy over staging a production of *Lohengrin* in Paris made the work a *cause célèbre* of the Decadent movement from 1885 to 1887.[5] "La question Lohengrin" inspired countless articles, including an entire issue of the *Revue wagnérienne* directed by Laforgue's friends Dujardin and Wyzewa.[6] The work was seen to embody a prominent concern, and cliché, of the period, the protest of the sensitive artist against a rationalist world, and was adopted as a symbol of the new tendencies in art.[7] The special relevance of this work to the Decadent imagination made it a particularly appropriate vehicle for Laforguian parody. The legendary hero, Knight of the Swan—devoted to virtue and righteousness, his true kingdom the sky, and his primary attribute one of the most prominent images of Decadent art—becomes, with only a slight nudge from the parodist, a Decadent idealist committed to purity, freedom, and, disastrously for Elsa, chastity. The catastrophic wedding night of the original provides the ideal setting for a parodic treatment of that favorite Decadent (and Laforguian) theme, the relation between the sexes.

In *Lohengrin,* Laforgue makes fun of the stock pessimistic attitudes of the late nineteenth century toward women and sex, as described in chapter 2. Elsa embodies the famous Eternal Feminine, the involuntary and unconscious accomplice of Nature in its programme of self-perpetuation; she is accordingly committed to the goal of procreation, and all her efforts aim to persuade Lohengrin to do what is, for her at least, *la plus naturelle des choses* on their wedding night. She is adorably flirtatious, vainly proud of her beauty, a coquette, more interested in fixing her hair and face than declaiming on the injustice of her misfortune. She is skillful at contriving to land in the arms of a reluctant Lohengrin, although in return she receives not the desired caress but only the "paroles bien senties" (151) of a sensitive and chaste poet. She is especially proud of her swanlike neck which, for obvious reasons, particularly appeals to Lohengrin. She is completely closed to otherworldly considerations, the "responsabilités transcendantes" (159) that morbidly obsess the hero: she is merely a "jeune fille" (137), a "pauvre personne du sexe" (129), an "esclave séculaire et sans malice" (163), bored with the "cultes platoniques" (149) of her fellow vestals and their idol, the moon, which she scornfully dismisses as "une marâtre, une glabre idole de vieux" (139). In a parody of Schopenhauerian language, the narrator imagines that she may even be a spy for the Ideal, who will be rewarded on the day of reckoning in a female afterlife according to the number and quality of dupes whom she tricked into working for the Ideal during her lifetime (163).

Although she professes to love music ("tu sais, j'adore la musique, moi!" 139), her only songs are little girls' rounds, neither example of which reassures Lohengrin about her motives: the first is on the theme of Samson and Delilah, the second on a young girl's painful desire for love. She does not understand Latin ("Je ne suis pas si pédante que cela!" 137), and justifies her ignorance by a cliché from an old school manual: "Il paraît que le latin dans les mots brave l'honnêteté, je l'ai lu dans un vieil almanach" (137).[8] Recycling and trivializing Boileau's famous line in this way calls attention to the methods (however more deliberate) of the larger parody and also serves a particular purpose in it: its prescription means that Elsa is immune to the "Crescite et multiplicamini" issued forth so suggestively and, for Lohengrin, terrifyingly, by the organ at the wedding.[9] Elsa does not need to know Latin: *crescite et multiplicamini* is part of her natural female understanding.

Lohengrin, on the other hand, represents in the extreme the Decadent hero's attitude toward women: he is eager to love as a way to the metaphysical Ideal, but is fully aware of its deception, which through women dupes men into submitting to the ongoing process of nature. He is obsessed with purity and venerates such stock Decadent images as the moon, the Milky Way, silence, whiteness, and night. This is a knight of the most literal shining ("radieuse," 129) armor, a pure crystal one; he rides a snow-white swan, an "avalanche fait cygne" (129), as a less parodic knight would a white horse ("chevauché," 129). He is terrified at the prospect of sexual union with Elsa, whom he prefers to regard as a virtuous "rosière" and a "divin spécimen humain" (135), the oxymoron comically embodying the contradiction: if Elsa fits his image of the divine, she will nevertheless turn out all too human a specimen. His only contribution to the singing is a morbid variation on the already depressing "Roi de Thulé." He cannot stop his teeth from chattering during the marriage ceremony (137), and spends the wedding night trying to avoid his marital duties. He tries to prepare himself by running through his mind the cliché of nineteenth-century moral relativism, "tout est permis"—Hamlet's excuse for gratuitous brutality here applied to a different sacrilege, sex. Even her swanlike neck cannot divert his attention from his Schopenhauerian preoccupations: her Adam's apple reminds him of the Fall of Man, "les plus mauvais jours de notre histoire" (169). Conscious of the deception by which the rest of humanity is manipulated, Lohengrin, true follower of Schopenhauer, resists love and pledges himself to the most rigorous chastity, a literal *mariage blanc* for this lover of things white. At heart, the man who, by his own admission, is "un peu hypocondre par nature" (133), who considers himself an artist and a man of genius, who, in a comical revision of a set formula, is the *lys* - rather than the *dieu - fait homme,* is in fact still a lily, or rather a virgin as, in the end, he undergoes his own literal Assumption into the heavens. Elsa can only look on in dismay as Lohengrin's earnest prayer comes true, and his pillow miraculously metamorphoses into a swan to carry him off into the sky, a parodic version of Flaubert's St. Julien.

Accordingly, the dialogue between the two lovers is throughout a comical exercise in misunderstanding and failed communication. Elsa searches for compliments, Lohengrin dodges the issue; he expresses a sexual fear, she answers with an inanely literal cliché. He hears the deathly sound of an owl hooting in the night, she the murmur of germination (153); to his association of the villa with the common grave ("Cette Villa-Nuptiale sent la fosse commune," 153)—sexual union is the demeaning fate of all mankind—she replies with a consoling "nous sommes tous mortels"; to his reservation that she is "un personnage avec qui il faut compter" (143), she returns an optimistic "Mais les bons comptes font les bons amis." She loves the moonlight for its effect on his appearance; he admires it for uplifting the soul (143). Where he trembles at the threshold of the nuptial villa, she claps her hands with glee to find themselves at last *chez eux* (145).

Laforgue gives the story a major parodic twist by making Lohengrin's role in the order of the Grail not to protect the lady's name and honor and defend the cause of virtue, but to achieve the emancipation of women. He is a self-professed feminist whose main task is to lead future crusades for the liberation of women, that is, free them from their Schopenhauerian enslavement to Nature and redeem the "petite soeur humaine et si terre à terre," the earthly, and all too earthy, sister (173). He accordingly descends from the sky in order to learn "la vérité sur la Jeune Fille" (165) in preparation for his future mission. But with high irony, Laforgue keeps Lohengrin's crusade well in the future: far from learning the truth about the *Jeune Fille,* he fails even to understand his chosen one and reveals himself a victim of the most standard Decadent attitudes. So little does he know Elsa that, after a disastrous evening of misunderstandings, he confuses her with his swan and his pillow. As his final prayer makes clear, Lohengrin wants an Elsa who is as soft as the pillow, as pure as the swan, as white as both, and most importantly, like the swan, "ne chantant jamais," especially those disturbing "rondes de petites filles" with their insinuating, and for him morbid, reminders of his marital duty.

Lohengrin's failure with Elsa does not augur well for his role in the women's crusade; the only sign of his liberal attitudes in the entire story is his declared intention to ask for Elsa's hand from her mother rather than her father (133), but Laforgue ironically thwarts even this token effort by making her an orphan. Indeed, Lohengrin ends by leaving the plan of female emancipaton to his father, Parsifal, the relation happily preserved in the "fils de Parsifal" addition to the title. The parodic hero fails in even a parodic mission: returning to the heights of the Schopenhauerian "Métaphysique de l'Amour" (173), to the land of meditative freedom and "glaciers miroirs," he imprisons himself in the very attitudes that it was his knightly purpose to dispel. His ideal land is the self-reflecting one of egoism, at once his *raison d'être* and the cause of his problem;[10] Laforgue thus portrays the character of an entire movement, whose egoism is a source of being, and likewise an utter human failure.

The Epigraph

As with the preceding tales, Laforgue introduces *Lohengrin* with an epigraph to guide our interpretation:

> A côté de son cher corps endormi, que d'heures des nuits j'ai veillé, cherchant pourquoi il voulait tant s'évader de la réalité.
>
> A. Rimbaud

Taken literally, the epigraph relates directly to the parody through its central themes, the lovers and the escape from reality; Elsa becomes the speaker, kept awake wondering why Lohengrin so wishes to flee reality. Even before the story begins to unfold, the epigraph thus identifies Lohengrin's real (though unexpressed) desire—evasion—and its tragi-comic consequence: the two lovers perpetually doomed to mutual misunderstanding. It presents the main theme of the story to follow, but in the past tense, as though spoken after the events of the story have taken place.

The source of the epigraph suggests its more complex relation to the story. Rimbaud was consistently associated with Decadence in the period;[11] relative to the story, the epigraph thus provides a Decadent commentary upon Decadence, as does the parody itself. Moreover, it functions as a kind of parody-within-the parody, for its source, Rimbaud's "Vierge folle" ("Délires I," *Une Saison en enfer*), itself transforms the Gospel episode of the Divine Bridegroom and the Foolish Virgins. Rimbaud's foolish virgin is enslaved rather to an infernal bridegroom reminiscent of Lohengrin himself: "Je n'aime pas les femmes. L'Amour est à réinventer, on le sait; . . . Je suis de race lointaine: mes pères étaient Scandinaves"; like Laforgue's hero, he wishes to change life by making women his "bonnes camarades"; unlike Lohengrin, however, he knows that he must one day depart for a faraway land. The virgin, submitted to his will while understanding neither him nor his ideal, prays that, if he must disappear miraculously, she may know of it: "Un jour peut-être il disparaîtra merveilleusement; mais il faut que je sache, s'il doit remonter à un ciel, que je voie un peu l'assomption de mon petit ami!"

The parallel between the poem and Laforgue's parody is striking: both end with a reference to the assumption of the hero. The epigraph thus provides a clue to the outcome of the parody, in which the hero is taken up into the sky as the foolish virgin of "Vierge folle" imagines her master will be. *Lohengrin* realizes the Assumption that is only projected in the source of the epigraph. But Lohengrin's assumption is a comically spectacular one, a trivialized version of the revolt embodied in Rimbaud's poem, whose hero departs in order to convert others: Lohengrin's "revolt" consists of a childlike, terrified escape from a reality, and specifically a sexuality, to which he cannot reconcile himself. His flight is an abdication (or at least an evasion) of his duty, not, as for the infernal bridegroom, a fulfillment of it. The epigraph thus provides at the start, and from within, a model which the parody then transforms. But if Laforgue thus mocks the revolutionary aspects of Decadence, its canon of purity, idealism, evasion, and Schopenhauerian misogyny, he nevertheless reminds us that it is these very aspects which the parody celebrates and recalls, as the speaker of the epigraph does here. Indeed, *Lohengrin* ends by alluding to a "certaine petite fête de l'Assomption" (173), celebrated regularly by poets on similar evenings. As I have argued in chapter 1, the parody mocks its target and itself but ensures a further version, thereby extending them into the future, just as the epigraph rewrites the Gospel story and in turn gives rise to the parody.

The Story

The plot follows the general lines of Wagner's: part 1 includes the assembly scene and the accusation of Elsa, her prayer to the knight in shining armor who will champion her, the sounding of the summons, the arrival of Lohengrin, and the marriage ceremony; part 2 dramatizes the wedding night and its final catastrophe. Laforgue alters the story considerably, however, in accordance with the new context and purposes of the parody. In both works, Elsa is accused of having a lover; but whereas in Wagner (as well as in the legend from which his version derives) this is merely the alleged motive for the offense with which she is charged—murdering her brother—it here becomes the offense itself: Elsa the vestal virgin has betrayed the cult of the moon by her sexual relations with Lohengrin and is brought to trial for her transgression.

The wedding night is troubled not by doubt planted in her mind by her two enemies (Laforgue omits the whole Wagnerian subplot involving Frederick and his sorceress wife, Ortrud, who out of jealousy conspire to bring Elsa to ruin), but rather by the ludicrous disagreements between the lovers. In Wagner, the swan is metamorphosed into Elsa's brother at the end; Laforgue instead metamorphoses Lohengrin's pillow into the swan, which then carries him back to the land of his father. The final flight of the swan, returning Lohengrin to the land of the Grail, comes from the pre-Wagnerian version of the story by Wolfram. In this way, Laforgue confronts Wagner's version with the one that inspired it and thus calls attention to the parody, itself based on an earlier work. Moreover, he uses this parodic signal as a vehicle of parodic meaning: the swan arises purely out of Lohengrin's pillow and the force of his will, and his departure represents not the tragic failure of faith and love, but the comical failure of Lohengrin to deal with the reality of sex. Wagner's hero consoles his beloved by restoring to her her lost brother; Laforgue's merely returns to his former existence, leaving Elsa to an unidentified fate, with only the suggestion of the epigraph to remind us of her lonely future.

The most blatant alteration to the plot concerns Lohengrin's identity, for Laforgue immediately violates the most central and traditional feature of the story in all its versions: the proscription on the hero's name. As in the legends of Cupid and Psyche, and Jupiter and Semele, Elsa is forbidden ever to ask her lover's name, and the fatal events of the ending ensue from her doubt and her consequent failure to keep her promise. Laforgue draws particular attention to the parody by making Lohengrin's first words to the assembly state his name and origins:

> ... J'arrive tout droit du Saint-Graal. Parsifal est mon père, je n'ai jamais connu ma mère. Je suis Lohengrin, le Chevalier-Errant, le lys des croisades futures pour l'émancipation de la Femme. Mais, en attendant, j'étais trop malheureux dans les bureaux de mon père. (Je suis un peu hypocondre par nature.) (133)

In breaking the primary convention of the story, the hero's first words also provide a clue to his unusual behavior to follow. "Je n'ai jamais connu ma mère": this clause, included so casually, likewise explains his parenthetical hypochondria, that Decadent synonym of *spleen* and *ennui,* and his attachment to the Ideal. Lohengrin's anguished sexuality is due to the fact that he never knew his mother. Indeed, in the final apotheosis, he will become a child again: "tel un enfant, un incurable enfant, je vous dis" (171). Laforgue treated this theme frequently, explicitly relating the loss of the speaker's mother to his desire for love and his poetic propensities[12] and thus reconciling the Romantic cliché of the orphan-poet-hero with the psychological interests of the late-nineteenth century. Lohengrin wants a mother, and thus he turns to Elsa, to his pillow, and finally to the swan, which alone can fill the role and carry him back to the unthreatening egoism of childhood.

The scene opens on a public square, set for a "soir de Grand Sacrifice" (107); Wagner's assembly of nobles is transformed into a society of vestal virgins and a "Concile Blanc" of high priests of the moon, and Elsa's trial for murder into a sacrifice to the goddess of the night sky. The bells prophetically toll Elsa's likely fate in a parodic *Nox Irae*. The setting reflects the stock Decadent ideals of sterility, darkness, cold, stillness, silence, and the chaste moon: the crowd of onlookers is, in a Laforguian invention, "*albement* ivre"; the vestals dress entirely in white; the platforms are "inviolablement drapées de linges" (107) and the balconies with shrouds (109); the sacred bird is the white gull (111); the rose window of the "Basilique du Silence" has a "tombale efflorescence" (109);[13] the moon casts a pale cold light on the chalky façades. Elsa complains of being a pariah among bourgeois (127), but the cliché applies only parodically to her situation, for they are actually Decadent to the core, and she a typical Laforguian *bourgeoise*.

The stock liturgical metaphor of Decadence dominates part one.[14] It is particularly appropriate to Laforgue's parody, for in addition to its Decadent associations it has medieval ones too: in the relation of the Grail theme to secular love (as in the *Lohengrin* story), and in the Christian tradition of love as a communion and of communion as the symbol of the love between man and God. Laforgue applies liturgical formulas to that pagan goddess of purity and chastity, the moon, and describes the marriage ceremony as a communion ritual and the wedding night in the terms of the Catholic Mass. Sexual union, from the hero's point of view, is not just a sacrifice but, more parodically, a sacrilege.

The priests and vestals do not keep the cult of the Virgin consistent with the medieval context of the original, but worship another chaste lady, Notre-Dame la Lune. Laforgue parodically replaces the virgin queen of heaven with the Romantic virgin queen of the night heavens.[15] He insists on this connection, and thus on the distortion, by applying religious, and specifically Marian, terms to the moon, or altering them to fit it. The "Salve regina, mater misericordia" literally salutes the moon's rising but is deformed to a more appropriate "Salve regina des Lys" (111): the "implacable" (107) moon is hardly a merciful mother and indeed represents the purity and chastity of the lily, as does Lohengrin himself, the "lys des croisades futures pour l'émancipation de la Femme" (133), and the "Lys fait homme" (145). The moon carries the epithet of the Virgin, "Immaculée Conception" (113), and a "hail Mary" parodies the "Je vous salue, Vierge Marie, pleine de grâce," to suit the nocturnal, sterile character of the lunar Virgin: "Je vous salue, Vierge des nuits, plaine de glace" (113). Such a clear parody-within-the-parody not only reminds the reader of the status of the story as a whole, but also signals the target, the "religion" of Decadence here represented by the ludicrous high priest who utters it, and later by Lohengrin himself. Her appearance in the sky is greeted by an abridged version of Palestrina's *Stabat,* a comically literal "there she stood." Laforgue never tells us what was expurgated from this version of the traditional prayer commemorating the sorrows of Mary at the Cross, but we may assume that it has to do with the part significantly omitted from the title, "mater dolorosa." Laforgue's moon may hardly be associated with motherhood, however chaste a maternal model she may follow; and far from suffering herself, she rather instills it in others, especially in reluctant vestals like Elsa.

Laforgue also applies to the moon epithets traditionally associated with Christ, and deforms them to suit the parodic context. The "hostie du salut" or *salutaris hostia* becomes a more ominous "hostie du Léthé," the pun playing literally on the appearance of the moon's host-like white disc in the night sky and, ironically, on the Decadent's notion of salvation, death. With an echo of the

Christian transfiguration, she is a "miroir transfigurant" (111), whose light quite literally transforms the scene, while serving the cherished decadent function of the narcissistic mirror, as do the "glaciers miroirs" to which Lohengrin returns at the end. Her eucharist-like face ("hostie," 111) on the "ciboire" of the ocean provides a visual image of the marriage sacrifice to take place shortly in the cathedral square.[16] But Laforgue derides this object of idolatry by comparing it to a more contemporary and highly incongruous one, the helium balloon, "quelque expérience aérostatique des temps nouveaux (oui, une lune naïve en son énormité comme un ballon lâché!)" (109).[17] The moon also represents the figurative death to which the Decadent aspires, the mystical tranquillity of the Unconscious. Lohengrin's flight into the sky may, as he prays, take him "par-delà les berges de la Voie Lactée et les giboulées d'étoiles, et le cap fallacieux du Soleil, vers le Saint Graal" (173), but one senses that he may end up at the moon, that symbol and harbor of death, egoism, purity, and unconscious bliss, "notre maîtresse à tous" (125).

The sacrifice begins with the rite of the Vestals. With a certain "coquetterie bien excusable" (113) that parodically borders on striptease, they expose their young breasts, "comme autant d'hosties, comme autant d'aspirantes lunes" to the caress of the moon's sacred ray, "venu de si loin à travers les infranchissables lagunes de la mer" (115). The narrative comically calls attention to this phrase by repeating it *verbatim* from the High Priest's prayer; what eventually crosses the supposedly "infranchissables lagunes" of the sea is Lohengrin himself. One begins to understand Elsa's fall; her experience as a vestal, caressed by the moonlight from across the water, has well prepared her for it. *The chariest maid is prodigal enough / If she unmask her beauty to the moon.*[18]

The accusation against Elsa is absurdly precious, full of comical euphemisms, periphrasis, and double entendres:

> Elsa, Vestale assermentée, gardienne des Mystères, des philtres, des formules, et du froment des brioches nuptiales, qu'as-tu fait de la clef de ton répertoire? Ah! ah! tes seins savent une autre caresse que celle si lointaine de la lune, ta chair est inoculée d'une autre science que le culte; des mains profanes ont dénoué ta ceinture et brisé le sceau de tes petites solitudes! (117)

It finally trails off into an unfinished "Dans la nuit du . . . etc, etc." The narrative neglects to elaborate not only because the accusation consists only of suspicions (117), but also because we already know about her vision of the shining knight from the original story. The incomplete accusation reminds us conspicuously of the parody's dependence on a familiar model, and accordingly develops the parodic distortion instead, Elsa's fall from innocence.

Stripped of her symbolic cult costume, her chastity buried with it in the "nécropoles sous-marines" (119), Elsa stands before the crowd, exposed not *à nu,* but in a peculiarly Decadent gown, itself an eloquent emblem of her crime:

> Ce qui fait qu'Elsa apparaît en fiancée, au bon peuple. — Oh! intéressante et promise, en longue blême robe étoilée de bas en haut d'oeils de plume de paon (noir, bleu, or, vert, comme on sait, mais il est beau de le rappeler), épaules nues, bras angéliquement laissés à leur nudité, la taille prise juste au-dessous de ses jeunes seins par une large ceinture bleue d'où pend une plume de paon à l'oeil plus magnifique encore, et sur ce joyau d'oeil central la pauvre tient pudiquement croisées ses petites mains aux longues mitaines bleues! (119–121)

Like Ruth and, as we shall see, Salomé, Elsa is associated with one of the most prominent of Decadent images, the peacock-feather eye. The narrative leaves no doubt as to its sexual connotations: she appears "en fiancée"; she keeps her hands folded "pudiquement" over the huge eye, the "joyau d'oeil central" hanging from her belt, recalling the "ceinture dénouée" (117) of her solitude evoked earlier; the narrator's parenthetical aside suggests a voyeuristic pleasure in recalling their variegated color. The punishment promised for her thus fits the crime: burning out her eyes (119) reflects the fate of the sexual peacock-feather ones and thus becomes a symbolic sterilization, an appropriate sacrifice to the violated cult of the chaste moon.

The horn having been sounded, and no response returned, Elsa interrupts the normal course of the story by decisively taking matters into her own hands and summoning Lohengrin herself. Her prayer contains many of the lover's clichés that Laforgue employed in his late poems, and to readers familiar with these the parody clearly parodies his own work. Even without this knowledge, however, Elsa's prayer proclaims itself a parody, first, by its exaggerated catalogue of lovers' clichés and, second, by its comical puns and double entendres. It includes the stock qualities of the Laforguian lady: her succulent eyes, her eighteen years, her moon-like elbows, her "bouche triste."[19] She uses the traditional formulas of the adoring lady: she is mad with love, has heart flutter, promises to follow him around crazily, will shine in his light, is at his mercy; she is a flower, a servant, a jewel, the Sulamite of the Song of Songs.[20] Many of these Laforgue deforms slightly so as to create a comically sexual innuendo:

> Ah! j'ai la chair encore toute évanouie de votre vision et (mettant la main sur son coeur) mon petit cratère m'en fait mal, et je m'en ai découvert des tas de trésors! Car votre fantaisie, si noble, sera toute ma pudeur, savez-vous. . . . Dites, venez m'assumer, vous ne vous en mordrez certainement pas les doigts. — *Angelus! Angelus!* Je suis la Sulamite! Je n'ai que la pruderie d'une fleur . . . .
> Tenez, je vais vous l'avouer, le goût de ma robe vous fera éclore mainte papille famélique! . . .
> Oh! Je vous comprends d'avance! Oh! Je vous en suivrai partout avec des yeux fous! Et je resterai si constamment suspendue à la lumière de votre front que j'en oublierai de vieillir; oui, j'irai si enchâssée dans votre sillon de lumière, que j'en deviendrai un petit diamant que l'âge ne saurait entamer! (125–29)

Laforgue increases the irony by making the ludicrous prayer work, as all look on in amazement—including the moon itself—:

> De l'horizon, au ras des flots résignés, dans l'enchantement de la Pleine-Lune écarquillée, s'avançait, merveilleusement et le col en proue, un grandissime cygne lumineux, chevauché d'un éphèbe, en armure radieuse, tendant les bras, sublime de confiances inconnues, vers le Rivage-Tribunal! . . . (129)

The curious metaphor of the swan's neck as a prow alludes playfully to the original, in which Lohengrin arrives riding not atop the swan but in a boat pulled by one. The parodic image simultaneously preserves and distorts the original by transferring the boat's prow to the swan. Laforgue comically extends the metaphor by making the swan depart like a boat, "à pleines voiles" (133). This does not merely signal the parody by recalling the original, but also provides Laforgue with an appropriate and significant pun: when Lohengrin sends the swan back to the land of the Grail, the narrator comments, "O sublime façon de brûler ses vaisseaux!" (133). The swan replaces the literal "vaisseau" that Lohengrin should have had with him and, parodically, did not. Moreover the pun is ironic, for Lohengrin's "sublime way" of burning his ships does not burn them at all: the swan comes back later and carries him away into the sky.

Laforgue makes the relatively minor episode of Lohengrin's adieu to the swan a crucial factor for understanding the hero's psychology, his relations with Elsa, and the real role of the swan in the story. It suggests for the first time the connection between Elsa and the swan in Lohengrin's imagination, which will motivate the fantastic parodic ending. He affectionately calls the swan his "petit coeur," a term more appropriate to Elsa, and associates Elsa's beauty with her "col de cygne" (133), that quality which reminds him of the swan. Indeed his greatest disappointment will be to discover that she is not a swan at all but rather "un personnage, un personnage avec qui il faut compter" (143). Although the swan disappears from the action until its dramatic reentry at the end, it remains in Lohengrin's image of the ideal woman. He simply trades the swan for Elsa, and if the disaster of their wedding night persuades him that he has made a bad deal, there is no objection to another exchange; he has only to revoke her and be united once again with the swan. Elsa certainly cannot take its place, particularly as a "cygne quadrige" (131), carrying him back to his sterile Ideal.

The marriage ceremony rehearses the sexual union meant to take place afterward. "La pure nappe est mise! Voici la brioche. Dites-vous: voici ma chair et voici mon sang" (135): the sacrifice of the Mass, with the wedding bells chiming the alarm ("tocsins," 135) prefigures the sacrifice of the lovers to follow.[21] The parodic nature of the ceremony is signalled by the sexual associations of the liturgical imagery, transforming the sacred ritual into a sacrilege ("cela se déroule à grand renfort de sacré," 137). Lohengrin and Elsa kneel at the altar, as they had earlier fallen to their knees to acknowledge their love (135),[22] and take communion "éperdument" (137); Lohengrin's despairing "larmes lustrales" replace the more traditional nuptial lustration; the wedding hymn urges them to spur their "hanches défaillantes" (139). The famous Wagnerian wedding march to which they file out becomes a suggestive "Allez enfants, la nappe est mise," thus confirming the sexual connotations of the earlier "set table," the nuptial altar. The rhyme "Oh! la nappe / Des agapes!" completes the metaphor with the Christian "agape," the love feast, evoking with significant irony the Last Supper. The sacrifice is accomplished: the two lovers go off to be martyred for the cause of Nature on the cross of love, or to what the narrative more discreetly calls their "duo." The metaphor of the duet reminds us of the parodied work, Wagner's opera, where a duet would be appropriate; here it is ironic, for the duet of the lovers will be inharmonious and the two parts totally out of step. The moonlit scene outside prophetically proclaims the failure of the marriage before it has even begun: "L'éblouissante hostie est au zénith! Et l'on aurait presque envie de détacher les gondoles pour aller là-bas, sur l'eau miroir, capturer avec un filet son immobile image si en hostie éblouissante!" (141). *"Presque* envie": escape to the moon will soon become Lohengrin's all-consuming desire, and ultimately a reality.

The second half of the story takes place in the Villa-Nuptiale, a bizarre honeymoon establishment reserved for newlyweds in their first week. Like the lonely tower of *Hamlet* (6f.), it stands forgotten on an inlet in an artificial garden, a labyrinth of flowered paths; the nuptial chamber is a gothic garret, its windows giving out onto the "solitudes" (159) of the sea. Its interior contains all the long corridors and spiral staircases of Decadent psychology and represents the aquarium-like, unconscious chambers of the human sexual imagination that Laforgue depicted elsewhere in similar terms, notably in *Salomé*. In it one encounters sonorous, echoing, labyrinthine corridors lined with Baudelairean twisted yew trees, the lonely, hollow echo of fountains dripping onto marble terraces, white peacocks strutting about in the moonlight, spiral staircases, empty rooms, mirrors with the names and dates of earlier nuptial victims engraved on them.[23] Lohengrin's fears are projected onto the decor, with its images of strangeness and death: the weathervane is not the traditional cock, but an ominous and parodic Baudelairean cat that meows.

The parodic marriage consummation takes place in two stages. A preliminary bathing in an ornamental pool rehearses the experience of the bridal bed itself: they enter "édéniquement nus" and lie down ("s'étendre") "comme dans des couvertures idéales" (147); Elsa is in the water up to her neck (149), as she will be in the fur covers of the bed. She fits in perfectly with the sexual aquatic atmosphere: her hair, let down and spread about her on the surface of the water, is compared to seaweed and makes her head appear an "inhumaine fleur lacustre" (149) on the stem ("tige," 149) of her neck. This bathing preview does not augur well for the real thing: while Elsa stretches her slim figure, Lohengrin, with his legs "trop croisées," maintains a discreet "pose sofalesque" (147), a Laforguian invention that ludicrously expresses the hero's *pudeur;* his assurance of love takes the form of a cordial handshake. Although Elsa has an almost asexual physique (with which no Decadent could quarrel)—firm hips, long legs, a flat chest—the reader is nevertheless reminded in a parenthesis of the more threatening qualities of the sensuous female: "Elsa s'étirant sous la lune, maigre, toute en lignes dures et gauches (Je hais ces inflexions molles qui coulent d'avance par la satiété à la pourriture), hanches fières, jambes à galoper par les haras pierreux; et le buste droit sans honte de ses deux seins si peu joufflus qu'elle pourrait les cacher sous des soucoupes" (147).[24] As often in Laforguian parody, the seeming objectivity of the third-person narrative is broken by the intervention of this "je," who reminds us remarkably of Lohengrin. Supposedly outside the story with the reader, the narrator in this way appears to participate in it enough to resemble the hero. The parody may in fact be one of those commemorative celebrations by Lohengrinian poets to which the final line alludes.

The scene in the nuptial chamber provides the occasion for a brilliant parody of Decadent attitudes toward women, as Lohengrin launches a vicious attack on the Eternal Feminine:

> — L'Eternel féminin! voilà, petite soeur, ce que c'est que t'avoir laissé faire humanité à part. Et si nous nous mettions, nous, à organiser l'Eternel masculin?
> — Oh, allez! c'est fait . . .
> — Et les hommes de génie! Pourquoi les faites-vous souffrir tout particulièrement, les hommes de génie? D'où, cet instinct qui confond le penseur à certaines heures? . . .
> — Je ne sais pas, puisque c'est un instinct.
> — Eh bien, c'est pour leur faire suer des chefs d'oeuvre, que vous les

faites particulièrement souffrir! Vous savez que c'est surtout les chefs d'oeuvre hallucinés de ces malheureux qui vous redorent à chaque génération votre blason pour mieux attirer la génération suivante à vos filles.
— Eh bien? puisque tout le monde y gagne! .... (161)

Ironically, just when he identifies the situation from which women should be emancipated, this future crusader proves himself singularly uninterested in doing so, and instead he proposes to arrange an "Eternel masculin" with which to combat the enemy.[25] The parody of course implies that he need only model it on himself. Indeed, in this dialogue Lohengrin reveals his thoroughly Decadent prejudices. In a Schopenhauerian move, he accuses women of inspiring artists in order to extend the species and keep the process going, making them sweat out masterpieces that will ensnare future generations of men for future generations of women.[26] The move is a play on the stock Decadent themes that art perpetuates and extends the illusion and deception of love, and that women inspire the artist, the work being a product of unfulfilled desire. Laforgue treats his hero with effective irony, for Lohengrin, presenting himself as the type of literary *homme de génie* that he here describes, has produced no such "chefs-d'oeuvre hallucinés" in Elsa's honor, but only a parody of panegyric, a diatribe. The cliché "redorer son blason," with its heraldic associations, is appropriate to his knightly station but in no way describes his behavior. The parodic hero cannot even produce the Decadent poet's habitual consolation for his anti-procreative attitudes, a work of art, a "chef-d'oeuvre halluciné," except perhaps the parody that is his life story; the narrative indeed suggests that the whole experience in the Villa may be "une nuit d'*hallucination*" (161, emphasis mine). Lohengrin is not quite a suffering man of genius; he is but a parody of one.

In another parody of Schopenhauerian attitudes, Laforgue makes his hero insult Elsa's slim hips for not proclaiming their procreative intentions honestly:

... je déteste en toi ceci, que, ayant des hanches sèches, bref anti-maternelles, tu marches cependant avec ce dandinement perpétuel de petit mammifère délesté depuis quelques jours à peine des kilos de ses couches (qu'est-ce qui vous fait rire?), oui, dis-je, ce dandinement, comme tout étonnée de se trouver si légère après neuf mois de corvée, et t'en allant plus légère que nature, comme profitant de ta légèreté d'entr'acte, avant que ça recommence, et faisant même de ce dandinement de délivrance un appât à de prochains obérateurs! Moi, j'appelle ça de l'aberration, de la légèreté. Tu saisis? (167–169)[27]

Her "anti-maternal" hips nevertheless move with a sway that expresses the buoyant freedom of one until only recently weighted down with child; they thus impertinently use this temporary freedom to lure future "encumberers." The humor derives not only from the parodic exaggeration and distortion, notably the absurdity of the argument, but also from the verbal play, the echo of *obérateurs* in *aberration* and the pun on *légèreté*. And in case we do not know how to take it, the parody provides us with the proper reaction in Lohengrin's parenthetical aside, conspicuous for its ambiguous "vous" in a paragraph otherwise exclusively in "tu": "qu'est-ce qui vous fait *rire?*"

The exchange of songs, meant as a diversion from their endless quarrelling, actually increases the tension and prepares the rupture of the ending. The songs are parodies in themselves and thus reflect the larger structure of the story. The famous epithalamium that opens Wagner's final act is here directly replaced by Elsa's more ominous ballad of Samson and Delilah, filled out by a proverbial formula unlikely to placate Laforgue's hero:

> Samson a cru en Dalila,
> Ah, dansons, dansons à la ronde!
> La plus belle fille du monde
> Ne peut donner que ce qu'elle a.

— Qui vous a appris cela? Si vous saviez quelque chose de moins epithalame. (163)

Her eyes raised not "au ciel" but, appropriately, only as far as the "ciel de lit," Elsa also sings a variation on the popular song, "Tu t'en vas et tu nous quittes,"[28] a strophe straight out of Laforgue's own "Complainte des pianos," embodying the ennui of the *jeune fille* without love:

> Tu t'en vas, et tu nous laisses,
> Tu nous laisses et tu t'en vas.
> Défaire et refaire ses tresses,
> Broder d'éternels canevas. (163)

Laforgue recycles his own verses in the parody, to which they are remarkably relevant—Lohengrin will indeed follow the prescription of the song and abandon Elsa at the end—and thus reflects the procedure of parody itself. In doing so, he also suggests the self-parodic nature of the genre: if the parodist's own verses can be reused in the parody, perhaps his other work, the parody, may be treated likewise.

In his turn, Lohengrin provides a morbid version of Gounod's (and Goethe's) "Roi de Thulé":[29]

> Lohengrin déclame d'un accent exemplaire:
>
>> Il était un roi de Thulé
>> Qui, jusques à la mort fidèle,
>> N'aima qu'un cygne aux blanches ailes
>> Voilier des lacs immaculés.
>> Quand la mort vint . . . (165)

The song is more "exemplaire" than merely in accent, however, for like Elsa's, it directly reflects the story; here we find the white swan, the swanboat ("voilier"), and the "lacs immaculés" which return in the "mers immaculées" of Lohengrin's final prayer (173). This parody-within-the-parody in fact plays a crucial role: it lets out the truth about the hero ("n'aima qu'un cygne aux blanches ailes"), prefigures the finale (Lohengrin's flight on his "voilier" swan into the "lacs immaculés" of the sky), and suggests the important relation, thus far unstated, between his final flight and spiritual death.

Indeed, in the last scene, Lohengrin, having failed miserably in his mission, reverts to a psychological childhood; the embrace that, in a more mature individual, should have been for Elsa's "col de cygne" is here given to the pillow. In answer to his prayer, the pillow metamorphoses into his beloved and unsullied symbol of purity—and escape—the taciturn swan, "pâle et ne chantant jamais" (171). Laforgue plays on the tradition that a swan sings before its death: Lohengrin's swan is not only immortal but provides significant contrast to Elsa, whose chatter and singing remind him of her terrifying femininity and his own conjugal duties.

> Oh! la fenêtre de la salle nuptiale éclata follement sous un cyclone de féerie lunaire! et voici que l'oreiller, changé en cygne, éploya ses ailes impérieuses et, chevauché du jeune Lohengrin, s'enleva et vers la liberté méditative cingla en spirales sidérales, cingla sur les lagunes désolées de

la mer, oh! par delà la mer! vers les altitudes de la Métaphysique de l'Amour, aux glaciers miroirs que nulle haleine de jeune fille ne saurait ternir de buée pour y tracer du doigt son nom avec la date! . . . (173)

The capital letters signal the parody and its object; returning to the "altitudes de la Métaphysique de l'Amour," Lohengrin reverts to the most pessimistic and Decadent attitude possible, precisely chapter 44 of Schopenhauer's main work, which carries this title, and in which love is never physical, only metaphysical. Lohengrin retreats into the "glaciers miroirs" of sterility and egoism, in contrast to the mirrors of the Villa-Nuptiale which record its victims and their dates (159). The hero triumphs, but only by disappearing forever into the deathly limitations of the self.

Laforgue makes the lesson embodied in the hero a lesson of nineteenth-century literature as well. Decadent attitudes to women, sexuality, and procreation may lead not only to moral sterility but also to silence, Lohengrin's silent, frozen atmosphere of *liberté méditative*. But the story suggests that a way out of such silence may lie in a form that mocks, subverts, and transforms these attitudes, that is, in a parody like this one, which saves Lohengrin from the oblivion of his remote lunar exile:

> Et c'est depuis lors, qu'à de pareilles nuits des poètes célèbrent froidement et inviolablement dans leur front certaine petite fête de l'Assomption. (173)

This line returns us to the opening line: "Oh, qu'ils sont irréparables, *même en imagination seulement*, les soirs des Grands Sacrifices!" (107, emphasis mine). The events of the story represent one of those "irréparables" evenings, which the parodist revives "dans [son] front" (173) or "en imagination seulement" (107). He is one of the poets suggested in the final line, who on similar evenings has had his own celebration, commemorating, in the particular way that parody does, the ongoing Lohengrinian problem, the perpetual fear of giving oneself to love. Moreover, the plural forms and "pareilles" imply that the process does not end here. In a manner consistent with the self-reflexivity of parody, Laforgue's extends its story further; the parodic assumption of this Virgin gives rise to future celebrations, and presumably future parodies, thus ensuring both the progress and continuity of the traditions it embodies.

6

Salomé

In a letter, Laforgue himself acknowledged Flaubert's *Hérodias* as the model for *Salomé*.[1] The title immediately signals the distortion, for the parody's heroine is not Herodias but her daughter, a minor figure of Flaubert's work here drawn into the foreground. Although, as with *Lohengrin*, this reminds us of the status of the parody as a "second generation," the filial relation is not quite the same. The title of *Lohengrin* identifies him as "fils du Parsifal," and the plot follows Wagner's *Lohengrin*; *Salomé*, on the other hand, follows the plot of the "mother" story, *Hérodias*, but recasts the daughter in the role of heroine. (Salomé herself hardly figures at all in Flaubert's novella, in which she appears only for the short scene of the dance and utters only the few fatal words dictated by her mother.) This fundamental tension, between the recognizable plot of *Hérodias* and the substitute heroine, Salomé, creates a constant disjunction that keeps the parody ever present in the reader's mind. It plays with an irony of the Salomé tradition itself, the frequent conflation of mother and daughter, as in Mallarmé's *Hérodiade* and the many paintings so entitled which picture her in the posture belonging to Salomé—receiving the Baptist's head on a platter.[2] Whereas usually Herodias takes on the attributes of Salomé, in Laforgue we have the reverse, an unadulterated Salomé in a story that belongs largely to Flaubert's Herodias.

The Salomé figure is especially appropriate to Laforgue's target: "déesse de la Décadence,"[3] "métaphore de la Décadence,"[4] Salomé was one of the most prominent images of Decadent art. She appears in works by Flaubert, Mallarmé, Huysmans, Laforgue, Gustave Moreau, and Odilon Redon, to name only the major ones;[5] she is a symbol of the *femme fatale,* the blood-thirsty, castrating woman, killer of prophets, temptation and lubricity personified.[6] Laforgue parodies the themes, attitudes, obsessions, and stylistic features of Decadence by means of one of its emblematic stories. He plays on Salomé's ubiquity and parodies the entire genre, integrating into his narrative elements from a variety of Salomé sources besides Flaubert, notably Moreau's paintings on the theme ("Salomé dansant devant Hérode" and "L'Apparition") and Huysmans' elaborate description of them in *A Rebours.*[7] In addition, Laforgue transforms the Salomé figure according to the heroine of another of Flaubert's Oriental novels: daughter of the tetrarch, guardian of the Iles Blanches Esotériques, and their values, high priestess of the night sky, incarnation of the moon and its cult of purity, atrophy, sterility, and artifice, a bard whose ravings are supposed to enchant, an allegedly committed virgin whose "initiation" brings death to her lover and to herself, Salomé is a parodic Salammbô.[8]

Integrating *Salammbô* into the complex of Salomé models plays on the close relation between them during the period. *Salammbô* was considered not only a sister novel to *Hérodias* but also a precursor of Decadence. Huysmans placed it in des Esseintes' library and coupled it in his hero's affections with *La Tentation de Saint-Antoine,* that other model for Decadence.[9] He directly compares Salomé to Salammbô in chapter 5: contemplating Moreau's "Salomé (dansant devant Hérode)," des Esseintes likens her to Salammbô by her headdress: "en la mitrant d'un certain diadème en forme de tour phénicienne tel qu'en porte la Salammbô."[10] However, the presence of *Salammbô* in Laforgue's story does not merely support the Salomé motif but actually qualifies the character of the heroine herself. The destructive *femme fatale* of the nineteenth-century Salomé tradition is also, like Salammbô, a bard and priestess tormented by desire, dissatisfied with her science, and whose sexual sacrilege will bring about her downfall.

Although (and perhaps even because) its parodic relation to *Hérodias* was understood from the beginning, *Salomé,* of all the *Moralités,* has suffered the most from unfavorable critical opinion.

It is taken to be less subtle, less sophisticated, less interesting, and by all accounts less delightful than the other stories. F. Ruchon judges its humor "facile et un peu lassant à la fin";[11] W. Ramsey denounces it as a witty but disappointing imitation of *Hérodias* "verging dangerously on that of the class yearbook."[12] But to see *Salomé* as merely a burlesque version of *Hérodias* is incorrect and misses the point of the parody. As M. Praz observes, Flaubert's story cannot explain Laforgue's, too many aspects of which remain unmotivated and unintelligible, most especially the character of his remarkable heroine.[13] *Salomé* does betray its status as Laforgue's first effort, and he himself expressed misgivings about its heaviness:[14] it contains many of the rather tiresome aspects of his early "cosmic" poems, such as the vocabulary of philosophical pessimism, Buddhism, and mysticism, underwater and lunar imagery, and an extreme sense of the artificial and contrived. However, this did not prevent him from adding to the revised version a long and ponderous passage, the Aquarium section of part two, containing precisely these features. He clearly wished not only to include them, but to emphasize them. Indeed, such language, imagery, and thematic material are commonplaces of Decadent art, including Laforgue's own; the peculiarities of *Salomé* thus are frequently sources and signals of the parody.

Laforgue modifies Salomé from a destructive woman to a mystical bard, and insists on the difference, by a crucial alteration to the legend. The central episode of the traditional story, the essential aspect of the whole genre, never takes place: Salomé does not dance, but rather talks. More precisely, consistent with her Salammbô model, she chants, though Salomé's is not a hymn to the goddess Tanit but an incomprehensible and unbearably tedious improvisation on nothingness. This change in the character of her art reflects the fundamental change in the Salomé figure itself: a pseudo-philosopher devoted to the mystical Unconscious, this Decadent heroine is also a Decadent poet, and Laforgue's story a conspicuous self-parody. Ultimately, it reverses the implications of the legend: she is a *femme fatale*, but her plans backfire and she destroys herself. *Salomé* embodies especially well the characteristic ambivalence of parody described in chapter 1: a work that is itself one of the supreme examples of Decadence sends the whole Decadent edifice hurtling to the ground, like the heroine herself who tumbles over the cliff at the end. Laforgue's story smashes Decadence upon the rocks of the real world and counsels, instead, a less extreme version of the pure poet.

The Epigraph

Salomé begins with a peculiar Vietnamese proverb:

> Naître, c'est sortir; mourir, c'est rentrer.
> —Proverbes du royaume d'Annam recueillis par le père Jourdain, des Missions Etrangères.[15]

A proverb figuratively expresses a familiar truth common to a given culture and proven by usage. It carries the authority of tradition and has connotations of universality. Used as an epigraph, it applies a general formula to a specific work and thus establishes by implication the universality of the work itself. Since a proverb crosses historical boundaries, the realm of influence of a proverb-epigraph, unlike that of an epigraph taken from a single literary source, includes not only the story to which it directly applies but also the world of the reader. This last feature makes it particularly appropriate to parody, which constantly seeks to relate itself to the reader by alerting him to its methods, signalling the medium, calling attention to the parodist's status as a reader, and so on. The universal pretentions of the proverb-epigraph suggest that the parody likewise may have general significance for the reader, whatever the distance implied by its setting, its comicality and exaggeration, or its status as a formal work of art. Laforgue's choice from an alien culture is especially appropriate to *Salomé,* for it underscores the contemporaneity and relevance of this most exotic and Oriental of stories.

The text of the epigraph describes the process of life, the "sortir" of birth and the "rentrer" of death, thereby identifying at the outset the "moralité" of the parody. Salomé goes out of herself, is born through her relations with the Baptist, but makes the fatal mistake of trying to go back, and dies for it. Destroying the evidence of her transgression by having the Baptist beheaded does not suffice to keep an inexorable truth from realizing itself. Salomé did not have the common wisdom of the epigraph, but the reader is armed with it beforehand and may use it to interpret her story. The epigraph also reflects the theme of cyclical revolution that runs throughout the tale: not only the cycle of life, but also the revolution being celebrated when the story opens and completed by Salomé's fall at the end.

The Story

The story generally follows the four parts of *Hérodias*: the opening scene at the palace that introduces the tetrarch; the visit to the subterranean rooms of the building and the cell where the Baptist is imprisoned; the anniversary banquet, the dance of Salomé, and the decapitation of Iaokanann; and finally, the removal of the head. Like *Hérodias* and *Salammbô*, *Salomé* opens with a description of the court on an anniversary holiday:

> Il faisait ce jour-là deux mille canicules qu'une simple révolution rythmique des Mandarins du Palais avait porté le premier Tétrarque, infime proconsul romain, sur ce trône, dès lors héréditaire par sélection surveillée, des Iles Blanches Esotériques, dès lors perdues pour l'histoire, gardé toutefois cet unique titre de Tétrarque, qui sonnait aussi inviolablement que Monarque, outre les sept symbolismes d'état attachés à la désinence *tetra* contre celle de *monos*. (179)

Unlike the tetrarch's birthday festivities in *Hérodias*, or the victory feast in *Salammbô*, *Salomé's* celebration commemorates a literal palace revolution, in which the lowly Roman governor ascended the throne as the first tetrarch. The theme of revolution introduced in the epigraph is thus restated prominently in the very first sentence. But Laforgue includes an initial parodic irony: "rythmique" suggests that the revolution will recur regularly, perhaps even at two-thousand year intervals, and hence does not augur well for the present regime; the "jours caniculaires" are indeed traditionally unlucky. Accordingly, the civilization born of a revolution will die at the hands of another one, Salomé's fatal tumble and the Baptist's implied ascension at the end.

That Salomé is supposed to inherit the throne, however, is clear from "héréditaire par sélection surveillée": Laforgue's play on the nineteenth-century concept of heredity and Darwinian natural selection blatantly relates the civilization of the Isles to the late nineteenth century, thus signalling the modernizing principle of the parody. The July setting ("canicules") and the theme of revolution suggest what will shortly be made explicit, the anachronistic likeness of the celebration to the anniversary (since 1880) of another famous revolution, as in *Hamlet*, the French national holiday. Laforgue later attaches the epithet "de juillet" to the sun (181) and the exotic fish in the pond (191), calls the holiday specifically a "fête nationale" (187, 239), and gives it the stock attributes ("pétards et orphéons, pavoisement et limonades," 187) of its late-nineteenth-century French counterpart, the fourteenth of July.

The final clause, justifying the title of tetrarch by its etymology, would seem ludicrously irrelevant except for the remarkable fact that it is not quite right: "tetrarch" is not an appropriate name for the new monarch and, with Salomé's disastrous end, the story will prove that the term—and the office—are less "inviolable" than they seem. Furthermore, whatever the significance of the number seven to this dynasty of mystical Decadent tetrarchs, the fact remains that "tetra" means four and thus clashes with the "sept symbolismes d'état" with which it (as against "monos") is supposedly associated.[16] Such an inaccurate analysis, placed so conspicuously in the first sentence, provokes the humor of gratuitousness and warns the reader not to take the narrative at face value. The comical misuse of "tetra" reflects and calls attention to the methods of the parody itself which deliberately misinterprets another work and uses it for its own purposes. The parodist himself practices this kind of faulty, and suspect, philology. In exposing its own processes, the story declares itself a parody, and ensures that the reader will take it as one.

The Iles Blanches Esotériques are, as their ludicrous name implies, a Decadent's paradise, a closed, isolated, sterile, hermetic world that Salomé, in her role of "cariatide des îles" (227) must literally uphold. They are separated from the rest of the world ("archipel de cloîtres de nature," 197) and, as we are told here, have been lost to history for the past two thousand years, a detail signalling the return to history that is the parody, which revives the original story. They are governed by the tetrarch and the Mandarinat of the palace: *le Grand Maître des Bibliothèques, l'Arbitre des Elégances, le Conservateur des Symboles, le Répétiteur des Gynécées et des Sélections, le Pope des Neiges, l'Administrateur de la Mort,* and *l'Ordonnateur-des-mille-riens.* These titles are all suggestive of Decadent themes and play on the Oriental forms of *Salammbô* ("l'Annonciateur-des-lunes," "l'Ordonnateur-des-oeuvres") and on set expressions, such as *elegantiae arbiter* and "ordonnateur des pompes funèbres."

The inhabitants of the Isles exaggerate the stock characteristics of the Decadent. "Pâles, épilés, les doigts chargés de bagues, sacerdotalement empêtrés dans leurs coruscants brocards lamés" (195), they worship in the lunar, Lohengrinian "Basilique Blanche" and sing their hymn of praise to the Decadent god, Ennui: Laforgue converts the "Te Deum laudamus" to a "Taedium laudamus" (193), the familiar joke applied literally to the Decadent *taedium vitae.* The most energy that they ever mustered up was almost to carry out a stoning on an overly zealous Iaokanann. They are beardless, eat no meat, hold annual ceremonies in honor of the cult of the snow, and profess a philosophy of atrophy, elitism, and reclusion: "Les mandarins pensaient qu'il fallait atrophier, neutraliser les sources de concurrence sociale, s'enfermer par cénacles d'initiés vivotant en paix entre eux dans les murailles de la Chine, etc., etc." (221). The "etc., etc." directly signals the parody and keeps us from accepting the narrative as a transcription of reality by reminding us that it consists of clichés, so familiar a programme that we may complete it on our own. And in drawing attention to the parodist's role in the narrative, it leads us to question the reliability of the account. He leaves things out, and thus leaves his story open to suspicion.

As at the start of *Hérodias,* the tetrarch appears on the terrace, leans against the railing, and reviews in his mind the events that have preceded the narrative. Laforgue modifies the setting in all its details to fit his target. The monolithic palace, a "titanique masse funèbre veinée de blême," reflecting "mystiquement" the rays of the July sun (181), embodies the morbidity, mysticism, and anemia of its Decadent inhabitants. It is an elaborate affair, with inner courtyards, galleries, cellars, a hanging garden, and an observatory whose tower projects two hundred meters into the sky. The famous balustrade of Flaubert's story is here made of decorative faience, suitable to the aestheticism of the Isles, as are the city walls covered with yellow enamel flowers (183). The story opens not at dawn but at a silent, "stagnant" high noon (181), consistent with the lethargic, atrophic atmosphere of the place and the Decadent ideals it embodies.

The tetrarch's name, Emeraude Archetypas, parodies the conventional Hérode-Antipas: the simple addition of an "m" sound changes "Hérode" into a favorite Decadent image, the jewel, notably one known for its purity, and a new prefix for "Antipas" produces "Archetypas," the model and type of his kind, the crown jewel of Decadence, as it were. He is a disillusioned aesthete, a fatalist, a dilettante, an aging dandy wearing elegant gloves, Ennui personnified: like Baudelaire's monster, he slowly and sulkily smokes his midday houka and gazes at the sea, that Laforguian symbol of the Unconscious and mystical bliss.[17] The sacred fish pond of *Salammbô*,[18] so important to the novel's theme of violation, here becomes merely a Hamletic mirror for the tetrarch meditating on his wasted life. Nothing ever came of the omen that marked his birth, a lightning bolt that flashed *alpha* and *omega* across the sky; the second coming has been long in coming, and meanwhile he has spent many a high noon, like this one, thinking about this "tirelire mystique" (189) in which he had placed such hope. His scepticism and relativism console him to some extent, in a self-parodic Laforguian formula ("et puis, *alpha, omega,* c'est bien élastique," 189), but solve nothing.[19] Despite daily pilgrimages to the family necropolis, he cannot seem to resign himself enthusiastically to nothingness, as he had done so devotedly in the ascetic days of his youth.

The tetrarch's reflections are inspired by a near-catastrophe of the preceding day: the arrival of the Princes du Nord, countrymen of the radical socialist Iaokanann who is imprisoned in the basement of the palace. This version of the Baptist's name immediately evokes Flaubert's *Hérodias,* but Laforgue transforms him into a nineteenth-century socialist revolutionary, an *engagé* intellectual with gold-rimmed spectacles and an unkempt beard, his nose always buried in a pile of papers and pamphlets. He has been thrown into prison not for having disapproved of the tetrarch's adulterous and incestuous marriage to Herodias, but for having tried too enthusiastically to inspire a revolutionary consciousness in the lethargic inhabitants of the Isles. Significantly, Laforgue's Baptist, prophesying the coming of the people's revolution rather than the Messiah, had failed, according to the old adage, even in his own country ("déjà si peu prophète en son pays," 187). In this he resembles that former ascetic and *résigné*, the tetrarch, with his faith in allusions to the Book of Revelation. The likeness between them is supported by the importance of revolution to both: we are, after all, celebrating the anniversary of the revolution that brought the "infime proconsul romain" to power. Their history does not bode well for the third prophet in the story, Salomé.

In a manner typical of Laforguian parody, Salomé formally enters the story in one of the tetrarch's offhand, apparently trivial reflections—that in the light of the arrival of Iaokanann's countrymen, the Princes du Nord, he had done well not to have him beheaded: "Heureux encore! et cela grâce aux inexplicables intercessions de sa fille Salomé, de n'avoir pas dérangé le bourreau de sa traditionnelle sinécure honoraire, en l'envoyant vers Iaokanann avec le Kriss sacré!" (187). In a remarkable violation of the legend, Salomé has parodically interceded with her father to spare the Baptist's life. The reason for her "inexplicables intercessions" goes unstated, and remains so until the end, but already this detail focuses attention on her relations with Iaokannan. It also explains her resistance to marriage (189) and hints at her motive for the beheading, likewise suppressed: her secret sexual relations with him. The "Précurseur" of tradition becomes here "l'Initiateur" (241), and Salomé will make him pay with his head.[20]

The Princes du Nord are ridiculous bourgeois figures in military garb, "sanglés, pommadés, gantés" (191),[21] who profess an imperial state philosophy ("l'autorité armée, religion suprême, sentinelle des repos, du pain et de la concurrence internationale," 219ff.) and mouth maxims about progress: "Et tout honnête homme, d'ailleurs, professe / Le perfectionnement de l'Espèce" (221).[22] Ugly, tasteless, and inarticulate, they recite meaningless "salamalecs galants" (195) and wear a parodic symbol of honor, the "Toison de Fer" necklace whose "nullité artistique" (213) stands out glaringly among the exquisite aesthetic treasures of the Isles. They believe in a military ideal, detest declassed ideologues like Iaokanann, and express their self-satisfaction in banal clichés: "se félicitant eux-mêmes du bon vent qui . . . à pareil glorieux jour . . . en ces îles" (191). By letting their words trail off and not filling in the holes, Laforgue conveys the emptiness of their thoughts and the utter conventionality of their speech, and alerts us, as before, to the parodist's role in the narrative. But in making us complete the Princes' utterances ourselves, the text also establishes a relation between us. Like us, the Princes see the curious world of the Isles for the first time and are asked to interpret it ("Ce fut donc l'aquarium—mais est-ce que ces princes étrangers comprirent?" 207), along with the crucial recitation of Salomé in part three. They provide another model of the reader besides the parodist, and specifically a negative one: everything goes by them completely.

The tour of the palace in part two passes through Salomé's exotic apartments and produces a few first tantalizing glimpses of her. The Princes du Nord and their hosts arrive at the observatory "ah! juste à temps pour voir disparaître une jeune fille mélodieusement emmousselinée d'arachnéenne jonquille à pois noirs, qui se laissa glisser, par un jeu de poulies, dans le vide, vers d'autres étages!" (195). Nearly identical words mark their visit to the next stage, the hanging garden, where they notice her disappearing around a bend in the path, this time escortée by greyhounds and mastiffs, like her mother goddess, the chaste lunar Diana (197). The phrase returns as they arrive at Iaokanann's cell, in time to see her slip out the door (211). This disappearing figure motif is inspired by a structurally similar feature of Flaubert's narrative: Salomé repeatedly eludes Herod, who glimpses her several times before he finds out, at the moment of the dance, who she is. Long before her seductive dance, she has aroused his desire and thus guaranteed the fulfillment of her request.

In Laforgue's version, however, which abandons the theme of Herod's desire altogether, the recurring motif parodically calls attention to Salomé's bizarre dress ("emmousselinée d'arachnéenne jonquille à pois noirs"), which, unlike other aspects of her attire, does not belong to her traditional iconography.[23] The color yellow is everywhere associated with Salomé in the story: she is metonymically a "petite vocératrice jaune à pois funèbres"; the decor of her apartments ("oh! si jaunes!" 193), the color of the moon with which she is associated (205), and the stage itself in part three (215) all reflect her penchant for yellow.[24] But the insistence on "jonquille" in the thrice-stated description of her dress suggests another sense contained in the word, communicated by its synonym, the metaphorically more obvious "narcisse."[25] This detail is important: the repressed term not only suits Salomé's narcissistic character but also hints at the precise motive for the beheading. Her relations with Iaokanann take her out of herself, a privilege formerly reserved for the stars ("Salomé ne sortait guère d'elle-même qu'aux étoiles," 239). And only at the end do we learn that in fact it was the stars that gave her the idea for her sexual adventure, those sexually suggestive nebulas with their "évolutions giratoires" (241). Salomé aspires beyond her Decadent association with the chaste moon to the stars, but the aspiration entails a sacrilege. She violates the narcissistic code of the Isles and thus must dispose of the evidence. This loner, this "fuyeuse de fêtes nationales" (239), actually makes a most fatal contact. The symbolism of her dress suggests her motive in asking for the Baptist's head, itself the symbol of her only transgression, her one *sortie* out of herself.

Beginning at the top with the observatory, the tour works downward through the garden, menagerie, and aquarium, to the cellars. Each part comically provides relevant information about the parodic heroine. The observatory, with its fresco-painted mobile dome and gigantic equatorial telescope, reflects her otherworldly astronomical interests. In the "Salle des Parfums," she dabbles in the occult world of chemical compounds, a mad scientist somewhat like the Edison of Villier's *Eve future* or, as we shall see specifically later, Poe's doctor in "The Truth about Mr. Valdemar." She concocts special potions, the purity of which is marked by a persistent "sans" in a long list full of ludicrous verbal play: "des épilatoires sans sulfure d'arsenic, des laits sans sublimé corrosif, . . . des teintures vraiment végétales sans nitrate d'argent, hyposulfite de soude, sulfate de cuivre, sulfure de sodium, cyanure de potassium, acetate de plomb (est-ce possible!)" (197). The hanging gardens, reached by an endless, humid corridor and a door turned green with fungus and moss, prefigure the Unconscious world of the Aquarium. They have the same stillness, silence (197), and claustral (199) character; the "garulements distingués" of two Oriental bulbuls prepare the "garulement mystique" (233) of Salomé herself later on. The menagerie is equally bizarre, with sleeping fauves, swaying elephants, elongated giraffes, snakes incessantly shedding their skins, and groups of monkeys in curious *tableaux vivants*.

But it is the Aquarium that most completely embodies the Decadent Unconscious:[26] labyrinthine, silent, claustral, humid, and womb-like, it represents the "béatitude aveugle et silencieuse" (205) to which the Decadents of the Isles aspire, the Buddhist nirvana, perfect tranquillity, stillness, and satisfaction, unlike the tormented, restless existence of men, perpetually unfulfilled. The Aquarium contains caves, corridors, plains of fine sand disturbed only by the flapping tail of a fish; colonies of sea horses in a single tree on a desolate plain; hairy nuclei, a cemetary of mollusks, beds of truffles in orange velvet, and plantations of asparagus "confites et tuméfiées dans l'alcool du Silence" (203); fields of sponges, bulbous onions, corals, worms, and so on, "toute une flore foetale et claustrale et vibratile agitant l'éternel rêve d'arriver à se chuchoter un jour de mutuelles félicitations sur cet état de choses" (205).[27] And at the center of the underwater labyrinth, on a plateau, sits an octopus, a parodic "minotaure gras et glabre de toute une région" (205). But Laforgue treats the Aquarium with considerable irony, interrupting the narrative and attributing to the submarine flora and fauna some highly comical qualities. The coupling crabs, with their "after-dinner good humor," obviously enjoy themselves: "s'empêtrent en couples avec de petits yeux rigoleurs de pince-sans-rire" (201). A passing fish provides the only reading matter for eyes half-buried in the sand: "et dont c'est même tout le journal" (203). King crabs capsize and skirmish to give themselves a rub-down: "mais sans doute d'elles-mêmes ainsi pour s'étriller" (203). Bits of tripe float about and settle down elsewhere: "et, ma foi, s'y refaisant une existence" (203).

The Pope des Neiges interprets the "antique leçon" of the Aquarium for the Princes and the reader—beatitude, silence, stillness, blindness, total satisfaction, narcissism:

> Ni jour, ni nuit, Messieurs, ni hiver, ni printemps, ni été, ni automne, et autres girouettes. Aimer, rêver, sans changer de place, au frais des imperturbables cécités. O monde de satisfaits, vous êtes dans la béatitude aveugle et silencieuse, et nous, nous desséchons de fringales supra-terrestres. Et pourquoi les antennes de nos sens, à nous, ne sont-elles pas bornées par l'Aveugle et l'Opaque et le Silence, et flairent-elles au delà de ce qui est de chez nous? Et que ne savons-nous aussi nous incruster dans notre petit coin pour y cuver l'ivre-mort de notre petit Moi? (205)[28]

The still creatures of the Aquarium in their mystical state of torpor are models of ideal existence.[29] The underwater world expresses a pantheistic beatitude, as for Flaubert's Saint Antoine, but here that of the Unconscious self. It is precisely this narcissistic ideal that Salomé betrays in aspiring "au-delà de ce qui est chez [elle]," to the stars and to sexuality.

The most eventful moment of the visit occurs, as in *Hérodias*, in the basement of the palace at Iaokanann's cell, where the failed prophet has an appropriately parodic vision:

> Et soudain, on le vit se hausser sur ses pieds nus, les mains tendues à une apparition à qui il hoqueta les plus doux diminutifs de sa langue maternelle. On se retourna.—ah! juste pour voir disparaître dans un tintement de clés, sous le blafard de cet *in-pace,* une jeune forme décidément emmousselinée d'arachnéenne jonquille à pois noirs. (211)

"Apparition" makes the object clear: Laforgue parodies Moreau's painting by setting the scene before the beheading and reversing the roles. The familiar "juste pour voir. . ." identifies the apparition as Salomé, and Iaokanann adopts the celebrated pose (on tiptoe, barefoot, hands extended toward the apparition) that Salomé has in the painting. Whereas there Salomé is startled by her vision of the Baptist's head, which haunts and punishes her for her part in the execution, here Iaokanann is haunted by the vision—or glimpse—of Salomé. This parody of a Salomé work reflects the larger story, itself a parody, and conspicuously broadens the target from Flaubert to the whole late nineteenth-century Salomé genre and the Decadence embodied in it.

Moreover, Laforgue uses this parody-within-the-parody to reinforce the thematic inversions of his story. First, as her chant in the next section makes clear, Salomé herself is a prophet, having inherited the role from her father, although her message of atrophy and Unconscious *laisser-aller* is the direct antithesis of Iaokanann's socialist ideas of class revolution. Second, she takes revenge on her lover (as according to the painting the Baptist took revenge on her), but for a rather different kind of execution. Iaokanann's childlike outburst of tender words in his "langue maternelle" (we know that he can speak the language of the Isles, 185) suggests that Salomé the *femme fatale* has conquered him, but for yet another parodic reason: to satisfy her sexual curiosity.

The banquet scene of part three consists of a series of parodies leading to that of the dance. Laforgue transforms the palatial hall of all the Salomé representations into a tent ("un bariolé vélarium", 215), and if one is tempted to relate this to the tent in the dance scene of *Hérodias* or the banquet scene of *Salammbô*, the parodist makes his intentions clear: Salomé's is, rather, a circus tent, as "bariolé" suggests, with a succession of acts preceding the feature performance. Laforgue emphasizes the parodic nature of the theater by describing the stage explicitly as "une scène d'Alcazar" (215), a typical nineteenth-century café-concert, whose moorish style and name comically fit the Salomé context and parodically recall Moreau's interiors as described in *A Rebours*.[30] The performances are those of the circus ("la folle frise de cirque," 217): mountebanks, jugglers, and virtuosos, doing songs, dances, and pantomimes. A dancer dressed in the scaly costume of a serpent, and singing "Biblis, ma soeur Biblis, tu t'es changée en source, toi!" (217) provides a parody of Ovid's story of incestuous love,[31] which plays on the Decadent taste for this, and further reflects on the story, itself a parody of legend with an equally parodic dancer. Clowns turn the handle of barrel organs, "avec des airs de Messies qui ne se laisseront pas influencer et iront jusqu'au bout de leur apostolat," a burlesque preview of the proselytizing of that "petite Messie à matrice" later in the show, Salomé herself. Trapeze artists "aux ellipses sidérales," prefigure the parabolic arc traced by Iaokanann's head at the end as it falls into the sea, and Salomé's final tumble as she follows it. And three clowns act out the sense of Decadent metaphysics:

> Et trois autres clowns jouèrent l'Idée, la Volonté, l'Inconscient. L'Idée bavardait sur tout, la Volonté donnait de la tête contre les décors, et l'Inconscient faisait de grands gestes mystérieux comme un qui en sait au fond plus long qu'il n'en peut dire encore. Cette trinité avait d'ailleurs un seul et même refrain:
>
>> O Chanaan
>> Du bon néant!
>>
>> Néant, la Mecque
>> Des bibliothèques!
>
> Elle obtint un succès de fou rire. (217–19)

Laforgue here mocks Schopenhauerian and Hartmannian ideas by portraying the three terms of their philosophy as clowns in a pantomime, each playing out its own character. The parody is also a self-parody, with the parodist participating in the very Decadence that he mocks: Laforgue's own verses (the refrain)[32] and persona (the clown) are part of the circus act. And in the self-reflexive manner of parody, it prescribes the reception proper to it: "un succès de *fou rire.*"

As the moment of Salomé's appearance approaches, Laforgue provides another parodic dance, which this time closely—and hilariously—resembles the legendary dance of Salomé; a young ice skater "valsa sur les pointes comme une ballerine" (219) and leaves the stage skating on his hands, his fingernails becoming metaphorically the runners of the skates ("patinant sur les ongles d'acier de ses mains," 219). This inverted Salomé recalls Flaubert's *Hérodias,* in which Salomé finishes her dance by bounding across the stage on her hands. But Laforgue's skater specifically etches a gothic cathedral on the ice, and with this detail the scene also evokes the celebrated representation that allegedly inspired Flaubert in the first place: the portal of the Rouen cathedral depicting Salomé as an acrobat, dancing on her hands. The parody returns to the source of its alleged source, the "Salomé" behind *Hérodias,* and thus reminds the reader of its own structure, as well as its own potential for reusage in another, future work.

Consistent with the *café-concert* atmosphere, Laforgue's heroine is a cabaret *chanteuse*, a *chansonnière* who hams it up for the audience and accordingly gets her legendary reward. Dressed in a chiffon sheath she slowly descends the staircase, signals to the guests to take their seats, blows a kiss on her fingertips to her father, and, moving to center stage to be admired by all, totters on her toes, the only movement at all resembling a dance that she will make. For her number, rather, she adopts a pose parodically adapted from Moreau's Salomé paintings, in which she balances on her toes and holds her arms outstretched: "délicatement campée sur le pied droit, la hanche remontée, l'autre jambe infléchie en retard à la Niobide" (227). From her shoulders rises a large peacock-feather fan, providing a kaleidoscopic halo for her spectacular head: "une roue de paon nain, en fond changeant, moire, azur, or, émeraude, halo sur lequel s'enlevait sa candide tête, tête supérieure . . ." (223). Her face carries the typical "sourire crucifié" (223) and "yeux décomposés" of the Laforguian Eternal Feminine.

Here Laforgue explicitly links Salomé with Salammbô. Both have powdered hair, a symbolic gold chain about the ankles, a pink mouth, bare arms, a peacock-feather headdress, and a black lyre.[33] Both are associated with the moon: Salammbô follows its cycle and literally grows weak as it wanes; for Salomé, "pour faire un sort à la petite personne en question, la Lune s'était saigné à quatre veines" (227). Both descend the stairway slowly and, accompanied by the lyre, chant a nearly incomprehensible hymn. Although the subject of Salomé's parodic chant departs from Salammbô's incantation, Laforgue does not abandon it: Salammbô's tale of Masisabal, whose head was cut off, attached to the prow of his victor's ship, and carried along on the waves, returns at the end of the parody, when Iaokanaan's head, thrown into the sea, is likewise borne along by the waves. The parodic integration of *Salammbô* into *Salomé* here prepares us for the final scene, the conversion of the Baptist into another figure whose head floats on the waves, Orpheus.

Despite her resemblance to Salammbô, however, Salomé possesses a significantly distinctive trait: her unusually large head, her "candide tête supérieure," so heavy that it literally and figuratively inhibits her actions. "Que sa tête lui était onéreuse! Elle ne savait que faire de ses mains, les épaules même un peu gênées" (225). Her cumbersome head functions caricaturally, representing her overdeveloped faculty, her excessive cerebrality; she resembles the "théosophes hydrocéphales" (229) of her song. Her large head, her metaphysical preoccupations and the imbalance that they cause, keep her from performing the essential Salomé act, the dance, and inspire instead the parodic hymn. The heavy head is also consistent with the inversion of Salomé and the Baptist, and the theme of revolution, that the story has developed: in the last sentence of *Hérodias,* his heavy head is transferred to her.[34] Ioakanann's head will be buoyed up by the waters; Salomé's would be too heavy to float.

In a ludicrous prose replete with puns, alliteration, verbal play, periphrasis, and an abstract philosophical vocabulary, the hymn preaches the aesthetic and moral of the Unconscious—absolute harmony, passivity, and total submission to the Unconscious law of the universe:

> "Soyez, vous, les passifs naturels; entrez automatiques comme Tout, dans les ordres de l'Harmonie Bien-Veillante! . . . redevenez des êtres atteints d'incurie . . . L'inconscient *farà da se* . . . Et vous, fatals Jourdains, Ganges baptismaux, courants sidéraux insubmersibles, cosmogonies de Maman! lavez-vous, à l'entrée, de la tache plus ou moins originelle du Systématique; que nous soyons d'avance mâchés en charpie pour la Grande Vertu Curative (disons palliative) qui racommode les accrocs des prairies, des épidermes, etc.—*Quia est in ea virtus dormativa.*—Va . . ." (229–31)

This revolutionary rejects all divisions and hierarchies ("Loin, les cadres, les espèces, les règnes!" 235) and calls for self-consciousness to give way to the purer state of the Unconscious: "Est-ce une vie que s'obstiner à se mettre au courant de soi-même et du reste, en se demandant à chaque étape: 'Ah, ça! qui trompe-t-on ici?" (235). But Laforgue undermines her proposal to plunge into the "harmonieuse mansuétude des moralités préétablies" (235) and lose oneself forever, not only by making it consist largely of word play and interior rhyme ("Ça s'avance par stances, dans les salves des valves, en luxures sans césures, en surplis appâlis, qu'on abdique vers l'oblique des dérives primitives," 235), but also by suggesting from the beginning that she is aware of putting on an act:

Salomé, ayant donné cours à un petit rire toussotant, *peut-être pour faire assavoir que surtout fallait pas croire qu'elle se prenait au sérieux,* pinça sa lyre noire . . . et, de la voix sans timbre et sans sexe d'un malade qui réclame sa potion dont, au fond, *il n'a jamais eu plus besoin que vous ou moi,* improvisa à même. (227f., emphasis mine)

The narrative accordingly interrupts her opening sentence with an incredulous "se moquait-elle?" (229). Her performance is derided as a "sommaire abattage de théogonies, théodicées et formules de la sagesse des nations," and a "garulement mystique" (233). She herself weakens her credibility by her Latin quotation, whose authority she chooses badly: as always, Molière's joke ("Pourquoi l'opium fait-il dormir? parce qu'il a une valeur dormitive") ridicules purely verbal reasoning, and hers is verbal reasoning par excellence.[35] More ironically, the quotation reflects on the tedious, soporific chant itself, which may impress the islanders but simply bores the Princes du Nord, who look at their watches and wonder when she will be put to bed (237). Salomé is a fake and a hypocrite: in a symbolic gesture, she resolutely breaks her lyre over her knee and silences herself forever.

Although she forsakes the tradition of the dance, Salomé remains true to her heritage by asking for the head of Iaokanann on a platter. Laforgue's story has none of the traditional explanations (the ire of Herodias, the wrath of Salomé for having been scorned), but has provided sufficient clues to the parodic one, which he makes explicit in part four as the heroine holds court with the night sky:

Ah! chères compagnes des prairies stellaires, Salomé n'était plus la petite Salomé! et cette nuit allait inaugurer une ère nouvelle de relations et d'étiquette!

D'abord, exorcisée de sa virginité de tissus, elle se sentait maintenant, vis-à-vis de ces nébuleuses-matrices, fécondée tout comme elles d'évolutions giratoires.

Ensuite, ce fatal sacrifice au culte (heureuse encore, de s'en tirer à compte si discret!) l'avait obligée, pour faire disparaître l'Initiateur, à l'acte (grave, on a beau dire), nommé homicide. . . .

Allons, c'était sa vie; elle était une spécialité, une petite spécialité. (241)

This otherworldly creature aims beyond the Decadent Isles and their lunar ideal and seeks to emulate the stars, most of all those stellar representations of the Unconscious, the nebulas, "les amorphes, les perforées, les à tentacules," and especially Orion, "ce pâté gazeux aux rayons maladifs" (241), the mystical nebula of her puberty (243). Indeed, this has inspired the sacrificial and sacrilegious act of sexual initiation. She is now "fécondée tout comme elles d'évolutions giratoires," and can proudly look Orion in the eye (243). She even dresses according to the night sky: diamonds twinkling in her hair, and a deep-mourning violet gown with golden polka dots, like the dark heavens flecked with stars.

But if Salomé has discreetly made for herself a place in outer space, she nevertheless is determined to dispose of the evidence, Iaokanann's head (now referred to more intimately as "Jean," 241). Her passion for scientific experiment makes her try to send electric currents through it, like Poe's *in articulo mortis* experiments in magnetism, an effort that here parodically yields only grimaces.[36] But she has skill with chemicals too, as the Salle des Parfums attests, and she thus prepares the head elaborately:

> Or là, sur un coussin, parmi les débris de la lyre d'ébène, la tête de Jean (comme jadis celle d'Orphée) brillait, enduite de phosphore, lavée, fardée, frisée, faisant rictus à ces vingt-quatre million d'astres. (241)

The parenthetical aside, specifically likening the Baptist's head to that of Orpheus, integrates into the parody another famous Moreau painting related to his Salomé ones, "La Jeune Fille thrace portant la tête d'Orphée," in which Orpheus's head indeed rests on his lyre.[37] This suggests Salomé's plan—rolling it into the water—and also prefigures the end of the parody and its symbolism: the rise of a new, true bard to replace the ineffectual and fallen Salomé.

Significantly, the head here sits on the pieces of her shattered lyre, symbol of her "shattered" purity and powers. Accordingly, she places her greatest treasure, the Orion opal from her crown, "comme une hostie" (243) in his mouth. She may intend to bury with him this symbol of her puberty (243), but as a host it is also a sacrificial offering, thus ensuring his salvation. Like another parodic Salomé, Stendhal's Mathilde de la Môle—as outrageous an example of Romanticism as Laforgue's heroine is of Decadence—Salomé gives the head of her lover a last kiss. But if Mathilde's macabre actions derive from her desire to bury her lover's head with her own hands, Salomé's "petites mains de femme" are more

Salomé

violent, grasping the "géniale caboche" and tossing it over the cliff into the sea:

> L'épave décrivit une phosphorescente parabole suffisante. Oh! la noble parabole!—Mais la malheureuse petite astronome avait terriblement mal calculé son écart! et, chavirant par-dessus le parapet, avec un cri enfin humain! elle alla, dégringolant de roc en roc, râler, dans une pittoresque anfractuosité que lavait le flot, loin des rumeurs de la fête nationale, lacérée à nu, ses diamants sidéraux lui entrant dans les chairs, le crâne défoncé, paralysée de vertige, en somme mise à mal, agoniser une heure durant. (245).

The pun on "parabole" (parabola and parable) makes the arc traced by the Baptist's head a literal allegory for Salomé: she indeed follows suit, but parodically, falling over the railing and crashing headlong into a hollow of the rocks below. This "petite astronome" (243) resembles that of the famous fable, "l'astrologue qui se laisse tomber dans un puits," and reflects a similar *moralité*: she who can measure the exact position and magnitude of the stars cannot correctly calculate the distance to the edge of her own parapet, and she pays for it with her life.

But however artificial her past, Salomé utters, at last, "un cri humain," and thus her gruesome end seems unwarranted. Even the famous Laforguian irony is rarely so gratuitously harsh as to condone such brutality. Here the answer again derives from the parody, which distorts a feature of Moreau's "Apparition" as Huysmans describes it in *A Rebours*. There the gems of her costume seem to come alive by the light emitted by the Baptist's nimbus, and stab her with fiery sparks:

> Sous les traits ardents échappés de la tête du Précurseur, toutes les facettes des joailleries s'embrasent; les pierres s'animent, dessinent le corps de la femme en traits incandescents; la piquent au cou, aux jambes, aux bras, de points de feu, vermeils comme des charbons, violets comme des jets de gaz, bleus comme des flammes d'alcool, blancs comme des rayons d'astre.[38]

Laforgue parodically ignores the metaphor and stabs his heroine quite literally with the jewels, each representing a star, with which she has dressed her hair. Moreau and Huysmans depict the Baptist's posthumous revenge on his executioner; Laforgue's Salomé is punished, more appropriately, by the very emblems of her otherwordliness and artificiality, her star diamonds. She finds her longed-for place "loin des rumeurs de la fête nationale," but far, as well, from the observatory and even farther from her goal, the nebulas, as the text tells us with ironic banality: "Quant aux lointains du ciel, ils étaient loin" (245).

Significantly, Iaokanann's head becomes a kind of star, a "phosphorescente étoile flottante ... sur la mer," somewhat closer to earth than Salomé's distant ones. Like the head of Orpheus, it is buoyed up and carried along by the waters, and the allusion suggests that it will, like his, ultimately reach land and survive. Iaokanann thus takes over for Salomé, who, in a parody of the last line of *Salammbô* ("Ainsi mourut la fille d'Hamilcar pour avoir touché au manteau de Tanit"),[39] dies:

> Ainsi connut le trépas, Salomé, du moins celle des Iles Blanches Esotériques; moins victime des hasards illettrés que d'avoir voulu vivre dans le factice et non à la bonne franquette à l'instar de chacun de nous. (245)

In a manner typical of the genre, the explanation of Salomé's accident becomes a commentary on the parody itself. Laforgue comically implies that the "hasards illettrés" which constitute the parody do not account for her end; her fate does not result merely from a parodic need to alter the original. Decadence actually kills itself and thwarts its own aesthetic purposes. However, he also reminds us that it has permitted the parody by which, transformed, it lives: Salomé herself made the Baptist a "shining star" and a new Orpheus, by her preparation of the head in phosphorous and by her bold venture out of herself, her sacrificial gift represented by the Orion opal placed so carefully in his mouth.

Moreover, consistent with the self-reflexivity described in chapter 1, the parody here does not have the final word. It is merely another text, subject to the same critical treatment that the original and target have undergone. The qualifying aside about Salomé ("du moins celle des Iles Blanches Esotériques") admits openly the existence of other Salomés, other versions that are, or will be, as valid as this one. And the irony of the last line (the quaint "à la bonne franquette" and the literary "à l'instar de") in fact directs the mockery at "chacun de nous," the parodist and ourselves. The story has brought Decadence under fire, but ends by reminding us that the solution proposed in its stead may be no less absurd. For every artificial, Decadent Salomé there is, on the other side, a ludicrous, bourgeois Prince du Nord. Laforgue thus proposes a new text altogether, with the lesson of the parody at issue. Only this Salomé has died, only this *Salomé* has ended; the ironic last sentence suggests another parody, with another heroine, "à l'instar de chacun de nous."

7

Persée et Andromède, ou le plus heureux des trois

Persée et Andromède differs from the preceding tales in two important ways.[1] First, it has a more complex narrative structure, of which we become aware only at the very end: in a surprising epilogue, the narrator and a member of his audience discuss the truth of the story just told. As we shall see, this dialogue reflects back upon the story through its content and as a narrative device is consistent with the self-reflexive nature of parody: the narrator becomes a character in the story itself. This turn is all the more unexpected because the text gives no prior indication of it; the story appears to be in the authorial third-person omniscient, until the epilogue introduces the narrator himself, and thereby reminds us that the parody is a story told rather than an experience lived. In this way, it carries out the merciless lesson of the genre; it denies us at the last moment the relief that accompanies a normal dénouement and thwarts the most basic literary trust, by which we willingly accept the authority and veracity of the omniscient point of view. The epilogue to *Persée et Andromède* forces us not only to acknowledge that the story is a fiction (the devices of parody within the story would alone accomplish this) but, more radically, to question the truth of the metafiction, the epilogue itself. It realizes in a highly sophisticated form the self-reflexivity described in chapter 1, whereby the parody challenges the very message of the genre (i.e. the scepticism that it maintains about the truth and authority of representations). Moreover, it carries out a main objective of parody, literary regeneration: in its ending, the story creates another story which encompasses it and features the parodist as a character. In closing the work, it uncovers a new one, like parody itself, which in seeming to end a tradition actually renews and transforms it.

Second, although *Salomé* and *Le Miracle des Roses* revolve around a heroine, and *Lohengrin* gives Elsa at least half the stage, only *Persée et Andromède* features a heroine comparable to Laforgue's otherwise unparallelled heroes. She is not, like Salomé, a charlatan Decadent poet, nor, like Ruth, a macabre and sadistic *névropathe;* nor even, like Elsa, a simple Eternal Feminine. In *Persée et Andromède,* the text expresses the psychology of the heroine. We know her every thought, whim, desire; we hear her private lamentations, witness her solitary caprices, follow her into her secret hideaways. Only with Hamlet and Pan do we have such intimate relations, and the likeness is significant: Andromède is to a great extent the female counterpart to Laforgue's two most distinctive heroes, the feminine version of the stock 1880s sensibility that suffers from ennui, *taedium vitae,* and especially, the loneliness of a life without love.

Andromède resembles Laforgue's heroes also in her very character. Like Hamlet, she is moody, egotistical, impatient, perpetually impulsive and restless, tormented by ennui, and overwhelmed by a sense of futility. She spends her time gazing out at the sea, despairs of its awesome immensity, and answers its laments with her own wounded-animal moans. She capriciously changes her mind from one moment to the next, galloping round the island, stopping abruptly to admire her image in her mirror-pool and immediately despairing of how ordinary and "sans distinction" it is (257), or tormenting the Dragon and then embracing him "selon sa câlinerie familière" (252). She longs to be cured of her ennui, her illness, her wound, her child's "bobo," her intolerable solitude. Like Pan in the final tale, Andromède is starved for love, and all her thoughts, feelings, and actions derive from the unfulfilled desire of the adolescent. "Aimer! aimer! crie la pauvre Andromède" (254): desire for love is the source of her ennui, a budding sixth sense forever frustrated, to which nothing responds (263). Like Hamlet's sixth sense, "ce sens de l'infini," Andromède's desire for love is also a desire for the Infinite, as the cosmological poem which she recites in part two makes clear: for the Laforguian imagination, these constitute one and the same impulse, the human aspiration toward the Ideal.

Andromède is not simply Hamlet or Pan in the form of a delightfully thin *jeune fille,* however. She represents (or, through the story, comes to represent) the feminine ideal of Laforgue's imagination, the appropriate companion for the poet-hero, with his metaphysical and sexual doubts on the one hand, and his sentimental "bon coeur" on the other. The Decadent heroes of the *Moralités* are all exaggerations of this figure, with their conflicting pessimism and sentimentality. However, this story features a more moderate example, a former nihilist who has suffered, and in so doing has learned his lesson: the Dragon, who, through misfortune, has discovered the truth about life and is thus worthy of being reborn. Andromède's adolescent crisis corresponds to his former puerile revolt against life, and her *jeune fille*'s ennui to his own more metaphysically inspired pessimism. But if Laforgue represents the female variety of the Decadent *mal* as personal and sexual, and the male variety as metaphysical, he takes care to establish the identity of the two: it is a source of humor in Hamlet and Pan, who confuse them constantly, and in *Persée et Andromède* it constitutes the wisdom of life that the Dragon expresses in his "petit poème sacré," as we shall see. With her fierce independence and pride, her sentimental loyalty, and her Laforguian "grand coeur" (274), Andromède is an excellent match for the Dragon; she will accordingly follow his example and, in the face of sorrow, learn the truth which has lain all the while unnoticed before her eyes.

Like the other characters, these two are exaggerations: the touching humor with which they are treated and the fairy-tale quality of the story itself make this clear. But the exaggeration expresses a fantasy and although living in our fantasies may bring us the unfortunate fate of Salomé or Hamlet, keeping them at a distance as ideals to be approached may rather bring us the wisdom of the Dragon: "L'Homme n'est qu'un insecte sous les cieux; mais qu'il se respecte, et il est bien Dieu" (263). Andromède is the Laforguian vision of the ideal modern woman, (as the monster is that of the man) a comically charming solution to the problematic relation between the sexes in the contemporary world; and the optimistic story is a gentle statement of faith in the power of life to bring about a measure of human happiness. If the moral of the story is that the monster may miraculously come out the winner, perhaps the monstruous idealism of the story itself may also surprise us and come true.

The story of Perseus and Andromeda comes from an appropriate source for a parody of Laforgue's sort, Ovid's *Metamorphoses* (IV, 604–803), itself a playful retelling of legendary stories. In response to an oracle, the Ethiopian princess Andromeda was to be given in sacrifice to a sea monster sent by Neptune to ravage the country as punishment for the insolence of her mother, Cassiopeia, who had boasted that she was as beautiful as the Nereids. Andromeda was thus bound to a rock and exposed, but was saved by Perseus, who arrived on the winged horse Pegasus, born of the blood of the Gorgon Medusa. Perseus had killed Medusa, and thus he carried on his shield the symbol of his victory, the redoubtable head, with its power to petrify all on whom it set eyes. Having slain the dragon and won Andromeda as his bride, Perseus later turned the Gorgon's head against Phineas, to whom Andromeda had been formerly betrothed, and also against Polydectes, who refused to believe that Perseus had actually killed it. Certain episodes of the story are conventional subjects in the visual arts: Perseus showing Andromeda the Gorgon's head in a mirror, Andromeda chained to the rock, and especially Perseus delivering Andromeda, interpreted by such masters as Veronese, Titian, Guercino, Rubens, Coypel and Puget, the latter with a famous example in the Louvre. There is some evidence that Laforgue himself did a sketch of the last subject during his time at the Beaux-Arts, for he mentions it in his notes.[2]

But Laforgue's parody does not keep to the model given by the title; into the legend of Perseus and Andromeda, it integrates that of *Beauty and the Beast*, which ensures that the other will be thwarted parodically at every turn. The central episode of the traditional story—*Perseus delivering Andromeda*—has no function in the parody, for Persée does not deliver Andromède and does not even need to do so: she is not the Dragon's prisoner but his darling little ward, whom he has reared from infancy on a faraway desert isle. She calls him uncle (251), teacher, friend, foster father (275); and the closest that he can come to being her captor is in a parody of a cliché: "Tant que je vivrai, je serai votre geôlier sans peur et sans reproche" (265). This jailer is really, according to the conventional *chevalier sans peur et sans reproche*, a knight. Laforgue's parody reverses the traditional situation: it is the Dragon who needs to be delivered, not only from his monster's exterior, but also from the captive tyranny of Andromède's "passagères lubies de croissance" (275), her incessant demands, her impulsive *volte-face*, her unpredictable adolescent *coups de tête* (277).

Andromède does need to be delivered, however, in another, more modern sense: "Où va-t-elle ainsi, ô puberté, puberté! par le vent et les dunes, avec ces abois de blessée?" (255). Andromède longs to be freed of her maidenhood, her solitude, exorcise her "poor being," cure her virginal "wound." Laforgue's Persée is incapable of doing this, for he is an outrageous egotist, cocksure, petulant and rude, "le petit chéri des dieux" (270) with affected speech and manner, a "vilain héros d'Opéra-comique" (275), as Andromède puts it, merely a parody of a hero. Only the Monster-poet, "homme distingué qui a eu des malheurs," can save Andromède and win her, but she must free him first by her kiss, liberating the fine young man from his shimmering monster's skin. Laforgue's ideal love is a reciprocal affair; Andromède is delivered from the lonely rock of her virginity, but only by loving the Dragon truly, for himself alone.

Unlike the preceding stories, *Persée et Andromède* carries no telling epigraph; however, its subtitle provides the first parodic deformation, which signals the parody and indicates its other, unnamed model. "Le Plus Heureux des Trois" is the title of a vaudeville play by Labiche. Its plot bears no relation to Laforgue's *Moralité*, but placing its title alongside *Persée et Andromède* casts the ancient legend into comic light, creating a vaudeville *Perseus and Andromeda*, as it were.[3] More importantly, the subtitle has proverbial echoes, as in the famous *moralité* of La Fontaine:[4] "le plus âne des trois n'est pas celui qu'on pense," which intertextually provides the natural, though unstated, sequel ("n'est pas celui qu'on pense"). The subtitle calls attention to the suppressed character of the three, the one "of whom we would not think" in a story of Perseus and Andromeda—the Monster-Dragon. It immediately signals the parody, for by alluding to him as the luckiest of the three, it inverts the story, making the defeated villain of the original the victorious hero of the parody, in a manner typical of the genre. It also identifies the second model, since the most obvious story in which a dragon triumphs happily is *La Belle et la Bête*. Indeed, in a parody, the winner is precisely not the one that we expect, for it is the purpose of parodic distortion to disappoint our expectations. This fundamental principle of the genre actually constitutes the moral of the *Moralité* itself, stated explicitly in the final line: the disdained Monster was worthy of being the luckiest of the three. *Persée et Andromède, ou le plus heureux des trois* thus offers an apologia for parody itself; the lesson of the story is that of parody in general. Laforgue makes this point clear throughout by presenting the characters' destinies as plots of pre-established stories: following the plot, changing the plot, fixing the plot, parodying the plot are all bound up in questions of will and self-knowledge. The story explores metaphorically not only the dangers of imitation but the importance, in art and life, of interpretation and transformation. Destiny may be fulfilled, but it can nevertheless be altered and choices made; and life, like a good parody, may turn out as we least expect.

The Story

The story consists of three parts followed by the epilogue. In the first two, we discover the remote, isolated setting of the island and witness a typical day in the life of its two inhabitants, Andromède and the Monster-Dragon. The third section contains the major episodes of the parody: Persée arrives on his winged horse and slays the Dragon, but is chased away by Andromède, who wants none of him; the Dragon then metamorphoses into "un jeune homme accompli" (277) by the power of her kiss.

Part one opens with a highly subjective description of the setting: the lonely island and the sea, immense, indifferent, mysterious, monotonous, resistant to man: "Bref, pas l'étoffe d'une amie (oh, vraiment! renoncer à cette idée, et même à l'espoir de partager ses rancunes après confidences, si seul à seul qu'on soit depuis des temps avec elle)" (249). This curious parenthetical remark immediately points to the parody: the sea, which in the original produced the enemy Monster to devour her, here itself functions as the enemy ("pas l'étoffe d'une amie"), keeping Andromède prisoner and ignoring her unhappy moans with its uncaring vastness and impenetrability. But the parenthetical aside renders "amie" ambiguous and introduces a point of view appropriate, rather, to the Dragon: is Andromède the stuff of which a beloved is made, or will he have to give up the idea after all this time spent alone with her on the island? Laforgue uses the parodic signal to hint at the second model and thus provides us from the beginning with the foremost tension of the story.

The initial impression of overwhelming monotony is belied by an extraordinary metaphorical richness: the frothing of the waves compared to a flock of sheep that swim, go under, reappear; the winds frolicking above them, whipping up the spume in iridescent spray; the ray of sunshine on the waves creating a rainbow, like a bright dolphin that surfaces and then plunges back again into the water. But the contradiction only communicates all the more clearly Andromède's problem: the figures of these comparisons disappear literally back into the depths from which they arose. They are the products of her active imagination, always projecting beyond what is at hand a world that will never reach her own, like the sheep "qui jamais n'arrivent" and the dolphin that, no sooner spotted, disappears from sight. On this desert island surrounded by an unending expanse of ocean "à perte de vue," where time is measured by the regular migration of screeching, untamable birds, Andromède lives enough in her imagination to be dissatisfied with her reality, as each new hope fades into the overall gray of the sky or drowns in the monotonous rolling of the waves.[5]

We meet Laforgue's Andromeda not in the traditional pose— bound to the rock and exposed to the elements—but lying comfortably on her stomach and propped up on her elbows, in a protected inlet harboring two caves padded in eiderdown and algae. In the ignorance and innocence of her solitary existence, this child of nature is "irréprochablement nue," and "n'a pas la face et les mains plus ou moins blanches que le reste du corps" (255), but rather an even, healthy tan all over, of the same terra-cotta color. Laforgue's comical allusion to the mottled consequences of wearing clothes distinguishes Andromède from the ordinary *jeune fille*, whose face and hands are more exposed than the rest of her person, or shaded by protective hat and gloves. His heroine, rather, is tall, thin, and angular with proud, straight, hips and long legs on which she bounds around the island like a stilt bird among the marshes (255). Her long neck balances a small childish head with a rich fleece of silky red hair down to her knees. She has two childish "hints" of breasts, which the narrative comically attributes, in a parenthetical aside, to her wild existence in the open air: "(et quand et comment auraient-ils pu se former, toujours à aller ainsi contre le vent, le vent salé du large et contre les douches furieusement glacées des vagues?)" (256). Even her eyes reflect her surroundings: sometimes, like Hamlet's and Ruth's, as piercing as a sea bird's, sometimes taking on the colorless gray of the sea itself, with all the monotony contained in those "eaux quotidiennes" (256).[6]

Andromède's freedom from the constraints that civilization places on a normal *jeune fille* has also had a significant effect on her personality. She speaks her mind and takes no pains to conceal her feelings, a trait later to serve her well in getting rid of Persée. Proud, obstinate, and headstrong, she is at home with the elements, braves the most violent waves even as they toss her, in a stupor, onto the beach, and scrambles fearlessly up and down the cliffs. But whereas she may formerly have enjoyed her uninhibited life on the remote island, lately she has been experiencing some inexplicable "palpitations de coeur" (261) that make her behave unpredictably. Like Hamlet, she is restless and inconsistent, and cannot keep to one activity long enough to carry it out; she thinks of ending her misery by drowning herself in the sea (258), jabbing herself with a bit of flint (263), or simply wasting away (264), but ultimately lacks the spirit to do so. All her thoughts center on freedom: in a desperate effort to escape the lonely existence of the island, she pelts the migratory sea birds that pass overhead with stones from a slingshot to arrest one and have it carry her away. Laforgue describes her metonymically in terms of her condition: this "puberté sauvageonne" (255) is coming of age, and as there is no one else about, she takes her adolescent crisis out on her old friend and guardian, the Dragon.

Laforgue has converted Ovid's ferocious Dragon into a mild, kindly creature who suffers Andromède's growing pains with the patience of a saint. He retains from his legendary predecessor his association with the sea, although Laforgue comically transfers this to his luxurious exterior: a skin shimmering with all the precious jewels of underwater Golcondas, lashes fringed with variegated cartilaginous trim, large eyes of a watery glaucous color. He speaks with "une voix d'homme distingué qui a eu des malheurs" (251), the first signal of his association with *Beauty and the Beast*. He is a "gentleman accompli, savant industrieux, poète disert" (274), who, changed into a dragon as punishment by the gods of life for preaching a doctrine of nihilism in the groves of Arcadia, has seen through illusion to nothingness, achieved the wisdom of resignation, and returned to the values of life, love, and self-respect. The text makes his new position clear in a comically appropriate comparison. The Monster polishes pebbles for Andromède's catapult, "— tel le sage Spinoza devait polir ses verres de lunettes" (255), an allusion to Spinoza's well-known trade as a lens-maker; but the humor, and the telling dash, expose the false pretense, point to the real source of comparison—not the polishing but the wisdom of resignation. The Monster has the acceptant philosophy of the man considered the prototype of Schopenhauer and Hartmann. His sacred poem, recited by Andromède in part two, will in fact translate Spinozian pantheism into the more contemporary Hartmannian system of the Unconscious.[7] Laforgue makes the connection indirectly, by a detour through the polishing motif common to both: a method appropriate to parody, which does similarly on a larger scale, using a trivial likeness to produce humor, and thus to lead the reader to the real connection between the parody and the work parodied.

Persée et Andromède

The Monster-poet puts his literary talents to use by giving Andromède a distinctive version of *Pyramus and Thisbe:*

> Le Monstre croit à propos de prendre la voix de fausset de cette pauvre enfant qui mue, pour railler ses doléances romanesques, et il commence d'un ton détaché:
> — *Pyrame et Thisbé.* Il était une fois . . .
> — Non! non! pas d'histoires mortes, ou je me tue! (254)

The story-within-a-story is here specifically a parody: the serious, tragic legend told comically as a fairy tale in Andromède's falsetto voice, and intended to mock her "doléances romanesques." As we have seen in chapter 1, the parody-within-the-parody functions as a model for the larger story. This example is all the more significant in that both come from the same source, Ovid's *Metamorphoses* IV. The Dragon-poet who takes *Metamorphoses* IV as the material for a parody represents that other poet who uses an episode from the same book, the parodist himself. Moreover this scene reflects the parodist's ambivalent attitude (mocking and admiring) toward the target: the Monster makes fun of Andromède, whom he nevertheless loves dearly. She, on the other hand, is insensitive to parody and misses the joke completely, as her threatening to imitate the story's tragic outcome attests. She suffers from the conventional parodic problem, taking stories as models to follow in life, not, like the Monster, to transform into other fictions. Her adolescent egoism keeps her from seeing that the solution to her "doléances romanesques" lies not in the romanesque version but in a parody. Indeed, having learned her lesson, she will follow the Thisbe model only parodically: upon seeing her dead lover she will kill herself only with remorse, and will give him the regenerative kiss.

Andromède displays no greater skill in interpreting the riddle by which the Dragon communicates her parodic, *Belle et la Bête* destiny:

> — O Monstre, ô Dragon, tu dis que tu m'aimes, et tu ne peux rien pour moi. Tu vois que je dépéris d'ennui et tu n'y peux rien. Comme je t'aimerais si tu pouvais me guérir, faire quelque chose! . . .
> — O noble Andromède, fille du roi d'Ethiopie! le Dragon malgré lui, le pauvre Monstre ne peut te répondre que par un cercle vicieux: Je ne te

guérirai que lorsque tu m'aimeras, car c'est en m'aimant que tu me guériras.
— Toujours le même rébus fatidique! Mais quand je te dis que je t'aime bien! (252f.)

Andromède does not see the obvious: she cannot decipher the riddle although the solution literally stares her in the face. She longs for society (253) even while the answer to her yearning lies—or crouches—in the cave next door. Not until the Monster is lost will she recognize her feelings for him and acknowledge the cause of her blindness: "oh, curiosité trois fois funeste!" (275), her fatal curiosity for a world other than her own. Here she rebels against the "destinée" (253) that keeps her on the island. But the Dragon's answer presents the peculiar dilemma of parody: which destiny of the two will ultimately unfold? Which story will prevail, *Perseus and Andromeda* or *Beauty and the Beast*? The Monster's alternative suggests not only the play of texts by which all parody operates but also the particular message of this one: perhaps destiny, like the story, may be tampered with after all, and, as the subtitle suggests, the one least expected come out the winner.

Andromède has two principal outlets for her hypertrophic adolescent energies. The first, a natural basin of water carved into the top of the cliff, serves her as a mirror into which she gazes at her image. She is a modern female Narcissus, with a bit less pride but the same egoism and self-ignorance:

> ... elle cherche à approfondir le sérieux de ses yeux; et ses yeux ne se départent pas de leur profondeur. Mais sa bouche! Elle ne se lasse pas d'adorer l'innocente éclosion de sa bouche. Oh! qui comprendra jamais sa bouche? ...
> ... Mais elle a beau se mirer! Tout comme elle-même, son visage attend toujours, sérieux et lointain. (256f.)

The lesson of the mirror remains ever the same and Andromède, unlike Narcissus, knows why. She even wishes she could be another in order to be able to look into her own eyes, "les interroger," "les épier," "rêver de leur secret." Andromède does not understand that she will know herself only when she turns away and toward another. But already the knowledge is being forced upon her: the rain troubles the purity of her mirror, as the death of the Monster will later shake her egoism.

Andromède's second answer to her growing pains involves erotically therapeutic encounters with the elements. Lying on her back in the wet sand, she abandons herself to the waves ("Les yeux clos, Andromède la reçoit ferme, avec un long sanglot d'égorgée," 258) and the rain showers ("et toute gémissante sous la grande rumeur diluvienne, elle reçoit l'averse," 259), but these satisfy her adolescent's desire only momentarily. Her final attempt to "exorcise"[8] herself (260) with one of the passing sea birds produces a brilliant parody of her traditional posture:

> Elle pousse un long piaulement d'appel, et s'affaisse contre le roc, les bras en croix, et ferme les yeux. Oh! que cet oiseau fonde sur sa petite personne prométhéenne exposée là par des dieux, et, perché sur ses genoux, commence, d'un bec implacablement salutaire, à lui retirer le brûlant noyau de son bobo. (260)

"Prométhéenne," apparently incongruous for this story, clues the reader in to the parody: Laforgue diverts the adjective from its sense of human grandeur and enterprise to allude more literally to the specific situation of Prometheus himself, bound, like Andromède, to the rock. But if Andromède, watching the great bird, resembles the original Andromeda observing the arrival of Pegasus, Laforgue deals us yet another parodic blow, for her explicit fantasies belong to a different mythological story altogether: the bird that tore out Prometheus' liver here becomes, in Andromède's hopeful imagination, the swan ravishing Leda. Laforgue freely integrates the stories, transforming the Prometheus and Leda ones into metaphors that clarify the parody. The reference to Prometheus both deforms and identifies the *Andromède enchaînée* episode; the allusion to Leda interprets the sexual nature of Andromède's captivity and the particular deliverance of the "bec salutaire" which she awaits.

But the answer to Andromède's loneliness lies in yet another "légende" (261), the Dragon's "petit poème sacré." Laforgue transforms Poe's *La Vérité sur le cas de M. Valdemar* according to Decadent evolutionary theories and produces the ludicrously appropriate title *La Vérité sur le Cas de Tout*.[9] Laforgue plays on Hartmann's identification of the Unconscious with the All (Tout, Un-Tout, Tout-Un): Poe's tale of a doctor's efforts to explore the unconscious mind of a corpse immediately after death becomes a cosmological poem in which the Unconscious provides the truth about everything.[10] It parodically reduces evolutionary metaphysics to eleven basic axioms reflecting the wisdom of acceptance: "Au commencement était l'Amour, loi organisatrice universelle, inconsciente, infaillible. Et c'est, immanente aux tourbillons solidaires des phénomènes, l'aspiration infinie à l'Idéal" (261). Love is the logos of this Gospel, the unconscious law which governs the universe, and reflects man's aspiration toward the ideal.

According to the poem, the impulse toward the ideal objectifies itself in worlds that are born, develop, and then disintegrate to make room for new ones. The place of the earth in this overall pattern is relatively insignificant, merely a miniature reflex of some monumental "Grande Evolution Inconsciente dans le Temps" (262). But the Dragon's poem subverts this pessimism and denies the importance of the cosmic pattern by affirming sentimentally that the negligeable earth is nevertheless all that we have to satisfy our human senses:

> Mais la bonne Terre descendue du Soleil nous est tout, parce que nous avons cinq sens, et que toute la Terre y répond. O succulences, émerveillements plastiques, senteurs, rumeurs, étonnements à perte de vue, Amour! O vie à moi!
> L'Homme n'est qu'un insecte sous les cieux; mais qu'il se respecte, et il est bien Dieu. Un spasme de la créature vaut toute la nature. (263)

Laforgue converts this review of fin-de-siècle pessimistic cosmology to a moral for the Decadent himself: it asserts the power of love to redeem human existence from insignificance. This commonsensical wisdom is the lesson that our former nihilist, the Dragon, has learned over the years of his punishment. The poem follows the pessimism of Decadence through to its despairing conclusion and finds that the only way out is to turn back to standard, commonplace human values of love and self-respect.

Andromède once again does not appreciate the message. "Ce n'est que la douceur des leçons apprises" (263): it offers the temporary comfort of an old lesson learned by heart but not the peace of mind of a lesson learned. She thinks it inadequate to her situation, for though life may satisfy the five senses, she has a sixth sense to which nothing responds. The real meaning of the poem escapes her: her pubescent sixth sense can indeed be satisfied, and by the fundamental law of life which the poem describes. Her hopes for love will be fulfilled not by appealing to an uncaring sky and sea or to her own frustrating imagination, but rather by understanding her reality, reading her own story rightly.

The opening of part three teases the reader with a false conclusion relevant to the parody: returning home for the customary evening routine of watching the sunset, Andromède finds that the Monster has disappeared and, in despair, bitterly reproaches herself for having tormented him. Laforgue inserts the dénouement of *Beauty and the Beast* into *Perseus and Andromeda* too early, before the latter has properly started up (Perseus himself has not yet appeared). But the Monster comes back; the false dénouement signals the parody, points specifically to the source of its distortion (*La Belle et la Bête*), and previews Andromède's later, proper self-reproach. Laforgue shows that the story can be interrupted, rearranged, mixed and matched, and thus exposes the procedures of his own parody.

Before bringing in Persée, Laforgue includes an elaborate parody of the stock Romantic sunset.[11] In keeping with the Decadent target, his sunset is a theatrical show staged by expert technicians and "artificiers," and parodically presents the ambiguous spectacle of a monarch's execution. The imperial Turkish "Sublime Porte" here becomes the gate through which the pasha retreats into death, and the sun into night. The scaffolding and sets go up, the lighting is given its final touches, the curtains are opened, but the setting of the triumphal march is parodically a slaughterhouse: "l'abattoir est prêt."

> L'Astre Pacha,
> Son Eminence Rouge,
> En simarre de débâcles,
> Descend, mortellement triomphal,
> Durant des minutes, par la Sublime Porte! . . .
> Et le voilà qui gît sur le flanc, tout marbré de stigmates atrabilaires.
> Vite, quelqu'un pousse du pied cette citrouille crevée, et alors! . . .
> Adieu paniers, vendanges sont faites! . . . (266)

The splendid sun becomes through this vulgarizing ritual first a humiliated victim mottled with the wounds of the stigmata, and then that ludicrous and traditionally parodic vegetable, a broken pumpkin,[12] kicked by some disdainful foot over the edge of the horizon into nothingness. The confusion that ensues, as the court rapidly empties, further metamorphoses into the rapid flight of an army, surprised by the fall of the sun-king and the subsequent invasion of night. The parodic sunset, so similar to those of Laforgue's *Derniers Vers*,[13] not only reflects the larger parody but also has significance for interpreting it, for it acts out an axiom from the Dragon's poem: "(Mais comme rien n'est plus chatouilleux aux organismes supérieurs que se sentir mourir tout en sachant qu'il n'en sera rien, le crépuscule et l'automne, le drame du soleil et de la mort sont esthétiques par excellence)" (261). Indeed, this supreme aesthetic moment has the proper effect on both characters, the pleasure of feeling oneself die while knowing that one is not, the principle of love in its aesthetic manifestation.[14] But the sun's dubious glory, represented by the process of vulgarization (from royal oriental pasha to ludicrous pumpkin, from court scene to one of panic and pillage), reflects the ambiguous experience of love itself: this source of human pleasure is also man's unromantic concession to the superiority of Nature.

Laforgue finally introduces the long-awaited third person, the Persée of the title: "Oh! bénis soient les dieux qui envoient, juste au moment voulu, un troisième personnage" (267). The formula to the gods is incongruous in a story where the nineteenth-century Unconscious has had more than its due share of exposure. But the humor calls attention to the idea of a governing force, a higher plan implied by "juste au moment voulu." The moment is right because, unless something happens, Andromède and the Dragon will merely retire and then "recommencer une journée pareille" (267), and the story will become merely the routine pattern of life on the island. But in a tale of *Persée et Andromède,* we need a Persée; in a story of "le plus heureux des trois," we need a "troisième personnage": the beneficent gods are actually the plot of the original story. In keeping with the parody, however, this essential character will be utterly superfluous. Persée's arrival seems to put the story on its proper course, but this is deceptive. The parody of the *Metamorphoses* will contain some metamorphosing of its own, of the Dragon into a fine young man, and *Perseus and Andromeda* into *Beauty and the Beast: le plus heureux des trois n'est pas celui qu'on pense.*

One has the disturbing impression that *Persée et Andromède* will dispense entirely with the central episode of the legend, Perseus' killing of the Dragon, for Laforgue's hero, with a mere "Allez, hop! à Cythère," seems content to whisk his fiancée away without fighting him at all. But the Dragon does not permit the story to end so easily, or so differently from the plots that he knows: Persée cannot take away Andromède without killing him first, as he has told us, and thus he summons up his traditional monster's qualities and launches a conventional attack, rearing ferociously, breathing fire, and recalling Persée to his role. Once again, however, the plot is interrupted, for Persée stops short of stabbing his enemy and opts for an untraditional (and more lethal) solution, the Gorgon's head:

> Persée l'empoigne par cette chevelure dont les noeuds bleus jaspés d'or lui font de nouveaux bracelets et la présente au Dragon en criant à Andromède: Vous, baissez les yeux!
> Mais, ô prodige, le charme n'opère pas.
> Il ne veut pas opérer, le charme!
> Par un effort inouï, en effet, la Gorgone a fermé ses yeux pétrificateurs. (270f.)

In the most remarkable parodic twist of the story, the fearsome and inescapable Gorgon head will not work its charm. Persée is such a parody of his heroic predecessor that even his most reliable weapon fails him at the crucial moment, serving only to add more bracelets to his already foppishly bedecked arms. The Gorgon's action is "inouï" precisely because it is parodic: the head figured not in the original legend of Perseus and Andromeda, but only in one of Perseus's later adventures. Persée gets what he deserves: if he ignores tradition, he must expect others to do the same. The willfulness of the Gorgon to defy his expectations might have prepared him for Andromède's rebellious and equally unexpected refusal to accompany him later on, but does not: Persée remains the model of a bad reader, a lesson to the reader of the parody.

Exploiting the creative implications of parody, Laforgue makes this distortion the material of another one, ultimately creating another story; the Gorgon closes her eyes because she has recognized the Monster as her old friend and neighbor, from the days when he was guardian of the Hesperides and she lived nearby with her sisters. The legendary Gorgon Medusa indeed lived with her sisters near the Hesperides, but the Dragon that kept watch over the gardens belongs rather to the legend of Heracles, who killed it and escaped with the celebrated golden apples. Mingling the two stories in this way reflects the procedure of this parody, which integrates its two models by their common elements of Monster and maiden. It also comically recalls the Ovidian original, which links all the important stories of mythology into a continuous narrative, however tenuous the connection. Laforgue insists on this later, when the Dragon, after his rebirth, tells his past history, encompassing several legends that involve a dragon, from the guardian of the Hesperides killed by Heracles, to the guardian of the golden fleece slaughtered by Jason, to the guardian of Andromeda. In addition to reminding us of the *Metamorphoses* model, the dragon's tale reflects on the story itself: the Monster's history of metamorphosis makes him especially eligible for a further one, into "un jeune homme accompli."

The parodic significance of the Gorgon's refusal is brought out by the reactions of Persée and Andromède themselves:

> Persée attend toujours, le bras tendu, ne s'apercevant de rien. Le contraste est un peu trop grotesque entre le geste brave et magistral qu'il a pris ainsi et le raté de la chose; et la sauvage petite Andromède n'a pu retenir un certain sourire; un certain sourire que Persée surprend! (271)

Here Laforgue gives us in miniature the procedure of the larger parody and the reaction that it should provoke. The grotesque contrast between Persée's magisterial gesture and the utter failure of his effort reflects the disparity between the legendary original and the parody's distortion, "le raté de la chose." This time Andromède understands the parody rightly and has the proper response: she cannot keep from smiling, a model for the reader himself.

Persée's failure with the Gorgon makes him resort to his traditional weapon, the sword. With characteristic theatricality, he kills

Persée et Andromède

the Monster easily, but gets carried away with the importance of his role:

> Le Monstre est mort. Mais Persée est trop excité, malgré l'infaillibilité de sa victoire, et il faut qu'il s'acharne sur le défunt! et le larde de balafres! et lui crève les yeux! et le massacre, jusqu'à ce qu'Andromède l'arrête.
> — Assez, assez; vous voyez bien qu'il est mort. (272)

The allusion to the infallibility of Persée's victory reminds us that it is not only definitive—the Dragon is really dead—but also predetermined by the plot of the original: he need not be so violent, for his triumph is already ensured by the legend. But Persée wants greater honors than the ones already reserved for him, and this excessive egoism will cause him to lose his prize. There is no objection to changing the story, but, as the Gorgon proved earlier, the other characters may do likewise, notably the heroine, who here chases him unceremoniously out of her life: "— Allez-vous-en! allez-vous-en! Vous me faites horreur! J'aime mieux mourir seule, allez-vous-en, vous vous êtes trompé d'adresse" (273). Persée *has* got the wrong address, having landed in a parody where things do not turn out as they ought. Natural Andromède is too wild and independent to fit into the easy, elegant atmosphere that produces such an *opéra-comique* hero as himself. Persée is just as glad to be relieved of his role, and merely pays the insult back in kind: "Vous n'avez déjà pas une peau si soignée" (274). But we do not need him to tell us that Andromède's skin is not so "soignée"; her even, weathered, terra-cotta tan was described early on with admiration. Persée's intended insult is actually the utmost mark of approval, thus guaranteeing the inversion of the parody: Persée departs and the Monster emerges as the hero; *Beauty and the Beast* takes over from *Perseus and Andromeda*.

Indeed, Andromède's remorse at the Monster's death makes her admit her love for him and administer the *Beauty and the Beast* kiss. He in turn tells her his life story: this "Dragon à trois têtes" (276) is the dragon of every legend that includes one. As we have seen, this reflects comically the procedure of the *Metamorphoses* themselves, but also suggests the creative function of parody and its capacity to renew literary tradition: with the loss of his third and last head at the hands of Persée, the Monster's life story should end but does not. It is miraculously transformed and continued, like the parody's model (or indeed its target) which seems to die but is reborn. Parody deals the supposedly final blow and gives the regenerative kiss: it is less like Persée than Andromède, who plays at tormenting the Dragon and then puts her arms affectionately round his neck. Here, the Dragon's fate functions as a direct metaphor for the parody at hand as well, which appears to draw to a close but is unexpectedly continued in the epilogue.

Andromède is so overwhelmed by the Monster's metamorphosis and the parodic turn of events that she at first risks having one of her recurrent "coups de tête" (277). But the story has had its effect. She accepts the Dragon's practical wisdom that life must be lived, however many surprises it entails along the way: "Mais il faut bien vivre, et vivre cette vie, quelque grands yeux étonnés qu'elle vous fasse ouvrir à chaque tournant de route" (277). She has learned her lesson, and that of parody generally, which likewise surprises the reader at every turn but must be accepted and followed, with the faith that in the end there will be, if not a moral to explain it, as here, at least a modicum of pleasure in the reading.

The heroine's reaction here is important, for it prepares us for the most startling "tournant de route" of the narrative thus far. As the new couple lands in Ethiopia, home of Andromède's father, we are forced, by an extraordinary parenthetical aside, to abandon the story altogether:

> Et [ils] abordèrent le troisième jour en Ethiopie, où régnait l'inconsolable père d'Andromède (je laisse à penser sa joie). (278)

Although we have witnessed a great deal of authorial intervention over the course of the story, we are not prepared for the casual appearance of this parenthetical "je," for we have nowhere encountered the first-person singular outside the direct speeches of the characters themselves. Here the story-within-the-story first identifies itself; the narrator drops his mask of authorial omniscience and becomes a character. With this interruption of the narrative just as it seems to approach its end, we are denied both the reality and finality of the story; the events which we witnessed were actually a tale recited, and we must suffer the frustration of not seeing it reach the happy conclusion toward which it is heading. We are left to imagine the joy of Andromède's father at this reunion, but the text refuses to affirm it and thus leaves us ever imagining. Moreover, if we have learned the lesson of the parody, we must imagine the unimaginable, the unexpected, the unconventional, the "inouï" (271), the parodic: the story has a future beyond this apparent ending, and it may not be as we expect. The parody invites the reader to be an author too, and perhaps even to follow the example of that other reader-author, the parodist.

But tearing us from the lovers and putting us in a present which, according to the conventions of narrative, we had willingly suspended, the "je" serves as a bridge between the story and the epilogue. This presents a polite gathering to which we might easily belong, for the narrator discusses the story which he has just told, and which we have just read. Outside the context of parody, the relation of the epilogue to the story is unclear and its content puzzling; however, read in terms of the self-reflexive and specifically self-critical function described in chapter 1, it becomes a commentary on the preceding tale and, even more importantly, on itself:

— Ah! ça, mon cher monsieur Amyot de l'Epinal, vous nous la baillez belle avec votre histoire! s'écria la princesse d'U.E. (en ramenant un peu son châle, car cette splendide nuit était fraîche). Moi qui avais donné tout autrement mon coeur à cette aventure de Persée et Andromède! Je ne vous chicanerai pas sur la façon dont vous avez travesti ce pauvre Persée. (Je vous le pardonne en faveur de la main de maître dont vous m'avez flattée, à l'antique, s'entend, sous les traits d'Andromède). Mais le dénouement de l'histoire! Qu'est-ce que ce Monstre à qui nul ne s'était intéressé jusqu'ici? Et puis, cher monsieur Amyot de l'Epinal, levez donc un peu les yeux vers la carte céleste de la nuit. Ce couple de nébuleuses, là-bas, près de *Cassiopée,* ne l'appelle-t-on pas *Persée et Andromède?* tandis que tout là-bas, cette file sinueuse d'étoiles, c'est, avec son air de paria, la constellation du *Dragon,* qui vivote entre *la Grande Ourse* et *la Petite Ourse,* ses pareils mal léchés? . . .
— Chère U . . . , cela ne prouve rien. Les cieux sont sereins et conventionnels; autant vaudrait dire que vos yeux sont simplement bruns (vous ne le voudriez pas). Non; car voyez de même, d'autre part, là-bas, près de *la Lyre,* qui est ma constellation, n'est-ce pas *le Cygne,* qui est la constellation de Lohengrin et a la forme d'une croix en souvenir de Parsifal?

Et cependant vous avouerez que moi et ma *Lyre* n'avons rien à voir avec Lohengrin et Parsifal?
— C'est vrai, c'est paraboliquement vrai. Mais il n'y a jamais moyen de discuter et de *s'instruire* avec vous. Allons, rentrons prendre le thé. Ah! à propos, et la moralité? J'oublie toujours la moralité. . . .
— La voici:

> Jeunes filles, regardez-y à deux fois
> Avant de dédaigner un pauvre monstre.
> Ainsi que cette histoire vous le montre,
> Celui-ci était digne d'être le plus heureux des trois. (278f.)[15]

The narrator's name itself reflects significantly on the story and is crucial for interpreting the epilogue: as the famous translator of Plutarch's *Moralia* and the *Ethiopica* of Heliodorus, Amyot provides an appropriate precedent for this teller of an *Histoire éthiopienne*, itself a *Moralité*. But our Amyot may be distinguished from his Renaissance ancestor by his family name, which in the nineteenth century could not fail to recall the most famous product of that region, the popular *images d'Epinal*. "Amyot de l'Epinal" thus alludes to the parody: an Ethiopian story and moral work, translated from the ancient into a popularized, and trivialized, version. The narrator is a parodist, and his words should thus be taken as critically as those of the parody itself.

The Princess begins by scolding the narrator for trying to deceive the audience with his unorthodox version of the legend ("Ah! ça, mon cher monsieur Amyot de l'Epinal, vous nous la baillez belle avec votre histoire!"). She knows the original *Persée et Andromède* and objects to the triumph of the Monster at the end of this one. The parody is false, merely a deception, because of its infidelity to the original. To support her view of its falsity, she cites the version of this legend written in the night sky: the nebulas Persée and Andromède form a couple on one side of the heavens, while far from them is located the appropriately sinuous constellation of the Dragon, looking the part of the outcast ("avec son air de paria"). Clearly the Princess thinks that this astronomical separation is definitive and should remain authoritative; the Monster should not win Andromeda. The night sky contains the true version, consistent with her knowledge of the original.

But the Princess weakens her case considerably by her strange reference to the two Bears. Without it, we would attribute the Dragon's "pariah look" to his separation from Perseus and Andromeda. However, the Princess evokes the Bears as further proof that the Dragon is a real outcast (and therefore unworthy of Andromeda): he keeps like company, the Bears are "ses pareils mal léchés." She thus betrays the fatal flaw in her reasoning which is inspired by nothing more than a cliché. For the Princess, the Dragon belongs with the Bears because he is *un ours mal léché,* an unpolished, uncouth individual. Her belief in the truth value of the stars' story rests on a cliché; it is no more or less true than the version which she has just heard and condemned for its falsity and deception.

The narrator's response aims at defending his unorthodox version by discrediting the one told in the heavens ("cela ne prouve rien"): that one is conventional, and the conventional story is not always true. To prove his point, he calls upon another story told similarly in the sky: his constellation, Lyra, is close to Cygnus, the constellation of Lohengrin in the form of a cross reminiscent of Parsifal (just as the Dragon is near the Bears, and Perseus near Andromeda). However, to show that this proximity signifies no real relation, and may in fact be false and deceptive, he poses a rhetorical question demonstrating that he and his Lyra have nothing to do with Lohengrin and Parsifal ("Et cependant vous avouerez que moi et ma *Lyre* n'avons rien à voir avec Lohengrin et Parsifal?"). The narrator argues not for the truth of his unusual version, the parody, but merely for the possible falsity of the conventional one. Both may in fact be false, fictions, but the conventional one is not truer than the parody.

The Princess is obliged to agree ("c'est vrai, c'est paraboliquement vrai"); the narrator's constellation example has the truth of a parable. But the adverb, usually reserved for the geometric sense of "parabole" (parabola), calls attention to the term.[16] A parable is, according to the Biblical formula, impenetrable for those who do not believe, intelligible for those who do. If, as she here somewhat petulantly admits, the Princess is unable to learn from the narrator, it is because she has not learned the lesson of the parody itself. She who sees herself "à l'antique" in that other princess of the story, Andromède, has not reached *her* same wisdom, that is, the knowledge that life and stories are a series of surprises which must be accepted and met, "quelques grands yeux étonnés qu'elle vous fasse ouvrir à chaque tournant de route." The Princess is vain enough to see Andromède as a version of herself, but foolish enough to miss the moral of her story. As with Andromède before her education, the egoism of the Princess is a barrier to understanding both herself and stories. Small wonder that she "always forgets the moral." The rhyming *moralité*, with its formulaic resemblance to *poésie populaire*, expresses the lesson that Andromède herself learned; but it holds a particular warning for the Princess, who disdains that most conspicuous monster of all, the parody itself, which, after *Perseus and Andromeda* and *Beauty and the Beast,* unexpectedly turns out, like the Monster, to be "le plus heureux des trois" and to have a life of its own.

By placing us readers in the company of the Princess hearing the story, Laforgue makes us see ourselves in her, and in this way issues a warning. A parody is only deceptive and false for those who take stories to be real, as the Princess did the tale told in the sky. We should learn the lesson of this story, and of parody generally, and take them all as fictions, to be told and even, like this one, retold. The rhyming moral itself implies the possibility of alternative versions: "*un* pauvre monstre," of which "cette histoire" and "celui-ci" are merely a particular case; other monsters, other parodies, remain to be created and may even survive their models.

But the parody has also taught us, through its structure and the narrator's name, to doubt the narrator himself. He is a parodist, and his words should be interpreted critically, however much they agree with the sceptical message of the genre—that stories are fictions and must not be taken as true or final. Indeed, in a radical turnaround that questions this, the very message of parody, Laforgue includes a final irony which ensures the parody's relentless criticism of itself. The narrator's confident assertion that the skies are unreliable for measuring truth, on the grounds that he and his Lyra have nothing to do with Lohengrin and Parsifal, is called into question by the easy and conspicuous pun on "*Lyre*": on the con-

Persée et Andromède

trary, the parodist's lyre has certainly had something to do with Lohengrin and Parsifal, just two stories previously, in the obviously related title, *Lohengrin, fils de Parsifal*. Perhaps proximity *does* signify a relation, after all, and the parodist's point about the falsity of stories is wrong. Moreover, his reasoning may be not simply faulty but, worse still, deliberately specious, and his intentions as deceptive as those of which the Princess first accused him. The parody refuses to make the charge openly; the narrator is, after all, distinct from the parodist of the other stories, and his point made in the ambiguous negative-interrogative form. But, given the highly contrived parallel, the connection cannot be missed, and the parody thus undermines itself. Laforgue takes the scepticism of parody to its furthest extreme, casting into doubt not only the truth of the original, but, more radically, the very scepticism of the parody. He thus creates the most monstrous *tournant de route* to confront even the sophisticated reader of parody, who with wide-eyed surprise can only carry on, taking the story as a fiction, even if it turns out to be *true*.

8

Pan et la Syrinx, ou l'invention de la flûte à sept tuyaux

Laforgue was interested in the figure of Pan from early on.[1] He had read Mallarmé's "Après-midi d'un faune" (1876), featuring the same legend and themes: the faun's pursuit of the nymphs who escape him, desire as the pursuit of the unattainable, and the consolation provided by art.[2] It had definite Decadent associations, since Huysmans made it a favorite of des Esseintes and described it at some length in *A Rebours*. The subject may also have been suggested to him by the recently completed *Persée et Andromède*, which has the same source, Ovid's *Metamorphoses*. It of course is prominent in history painting from the Renaissance onward, in works, for example, by Jordaens, Poussin, Pellegrini, Tiepolo, and Boucher.

The legend of Pan and Syrinx as told in *Metamorphoses* I (689–712) recounts the god's pursuit of the chaste nymph in the mountains of Arcadia, and her metamorphosis into marsh reeds by the nymphs of the stream Ladon, her father, in answer to her prayer. Pan's sigh of disappointment at losing the object of his desire produces sweet music as it stirs the reeds and inspires him to invent the reed-pipe; his relations with the maiden are in this way consummated but displaced to the level of art. The story arises in answer to a question posed by Argus to Mercury, disguised as a shepherd, about the origin of the reed-pipe, and thus functions as a myth.

Pan et la Syrinx carries no epigraph but, like *Hamlet* and *Persée et*

Andromède, has a subtitle which, qualifying the original title, immediately signals the parody: "L'invention de la flûte à sept tuyaux" identifies the outcome of the story *avant la lettre* and likens it to its Ovidian model. The subtitle validates the pretext of the original and makes it a central theme of the parody. Indeed, Laforgue gives to Pan's music making as important a place as his more traditional pursuit of Syrinx. *Pan et la Syrinx ou l'invention de la flûte à sept tuyaux* recounts the Artist's desire, his search for an expression equal to his ideal, but ever fugitive, inspiration.

Several aspects of the traditional story make it relevant to Laforgue's aesthetic and metaphysical concerns. As we have seen, the impossibility of sustained love constitutes a major theme of Decadence, which he treated in all his writings. Pan's failure to possess Syrinx except through his art lends itself easily to a Laforguian interpretation of the relation between love and artistic creation, woman and poet. Art provides a substitute for love, which is ever fugitive and unattainable, an Ideal glimpsed and vigorously pursued but inaccessible except in song. Furthermore, it compensates for the loss of love by ensuring poetic creation: the metamorphosis of Syrinx into marsh reeds furnishes the instrument by means of which Pan produces his music; and her disappearance is likewise the source of his inspiration, in the form of nostalgia. The conventional aspects of the legend correspond well to the pessimism of the late nineteenth century. Pan's relentless pursuit is futile and wins him only the *pis-aller* of art; but art is nevertheless the greatest of compensations and, as Syrinx herself remarks, the most viable and durable source of human happiness.

Mallarmé's treatment of the myth in "L'Après-midi d'un faune" features many of these themes. The faun's wish to "perpetuate" the nymphs, expressed in the first line of the poem, reflects both his erotic and his aesthetic desire. Laforgue puts this idea more directly—"l'art, c'est le désir perpétué" (304)—but parodically makes it the wisdom of Syrinx herself, who condescendingly imparts it to Pan. The faun's uncertainty, throughout Mallarmé's poem, about the reality of his erotic experience ("Aimai-je un rêve?", l. 3), and the italicized verse in which he remembers and reenacts it, resemble Pan's songs at the beginning of Laforgue's story:

> *En rêve, je l'ai vue,*
> *La petite Eve bienvenue!*
> *Epiphanie, Epiphanie!*
> *Mais ce n'était que mon génie.* (285)

Both works represent the essence of desire—the unattainability of the object—and its sublimation into art, the "solo long" and "sonore, vaine et monotone ligne" of the poem, the "long et unique sanglot" (290) and "gamme nostalgique" (310) of the story.

Like the other *Moralités*, *Pan et la Syrinx* modernizes the story and its significance by converting traditional themes and *topoi* into contemporary Decadent ones. The relatively simple theme of art as a product of loss is inserted into the complicated evolutionary and pantheistic metaphysics of Decadence. Pan's pursuit of Syrinx becomes a metaphor not only for the inevitable failure of love but also for the general condition of man, endlessly in pursuit of an unattainable ideal toward which everything in the universe aspires. The elusiveness of love reflects on a larger scale the metaphysical problem of the late nineteenth century. But it is in the very nature of love both to disappoint and to inspire: hence Laforgue's Syrinx, in contrast to the original heroine, personally urges the breeze to hand over her soul to the inconsolable Pan. The Ideal gives over some of its mystery, in the form of inspiration and aesthetic emotion, to one who has suffered loss.

Laforgue parodically undercuts even this already pessimistic consolation by suggesting that the artist's new creation, product of his loss, has no practical significance, makes no change in the world whatsoever, except to restore him to his futile pursuit. Pan's new song—a vehement imprecation against the sterile, insensitive moon—has no effect on the immovable Diana; it merely sets him once again on a quest for the ideal and with it, a new round of desire and frustration. Art dispels the illusion of our hopes for the Ideal but creates another one and returns us to the quest, enabling, or rather obliging, us to live. Pan's experience reflects and confirms the workings of parody itself, undermining our belief in the truth or authority of one work but making from that a new one which enables the process to continue.

Laforgue's hero has three major concerns, from which derive the main parodic alterations to the story. The first carries to an extreme—and renders ludicrous—the frustration of the Mallarmean *faune vierge:* "Immortel et jeune, Pan n'a jamais aimé comme lui et moi l'entendons" (283). The ancient master of seduction—a companion in revels of Dionysus, and renowned for his lasciviousness and eroticism—becomes in Laforgue's version a lovesick, love-starved, lonely insomniac who whiles away the hours voicing his complaint on a very inadequate pipe, and imagining the ideal lady who would come adoringly into his "bras prospères" (286). As with Hamlet, Pan's fantasies are exaggerated, egotistical, and wholly unsuited to the reality that will present itself to him in the delicious, but resistant, form of Syrinx.

Pan's second parodic problem lies in the metaphor of his erotic life, his music making. This god of woodland song is dissatisfied with his rudimentary pipe, with its limited four-note range, and wants a better one. His "imparfait et monotone pipeau-galoubet" (283) does not suffice to express his current inspiration, the pain of unfulfilled desire: "Que faire, quand on *aime,* sinon attendre ainsi en plein air en essayant de s'exprimer par l'art?" (283). He indeed awaits and sings, but the old and faithful companion, the "vieux biniou," the "galoubet à deux sous," will not even communicate his desire, much less satisfy it. Laforgue's unhappy artist longs for a more sophisticated means of expression, "une flûte plus compliquée" (288), and he will get one, ironically, with the loss of Syrinx, whose metamorphosis engenders the new invention. Pan is fulfilled in one way as he is frustrated in another: his wishes for his art come true, but only at the cost of his beloved.

Pan's love and his music are repeatedly associated with his third problem, a typically Decadent, Laforguian, and parodic one. The Mallarmean ambiguity of the faun's past experience—dream or reality—is here converted into Pan's fundamental inability to grasp the present, particularly where Syrinx is concerned: "Qu'il se persuade et se pénètre d'abord qu'elle est là, et que c'est du présent!" (288). This recurrent wish accounts for both his failure with the nymph and the failure of his art to express "la chose qu'est la chose" (300). Pan indeed has trouble dealing with reality. When he finally ventures a declaration of love, he immediately discredits it, retracts it, or provides Syrinx with objections to use against him (290). He considers throwing himself at her feet to dazzle her, but refrains, and instead of returning her smile with a "brave sourire" (291) of his own, shrugs his shoulders and feigns a nonchalant look. In the end, after losing her to the river, he reproaches himself for not acting more decisively from the beginning:

> ... Et c'est encore une fois que je n'aurai pas eu la présence d'esprit de me pénétrer du fait de la présence des choses! J'aurais pu la dévisager pour toujours et l'écouter pour jamais et prendre sa formule sur le vif! Au lieu de cela, j'ai pensé, à quoi? à tout? Et c'est passé. Oh! que je suis donc incurablement en Tout! Que je suis insouciant! Oh! qui jettera un pont entre mon coeur et le présent! (308)

Pan's rhetoric gives an idea of his problem. His free mélange of clichés is comical—*présence d'esprit / présence des choses,* and the double-entendre in *prendre sur le vif*—but it also reflects the love of talk and the reluctance to act that Laforgue consistently mocks in the sensibility of his age. Pan is too busy thinking and talking to seize reality when it offers itself. The story provides an answer to his question of bridging the gap between his heart and the present, by implying that reality and the present may only be grasped once they have passed. Only when Syrinx has escaped him does he manage to act decisively and effectively; "sans hésiter, sans se gratter l'oreille ni tirer sa barbiche pointue" (306), he captures her spirit as it floats through the reeds in his arms and encloses it within the brand-new flute. He ultimately learns that reality is best understood in art and that the most perfect art derives from nostalgia and regret. Only after he has loved and lost does he invent a perfect flute, create a purer song, express "la chose qu'est la chose," the soul of the lost Syrinx, and live tolerably, if not happily, ever after as an artist.

Through these three related themes, Laforgue explicitly threads the one of modernity. Pan is concerned with the modern quality of his love: "Et tout l'Olympe parlera du génie de Pan et de ses amours si nouvelles, si pleines d'un caractère moderne" (300). Syrinx herself has the characteristics of a "new woman," and her determination to preserve her indépendance and solitude reflects the wave of the future, "un signe de temps nouveaux" (305). Pan worries that his genius will not meet the challenge of the new era,

Pan et la Syrinx

"cette révélation de temps nouveaux auxquels son génie ne va peut-être pas suffire" (305). All this calls attention to the principle of the story itself, by which the ancient legend is modernized, and suggests the relevance of the parody as a modern creation. Pan's hopes for a modern love are disappointed, but he creates a modern flute ("des plus nouvelles") and a modern song, a "miraculeuse gamme d'ère nouvelle" (306), paradoxically expressing "la chose qu'est la chose" with the aesthetic distance provided by time. Pan's song grasps the spirit of the present through a backward glance and produces modern song, the soul of Syrinx preserved in the new flute and transformed into sound. The story argues for the importance of memory in seizing the quality, significance, even truth of an ephemeral moment, and in producing thereby a truly modern art.[3]

Laforgue makes his Pan and Syrinx a thoroughly modern couple, who interrupt their legendary chase to discuss the nature of love and art, the perpetual misunderstanding between the sexes, the metaphysics of the Ideal, even the etymology of *aimer*. The chase itself is as much a battle of wits as a contest of strength and endurance. Pan retains his traditional half-goat, half-human form, but otherwise is a frustrated 1880s artist. He is neurotic, obsessed with love, and filled with the principles of Decadent philosophy, especially a pervasive fatalism, which he evokes constantly and indiscriminately: "arrivera ce qui doit arriver" (290), "tout est dans tout," and "Je saurai la prendre par quelques considérations fatalistes" (301). He pities himself for being misunderstood and unwanted, and insists on his "bon grand coeur" (294), his "belle âme" (285), his "âme d'un grand pasteur" (296), and his "tristesse de génie" (294). He has difficulty sleeping, suffers from fever, and is troubled by dreams. He has mournful eyes and the traditional expression of tension and stress, clenched teeth (288). We are told parenthetically that he no longer does exercises: although "immortel et jeune" (283), Pan is old before his time, worn out by the "antinomies irréductibles" of his endless meditations (288). The extent of his desperation at the point where Syrinx enters the story may be measured by the fact that he is willing to accept "la Femme" without further ado: "Et aujourd'hui, malade de grand amour comme il l'est, il accepterait la Femme sans discuter. . . ." (288).

But the text parodically associates this Decadent, Hamletic hero with a less complicated character, whose legendary violence and crudity call into question the innocence of Pan's behavior: Shakespeare's Caliban ("il se roule devant elle dans les thyms, comme un sale Caliban, et gémit," 292). The integration of the rough primitive of *The Tempest* into the suffering hero undermines Pan's careful metaphysical arguments for the inevitability of his love for Syrinx and suggests his real motivation, the thoroughly more Pan-like sensuality of Caliban. But the choice of Caliban is not arbitrary: in the end, Pan inverts his role, from Caliban to something more like Ariel, a true artist, who, "au-dessus du Présent," seizes the present only in being detached from it in regret.[4]

The beauty of Laforgue's Syrinx is calculated to throw Pan into the sort of frenzied panic that he traditionally inspires in others. She has the qualities of the typical Laforguian lady: predictably large "heavenly" (288) eyes, an "otherworldly" (288) mouth, her hair put up in a large diadem atop her head, long, perfect legs, and pale "lunar" breasts.[5] She is fair, modest, and virginal, with a nostalgic, clear voice, a disarmingly direct and intelligent gaze, and, much to Pan's surprise, a streak of independence and pride reminiscent of Andromède's. If Pan is Caliban, Syrinx is a Wagnerian Valkyrie, as much a warrior maiden as a helpless victim, who repeatedly cries the famous "Hoyotoho, Heiaha!" (298 passim) of Brunnhilde herself. She resists his advances with scornful *hauteur* and guards her independence jealously; a companion of chaste Diana, and as hard-hearted, she is untroubled by the sexual desire that so torments Pan. She inspires a love like that of Diana herself, "dont les amours n'ont pas de lendemain, mais seulement des veilles" (303), to be approached but never fulfilled, as Pan later learns. Unlike him, she lives an orderly life with adequate, uninterrupted sleep, no fevers, plenty of exercise, and a clear moral code to follow, all of which will serve her well during the chase. She resists the sensuality of the night: "O crépuscule, tu ne me touches pas, tu ne me toucheras jamais! la volupté positive ne saurait filtrer dans le ciboire de mon être!" (302); unmoved by Pan's pragmatic arguments about loneliness and oncoming winter, she proclaims her ability to live on new-fallen snow (304). She is repeatedly described as "inhumaine" (305), "surhumaine" (288, 295), a "divine enfant" (299) and "déesse" (291), not only because she is a nymph, but also because she embodies an Ideal well out of the reach of men, even half-men, half-gods, like Pan. She represents the lunar ideal that has attracted and tormented most of the heroes of the *Moralités,* here transformed, according to the legend, into an elusive beloved.

Laforgue plays with the old pun by which Pan is associated with the all. According to his name, the hero should be everything, but is actually rather little:

> [Syrinx] — . . . Vous êtes bien réaliste.
> — Je suis Pan.
> — Pan qui?
> — Je suis . . . bien peu en ce moment, mais en général je suis tout, je suis le tout s'il en fut. Comprenez-moi, c'est moi qui suis et la plainte du vent . . .
> — Et Eole, alors?
> — Mais non, comprenez-moi! Je suis les choses, la vie, les choses, classiquement, en un sens. Non, je ne suis rien, rien. Ah, je suis bien malheureux! Si, du moins, j'avais un instrument plus riche que ce galoubet! je vous chanterais tout ce que je suis! (291f.)

The exchange comically points up all the contradictions in Pan, who rather than everything is nothing at all, except perhaps unhappy; whose name leaves little trace in reality of its sense of "les choses" except for the "realistic" character that Syrinx notices in him; whose "all" is so unapparent as to demand a surname ("Pan qui?"); who, alleged symbol of the universe, is less well-known as the wind's lament than Aeolus and suffers the added indignity of a hint of superfluity. Pan has a problem of identity because he cannot express himself properly, a relation underscored by the punning "je vous chanterais *tout* ce que je suis": not only all, but the All, Pan, ultimate subject of his own song.

Laforgue also gives a Decadent twist to Pan's name by exploiting the Hartmannian sense of "Tout," the universal law: "Voulez-vous vous laisser être tout pour moi, au nom de Tout?" (292). Pan's declaration is, as Syrinx remarks, realistic, based on the practical consideration that it is in the nature of things for them to love ("Oh, vous, là! Et moi, ici! Oh, vous! Oh, moi! Tout est dans Tout!" 296). This last, his favorite expression, occurs at least eight times; the old axiom, used in normal circumstances to express the comical futility of complicated cosmic theories, becomes a serious expression of the Decadent one. Pan speaks in a "pantheistic" voice not only because of the obvious play on his name, but also because he is a pantheist in the most literal nineteenth-century sense, a follower of Spinoza, Schopenhauer, and Hartmann, who subscribes to the doctrine that the All—be it God, the Will, or the Unconscious—is the immanent cause of everything, and everything is contained in it. Syrinx, on the other hand, is "spiritualiste" (296), believing in the superiority of spirit over matter, and the total separation of the two. Laforgue's allegory suggests that, though the artist may be a pantheist, ever pursuing the Ideal, the Ideal remains resolutely, like Syrinx, spiritualistic, forever distinct and beyond his reach.[6]

The two main characters present striking similarities to those of Laforgue's other lunar story, *Lohengrin,* except that the roles are reversed. Syrinx has many of the characteristics of Lohengrin himself: egoism, chastity, a cult of sterility, devotion to the moon, resistance to love, associations with images of purity. Pan, on the other hand, has the sensuality and earthiness of the "terre-à-terre" Elsa. This inversion suggests a certain self-parody on Laforgue's part, with the consequences that always derive from such: calling attention to the parodic status of the work at hand and its susceptibility to parody in its turn. If *Pan et la Syrinx* can invert another *Moralité,* surely it, as a *Moralité* itself, may be treated likewise. In his final story, Laforgue implies that the earlier scheme of *Lohengrin* may be changed, or interpreted differently, as easily as it altered its Wagnerian model. The Decadent myth of the pure, innocent, sincere man ever at odds with the fearsome sexuality of the Eternal Feminine is here inverted, and its truth therefore undermined. Laforgue demonstrates the pliability of any commonplace belief, the adaptability of any story; but he also brings out the creative possibilities of parody, which may regenerate itself in the parody of a parody, producing ultimately another fiction.

The Story

Laforgue preserves in his plot the main events of the legend: Pan's meeting with Syrinx as she comes down from Mount Lycaeus, his pursuit, her metamorphosis into the marsh reeds, and his invention of the reed-pipe. The text twice reminds the reader explicitly of its alleged fidelity to the original, thereby drawing attention to the parody, to the distance between the story and the original. As Pan sets off in pursuit of the fugitive Syrinx, the narrative comments: "Et la légendaire poursuite de la nymphe Syrinx par le dieu Pan dans l'Arcadie commence" (294); and later, when Syrinx takes up her flight again: "Et la légendaire poursuite de la nymphe Syrinx par le dieu Pan continue . . ." (299). The latter phrase provides a surprise for there is no "continuation" in the traditional version, where the chase is a single event; it expresses the status of the parody itself as a continuation of that first "legendary pursuit." Similarly, Laforgue often signals the distinction between present and past, a device which seems to preserve the original and to deny the modernization of the parody, whereas it actually points up a conspicuous relation between them. For example, an acknowledgment of historicity, such as "O longue journée légendaire, tu es loin, tu ne reviendras plus! . . . Cela se passait en Arcadie avant la venue des Pélasges" (294), actually reminds the reader of the present time of the narrative and thus calls attention to the parodic modernization that it is meant to deny. Here, the assertion is further belied by "légendaire": the chase and the day are legendary in so far as they have already been told and relate to the present; although they will not happen again, they may nevertheless be retold, reenacted, as in this *Moralité légendaire*.

The first sentence places the story in Pan's conventional Arcadia (283), but it is immediately undermined by the narrator's comment that this might just as well be anywhere: "Tout le monde a passé par une belle matinée d'été dans une vallée folâtrement merveilleuse, tout le monde dira: 'Je sais ce que c'est'" (283). This aside serves Laforgue's parodic and modernizing purposes by destroying the specificity of the story's time and place, universalizing them, and thus likening Pan's situation (if not his story) to that of "tout le monde," including ourselves. If we recognize the setting and surroundings, perhaps it is because we have seen them before, in the original, for example, or even in our own experience: this is the legend of Pan, but transposed into the world of the contemporary reader. Moreover, if we know Pan's lovely summer country morning, perhaps we are also implicated in what goes on there. Laforgue thus subtly works the reader into the parody.

Laforgue's insistence on the unspecificity of Pan's surroundings, however, does not prevent him from dwelling lyrically on the beauty of the setting: warm sunshine pouring its rays into the valley like the full waterfulls of spring, a foaming flood of Champagne bathing the groves and hillsides;[7] a radiant summer morning with fragrant thyme, buzzing bees, chirring cicadas, grazing animals, warbling birds, lush vegetation, all reminding Pan of the "universal bonheur si insaisissable" (285) that eludes him. Laforgue's Arcadia is the idyllic one of Virgil and, later, the European Renaissance, a land of youth, beauty, harmony, and happiness reflected in the interior rhymes of the language itself: "O milliards de prismes d'optimisme! O Jeunesse, ô beauté, ô unanimité! Oh, du soleil!" (283). The subjectivity typical of Laforguian narrative here serves the theme of universal harmony, and emotion is integrated easily into the description of the fine weather: "il fait heureux à perte de vue" (285). The well-being of Nature reminds Pan all the more clearly of his inability to follow its example: "— Et c'est la radieuse matinée, et tout le soleil et l'universel bonheur si insaisissable! Et voilà; à lui de s'arranger pour être heureux, comme cette matinée s'est arrangée pour être heureuse" (285). "Insaisissable" provides a conspicuous clue to the sense of Pan's later chase: that primary "être insaisissable," Syrinx, represents the "universel bonheur" which he strives in vain to possess and express.

As the story opens, Pan is playing out his "doléances très personnelles" (283) on his pipe. This gives him the occasion to develop his philosophy of love, which he derives in a ludicrous display of typical etymological ingenuity:

> — O femme, femme! toi qui fais l'humanité monomane! Je t'aime, je t'aime! Mais qu'est ce mot: Je t'*aime*? . . . *Aime* ne me dit quelque chose que lorsque j'associe à ce son, et par une inspiration non fantaisiste, le son du mot britannique *aim* qui veut dire *but*! — Ah! *but,* oui! "Je t'*aime*" signifierait ainsi: "Je tends vers toi, tu es mon but!" (286)

The verbal trick points up the flaws in Pan's method: if he associates the French *aime* with the English "aim" (*but*), he might also associate the French *but* with the English "but" (*mais*), which fits nicely into his own exclamation, "Ah, *but,* oui!." Pan uses the etymological argument repeatedly to justify his behavior to Syrinx: "Mais, que je t'aime, que je t'aime, que tu es donc mon but!" (295); "Parce que je vous *aime,* vous êtes mon but!" (296, cf. also 297, 303). The argument is wrong, however, like the philosophy which it is evoked to support; if to love means to aim toward, to take the beloved as a goal, it follows, contrary to what Pan thinks, that the object must remain out of reach. Only Syrinx, ironically, understands the consequences of this, as she will observe later: "le bonheur est dans la poursuite de l'Idéal" (297).[8]

Pan's songs paint a portrait of the lady of his dreams in recognizably Laforguian free-verse lines, many direct from Laforgue's own poems:[9]

> *L'Autre sexe! L'Autre sexe!*
> *Oh! toute la petite Eve*
> *Qui s'avance, ravie de son rôle*
> *Avec les yeux illuminés*
> *D'hyménée . . .* (284)

One might have expected Syrinx, or Echo, or at the very least a classical name, but Pan's ideal feminine is the model of the Eternal Feminine, Eve. However, Pan's image is not the standard destructive woman, but the adoring lady, eager to play out her role of victim and to throw herself into his prosperous arms:

> *Oh! dites, dites!*
> *La petite Eve descendant des cimes,*
> *Avec sa chair de victime*
> *Et son âme tout en rougeurs subites! . . .*
> *. . .*
> *Puis, proclamant, fièrement campée:*
> *"Je ne suis pas un petit paon,*
> *"Je ne suis pas une poupée!*
> *"Je me suis tout échappée*
> *"Pour venir échouer sur le coeur du grand Pan!*
> *"Oh! je suis pure comme une tulipe*
> *"Et vierge de toutes espèces de principes!*
> *"Avril! avril!*
> *"Mon bonheur ne tient qu'à un fil!"*

> ...
> *Oh, ce sera tant toi!*
> *Ingénieusement je t'emmènerai*
> *Au plus profond des bois,*
> *Là où il fait le plus frais;*
> *Et puis, tu pourras t'étirer sur le gazon,*
> *Après tant d'après-midi virginales,*
> *Et t'abandonner à la bonne saison*
> *Dans l'assourdissement des cigales.* (284-6)

As in all the other stories, this autocitation implicates the author, and with him the reader, in the parody.[10] The fact that it is Pan who recites them makes the self-parody all the more ironic. The parodist may be an artist and a lover, like Pan, dissatisfied with his art, disgusted with his song, always seeking an Ideal that remains resolutely out of reach; but he may also, like Pan at the end, produce from that effort a song eminently adequate to the "ère nouvelle," the parody itself.

Pan's essential problem of misjudging reality is apparent from the comical discrepancy between the image of the beloved in his songs and the harsh reality of Syrinx that they miraculously conjure up. She indeed "descend des cimes," of Mount Lycaeus (292) and approaches him in the sunshine; he will have ample occasion during the chase to remind her of her "chair de victime" and the cool deep wood where he plans to lead her; she has "regards ravis" (287), and is as "pure" and "fièrement campée" a lady as he is ever likely to encounter. But the resemblance ceases there, for the independence attributed to her in the song will rebound upon Pan himself. The proudly proclaimed "Je ne suis pas un petit paon" of the song finds its parodic equivalent in her haughty accusation: "Me tenez-vous pour un animal, un petit animal classé? Savez-vous que je suis inestimable!" (296). Pan, of course, would love to consider her a little animal, particularly "aux abois," as he fantasizes several times, but Laforgue turns this back on the hero by giving Syrinx total control over the pack: she has a "voix habituée à lancer et retenir les meutes de Diane" (296). The comical echo of "Pan" in "paon" further turns Pan's song against himself. Syrinx is not a figurative little Pan, a child of his imagination, a creation of his fantasies to serve the same, but rather an individual, "toute vivante et en chair et en os" (287). Even Pan notices a contrast between her appearance and his image: "elle ne paraît guère pressentir qu'elle est au monde pour s'abandonner comme cela à la belle saison dans l'étourdissement des cigales" (287f.). The words come from his verses; the reality of Syrinx will largely parody the illusion of his songs.

Here Laforgue revises a standard Decadent theme—the deceptive innocence of the lady's face which belies her sexual function—to point to the parody: Syrinx does not look as though she was born to abandon herself, or otherwise to fulfill Pan's fantasies, precisely because she has no intention of doing so. On the contrary, she has an extraordinary determination to preserve her virginal solitude: "Sachez que mon orgueil de rester moi-même égale au moins ma miraculeuse beauté" (296). Pan misjudges reality because he interprets it according to his own desire, in flagrant contradiction to the facts, especially that of Syrinx's will. His experience with her is a series of disappointed expectations, humorously portraying not only the inevitable misunderstanding between the sexes and the folly of the egotistical sensibility, but also the lesson of parody itself. Pan interprets reality according to a fiction and thus functions as a warning lest the reader do likewise. Unlike the hero, however, the reader of parody, constantly reminded of the fiction on which it is based, benefits from the aesthetic distance and hindsight that Pan will find only in loss.

Significantly, Syrinx's presence inspires him only to parodic lyricism, as he succeeds in singing the "antique ballade," "Je suis dégoûté des fraises des bois":

> *Je suis dégoûté des fraises des bois,*
> *Depuis que j'ai vu en rêve*
> *Ma petite Eve*
> *Me sourire mais en mettant un doigt*
> *Sur les lèvres.*
>
> . . .
>
> *Mystère et sourire,*
> *O mon beau navire!*
> *Sourire et puis chut*
> *Ah! tais-toi, mon luth!* (287)

The first line makes clear that the song is a parody, all the more ironic coming from the lips of the pastoral woodland god. The comical final couplet, with its "chut"/"luth" rhyme and its indelicate command to the instrument, parodically undercuts not only the preceding song but also the most basic symbol of lyric poetry itself. This poet does not take up his lute, according to poetic convention, as in the famous formula of Musset ("Poète, prends ton luth"), but tells it unceremoniously to shut up. The parody within the parody reflects on the larger story, all the more so in that it is, like the *Moralité,* an "antique ballade," the ancient story retold comically by a modern poet; it also provides an example of Pan's unsatisfactory songs, his inability to create a lyric adequate to the seriousness of his desire and inspiration.

The interview between the two is characterized by awkward silences, misunderstandings, and a repartee that threatens to become outright bickering. Her frank gaze, clear, direct speech, and resolute actions contrast sharply with his periphrasis, changes of mood, and uncertainty. Syrinx herself reproaches him for being oblique and refuses to let him blame his inadequate flute for it:

> — Voyez, les hommes ne peuvent jamais être clairs devant la femme! Ils devraient faire leur déclaration en bon français, c'est-à-dire en noble et léger dialecte ionique. Non, il leur faut tout de suite de la musique! la musique si communément infinie!
>
> Pan se dresse furieux!
>
> — Et vous autres! Rien que le son de votre voix! Vous, tenez, la seule musique de votre voix! Est-ce plus loyal, ça? Oh! oh! misère! misère des deux côtés, en vérité! (292)

Pan throws the ball back by evoking one of his *idées fixes,* the stock Decadent deception of women, whose very voices charm like music, but this does not gain him much of an edge. Syrinx remains self-composed while he vacillates between shyness and aggression, embarrassment and audacity, mournful lamentation and disinterested nonchalance, cries of love and dry philosophical arguments, pleas for pity and harsh sarcasm. Finally he resorts to more practical means and makes his declaration with the help of his old stand-by, the philosophy of necessity:

> — En somme! Voyez, ô noble vierge, ô qui que vous soyez, vous qui avez pourtant une forme connue! La journée s'avance et je n'ai jamais aimé. Voulez-vous vous laisser être tout pour moi, au nom de Tout?

Pan et la Syrinx

. . .
    La nymphe Syrinx se dresse lentement de toute sa beauté. Elle dit sobrement:
— Je suis la nymphe Syrinx; un peu naïade aussi, car mon père est le fleuve Ladon au beau torse, à la barbe fleurie. Je revenais du mont Lycée . . .
— Ah! Ah! une naïade, je vois! Vous devez me trouver bien laid, bien Caliban, bien capricant! Une naïade! Une cousine du beau Narcisse, fils du fleuve de Céphyse! Peste! Il était beau, hein, Narcisse? et distingué! (292f.)

But if Pan intends his clever sarcasm to wound her, it once again rebounds parodically upon himself. Taunting her with the Narcissus story is not likely to dispose her any more favorably toward his advances; it may rather remind her of the fate of the other nymph relevant to that story—Narcissus's mother, Liriope, ravished by the river-god Cephisus—and is apt to put her on her guard. Pan's mocking reminder of Narcissus's beauty, as opposed to his own Caliban-like ugliness, actually prepares Syrinx for his next move, and, instead of defeating her by humiliation, sends her, with a prayer to Diana, off in flight.

In typical fashion, Pan interprets the situation badly by calling on an inappropriate literary parallel:

il vient de lui passer sur le coeur, d'un éclair, la révélation de la grande et légendaire douleur de Cérès parcourant toute la terre et, poudreuse et mendiante, interrogeant les bergers, cherchant sa fille Proserpine disparue un matin comme elle faisait un bouquet de fleurs pour sa mère. (293f.)

Pan inaccurately compares his own misfortune to the legendary sorrow of Ceres, wandering the earth in search of her daughter. But although he may consider himself as unlucky as Ceres, Syrinx's feelings toward him can hardly be compared to Proserpine's devotion to her mother. The comparison may even work against him; the motif of abduction suggests that Pan is actually closer to Pluto than to the suffering Ceres. The humor of his sulking and self-pity permits the reader to see through the comparison altogether. Perhaps the hero is as much a Caliban as he sarcastically admits to Syrinx, not simply the bestial primitive but, more tellingly, the potential ravisher, as here and in the Narcissus story above.

Laforgue transforms the simple chase and capture of legend into a sustained test of wits and wills, broken by frequent discussions and repartee. Pan fails to move Syrinx with his "Tout est dans tout" rhetoric ("Ah, ces gens à formules!" 296), and his pantheistic and deterministic explanation that they are meant to give themselves over to the universal law of nature. Her request to have him describe her beauty becomes an exercise in late-nineteenth-century metaphysics:

> — Soyez donc bon à quelque chose, soyez mon miroir comme la conscience humaine essaie d'être celui de l'Idéal indéfini . . .
> — Ah! pas ainsi, mon idéal enfant! Cela vous donnerait trop de droit à l'insaisissable! (A pédante, pédant et demi!)
> — C'est reconnaître en passant que le bonheur est [d]ans la poursuite de l'Idéal, sans plus.[11]
> — A cela, je ne puis répondre que par une impolitesse.
> — Dites.
> — C'est que vous déplacez la question, le but. Vous n'êtes pas le but de ma poursuite; sous couleur de ce but même, vous n'en êtes qu'une étape entre nous. D'ailleurs, cela revient au même, puisque tant que je ne vous sais pas, vous êtes pour moi le but même, l'Idéal. Quand je vous aurai traversée, ô étape, pourtant absolue, je verrai au delà! (A pédante et demie, la vérité toute entière!) (297)

The terms and ideas come directly from the philosophy of Hartmann.[12] Human consciousness strives to reflect the Ideal; love represents the same effort; however, the beloved is not the ultimate goal, but only an intermediate one from which to gain access to the Ideal. The ideal promised by love is thus illusory, although, as Pan explains, still an ideal in relative terms. His parodically triumphant "A pédante, pédant et demie!" and "A pédante et demie, la vérité toute entière!" are weakened by the fact that he again does not see the implications of the argument. If Syrinx is an ideal, she can never be reached, however intermediate an "étape" she may be in absolute terms. The philosophy suggests what will in fact happen in the story: attaining the intermediate ideal must involve disappointment. Syrinx will be possessed, but only in loss and by her transformation into art.

Laforgue humorously exploits the theme of Arcadia to provide yet another instance of Pan's parodic inability to interpret reality. He looks on from the hilltop as Syrinx stops at a tombstone on the

Pan et la Syrinx

plain below, as if inhaling the scent of a flower, and then takes off again in flight:

> Il s'arrête à son tour un instant à ce tombeau de marbre blanc. Il se penche comme l'objet de sa poursuite, il n'y a pas de fleur à sentir, mais cette inscription à méditer:
>
> ET IN ARCADIA EGO
> "Et moi aussi, je vivais en Arcadie!"
>
> — Pauvres mortels, que de raisons ils ont de s'aimer, eux!
> Mais Pan et Syrinx sont immortels, rien ne presse. (300f.)

Laforgue thus inserts the famous subject of Poussin's painting into the story of Pan and Syrinx. This free recycling of materials calls attention to the parody and, as we have seen, is a common feature of the *Moralités'* method. The harmless, typical pastoral scene (Pan assumes that Syrinx has stopped "pour y sentir une fleur") is actually a more sinister reminder of death, the "Et in Arcadia ego" of the epitaph. As usual, he does not see the significance of the discrepancy between what he imagines and reality; if he did, he would know that his vision of pastoral revels with Syrinx will likewise meet with death. He translates the epitaph correctly, according to the convention of the painting: the dead man warns the carefree passers-by that he, too, once enjoyed the pleasures of Arcadia as they now do.[13] But his conclusion—that because of death "poor mortals" have particular reason to love—shows a typical lack of self-knowledge, for he does not see that the "Je" may apply to himself. The incident holds a foreboding message for his own situation: Pan and Syrinx, too, live in Arcadia. They may be immortal, as the narrative ironically reminds us here ("Mais Pan et Syrinx sont immortels, rien ne presse," 301), but the story demonstrates that their relationship is not. Like the subject of the epigraph, it will live on only in art, in the music of the flute, and ultimately in the parody at hand.

Laforgue places Pan's pursuit of Syrinx in the larger context of the night's stalking the world of nature: twilight weaves an invisible net and weakens the nymph's resistance, the landscape trembles and languishes with expressions of tenderness, and Pan, in his desire, is "ivre de nuit" (303). Once again, he calls upon a literary model to describe and explain his own sensual frenzy, the stories told by his companion Bacchus of his legendary conquest of India:

— ... Quoi, ne respires-tu pas cette nuit d'été par tous tes organes libres? O nuit d'été, maladie inconnue, que tu nous fais mal! Je ne sens plus que nous, moi! O riche nuit d'été, je me rappelle, maintenant, les enivrants récits que me faisait Bacchus de sa conquête de l'Inde! Je me souviens, et ne puis m'arracher de Delphes! Oh, furie de la flûte grêle crevant l'orage sulfureux de la fin du jour des vendanges et appelant les averses lustrales! Thyrses, et chevelures emmêlées! Mystères de Cérès, mystères et kermesses, et fosse commune! Astarté! Astaroth! Derceto! Adonaï! En rond dans la prairie déjà tiède de danses, avec tous les pensionnats des Sulamites, au charivari de toutes les flûtes salamboennes! Tout est dans Tout! (303)

Pan's legendary association with Dionysus here becomes yet another instance of his problematic habit of living according to his imagination. This parodic Pan knows no frenzy, no panic, at all, except for what he has been told, and has thus imagined. He cannot overcome the frustrating discrepancy between his own life and the stories told to him by Bacchus, between his uneventful existence in Delphi and the exciting stories that he has heard there. However, the fact that Delphi is not in Arcadia, Pan's traditional home and the setting of the parody, considerably undercuts the pathos of the contrast that he tries to draw. Pan's slip gives him away: he falsely sees himself as Dionysus (who does belong to Delphi). Although the images, with their erotic connotations, indeed derive from Dionysiac ritual, Pan adds his own peculiarly modern touches: the Laforguian "pensionnats des Sulamites," of whom Elsa is a good example,[14] and the "flûtes salamboennes," recalling Flaubert. Ironically, Pan will get a flute, but not the kind associated with the orgies of Dionysus, rather a product of the strictest, unhappiest chastity.

The image of the flute gives us pause: there is no flute in *Salammbô*, whose heroine plays the lyre, and no harp, as Laforgue himself reminds us in *Salomé*. "Salamboennes," rather, evokes the object of the heroine's devotion, the feminine principle, goddess of love and fertility: Tanit. Indeed, the names that Pan invokes ("Astarté! Astaroth! Derceto! Adonaï!") directly recall Salammbô's prayer to the goddess in chapter three of the novel: "Anaïtis! Astarté! Derceto! Astoreth!"[15] Pan transforms Salammbô's virginal hymn to Tanit into a licentious plea for sexual fulfillment, and uses it as a reason for such.[16] His "flûtes salamboennes" are supposed to express the sensuality of Salammbô's Tanit, like the more traditional flutes of Dionysus. But once again, he chooses his model badly. Salammbô dies in the end, and Syrinx will, for all practical purposes, follow suit; Pan's moon will turn out to be not the sensual Tanit, but the harshly chaste Diana.

Indeed, after Syrinx's plunge into the river, Pan takes advantage of his new flute to fulminate against the moon for her role in the misfortune of men, for attracting them under the false pretense of sex only to ensure her own chastity, for being no better than a man in a woman's form, for enslaving the Syrinx-like keepers of her cult and destroying their sexual desire with her spells:

> — . . . Jamais tu n'as rêvé de notre sexe, de notre sexe si légitime! Non, tu as été élevée dans les forêts et les grandes chasses en toute saison, et les rudes soies des sangliers, et le sang et les abois, et les douches des fontaines au fond des bois. Tu es un homme, un homme sublime et pâle, un planteur à pauvres esclaves blanches, et tu fouailles cruellement tes compagnes en chasse, et, par des incantations inavouables, tu leur cautérises leur pauvre sexe au fond des forêts claustrales! Oh! va, je sais tout! je ne suis pas un halluciné. Tout est dans Tout et j'en suis la brave sentinelle empirique!"
>
> Mais la Lune reste là, rondement aveuglante, seule dans tout le ciel . . . (309)

But Pan's supposedly enlightened attitude is belied by both the terms in which he acknowledges it and the events themselves. He expresses his new pessimistic understanding with precisely the same "Tout est dans Tout" argument that he has used throughout the story as a reason for loving. Although he maintains that he is not an *halluciné*, this claim is undermined by the narrative's conspicuous ambiguity about the reality of the recent events: we are told that Syrinx's plunge hardly rippled the surface of the water; the metamorphosis is described in the uncertain form of a question, suggesting that it may be simply an optical illusion ("Oh, là-bas, en face au ras de l'eau, est-ce encore sa tête adorée qui regarde encore immobile, ou simplement un bouquet de lys d'eau qui jouit dans son genre?" 305); and the breeze that whispers in Pan's perked-up ears conjures up a host of disparate, synaesthetic images:

> O frisselis alisé, baisers d'ailes, paraphes de rumeurs, éventails pulvérisant en chœur un jet d'eau du fond des parcs de l'Armide, mouchoirs de fées froissés, le silence qui rêve tout haut, éponge passée sur toute poésie! . . . (306)

Pan soon falls into another series of feverish nightmares ("des Mille et Une Nuits d'abjection," 309), and the text poses the question explicitly:

> O enchantement lunaire! Climat extatique! Est-ce bien sûr? Est-ce l'Annonciation? N'est-ce que l'histoire d'un soir d'été? (310)

Laforgue strongly suggests that the whole story may have been only a mid-summer night's dream, thus parodying the Mallarmean "Aimai-je un rêve?"; perhaps Pan's miraculous conception of the new flute may be explained only by recourse to the questionable reality of the Annunciation.

But if, following the Mallarmean model, the reality of the events is cast in doubt, that of the new flute is not. It may not be able to move Diana, but the final sentence, realizing the creative function of parody, suggests that it may be able to produce more stories, however unreal, however fictional:

> Heureusement, et désormais, il lui suffit, dans ces vilaines heures, de tirer une gamme nostalgique de sa Syrinx à sept tuyaux, pour se remettre, la tête haute, les yeux larges et tout unis, vers l'Idéal, notre maître à tous. (310)

The story is not only a *gamme nostalgique* like Mallarmé's poem, the experience revived in memory and song. "Désormais" explicitly indicates that the story does not end but will have a sequel, or even a replay, in Pan's future unhappy hours. The portrait of the sorrowful hero mournfully playing the flute returns us to the beginning, to the "Sur son galoubet matinal, Pan se plaint, Pan donne cours à des doléances très personnelles," with which the story opened; but here he plays on his new instrument. "L'art, c'est le désir perpétué": Laforgue perpetuates Pan's desire indefinitely and thereby guarantees future stories. The parody gives rise to an endless series of strivings and disappointments, as in the frustrated pur-

Pan et la Syrinx

suit recounted here, and thus to an endless series of works like itself. Perhaps the traditional story of Pan's many loves has only just begun, or begun to be retold, so many future "gammes nostalgiques," like the parody, to brighten one's "vilaines heures." It would thus follow the model of another famous example of continuous storytelling here parodically reduced to quantifying Pan's unhappy dreams, *Les Mille et Une Nuits*.

Conclusion

A study of the *Moralités légendaires* in terms of the theory and conventions of parody has a reciprocally beneficial effect: it elucidates the individual tales and also contributes to the theory itself. In comically transposing legendary and canonical stories into the contemporary world and modernizing them according to the tenets of 1880s Decadence, the *Moralités*, as we have seen, represent the anachronistic and intertextual principle of parody. The typical devices of this genre figure throughout the tales and provide the basis for interpreting them most effectively and comprehensively. Moreover, the *Moralités* are superb examples of the genre, for they realize many of its possibilities and implications, and thus enhance our understanding of parody itself.

The object of Laforgue's parody is modern art of the 1880s, and the ideas, themes, forms, and sensibility associated with it, known to him and his contemporaries as *décadence*. The reexamination of this term in chapter two yields a broader and yet more accurate notion of Decadence than is usually acknowledged. This revised conception has obvious importance in interpreting the *Moralités*, which play freely with the clichés and conventions of Decadence, and in doing so identify them, but it also matters for our understanding of modernism and its late-nineteenth-century origins. From such a study, Decadence emerges as the primary manifestation of the avant-garde during the 1880s, which had begun in the work of Baudelaire and continued in that of Verlaine and Mallarmé. The countless contemporary essays and articles on the

Conclusion

movement attribute to it a number of common themes such as pessimism, individualism, artifice, evasion, mysticism, the unconscious, and an emphasis on stylistic innovation. Significantly, an examination of this material also reveals that parody played an important, and thus far unrecognized, role in the movement, and with reason: it achieves one of the principal objectives of Decadence by realizing its fundamental aesthetic of modernity.

A study of the *Moralités* as parodies contributes much to our understanding of the genre overall and produces especially important, indeed revolutionary, findings in a number of specific areas. First, Laforgue's stories clarify the relation of the parody to the work parodied: the latter is at once the object of the parody's distortion and transformation, and the basic constituent of the parody itself. The parodist depends for his own creation on the very work that he alters, and therefore must display toward it an attitude both irreverent and admiring. The *Moralités* indeed express a definite sympathy for the originals with which they play and the Decadence which they mock. They also point up an important qualification about the parody's target, which need not be the parodied work; the original may be simply a vehicle for the parody, rather than an object of its mockery, and the target something altogether different. Laforgue rewrites a well-known original in order to target contemporary Decadence, including his own work. In most cases, he chooses an original that has some relevance to the Decadent target to make the parody all the more acute. His legendary subjects (Lohengrin, Perseus and Andromeda, Pan and Syrinx, even the medieval story of St. Elizabeth) are appropriate to the rampant use of legend in art of the period and as Dottin has noted, can be found in the work of Gustave Moreau;[1] *Hamlet* plays on the importance of the Hamlet figure and *hamlétisme* for the entire nineteenth century; and *Salomé* fits the vogue for Salomés and other *femmes fatales*. In a manner wholly appropriate to parody, Laforgue treats subjects with obvious or potential Decadent associations in order to make fun of Decadence itself.

A second principle of the theory confirmed by the *Moralités* is that a comic element, present in the concept of parody from its first usage, is implied by the distortion essential to it and the deception of expectations by which it operates. The comic element may vary in degree, but it is nevertheless an essential aspect of the genre. It may imply derision or ridicule, but frequently does not, this effect being weakened constantly by the parody's reliance on the object of its mockery; it more often involves irony, or simply humor and playfulness. The *Moralités* follow the latter pattern, generally treating the Decadent target with irony and the canonical original as an object of parodic play.

Third, the dual status of the parodist as reader and author guarantees a self-reflexive and self-critical aspect to parody. The analogy between the parodist (as a reader) and the reader of the parody ensures that the parody's effect will rebound upon itself: the parodist's treatment of his own reading suggests to us that we treat our reading, the parody, similarly. The *Moralités* call frequent attention to the analogy between parodist and reader by various means, particularly authorial asides. In addition, the tales bring out a formerly unidentified consequence of the self-reflexivity of parody, namely the expressed anticipation, within the parody, of other versions of its story and even the features that these may have. Examples exist in all the tales, evoking other Hamlets, other Salomés, recurrent feasts of the Assumption in *Lohengrin,* a sequel to *Le Miracle des Roses,* and, for Pan, countless future disappointed loves, endless rounds of pursuit and frustration. A more radical consequence of self-reflexivity occurs, as we have seen, in *Persée et Andromède,* with the frame provided by the epilogue, which calls into question not only the preceding story, but also the content of the epilogue itself, and with it the very message of parody as a genre. Parody implies the possibility of self-parody, and by its own logic necessarily calls itself into question. In proposing something new, it must also allow for a rewriting, even a parody, of itself.

Fourth, the theme of imitation central to parody has particular relevance for Laforgue's Decadent target, where the confusion of art and life, or the attempt to make life an art, is a dominant characteristic. By its distortion and transformation of another work, parody calls strict imitation into question and constantly reminds the reader of its consequences. The characters of the *Moralités* all learn the dangers involved in living a life that imitates art, a Decadent life of artifice. Only by abandoning the effort do they assure for themselves a future, as do the Monster and Andromède, who, in the manner of parody itself, choose not to follow the original story, but transform it and live happily ever after.

Fifth, the intertextual character of parody ensures the self-sufficiency of this genre, which has always been considered dependent on other ones for its interpretation. Parody retains within itself the original (and target) that it simultaneously transforms. The reader therefore does not need to know the parodied work in order to understand the distortion, which will be signalled in the text, usually by the devices of humor. Laforgue's *Miracle des Roses* provides a rare example by which to test this controversial point of the theory, for its model long remained unknown even while it was nevertheless perceived and understood as a parody. The elements of that story which ultimately led me to the discovery of its model actually function as guides to the parody, locating and identifying the distortion.

Lastly, in preserving the original within itself, and providing directly for future or alternative versions of their own stories, the *Moralités* clearly demonstrate that parody indeed fulfills the function first attributed to it by the Formalists: the continuation of literary history and the extension of literary traditions. Parody preserves and transforms, contains within one work both the old and the new, and thus represents in miniature the process of literary history. This suggests the crucial role of parody in the avant-garde: the *Moralités* prove that parody is far from being a conservative force; in mocking the avant-garde, parody makes it into the status quo and forces the creation of even newer forms. The process is consistent with Laforgue's expressed notion of modern art in general, a radical transformation of the past that produces something new, ultimately advancing the evolution of artistic forms and, consequently, the aesthetic sensibility. Along with the obvious case of the parodic *Moralités,* nearly all his other works reflect this aesthetic to some extent, transforming illustrious literary precedents according to the artist's new poetic purposes.

Unlike Laforgue's other works, the *Moralités* drew consistently high praise in the years following their publication in November

1887. The reviews display a number of common themes: the originality and modernity of the book in both language and conception, its poetic quality, the underlying seriousness of its vision, its relation to the artistic sensibility of the 1880s, its gently mocking irony, its themes of love and metaphysical ennui, and its principle of modernization. The stories are labeled "original," "incomparable," "unprecedented," "personal," even "works of genius," and are explicitly called "poèmes."[2] They are seen as studies in the psychology of modern love, containing, in their irony and pessimism, a sustained philosophy toward life. The main themes of the *Moralités*—love and ennui—reflect the dilemma of the modern sensibility, the inability to escape from one's solitude by either love or metaphysics, and the equally insistent compulsion to do so.[3]

The modernizing aspect of the *Moralités* dominates the critical articles and constitutes for all reviewers the most original and distinctive feature of the volume. They are perceived to express ironically the sense of the futility of existence that haunts the modern literary imagination. Hamlet, in particular, represents the contemporary mind. He is a Baudelairean figure, with an *ennui* less royal than that of his Shakespearean predecessor but more significant to the modern reader: "un Hamlet français nettoyé de ses brumes saxonnes, un Hamlet parisien même, moins déclamatoire, moins désorbité, moins épique que l'autre; par contre, plus aigu de volonté, plus ironique, plus spirituel, plus irrémédiablement et plus consciencieusement à vau-l'eau."[4]

Ironically, however, it is Camille Mauclair, editor of the first—imperfect—edition of Laforgue's "complete" works, who probably summed up best the quality and effect of the *Moralités* as parodies:

> Les *Moralités légendaires* demeurent un monument singulier et unique dans notre littérature . . . l'esprit philosophique de Jules Laforgue allait bien plus loin que le goût même de parodier . . . L'anachronisme appliqué à la légende en relie simplement le sens moral à notre vie; et la déformation n'en a pas lieu pour la seule facilitation du comique . . . elle commente, elle augmente, elle permet à l'écrivain une création originale.[5]

Like the others, Mauclair calls attention to the function of anachronism and to the relation of the stories to modern life. But in paying tribute to the transformative nature of Laforgue's parody, he also suggests the achievement of the *Moralités*, which indeed brilliantly realize the creative implications of parody, and affirm in this genre the originality that Laforgue required of all true art.

Notes

Chapter 1

1. Letter 44, c. 3 June 1886, in *L.A.,* 188.

2. The most complete one is by M. Rose, the first to have covered the field. See also G. Genette, L. Hutcheon (for twentieth-century parody), and C. Abastado, "Situation de la parodie." Joseph Danes's *Parody: Critical Concepts versus Literary Practices, Aristophanes to Sterne* appeared too late for me to take it into account, but it will be clear that I do not accept his premise that a general theory of parody is impossible due to the variety of specific works to which the term is applied and the close relation of each to a given literary and cultural context. His idea of theory as a prescriptive phenomenon, the "originating principles" on which a work is based (25, 205), is misguided; the claim that parody was theorized only in the last few centuries in no way prevents it from applying to works of other periods. A theory which is descriptive and abstract seeks to draw general features from the body of existing works.

3. See M. Riffaterre, *Semiotics of Poetry* and *La Production du texte.*

4. Genette and Hutcheon have admirable breadth but do not test their theories over the course of a sustained parodic work.

5. See letter 44 to Kahn (note 1); a jotting among his notes on Baudelaire records the idea behind *Salomé* as "une Salomé, moderne" (*E.P.L.* XIII, April 1891, 101); and he describes his Andromède as a more modern version of the ancient princess (letter 121 to Fénéon, 21 September 1886, *O.C.* 1922, V, 160).

6. "The Poet as Art Critic. Laforgue's Aesthetic Theory."

7. See especially "Notes d'esthétique," *Revue blanche* XI, 84, 1 December 1896.

8. Laforgue does suggest that the contemporary may be more *moving* to the contemporary viewer because closer to one's own ephemeral experience; he also maintains that the function of art lies in advancing the sense organ to which it appeals. But he insists on removing the scale of value for works themselves and judging them on their aesthetic originality, the same grounds on which, in his view, great works of the past are given their place in the "natural selection" of art.

9. *O.C.* 1986, I, 97–154. (See my article, "The Early Laforgue: *Tessa.*")

10. *O.C.* 1986, I, 214–16.

11. Laforgue's notes record other projects that reflect the modernizing and parodic method of the *Moralités*: "Une histoire de Jeanne d'Arc—à la lumière de l'Inconscient"; and "Contes pour la jeunesse—prendre les très populaires contes moraux et les raconter avec une psychologie réaliste en les faisant tous rater" (*Revue blanche* VII, 36, October 1894, 304, and VIII, 49, 15 June 1895, 553).

12. Laforgue's unsuccessful prose efforts include the early novel *Un Raté*, for which a collection of notes survives (*M.P.*, 8f. and J. L. Debauve, "Laforgue romancier. Une Tentative avortée: *Un Raté*"); an untitled one mentioned in a letter to Henry (57, 20 August 1882; *O.C.* 1986 I, 796); *L'Aveugle*, noted in his 1883 *Agenda* (22 September); a late novel, *Saison*, surviving in fragments (*Revue blanche* VIII, 49, June 1895, 555–60; *Mercure de France* 1206, April 1964, 616–23; *E.P.L.* IV, 22, January 1892; *Revue d'histoire littéraire de la France* 1964, 667); and some stories of 1885, *Histoires de femmes* (*Revue blanche* XI, 85, 15 December 1896, 543–47, and XII, 94, May 1897, 518–24), which D. Grojnowski suggests belong to *Saison* (*Feuilles volantes*, 171f.).

13. The alternative titles which Laforgue proposed also communicate his conception of the stories as "de vieux canevas brodés d'âmes à la mode": "Vieux canevas, âmes du jour," "Fabliaux d'antan," and "Sachets éventés," this last evoking the conventional image of the sachet (cf. Baudelaire, "Le Parfum") which, broken open, releases into the present a scent preserved from a former time.

14. See J. Pierrot's excellent section on the importance of legend in the literature and art of Decadence (*L'Imaginaire décadent*, pt. 2, ch. 3).

15. This is the traditional view, accepted by Hutcheon (26, 44, 51, 68), who equates the mockery of parody with a conservative force.

16. See, for example, Hutcheon (4), who argues that the Romantic aesthetic is responsible for the devaluation of parody: "What is clear from these sorts of attack is the continuing strength of a Romantic aesthetic that values genius, originality, and individuality. In such a context, parody must needs be considered at best a very minor art form." Laforgue's case confirms that this need not be so.

Notes

17. See letter 109 to Henry, 6 June 1885 (*O.C.* 1922, V, 128).

18. Letter 13 to Kahn, 19 February 1885 (*L.A.*, 72).

19. A. Baju considered the *nouvelle* appropriate to the Decadent sensibility for these reasons (*Le Décadent*, 12 June 1886, 1).

20. Laforgue died in 1887, while revising the *Moralités* for publication. The stories were originally completed as follows: *Salomé* (July 1885), *Hamlet* (August 1885), *Le Miracle des Roses* (June 1886), *Lohengrin* (July 1886), *Persée et Andromède* (August 1886), *Pan et la Syrinx* (November 1886). He worked on four other *Moralités*, which have not survived (letter 44 to Kahn, c. 3 June 1886, *L.A.*, 188): *Marlborough s'en va-t-en guerre*, *L'Amour de la symétrie*, *Corinne au Cap Misène*, and *Incomprise*. Nothing remains of the first two; of Corinne we have only a fragment from Laforgue's "Carnet" of 1884-5, repr. in D. Grojnowski's edition of the *Moralités* (354ff.). (Unless otherwise indicated, numbers in parentheses in the text refer to this edition.) *Incomprise* became *Les Deux Pigeons*, which Laforgue originally intended for the volume but removed in 1887 for being inconsistent with the rest (repr. in Grojnowski, 312–331). I do not study it here, because it does not follow the same parodic principle of modernization that the others do. It in no way tells the story indicated by the title in a "modern" way; the title functions metaphorically, even allegorically, vis-à-vis the action. Debauve (56) proposes that Laforgue's original manuscript contained five stories, with *Les Deux Pigeons* as the sixth. However, in offering his manuscript "prêt et ficelé" to Vanier on 25 December 1886, Laforgue twice specifies that it has six (see letter 32 to Vanier, Debauve, 127) and only later announces that he will add *Les Deux Pigeons* (letter 35 to Vanier, Debauve, 131). This accounts also for the manuscript title page, where *Les Deux Pigeons* figures last in the list of seven stories (coll. Bibliothèque J. Doucet, Paris, repr. in Grojnowski, frontispiece).

21. Grojnowski's theory (xvii) that this derives from a desire on Laforgue's part to begin and end the volume with a creator, Hamlet, the playwright, and Pan, inventor of the flute, is unconvincing. Many of the characters of the *Moralités* are creators, notably poets: not just Hamlet and Pan, but also Salomé, Lohengrin, and both the Monster and the narrator Amyot of *Persée et Andromède*, to name a few. Nor does the hypothesis account for the order of the stories in the volume as a whole.

22. See H. Markiewicz, "On the Definitions of Literary Parody"; F. Lelièvre, "The Basis of Ancient Parody"; U. Weisstein, "Parody, Travesty and Burlesque: Imitations with a Vengeance"; Genette; Hutcheon; and Rose.

23. T. Shlonsky, "Literary Parody. Remarks on its Method and Function," 798. L. Duisit (*Satire, parodie, calembour*) also uses mode.

24. Hutcheon retains *genre* on similar grounds (19).

25. On the problems posed by the distinction of terms, see Rose, es-

pecially ch. 2; Genette, ch. 6–7; Hutcheon, 38ff.; W. Karrer, *Parodie, Travestie, Pastiche;* Markiewicz, "On the Definitions of Literary Parody," 1266ff.; Weisstein, "Parody, Travesty, and Burlesque: Imitations with a Vengeance," 811; and Abastado, "Situation de la parodie," 16ff.

26. Although I cannot do justice to this topic here, I conceive of the basic differences as follows. Forgery aims to deceive by close imitation of its model; it lacks the distortion, the comic element, and the conspicuous self-identification associated with parody. Caricature involves the distortion of physical traits and applies normally to visual forms; like satire and unlike parody, it usually (though not always) targets something in the world, rather than a work of art. Pastiche exaggerates the traits of a given style and, like parody, even calls attention to this, but aims principally at imitation, capturing the spirit of the original text or writer, and places less emphasis on introducing original elements; parody aims rather at transformation, using the original for another purpose, and does not necessarily have the "à la manière de" quality of pastiche. Travesty and burlesque have traditionally designated the comical transposition of a serious work into a low style, as in Scarron's *Virgile travesti* of 1648; the application of a high style to a low subject; or a general inversion of values, such as lowering the gods. They are parodic, but not equivalent to parody, which covers a wider range of methods and effects and puts its comic distortion more directly in the service of a new aesthetic.

27. This conception of parody roughly agrees with what Rose terms general parody (33ff.), which "refunctions" the parodied work for a new audience and thus mirrors the process of composing and receiving texts. It resembles Genette's category of transposition, the transformation of a text (rather than strict imitation) for a "serious," rather than aggressively satirical or purely playful, purpose (36).

28. Cf. the definition of comedy as the representation of inferior men at *Poetics* 2.1448a16–19 and 5.1449a32. See now Janko, *Aristotle on Comedy*.

29. Markiewicz ("On the Definitions of Literary Parody", 1265) maintains that parody in the sense of comic imitation of a serious work is used only by the scholiasts, as the Greeks called parodies of didactic and philosophical poems *silloi*, and parodies of tragedy *paratragodein*. But contrast F. Householder, *"Parodia"* (8f.), who holds that the earliest usage of *parodia* applied to mock-epic and only later was given a nonhumorous application by the rhetoricians, "under the influence of etymological consciousness" and by the grammarians, who added a word to indicate the presence of humor. Hutcheon (51) seems to misunderstand this and uses it to argue, unconvincingly, against the comic element of parody.

30. Athenaeus 15, 697f–699c. See Lelièvre ("The Basis of Ancient Parody," 71) and Householder (*"Parodia,"* 2ff.).

31. Cf. Lelièvre, "The Basis of Ancient Parody," 81.

Notes 227

32. Hutcheon (32) maintains that the dual meaning of *para* has been neglected, to the detriment of the "nearness" sense; but this has in fact been noted by several scholars, along with its relevance to the meaning of parody, for example, Lelièvre ("The Basis of Ancient Parody," 66), Householder (*"Parodia,"* 2), and Rose, 33.

33. This is suggested by D. W. Lucas in his edition of the *Poetics* (65) and is consistent with the inverse relation of *parodia* to *rhapsodia* discerned by J. C. Scaliger in his *Poetics* of 1561 (I, 42): "Sic parodia de rhapsodia nata est ... Est igitur parodia rhapsodia inversa mutatis vocibus ad ridicula retrahens." For Scaliger, a parody was a comic version of the epic subject performed during breaks in the epic performance, which set a ridiculous version "praeter rem seriam propositam," that is, parodically, in its etymological sense. Cf. also Householder, *"Parodia"* (8).

34. Genette, 22.

35. On the Formalist concept of mechanization or automatization, see J. Tynjanov, "De l'évolution littéraire" (Todorov, 120–137) and "Destruction, parodie"; B. Tomachevski, *Thématique* (Todorov, esp. 301ff.); and V. Shklovsky, "L'Art comme procédé" (Todorov, 94).

36. Genette, 23.

37. See Riffaterre, "Parodie et répétition," on the role of repetition in parody.

38. H. Koller ("Die Parodie") implausibly argues that *parodia* originally designates not a noble form applied to absurd content but rather a phenomenon in epic performance: recitation contrary to the usual verse-melody. This view is followed by W. Hempel, "Parodie, Travestie, und Pastiche," 151f. Koller feels that Aristotle uses it in this sense in the *Poetics* passage already mentioned (1448a12). He cites Athenaeus 9.407a, where Hegemon is described as a reciter of Homeric epic who achieved new effects *like an actor,* and 14.638b, where ridiculous effects are attributed to parodies of hexameters, to argue that *parodia* applied first to a technical innovation in epic performance, and only later, in the scholia, to the comic imitation of another poet, as the term was later understood. Koller bases much of his argument on the fact that the noble form applied to absurd content existed before Hegemon. While this is true, notably in the *Margites* ascribed to Homer, it does not suffice to make the sense of *parodia* merely recitation or to change the basic elements of parody, for two reasons: (a) Aristotle associates parody with the representation of inferior persons and thus with the comic; (b) actual quotations of Hegemon are known, including comic tags like "the leg of a partridge" (quoted in Lucas, ad loc.), comparable to Aristophanes's famous "lost his bottle of oil" (*Frogs,* 1208ff.). This evidence shows that Hegemon's parody had to do not simply with performance, but with comical form and content as well. See now Janko, *Aristotle on Comedy,* 181ff.

39. Cf. Rose, 20; Abastado, "Situation de la parodie," 11; Weisstein, "Parody, Travesty and Burlesque: Imitations with a Vengeance", 807.

40. *Institutio oratoria* 6.3.97: "ficti notis versibus similes, quae *parodia* dicitur."

41. Cicero, *De Oratore* 2.64.257: "saepe etiam versus facete interponitur, vel ut est, vel paululum immutatus, aut aliqua pars versus." Cf. Demetrius, *On Style*, 150.

42. *Rhetoric* 3.11.1412a26–36.

43. Hutcheon, 15, 20, 26, 41.

44. *Rhetoric* 3.11.1412a19.

45. Hutcheon, 26, 20.

46. This equation is made by Hutcheon, 51.

47. Hutcheon, 60.

48. Markiewicz ("On the Definitions of Literary Parody", 1269) cites A. Morozov, author of a work on Russian literary parodies from the eighteenth to the early twentieth centuries (*Russkaia stikhotvornaia parodia*), who maintains that while the relation of the parody to the parodied work can be humorous, or even friendly and jocular, the parody nevertheless places the parodied work clearly on the plane of comicality.

49. M. Bakhtin, *Problèmes de la poétique de Dostoïevski*, 193ff.

50. Hutcheon, 65.

51. D. Baguley, "Parody and the Realist Novel," 96. This article demonstrates in detail the seemingly paradoxical continuity between parody and realism.

52. The view that the pleasure of humor comes from recognition has been held by theorists of the comic since Aristotle (*Rhetoric* 3.10.1410b6–12). However, to maintain that the pleasure in humorous examples of ambiguity, irony, and parody lies *solely* in our recognition of the cleverness of the author in showing it and our own cleverness in perceiving it (see Rose, 89; W. Booth, *Rhetoric of Irony*, 123ff.; cf. Hutcheon, 32) is inadequate: many jokes are clever, and we are clever enough to understand them, yet we may not take any pleasure in them. We might add a second condition, namely the perception of the relative appropriateness of the mockery to its object. If the humor seems excessive relative to its object, the pleasure is diminished or cancelled altogether. This includes the case where we are ourselves the object, and thus embraces the injurious, which *has* figured in theories of the comic since antiquity. Aristotle maintains at *Poetics* 5.1449a35 that the ludicrous, or the laughable, is never painful or injurious. Plato says in the *Philebus* (48c–49c) that too powerful a character inspires not laughter but fear. Freud, looking at humor and the comic from a very different perspective, held that the release of a strong emo-

Notes

tion by a comic situation greatly interfered with and lessened the comic; where feelings and interests are involved, the comic is inhibited (*Jokes and their Relation to the Unconscious*, 289, 293).

53. Lelièvre, "The Basis of Ancient Parody," 71; Markiewicz, "On the Definitions of Literary Parody," 1265; Hutcheon, 11, 44; J. Priestman, "The Age of Parody," 14ff.

54. See the dialogue between the priest and the barber: "— Parece cosa de misterio ésta; porque, según he oído decir, este libro fue el primero de caballerías que se imprimió en España, y todos las demás han tomado principio y origen déste; y así, me parece que, como a dogmatizador de une secta tan mala, le debemos, sin escusa alguna, condenar al fuego. — No, señor — dijo el barbero —; que también he oído decir que es el mejor de todos los libros que de este género se han compuesto; y así, cómo a único en su arte, se debe perdonar." (*Don Quijote de la Mancha*, I, 67).

55. See n. 15. Hutcheon claims that such parody is necessarily conservative, but the *Moralités* disprove this. However, it is sometimes so, as Priestman has shown in nineteenth-century parodies of Romanticism ("The Age of Parody," 106ff.).

56. Rose, pt. 2, ch. 3.

57. "Destruction, parodie," 67.

58. These remarks apply both to the original on which the parody is based and to its target.

59. Rose, 44.

60. *Problèmes de la poétique de Dostoïevski*, 124ff.

61. Rose, 79ff.

62. R. Poirier ("The Self-Reflexivity of Parody") discusses the topic in terms similar to Rose's: parody is self-reflexive in so far as it exposes the process of artistic creation, including that of the parody.

63. Barthes sees parody as an example of "écriture classique," which merely replaces one code with another and arrests the play of codes characteristic of modern writing (*S/Z*, 145f.; cf. 52). See my article, "The Reflexive Function of Parody: Self-Criticism and Creativity."

64. "Para mí sola nació don Quijote, y yo para él; él supo obrar y yo escribir; solos los dos somos para en uno, a despecho y pesar del escritor fingido y tordesillesco que se atrevió, o se ha de atrever, a escribir con pluma de avestruz grosera y mal deliñada las hazañas de mi valeroso caballero" (*Don Quijote de la Mancha*, II, 1068). The final sentence of part 1, which mentions a third sally to follow, suggests not another version but a continuation, with its famous and ironic result: the pseudonymous Avellaneda took up the challenge before Cervantes had published his own part 2.

65. See my article, "The Reflexive Function of Parody," which discusses this episode in detail and documents the existence of this self-reflexive feature in a number of parodies of different periods and literatures.

66. So too Hutcheon, 50.

67. The terms are J. Kristeva's. See "Bakhtine, le mot, le dialogue, le roman." Cf. Riffaterre, "Sémanalyse de l'intertexte" and *Semiotics of Poetry*.

68. "Sémanalyse de l'intertexte," 173.

69. See Weisstein ("Parody, Travesty, and Burlesque: Imitations with a Vengeance," 803); Hutcheon, 94ff.; cf. G. Lee (*Allusion, Parody and Imitation*) and J. G. Riewald ("Parody and Criticism").

70. "Destruction, parodie," 75. Cf. Hutcheon, 88f.

71. On the role of humor in signalling the intertext generally, see Riffaterre, "The Poetic Functions of Intertextual Humor." Repetition likewise allows the reader to perceive parody without knowing a specific parodied work: see Riffaterre, "Parodie et répétition," 87.

72. Here repetition, not being an aspect of the original form, would be a signal of the parody above.

73. Cf. M. Foucault, *Les Mots et les choses*, 62; Rose, 65ff.

74. See H. Levin, *Contexts of Criticism*, on the relation of parody to realism in *Don Quixote*.

75. Priestman's study of parody among the English *fin de siècle* aesthetes confirms that this was a function of Decadent ideology generally, and not simply a French phenomenon. See "The Age of Parody," pt. 3 ch. 5.

76. See P. Mourier-Casile, "Modernités à rebours," 151. Cf. J. Birkett, *The Sins of the Fathers*, who describes Decadence as "an attempt . . . to substitute fiction for history" (3).

77. "Literary Parody. Remarks on its Method and Function," 800.

78. Rose, 65; cf. Priestman, "The Age of Parody," 27.

79. ". . . luz y espejo de toda la caballería andante" (*Don Quijote de la Mancha*, I, 21); cf. "flor y espejo," II, 23.

80. On this term, see n. 35.

81. See A. Michel, "Tradition antique et philosophies de la décadence dans la littérature française autour de 1880," 57.

82. Rose, 108.

83. Cf. Bakhtin, *Problèmes de la poétique de Dostoïevski* (124f.); also Tomachevski, "Thématique" (Todorov, 301f.). Hutcheon (36) rejects the

Formalist concept of "evolution" for its ameliorative implications; however, there is little evidence of this sense in their work. Tynjanov, for example, defines evolution neutrally as change and substitution: "un changement du rapport entre les termes du système, c'est-à-dire un changement de fonctions et d'éléments formels, l'évolution se trouve être une 'substitution' de systèmes" ("De l'évolution littéraire," Todorov, 136).

84. Heine described it this way in 1837 (see Rose, 158). Cf. Shlonsky, "Literary Parody. Remarks on its Method and Function," 801.

85. Rose, 159ff. Shlonsky ("Literary Parody. Remarks on its Method and Function," 801) sees Sterne's work as parodying the eighteenth-century novel and leading to the stream of consciousness one.

86. Priestman, "The Age of Parody," 65; Baguley, "Parody and the Realist Novel," 95; cf. P. Waugh, *Metafiction. The Theory and Practice of Self-Conscious Fiction*, 70.

87. For Laforgue's main devices, see index, *Moralités légendaires*.

88. See n. 71.

89. Rose, ch. 3; wrongly criticized by Hutcheon, 20.

90. J. L. Borges, "Magias parciales del *Quijote*," 99–100.

91. Tomachevski compares the process of renewal or refunctioning that parody represents to this kind of quotation: "Le renouvellement du procédé est analogue à l'emploi d'une citation d'un auteur ancien dans un contexte nouveau et avec une signification nouvelle." ("Thématique," Todorov, 301)

92. Riffaterre argues that the epigraph tells us the essential in the work by a double detour: "saying it through another author, and letting it out in the guise of some trivial detail apparently unconnected with the subject, or through a seemingly superficial lexical similarity" (*Semiotics of Poetry*, 191).

93. This is consistent with the quarrel in *Pan et la Syrinx*, where Syrinx accuses men of needing music to express themselves, and Pan responds that a woman's voice is music in itself; women are endowed with art by nature.

Chapter 2

1. *L. A.*, 124.

2. *Le Temps*, 6 August 1885. Reprinted in Pakenham (9–22). When possible, I refer to this edition (which contains some of the major articles surrounding the Decadent-Symbolist controversy of 1885–86) because of its availability.

3. Bourde concentrates on Mallarmé, whom he ridicules for being unintelligible, and Verlaine, toward whom he is considerably more gracious; he also discusses Jean Moréas, Laurent Tailhade, Charles Vignier, and Charles Morice. Laforgue expected his formal novelty to appeal to Bourde, who admired this aspect of the new poetry. But for his article of 6 August, Bourde most likely could not have included Laforgue's only published volume, the *Complaintes,* since it had just come out in late July. The earliest review appeared on 9 August, and that one written by Mostrailles, pseud. for Trézenik, the book's printer.

4. Laforgue wrote two reviews of the *Complaintes* and, in the first, calls them the acme of Decadence (see below, 71f.). The seventy or so reviews of his work from 1885 to 1887 reprinted by Debauve (197–269) characterize him as a Decadent, either explicitly or by placing him in the company of the *chefs d'école,* Verlaine and Mallarmé: for example, the *Complaintes* are "un livre fou, plus décadent que les décadents . . . O Paul Verlaine, ô Mallarmé, voilà quelle race vous faites!" (*La Revue littéraire et artistique,* Debauve, 211). Whenever possible, I will refer to Debauve's volume, which makes easily available a large collection of reviews from the *petite presse.* I have found only a couple of articles on Laforgue not included there. Full references to other articles are given in the notes.

5. "Préface," *A Rebours,* 53.

6. Michel discusses Laforgue's use of irony as a way of realizing the philosophical goals of Decadence described in the system of Schopenhauer ("Tradition antique et philosophies de la décadence dans la littérature française autour de 1880," 67).

7. Teodor de Wyzewa, "Les Moralités légendaires," *Revue Indépendante,* n.s. 5, 14, December 1887, 343.

8. For a study of these figures as representative of Decadence, however, see Birkett, *The Sins of the Fathers.*

9. Only later did Decadence come to be equated more exclusively with them, when Symbolism was adopted for works of a more serious literary modernism. See below, 35f.

10. For Y. Vadé ("Mythe de la décadence and décadence du mythe") Decadence was in particular a resistance to the transformation of cultural myths under the influence of science, industrialization, and new social practices.

11. See J. Lethève, *Impressionnistes et symbolistes devant la presse,* 172.

12. Mallarmé, however, disliked the term *décadence* (*Oeuvres,* 1444).

13. For example, P. Bourde (Pakenham, 10): "Baudelaire est leur père direct, et toute l'école danse et voltige sur le rayon macabre qu'il a ajouté au ciel de l'art, suivant l'expression de Victor Hugo. M. Verlaine

... en est devenu l'une des deux colonnes ... l'autre est M. Stéphane Mallarmé"; the same relation is cited in Moréas's Symbolist manifesto (*Le Figaro*, 18 September 1886, Pakenham, 31), and in many of the critical articles reproduced in Debauve (211, 212, 224, 227, 232, 237, 263). In his review of the *Complaintes*, Laforgue himself called Baudelaire the "dieu et prophète" of the Decadent movement (Debauve, 193).

14. Minor writers often mentioned include: Charles Vignier, Charles Morice, Laurent Tailhade, René Ghil, Jean Lorrain, and Jean Ajalbert; the Goncourts are occasionally included in the context of style. Laforgue does not think highly of Vignier, Morice, or Ghil. See letters 52 and 23 to Kahn, c. 21 August 1886 and 1 May 1885 (*L. A.*, 214 and 107).

15. G. Michaud, *Message poétique du symbolisme*, II, 232. Cf. M. Décaudin, "Définir la décadence," 10f.

16. Pierrot's first chapter provides one of the most intelligent and accurate accounts of Decadence available thus far. See also A. E. Carter, *The Idea of Decadence in French Literature 1830–1900*; N. Richard, *Le Mouvement décadent*, and *A l'Aube du symbolisme*; P. Stephan, *Paul Verlaine and the Decadence 1882–1890*; K. Swart, *The Sense of Decadence in Nineteenth-Century France*; R. K. R. Thornton, *The Decadent Dilemma*; and the classic work on the subject, which after more than half a century remains a standard source, Mario Praz's *Romantic Agony*.

17. *Le XIXè Siècle*, 11 August 1885 (Pakenham, 27).

18. *Le Figaro*, 18 September 1886 (Pakenham, 31).

19. In his edition of *Les Déliquescences d'Adoré Floupette* (30), S. Cigada notes likewise: "... decadentismo e simbolismo sono termini diversi per designare lo stesso e unico fenomeno."

20. Anatole France makes the relation clear ("La Vie à Paris," *Le Temps*, 26 September 1886): "Un journal qui reçoit d'ordinaire les manifestations des princes, vient de publier la profession de foi des symbolistes. Ceux-ci étaient plus connus sous les noms de décadents et de déliquescents" (Pakenham, 45).

21. Seven of the post-September reviews reprinted in Debauve call Laforgue a Symbolist, ten a Decadent. A year later, the naturalist writer Paul Alexis comically cannot decide: "Les décadents (?), pardon, les symbolistes (???), viennent d'perdre un des leurs: M. Jules Laforgue" (*Le Cri de Paris*, 6 September 1887, Debauve, 249).

22. Debauve, *Guêpe*, 172. The quotation comes from Zola's essay on the Goncourts' *Germinie Lacerteux*, in *Mes Haines*. Although Laforgue keeps his distance from Naturalism, which he considered inconsistent with true poetry and relevant only to the novel, the quotation suggests that, in 1877 at least, it had some relation to the Decadent aesthetic that he would later embrace.

23. T. de Wyzewa, "Notes sur la littérature wagnérienne et les livres en 1885–1886," and "Notes sur la peinture wagnérienne et le salon de 1886," *Revue wagnérienne*, 8 June 1886 and 8 May 1886.

24. A. F. Claveau, "Les Décadents," *Le Gaulois*, 22 September 1886 (Pakenham, 43).

25. "Le Symbolisme," *La Vogue* II, 12, 4–11 October 1886, 400.

26. "Le Symbolisme et l'instrumentation poétique," *Revue de Semaine*, Warsaw, 2 February 1887. (A résumé is given in *Ecrits pour l'art*, 4, 7 April 1887.)

27. "Cet idéal et ces procédés se résument en ceci: mysticisme, alexandrinisme, schopenhauerisme et impressionnisme" (Debauve 194). For the quotation from the essay on Impressionism, see *M.P.*, 138.

28. See A. E. Carter, *Baudelaire et la critique française*, 19.

29. See Charles Bataille: "le Prométhée des moeurs énervés de notre décadence," and Barbey d'Aurevilly: "Son talent travaillé, ouvragé, compliqué avec une patience de Chinois, est lui-même une fleur du mal venue dans les serres chaudes d'une Décadence" (Carter, *Baudelaire et la critique française*, 15).

30. "Notes nouvelles sur Edgar Poe" (*O.C.* II, 320).

31. Cf. *A Rebours*, ch. 14.

32. See letter 39 to Ephrussi (9 April 1882, *O.C.* 1986 I, 767): "il y a longtemps que je pense et dis à qui veut l'entendre que si quelqu'un a du génie parmi nos poètes, c'est Bourget, au-dessus de Sully, de Coppée, de Richepin, etc. Quant au critique, à part les maîtres bien assis, il est encore le plus pénétrant, avec quelque chose de plus qu'eux tous, son âme." Cf. letters 27 (13 January 1882) and 38 (31 March 1882) to the same, *O.C.* 1986 I, 744 and 766; 41 to Henry (16 April 1882), *O.C.* 1986 I, 770; and 93 to Kahn (29 November 1883), *O.C.* 1986 I, 845.

33. ". . . ses deux volumes d'Essais de psychologie contemporaine dont on n'a pas assez compris la préface" (Laforgue, "Paul Bourget," Les Hommes d'aujourd'hui [1886], reprinted in Ruchon, *Stéphane Vassiliew*, 88).

34. Published by D. Grojnowski, "Un Inédit de Jules Laforgue, 'Paul Bourget.'" Laforgue never completed the article.

35. For a comparison of Laforgue's usage of this metaphor with the others,' see G. G. Rotelli, *Due Studi sul simbolismo: la metrica delle poesie di Rimbaud. Il tema liturgico nelle poesie di Laforgue*.

36. For the ideas of Taine on Decadence and their influence on Bourget, see Jean-Thomas Nordmann, "Taine et la décadence."

37. "Notes d'esthétique," *Revue blanche* XI, 84, 1 December 1896, 488.

38. Letters 38 to Ephrussi and 41 to Henry, 31 March and 16 April 1882, O.C. 1986 I, 766 and 770.

39. "Les *Moralités légendaires* de Jules Laforgue," 873.

40. "Pierrots (on a des principles)" and "Pierrots" II (*Imitation*); *F.B.V.* XXIII.

41. *Le Décadent*, nos. 1 and 4, 1886.

42. "Notes sur Schopenhauer," *Revue indépendante* II, February 1885, 381.

43. *Ibid.*, 379, 385ff.

44. See Jules Lemaître, "Joris-Karl Huysmans," *Revue contemporaine* I, 1885, 555; Emile Hennequin, "A Rebours," *Revue indépendante* I, June 1884, 212.

45. *Revue des deux mondes*, 15 March 1870. Laforgue quotes this article in *Tessa* (1877). (See my "The Early Laforgue. *Tessa*.") Cf. Bourget's essay on Dumas, 296.

46. Laforgue also read the Janet articles, and he quotes them in *Tessa*. He at least knew about Caro, since in a chronicle for *La Guêpe*, he notes the opening of Caro's well-publicized course at the Sorbonne (2 November 1879, O.C. 1986, I, 204).

47. French translations first appeared as follows: *Essai sur le libre arbitre*, trans. S. Reinach, Paris, G. Baillière, 1877; *Le Fondement de la morale*, trans. J. Bourdeau, Paris, G. Baillière, 1879; *Parerga et Paralipomena*, trans. J. Cantacuzène, Paris, G. Baillière, 1880; *Pensées, maximes et fragments*, trans. J. Bourdeau, Paris, G. Baillière, 1880; *De la quadruple racine du principe de la raison suffisante*, 1882; *Le Monde comme Volonté et comme Représentation*, trans. J. Cantacuzène, Leipzig, 1886. This edition of Schopenhauer's principal work was little known and difficult to obtain. A more well-known one by A. Burdeau (Paris, Alcan) was not published until 1888, after Laforgue's death. He could not have read it in the original German; as he does not explicitly mention having read Schopenhauer himself, it is possible that his knowledge came from secondary sources such as those mentioned earlier and from Hartmann's *Philosophie de l'Inconscient*, which refers to it frequently. For a history of Schopenhauer in France during this period, see R. Colin, *Schopenhauer en France. Un Mythe naturaliste*, and V. Hell, "Schopenhauer et le mouvement décadent en France."

48. From the interview with Challemel-Lacour, *Revue des deux mondes*, 15 March 1870, 311. Quoted by Bourget in the Dumas essay (296).

49. Translated into French in 1877. Bourget championed Hartmann also, and introduced Laforgue to his work in 1880. The works by Janet and Caro devote sections to his thought.

50. "Les Poètes maudits," *La France libre*, 3 October 1885 (Debauve, 208).

51. Pierrot, 159ff. See above, 40.

52. *O.C.* I, 677: "La femme a faim et elle veut manger. Soif, et elle veut boire. Elle est en rut, et elle veut être foutue... La femme est *naturelle*, c'est-à-dire abominable"; I, 694: "La femme ne sait pas séparer l'âme du corps... Un satirique dirait que c'est parce qu'elle n'a que le corps"; cf. II, 720: "dénuée de spiritualité."

53. "Complainte des voix sous le figuier boudhique."

54. "Feuilles," *Mercure de France*, April 1964, 618; *D.V.* IV and V. See also "Bobo" (*Le Symboliste* 2, 15 October 1886), and his notes in *Revue anarchiste* VI, 1 November 1893.

55. Jules Lemaître, "J.-K. Huysmans," *Revue contemporaine* I, 1885, 553.

56. "Le Pessimisme des écrivains," *Revue indépendante* I, September 1884, and 2, November 1884.

57. *Revue indépendante*, June 1884, 209. Laforgue knew Hennequin in 1886: see letter 124 to Dujardin, 4 December 1886, *O.C.* 1922, 5, 169.

58. "Paul Bourget," *Revue contemporaine* II, 1885, 76. Laforgue approved of this article: "Je trouve que l'étude de Ch. Morice donne une idée très intime de Bourget" (letter 109 to Henry, 6 June 1885, *O.C.* 1922, 5, 128).

59. "Les Déliquescences d'Adoré Floupette," *Revue contemporaine* II, 1885, 266.

60. See the Goncourts' *Charles Demailly*, ch. 58.

61. "Le Pessimisme des écrivains," *Revue indépendante* II, November 1884, 67.

62. See Paul Alexis, "Les Livres," *Revue indépendante* I, June 1884, 252: "Voici encore M. J.-K. Huysmans, qui, dans *A Rebours*... analyse en médecin et en psychologue un cas de notre maladie à tous: la névrose!" Cf. Lemaître's article cited above (n. 55).

63. See Pica, "Les Décadents," *Corriere del mattino*, 1885 (Debauve, 212).

64. *Le Capitan*, 2è année, no. 1, February 1884, 6.

65. For other examples, see Pierrot, ch. 4.

66. *La Basoche* (Brussels), I, 2, December 1884, 77f.

67. *A Rebours*, ch. 12.

68. Louis Desprez, "M. Paul Verlaine," *Revue indépendante* I, June 1884, 219.

69. D'Orfer, "La Décadence," *Le Scapin*, 1 September 1886. The

themes of Byzantium and the late Empire were exploited *à outrance* by minor writers, as in the tedious novels of Jean Lombard, *L'Agonie* (1888) and *Byzance* (1890).

70. Baudelaire uses them as such in *Le Peintre de la Vie Moderne* and the *Salon de 1859* (O.C. II, 709, 642). Cf. Bourget's essay on Renan, 43.

71. A. Baju, "Sadités," *Le Décadent* 14, 10 July 1886.

72. Laforgue mentions Nero also in his art notes and the "Complaintes-litanies de mon Sacré-Coeur," where the emperor is a figure for the speaker's heart: "Mon Coeur est un Néron, enfant gâté d'Asie, / Qui d'empires de rêve en vain se rassasie."

73. *A Rebours*, ch. 14. See also G. Kahn, *Symbolistes et décadents*, 313. Laforgue read and admired both the *Tentation* and the *Imitation* (letter 46 to Henry, 12 May 1882, O.C. 1986, I, 778); as we have seen, he revised the latter for the title of his second published collection, and took his epigraph for the *Moralités* from the former.

74. "Les Déliquescences d'Adoré Floupette," *Revue contemporaine* 2, 1885, 266. See Pica, "Les Décadents" (Debauve, 212); L. Desprez, "M. Paul Verlaine," *Revue indépendante*, June 1884, 219; Pica, *Letteratura d'eccezione*; Laforgue, "Les Complaintes de Jules Laforgue" (see above, 27).

75. *Le Constitutionnel*, 28 July 1884, repr. in *Les Oeuvres et les hommes*, XVIII, 174.

76. Laforgue specifically links the underwater world with the mystical nirvana of the Buddhists: "A l'Aquarium de Berlin—devant le regard atone, gavé, sage, bouddhique des crocodiles—comme je comprends ces vieilles races d'orient qui avaient épuisé tous les sens, tous les tempéraments, toutes les métaphysiques—et qui finissent par adorer, béatifier comme symbole du Nirvâna promis ces regards nuls dont on ne peut dire s'ils sont plus infinis qu'immuables" (*Revue blanche* VIII, 49, June 1895, 553). He uses this imagery extensively to parody Decadence in *Salomé*.

77. Cf. Rotelli, *Due Studi sul simbolismo*, 71ff. The minor writers use it frequently, as in Paul Marguerrite, "La Légende de Pierrot" (*Le Passant*, February 1888): "Puis [Colombine] le rabaisse, le fait boire, manger, et s'offre enfin, suprême hostie. Pierrot va communier."

78. "Remords" and "Platonisme."

79. See Rotelli, *Due Studi sul simbolismo*, 79ff.

80. See M. Mansuy, *Un Moderne. Paul Bourget. De l'enfance au Disciple*.

81. P. Adam, "La Presse et le Symbolisme" (*Le Symboliste*, 7 October 1886, 62).

82. Adam, "Le Symbolisme" (*La Vogue*, 4–11 October 1886).

83. Moreau ("Les *Moralités légendaires* de Jules Laforgue," 872) cites Barrès's *Sous l'oeil des barbares* (1888) as an example: "Le drame même qui se joue dans notre tête ne nous est plus qu'un spectacle."

84. See Paul Adam, *La Vogue*, 4–11 October 1886. Cf. the Larousse article of 1887–1890 (second supplement): "la recherche des mots étranges, totalement inusités" and "l'art de donner à deviner au lecteur les plus obscures énigmes"; Morice, *Revue contemporaine* 2, 1885, 76: "un amour essentiel pour le compliqué, seule expression naturelle d'idées qui ne sont pas simples; le sens de la philosophie du verbe—sons et couleurs; une aristocratie de fond et de forme qui est en exil; une complaisance en toutes les menues délicatesses de style et de métrique, assonances, allitération, etc., la malédiction de la rhétorique, la science des nuances"; "Critique littéraire. Les Déliquescences," *Ibid.*, 266: "Il existe aujourd'hui une école de poésie, formée de jeunes raffinés amoureux de la forme parfaite, abstraite et suggestive; poursuiveurs acharnés du mot rare, précis et nombreux; lanceurs de néologismes"; Wyzewa, "Une Critique," *Revue indépendante*, n.s. 1, 1886, no. 1, 74: "des poètes nouveaux ont encore perfectionné le vocabulaire musical de la littérature en détruisant les règles surannées de la césure, de la rime périodique, du rythme fixe. Ils essaient une prose rythmée librement, un emploi logique et intermittent de la rime et des alliances sonores des syllabes"; and Pica, "Les Décadents" (Debauve, 212): "Tous ces écrivains byzantins ont en commun une adoration pour la forme parfaite et suggestive et la recherche passionnée des mots rares et pittoresques." For a general discussion of Decadent style, see R. P. Colin, "Les Décadents: nuanceurs ou barbares de l'idée," and P. Dumonceaux, "Les 'Décadents' ont-ils renouvelé la langue?"

85. Morice, *Revue contemporaine* 2, 1885, 76. Cf. P. Adam, "Le Symbolisme," *La Vogue* II, 12, 4–11 October 1886.

86. A. F. Claveau, *Le Gaulois*, 1886 (Pakenham, 43); Sutter Laumann, *La Justice*, 19 July 1885.

87. The more important second edition of the *Déliquescences* appeared in July 1885. The *Complaintes* came out at the end of the same month and were reviewed principally from mid-August to mid-September. J. Lethève demonstrates the extent of the publicity that the Decadent question received in the following year: "D'août 1885 à octobre 1886, les articles deviennent si nombreux que le grand public ne peut plus les ignorer" (*Impressionnistes et symbolistes devant la presse*, 178).

88. *Lutèce* 192, 9–16 August 1885 (Debauve, 199).

89. R. Caze, *Le Voltaire*, 18 August 1885 (Debauve, 201).

90. *Paris illustré*, 1 October 1885 (Debauve, 207).

91. Ch. Vignier, *Revue contemporaine*, 1 September 1885 (Debauve, 204).

92. *Le Passant*, August–September 1885 (Debauve, 201).

93. Nautet, *Notes sur la littérature moderne*, II, 134; Wyzewa, "Notes sur la littérature wagnérienne et les livres en 1885–1886," *Revue wagnérienne*, June 1886, 164.

94. Letter to Laforgue, 28 September 1885 (Debauve, 285f.).

95. *La République française*, 31 August 1885 (Debauve, 194).

96. Laforgue's vocabulary in general was considered representative. There are over fifty Laforguian entries in the *Petit Glossaire pour servir à l'intelligence des auteurs décadents et symbolistes* by Adam et Fénéon (Paris, Vanier, 1888).

97. "Les *Moralités légendaires* de Jules Laforgue," 865.

98. *L'Art moderne*, 8 January 1888 (Debauve, 220f.).

99. F. Brouez, *La Société nouvelle*, 1888 (Debauve, 223).

100. See Thornton, *The Decadent Dilemma*, 21.

101. "Définir la décadence," 8.

102. *Paul Verlaine and the Decadence*, 118.

103. *The Decadent Dilemma*, 21, 25f. Birkett follows this, calling des Esseintes a "comic grotesque" and *A Rebours* the "ironic celebration of Decadence" (*The Sins of the Fathers*, 68).

104. *M.L.*, 9.

105. Priestman, "The Age of Parody," ch. 5, 198ff.

106. Priestman (*Ibid.*, 197) notes a parallel situation in England.

107. *M.L.*, 9.

108. In the first case (*Le Chat noir* 63, 31 March 1883), the national anthem ironically fits a particular type of "infirme": the deaf man, "Entendez-vous dans les campagnes / Mugir ces féroces soldats"; the armless cripple, "Ils viennet jusque dans nos bras"; the man without legs, "Marchons, marchons," and so on. The second stirs up the furor of tenants against the Concierge (quoted in Richard, *Symbolisme*, 14). The third (*Le Chat noir* 46, 25 November 1882) satirizes Zola and the literary ambitions of the *groupe de Médan*.

109. *La Parodie*, 1869–1870, 84ff.

110. 4 February 1882.

111. *Le Chat noir*, 16, 29 April 1882.

112. S. Travers (*Nineteenth Century French Theatrical Parodies*) lists hundreds of such examples which follow the standard pattern of the farces and pantomimes of nineteenth-century popular comic theater.

113. Pia notes this also: "C'est Laforgue qui a donné le *la*" (*M.L.*, 11).

114. See R. Siohan, "Les Formes musicales de la parodie et du pastiche."

115. *L'Art moderne*, 8 January 1888 (Debauve, 220).

116. No. 5 of Debauve's list of copyholders (190). Laforgue read some of Lemaître's works, presumably his reviews in the *Revue bleue*, and perhaps his verse. In 1877 he praises Lemaître's article on Flaubert (Debauve, *Guêpe*, 170). See also letter 24 to Kahn, ca. 11 May 1885 (*L. A.*, 111): "Lis-tu les choses que publie Jules Lemaître, un normalien devenu un mandarin tout à fait charmant?"

117. Other examples include a play on *Don Quixote*, "Dulcinée," in which Dulcinea reads *Amadis of Gaul* and becomes somewhat "donquichottesque" herself. An early play, "La Bonne Hélène," (1896), transforms events and scenes from the *Iliad* by following through the implications of Helen's questionable character: she is a good-hearted victim, and her freely given favors are seen as signs of her kindness. See X. de Courville, "Le Pastiche et la parodie chez Jules Lemaître," 31ff., and G. Durrière, *Jules Lemaître et le théâtre*.

118. *Le Chasseur de Chevelures*, 17, March 1893.

119. *Ibid*. For example, one plays on Musset's "La Coupe et les lèvres": "*Le coeur d'un homme vierge est un vase profond*, mais combien nous préférons, pour déposer les cannes et parapluies, les grands vases japonais du bazar de Yeddo, 68, rue Mogador prolongée...."

120. *Ibid.*; and no. 27, January 1894.

121. *Revue blanche*, May 1892, 278–287.

122. "L'Authentique Histoire de Barbe-Bleue," *Revue blanche* 21, July 1893.

123. *Le Décadent*, 27 November 1886; and 1 January, 1 February, 15 March, 15 May, 1 July, and 15 September 1888.

124. *Le Décadent*, 15 November 1888, 1 April 1889, 1 March 1889. See Richard, *Mouvement décadent*, ch. 12, 17, and 18.

125. *Symbolisme*, 271: "les flèches de Vicaire et Beauclair visaient surtout les copistes indiscrets, les nourrissons des Muses sèches et les suiveurs empanachés des plumes d'autrui."

126. Cf. Laforgue, "Complainte des grands Pins dans une Villa Abandonnée"; also letter 9 to Kahn, c. 27 December 1883, L.A., 53: "je suis très vanné."

127. See Claveau (Pakenham, 43). Cf. Trézenik, describing the goal of the followers of Baudelaire and Mallarmé: "faire flou, vague, opaque" (*Lutèce*, 19 April 1885).

128. *Lutèce*, 16 August 1885.

Chapter 3

1. Four of the six *Moralités* have subtitles: *Hamlet, Lohengrin, Pan et la Syrinx,* and *Persée et Andromède. Le Miracle des Roses* and *Salomé*, as titles, already differ from those of the works parodied. I shall discuss each in its respective chapter.

2. On the history of Hamlet in French literature and art, see H. P. Bailey, *Hamlet in France from Voltaire to Laforgue,* and D. Madsen, "The Figure of Hamlet in Baudelaire, Mallarmé, and Laforgue."

3. *A propos de Hamlet* (336).

4. Cf. "Pierrots" (*L'Imitation*): "Ils ont comme chaton de bague / Le scarabée égyptien."

5. Cf. Bourget's *Essais*, especially "Baudelaire"; Huysmans, *A Rebours*; and, interestingly, Taine's essay on Shakespeare in the *Histoire de la littérature anglaise,* which presents Hamlet as one whose overly impassioned imagination exhausts his will.

6. In a note, Laforgue described the categorical imperative as the second of the three Comtean stages of ethical evolution: "toujours les triades de Hegel. les trois stades de l'Inconscient. Il y a eu trois stades de l'éthique—théologique (le Décalogue), métaphysique (l'Impératif Catégorique), positiviste (l'altruisme sociologique)" (E. A. Holmes, "The Poetic Development of Jules Laforgue," Appendix D, I, 8).

7. The first *Hamlet* appeared in *La Vogue,* November 1886.

8. "Do you not know that in true death there will be no other self alive that can mourn your death nor, standing, mourn you lying there?"

9. "Thus he is indignant at having been created mortal, and he does not see that in true death there will be no other self who, alive, can mourn his own death, or standing, suffer what he feels lying there being lacerated."

10. *Revue blanche* XI, 84, 482. In another note he juxtaposes the Unconscious and the *templa serena* of *De Rerum Natura* II, 8 (*O.C.* 1986, I, 655).

11. Laforgue translates for himself here, suggesting that he was not using a translation when he wrote *Hamlet*. The epigraphs to *F.B.V.*, quoted in the original English, also indicate this. He does seem to have read *Hamlet* early on in the French translation of Le Tourneur (1779), however, as he mentions it in the *Guêpe* chronicle of 25 September 1879 (*O.C.* 1986, I, 197).

12. In this, Hamlet again resembles Laforgue's Pierrot. Cf. "Locutions des Pierrots" XVI (*L'Imitation*): "Je ne suis qu'un viveur lunaire / Qui fait des ronds dans les bassins, / Et cela, sans autre dessein / Que devenir un légendaire."

13. The stagnant pond is a standard motif of Decadence. See P. Stephan, *Paul Verlaine and the Decàdence*, 188; and P. Mathias, "De l'imaginaire au psychosomatique dans la sensibilité décadente" (*L'Esprit de décadence*).

14. Etching has definite associations with Decadence: the late nineteenth century experienced a well-documented revival of the art; it had macabre and dreamlike associations, as Baudelaire described it vis-à-vis Meryon's etchings of Paris; des Esseintes had a fascination for the etchings of Goya. Laforgue was especially interested in etching: he practiced it himself and championed the works of his friend, the German etcher Max Klinger.

15. E.g. J.-L. Barrault, *Cahiers Renaud-Barrault* (90ff.; cf. Arkell, *Looking for Laforgue*, 191); M. Dansel, *Choix de poésies. Hamlet* (66). Barrault notes that Laforgue also takes from Saxo the childhood friendship of Hamlet and Ophelia: "C'était ma petite amie d'enfance" (32). Laforgue may have known of Saxo's *Vita Amlethi* by an essay describing it, appended to most French translations of *Hamlet*, including the Le Tourneur one. For a study of Saxo and the Hamlet legend in general, see W. Hansen, *Saxo Grammaticus and the Life of Hamlet*; and G. Bullough, *Narrative and Dramatic Sources of Shakespeare*.

16. By a curious irony of literary history, research in the twentieth century has proposed that Shakespeare based Gertrude's description of the death of Ophelia (IV,vii) on the drowning of a certain Katherine—or Kate—Hamlet in the Avon in 1580. Laforgue would not have known this anecdote, but would surely have appreciated the coincidence: his own heroine—Kate, alias Ophelia—is truer than he imagined. (See E. Fripp, *Shakespeare Studies*, 1930, 128ff.)

17. The words come from Michelangelo's *Rime* CXXIII: "Caro m'e 'l sonno, e piu l'esser di sasso, / Mentre che 'l danno e la vergogna dura. / Non veder, non sentir, m'e gran ventura: / Pero non mi destar, deh! parla basso.

18. The first three of the five passages come, with slight variations, from *F.B.V.* XLVI, XXXIII, and XXXVII.

19. *Consolation à M. Du Périer*, 77–80.

20. J.-L. Barrault (*Cahiers Renaud-Barrault*, 92) traces this episode to the temptation scene in Belleforest's version of the Hamlet story (1570), where a friend of the hero Amleth warns him of Fengo's trap. But there is no bird (let alone a strangled one) in Belleforest; the friend warns Amleth only "avec certains signes." In Saxo, this sign is specifically a gadfly ("oestri") sent with a bit of chaff under its tail, but this is too far removed from Laforgue's episode to be relevant to it. The texts of both Saxo and Belleforest are reproduced in I. Gollancz, *The Sources of Hamlet*.

21. Cf. *A Rebours*, ch. 14: "En littérature, il avait, le premier, sous ce

Notes

titre emblématique: 'Le démon de la Perversité', épié ces impulsions irrésistibles que la volonté subit sans les connaître et que la pathologie cérébrale explique d'une façon à peu près sûre."

22. "Complainte des formalités nuptiales."

Chapter 4

1. Scholars have generally followed F. Ruchon (*Jules Laforgue*, 107): "*Le Miracle des Roses*, la plus moderne des *Moralités*, la seule qui ne soit pas la parodie ou remaniement d'un sujet antique." Even Pia (*M. L.*, 8) did not distinguish a model: "A l'exception des *Miracle des Roses*, dont l'héroïne n'est pas de haute extrace et dont le décor n'a rien d'irréel, toutes ses moralités se développent autour d'une ou plusieurs créatures d'origine mythologique." In her recent edition of Laforgue's art criticism, however, M. Dottin mentions in a footnote two *Miracle des Roses* by Gustave Moreau (*Textes de critique d'art*, 29).

2. Wyzewa, *Nos Maîtres*, 238.

3. *Revue universitaire* II, 1903, 424.

4. Letter 44, ca. 3 June 1886 (*L. A.*, 188): "Ces nouvelles sont: Salomé; Hamlet ou les suites de la piété filiale; le Miracle des Roses; Incomprise; l'Amour de la symétrie; Persée et Andromède ou le plus heureux des trois; Corinne au Cap Misène; Marlborough s'en va-t-en guerre. Seules la 4è et la 5è ne sont pas sur vieux canevas." *Le Miracle des Roses* figures third in this list. Of the two exceptions, "Incomprise" became *Les Deux pigeons*, and "L'Amour de la symétrie" did not survive.

5. This was an emblem of the evil eye in both Egyptian and Roman culture, and a favorite sexual symbol in Decadent art.

6. *Agenda*, O.C. 1986, I, 870.

7. Liszt's work (1867) was based on the M. von Schwind frescoes illustrating the life of Saint Elizabeth, painted for the Wartburg castle in 1855. Each section of the oratorio corresponds to one of the six frescoes.

8. *Agenda*, 24 May (*O.C.* 1986, I, 880): "Dès 8h.—La procession de la Fête-Dieu! Devant l'hôtel d'Angleterre—. . . Quelle horrible population tannée, déjetée, osseuse, abrutie, abêtie . . . Les valets s'étaient mis à la file des hommes aussi—en noir et gantés . . . Les petites filles, les garçons . . . des gens récitaient des chapelets."

9. *Agenda*, 26 August (*O.C.* 1986, I, 898): "—S Sébastien, le capitaine—Largartijo (*sic*) et Frascuelo—Mantilles, éventail—assaut de trains lents. Retour (notes)." Lagartijo and Frascuelo were famous matadors. The notes mentioned do not seem to have survived, although they may have been used for the preliminary version of the story, the Carton manuscript ([A] in Grojnowski).

10. Laforgue does not mention *Le Miracle des Roses* until June of 1886; however, E. A. Holmes ("The Poetic Development of Jules Laforgue," 331) notes that the earliest manuscript draft is written on the same paper and in the same hand as the early draft of *Salomé*, dating from the spring of 1885. Laforgue seems to have done a first version of *Le Miracle des Roses* around June 1885, and then taken it up again in the spring of 1886.

11. In this it somewhat resembles *Salomé*, based on the "Salomé" episode of Flaubert's *Hérodias*.

12. Cf. Hamlet's "allure traînarde" (24, 28).

13. Ch. 1, 37: "The other seedling behaved rather differently, for it fell in the morning until 11.30 a.m., and then rose, but after 12.10 p.m. again fell; and the great evening rise did not begin until 1.22 p.m." The French translation, *La Faculté motrice dans les plantes*, appeared in 1882. Laforgue does not identify the work, only the author.

14. *Semiotics of Poetry*, 191.

15. As others have noted, the town of *Le Miracle des Roses* is modelled somewhat on Baden-Baden, which the court visited annually in the spring (Arkell, *Looking for Laforgue*, 93ff.; Ruchon, *Jules Laforgue*, 107; Ramsey, *Jules Laforgue and the Ironic Inheritance*, 108). The evidence of the 1883 *Agenda* verifies this, for the details noted there reappear in the story: the Greek chapel, the fountain, the melancholy French horn, the local band, the bells in the valley, the *Fête-Dieu* procession, the Hôtel d'Angleterre. See 27 and 29 April, 14 and 24 May, and the Baden-Baden portion generally (*O.C.* 1986, I, 874–82). However, the fictional town also partakes of another stop on the court's rounds, Hombourg. The description of the festivities in the parody (59f.) matches Laforgue's notes on Hombourg in *E.P.L.* IV, 26, May 1892, 203f.

16. Laforgue elsewhere described the waltz in similar terms of poignant, autumnal nostalgia: "La poignance lointaine de ces valses, faites de souvenir—on les joue en automne solitaire après les casinos d'été où elles accompagnaient une illusion d'une vie idéale, linge, toilettes, repas fins, demi-saison, tous distingués et oisifs—ou l'année d'après, et ça dit le bonheur d'antan." (*E.P.L.* IV, 22, January 1892, 9)

17. Cf. *Agenda*, 27 April (*O.C.* 1986, I, 876): "Service à l'église grecque, pope noir à croix d'argent—nasillements insensés—portraits des Stourdza."

18. Lawn tennis was a recent invention, formalized by the English in 1877. Cf. Laforgue's notes on Hombourg (*E.P.L.* IV, 26, May 1892, 203): "le Casino et ses toilettes de Boston, et les quadrilles d'enfants sur la pelouse, et un ballon prêt à partir, et plus loin vu de la terrasse du casino la pelouse des lawntennisants"; and also letter 27 to Kahn on 6 August 1885 (*L. A.*, 120): "Je ne suis plus à Coblentz mais à Hombourg, une ville

Notes

d'eaux . . . pleine d'Anglais, fleurie de toilettes, encombrée de lawn-tennis, etc."

19. Laforgue witnessed the celebration of this holiday in Baden-Baden with contempt. See above, n. 8.

20. Laforgue left no explicit evidence of having read this work, except for its echo in *Le Miracle des Roses;* however, he read all Flaubert's other works, including the two novellas that accompany *Un Coeur simple* in the *Trois Contes* trilogy, and parodies them frequently in the *Moralités*. I consider it certain that he knew it; the parallels are more than coincidental. See below, 124f.

21. Cf. *A Rebours,* ch. 5: "un énorme dé à jouer où clignait une paupière triste."

22. All quotations from *Un Coeur simple* come from the Pléiade edition of the *Trois Contes,* 621f.

23. The little girls in white are a ubiquitous image in Laforgue, as in *D.V.* III, IV, and XII.

Chapter 5

1. Laforgue never mentions *Lohengrin* until after it appears in *La Vogue* (19 and 26 July 1886). It was probably written and given to Kahn for publication during his visit to Paris (21 June–14 July).

2. Wagner was inspired by Wolfram von Eschenbach and Wolfram by Chrétien de Troyes' *Perceval*.

3. Popular parodies of Wagner were numerous in late nineteenth-century theater, particularly at the Bouffes, and "Lohengrin" alone inspired several, though mostly after 1887: "Lohengrin à l'Alcazar" (February 1886), "Lohengrin II, ou Lohengrin à l'Eldorado" (November 1891), "Le Petit Lohengrin" (January 1892), "Lorehencin" (February 1892), "Lolo Beaugrain" (March 1892), and "Monsieur Lohengrin" (November 1896). See S. Travers, *Catalogue of Nineteenth Century French Theatrical Parodies,* 103.

4. The 1883 Agenda notes "Lohengrin" in February (*O.C.* 1986, I, 866); in April one of its melodies keeps running through his head (*Ibid.,* 876). For allusions in the poems, see "Les Linges, le cygne" (*Imitation*), and *F.B.V.* XXV and XXVII.

5. *Lohengrin* was announced in 1885 as soon to appear at the Opéra-Comique, but protests caused the production to be cancelled; it was given at the Eden Théâtre, 3 May 1887.

6. *Revue wagnérienne* 6, 8 July 1885 (cf. 8 February and 8 March 1886, and March and 15 May 1887). Laforgue read an article on *Lohengrin* in the

Revue illustrée (letter to Lindenlaub, 12 April 1886, in Durry, *Jules Laforgue,* 236).

7. Wagner himself assisted this interpretation by describing the tragic situation of the hero as parallel to that of the modern artist in society. See M. Kufferath, *Le Théâtre de Richard Wagner. Lohengrin,* 84.

8. *Art poétique,* Canto II, 175–76: "Le latin, dans les mots, brave l'honnêteté: / Mais le lecteur français veut être respecté."

9. Cf. "Un Mot au soleil pour commencer" (*Imitation*), where the same phrase is called the sun's "vieux prêche" and rejected in favor of the moon.

10. The original text had him returning "vers les altitudes de l'Egoïsme" (172).

11. "[Rimbaud], un des plus farouches décadents" (*Le Figaro,* 24 November 1886, in Debauve, 232). Cf. Huysmans' Preface to *A Rebours* (see above, ch. 2). Except for the selections published in Verlaine's *Poètes maudits* (1883), Rimbaud's poetry was relatively unknown until 1886, when Kahn published the *Illuminations* in *La Vogue.* Laforgue was impressed: see letter 44 to Kahn, 3 June 1886 (*L. A.,* 187), and also his notes on Rimbaud (*M.P.,* 129). In *A propos de Hamlet,* he specifically names Rimbaud (along with Bourget and himself) as a modern example of the Hamletic character.

12. See *Stéphane Vassiliew* and the "Complainte du petit hypertrophique."

13. In "Jeux" (*Imitation*), Laforgue applies the same image to the moon.

14. Of the key terms of the Mass that Laforgue uses, one finds in Baudelaire *ciboire, autel, ostensoir, Sainte Table,* and *encensoir.* This aspect of Baudelaire was noted by critics from the first. See, for example, Charbonnel: "Il y eut encensoirs, ostensoirs, autels, hosties et ciboires . . . L'amour fut une adoration ou même une communion de Sainte Table" (Carter, *Baudelaire et la critique française,* 61). For Laforgue's use of liturgical imagery in his poetry (although not in the *Moralités*), see Rotelli, *Due Studi sul simbolismo,* especially the quantitative tables (77ff.).

15. Cf. the moon of Chateaubriand: the "vierge blanche" of *Les Martyrs,* the "reine des nuits" of *Le Génie du christianisme* and, most importantly here, the vestal virgin of *Atala,* 130: "[La lune] se leva au milieu de la nuit, comme une blanche vestale qui vient pleurer sur le cercueil d'une compagne." Rotelli (*Due studi sul simbolismo*) notes nine occurrences of *Notre-Dame* in the *Complaintes,* all but one of which apply to the moon. See especially "Complainte à Notre-Dame des Soirs" and "Complainte de cette Bonne Lune."

16. Laforgue used these terms frequently in his poetry, sometimes together. See "Etats" (*Imitation*): "Elle est l'Hostie! et le silence est son ciboire." Rotelli notes seven instances of *ciboire* and seventeen of *hostie* (*Due Studi sul simbolismo*, 80, 82, 96, 98).

17. Cf. the balloon launching in *Le Miracle des Roses*, and *E.P.L.* IV, 22, May 1892, 204. In his *Guêpe* chronicle of 21 August 1879, Laforgue describes the explosion of the great balloon built for the 1878 Paris Exhibition: "Hier encore il se dandinait sur ses amarres, faisant des grâces devant les badauds ou montait cranement dans l'azur avec sa petite cargaison de philistins ébaudis, et maintenant . . . sic transit gloria mundi; traduction: voilà comment s'en va une fortune de 500.000 francs" (*O.C.* 1986, I, 188).

18. Laforgue used this line from Shakespeare's *Hamlet* as an epigraph to "Dimanches" XLIV (*F.B.V.*).

19. Cf. the Ophélie of *Hamlet*, who was eighteen; the succulent eyes of Salomé; the sad mouth of Kate.

20. Cf. the words of the lady in *D.V.* X. Laforgue used the figure of the Sulamite often. See "Complainte des Pianos dans les Quartiers Aisés," "Complainte de l'Orgue de Barbarie," "Complainte du Temps et de sa Commère l'Espace"; and "L'Aurore-Promise" (*F.B.V.* XXXV).

21. Laforgue used the metaphor of the mass for sexual union in the *D.V.* Cf. the "messes dont on a fait un jeu" and the "Grand'Messe" of IV.

22. This is a frequent metaphor in the *D.V.* Cf. "Dimanches" IV, "Solo de lune" VII, and "Sur une défunte" XI.

23. Cf. also "Climat, faune et flore de la Lune" (*Imitation*), which contains many of these, as well as most of Laforgue's terms and metaphors for Decadence: *Immaculée-Conception, nébuleuse, silence, ivoire, ciboires, blême, fontaines de Léthé, étangs, crayeux, nécropoles, crapauds, cygnes, paons blancs, cristal, fleurs fixes, cierges, lys, albes, lait, calme, amours blancs, miroir mort.*

24. Cf. Andromède (255f.) and Syrinx (293), who have the same characteristics.

25. Cf. Laforgue's ironic prose piece on this subject, "Bobo": "On l'a donc laissée dans la paresse, le miroir, l'esclavage, sans autre occupation que son sexe, sa seule arme et monnaie. Et elle a donc, à force de siècles de serre chaude, hypertrophié son sexe. Et elle est devenue le Féminin, l'éternel Féminin (comme s'il y avait un éternel Masculin!), franc-maçonnerie de faux frères, quoi. . . . Ah! nous avons laissé notre petite soeur faire humanité à part. On récolte ce qu'on a semé" (*Le Symboliste* 2, 15 October 1886).

26. Again, cf. "Bobo" (see previous note): "et c'est les génies qu'elle fait souffrir particulièrement pour leur faire donner des chefs d'oeuvre qui

la renouvellent aussi, la retransfigurent et alimentent la banque de la loterie."

27. Cf. *F.B.V.* XXXIV: "Je te crierai: 'Nous sommes frères! / Alors, vêts-toi à ma manière, / Ma manière ne tromp e pas; / Et perds ce dandinement louche / D'animal lesté de ses couches, / Et galopons par les haras!' "

28. "Tu t'en vas et tu nous quittes / Tu nous quitt' et tu t'en vas. / Si tu t'en vas, paye un litre / Paye un litre si tu t'en vas."

29. Cf. Laforgue's own "Complainte du roi de Thulé" on the same theme of pure love: "Il était un roi de Thulé, / Immaculé, / Qui, loin des jupes et des choses, / Pleurait sur la métempsychose / Des lys en roses, / Et quel palais!"

Chapter 6

1. Letter 109 to Henry, 6 June 1885, *O.C.* V, 128. *Salomé* was the first *moralité* that Laforgue wrote, not, as is commonly alleged, *Le Miracle des Roses*. *Salomé* is the first to be mentioned by name in his correspondence (letter 107, mid-May 1885, *O.C.* 1922, V, 124), and the first one completed. (*Le Miracle des Roses* contains older material and was initially drafted at the same time as *Salomé* but was finished a year later. See ch. 4, n. 10.) The theme interested him from early on; in 1882 he mentions working on a *Salomé* in verse (letter 56 to Henry, 5 August 1882, *O.C.* 1986, I, 795).

2. For example, Carlo Dolci and Paul Delaroche.

3. P. Jullian, *Esthètes et magiciens*, 132.

4. P. Mourier-Casile, "Modernité à rebours," 152.

5. Laforgue knew the relevant works of all these artists. For other Salomés, see Décaudin, "Un Mythe 'fin de siècle': Salomé"; and J.-P. Reverseau, "Pour une étude du thème de la tête coupée dans la littérature et la peinture dans la seconde partie du 19è siècle."

6. *A Rebours*, ch. 5.

7. Laforgue never mentions one of the most famous examples, Mallarmé's *Hérodiade*, two parts of which were not published during his lifetime. He did not meet Mallarmé until late October of 1885, and thus for *Salomé* he cannot have had access to Mallarmé's unpublished works. (A letter to Mallarmé from Kahn of 18 October 1885 asks permission to present Laforgue at one of the following Tuesday soirées; the meeting probably took place on the 27th. [coll. P. Pia, Vanderbilt University]). He may have read the "Scène" portion (1871), though this is uncertain (cf. letter 28 to Kahn, 10 November 1885, *L. A.*, 127). Huysmans quotes Hérodiade's invocation to her mirror in *A Rebours* (ch. 15, 219f.). There are some connections between the two heroines: Hérodiade, like Salomé, is associated with the night; she is narcissistic and claims to be committed to chastity,

while admitting at the end that she has been lying; the jewels of her hair are likened to stars; the poem is concerned with her nascent sexuality. But these can also be found in other works of the Salomé genre, as we shall see. If the language, themes, metaphors, even ideas of *Salomé* remind us of Mallarmé's, it may be because they reflect and parody those of Decadence, and Mallarmé, as we have seen in chapter two, was considered with Verlaine one of the two "pilllars" of the movement.

8. Laforgue read *Salammbô* and alludes to it frequently. *L'Imitation de Notre-Dame la Lune*, written at about the same time as *Salomé*, is dedicated to her.

9. *A Rebours*, ch. 14. Pierrot discusses the importance of *Salammbô*, *La Tentation de Saint Antoine*, and *Trois Contes* for the Decadent imagination (52ff.). See above, ch. 2.

10. Laforgue will work a variation on this headdress connection by also giving Salomé one of Salammbô's headdresses, but not the mitred one; rather, the peacock feather one that she wears at the end of the novel as she watches Mâtho die, before dying herself.

11. Ruchon, *Jules Laforgue, sa vie, son oeuvre*, 111.

12. W. Ramsey, *Jules Laforgue and the Ironic Inheritance*, 161.

13. Praz, *Romantic Agony*, 392.

14. Letter 44 to Kahn, ca. 3 June 1886, *L. A.*, 188.

15. I have not succeeded in tracing the epigraph. Denis Jourdain (1811–1871) served in the Société des Missions Etrangères in Indochina and wrote a *Grammaire franco-annamite* (Saigon, Imprimerie du gouvernement, 1872).

16. Laforgue added "sept" to the final version; the original one had merely the unspecified "symbolismes d'Etat."

17. The sea is appropriate to the Decadent ideal of the Isles. Cf. Hamlet's revery (9).

18. *Salammbô*, ch. 1.

19. Cf. "Dialogue avant le lever de la lune," *Imitation:* "Je veux bien vivre; mais vraiment, / L'Idéal est trop élastique!"

20. The love of Salomé for the Baptist belongs to a popular tradition, according to which he repulses her advances, and she thus asks for his head. (Heine used it in *Atta Troll*.) Laforgue alters this, however; Iaokanann most certainly, and fatally, does not resist.

21. Cf. Laforgue's description of the Prussian military in Berlin, *O.C.* 1922, VI, esp. ch. 2. He equates the imperial regime with the bourgeoisie generally, whose values he satirizes here.

22. Cf. Laforgue's "Dimanches" (*F.B.V.* LV): "Et professent / Le perfectionnement de notre espèce."

23. Laforgue uses it in the "Complainte du pauvre chevalier-errant": "Au fond de chapelles de mousseline / Pâle, ou jonquille à pois noirs, / Dans les soirs, / Feu d'artificieront envers vous mes sens encensoirs!"

24. Salammbô indeed wears a "tunique jaune" (*Salammbô*, 747).

25. Most commentators mention Salomé's peculiar costume but do not discuss its significance. Ruchon describes it as a "costume aussi saugrenu que l'âme de l'être qu'il revêt et qu'il pare" (*Jules Laforgue*, 102). Only R. Schaffner, in an aside, notices any relation between it and her narcissism: "Der Abscheu vor banaler Wirklichkeit ist der Grund für narzisshaft (jonquille) esoterisches Wesen" (*Die Salome-Dichtungen von Flaubert, Laforgue, Wilde und Mallarmé*, 100).

26. The Aquarium section of the story comes from Laforgue's prose piece, "L'Aquarium" (*La Vogue* 6, 29 May 1886). Grojnowski reprints Ruchon's line-by-line comparison of the two versions (346ff.). Laforgue always viewed the Aquarium in terms of the Unconscious and the mystical nirvana of Buddhism. See ch. 2, n. 76.

27. Laforgue associated the Aquarium with the womb explicitly in the "Complainte du foetus": "Adieu, forêts d'aquarium qui, me couvant, / Avez mis ce levain dans ma chrysalide!"

28. Cf. Laforgue's notes on the Berlin aquarium: "A l'aquarium—les fonds silencieux pour lesquels c'est toujours l'éternité, pour lesquels il n'y a ni printemps ni été ni automne ni hiver" (*Revue blanche* VII, 36, October 1894, 307).

29. Cf. *Revue blanche* VIII, 49, June 1895, 553: "Mais l'idéal c'est ces éponges, ces astéries, ces plasmas dans le silence opaque et frais, tout au rêve, de l'eau —"

30. "Dans un palais semblable à une basilique d'une architecture tout à la fois musulmane et byzantine"; and "le palais . . . ainsi qu'un Alhambra" (*A Rebours*, ch. 5).

31. *Metamorphoses*, 9.451ff.

32. "Litanies des derniers quartiers de la lune" (*Imitation*).

33. Cf. *Salammbô* (O.C. I, 718): "chevelure poudrée d'un sable violet"; "une chaînette d'or entre ses chevilles"; "une bouche rose comme une grenade ouverte"; "lyre d'ébène"; "une coiffure faite avec des plumes de paon étoilées de pierreries" (988); with *Salomé*: "[cheveux] saupoudrés de pollens inconnus" (223); "ses pieds . . . chaussés uniquement d'un anneau aux chevilles" (225); "les lèvres découvrant d'un accent circonflexe rose pâle une denture aux gencives d'un rose plus pâle encore" (223); "une petite lyre noire" (221); "une roue de paon" (223).

Notes 251

34. "Comme elle était très lourde, ils la portèrent alternativement."

35. She is also obliged to alter it, changing the original "eo" (referring to opium) to "ea," consistent with its feminine antecedent, "Grande Vertu Curative"; "dormativa" is simply wrong (it should read "dormitiva"), and one wonders whether the mistaken vowel was conditioned by the preceding "cur*a*tive" and "palli*a*tive," in a manner typical of Salomé's ludicrous assonantal speech. Editors have always emended the "a" to "i," but the manuscript versions reprinted in the Grojnowski edition read "dorm*a*tiva." This is unlikely to be a mistake on Laforgue's part, for the cognate French word preserves the "i," "dormitive." For the joke, see *Le Malade imaginaire*, 3è intermède.

36. Laforgue's play on Poe's *La Vérité sur le cas de M. Waldemar* in *Persée et Andromède* ("La Vérité sur le cas de Tout") originally figured as the tetrarch's Bible in *Salomé*. See below, ch. 7, n. 9.

37. The Baptist and Orpheus legends are related by the motif of the severed head, specifically, one that retains its powers even after it has been cut off. The likeness between Moreau's paintings of the two figures was perceived by Gautier: "Sur la grande lyre aux cornes rouges repose la tête d'Orphée, comme celle de Saint-Jean Baptiste sur son plat d'argent aux mains d'Hérodiade" (*Moniteur universel*, 15 May 1866, quoted in Reverseau, "Pour une étude de la tête coupée dans la littérature et la peinture dans la seconde partie du XIXè siècle," 177). Laforgue discussed the Salomé and Orpheus paintings in his art criticism (*Gazette des Beaux-Arts*, 1 August 1883, and *Le Symboliste*, 4, 30 October 1886).

38. *A Rebours*, ch. 5, 108.

39. *Salammbô*, 994.

Chapter 7

1. Laforgue had written a draft of *Persée* by early June 1886; he then revised it substantially in late July, precisely at the time he was making the important transition from the stilted syllabic meter of the *Fleurs de bonne volonté* to the more supple free verse of the *Derniers Vers*. The prose reflects his new manner: it abounds with repetitions, vocatives, independent descriptive phrases, and lyrical rhythms, and has many images and themes in common with the last poems, such as the sunset of part 3.

2. "— Ils apportaient tous les lundis une esquisse à Lehmann — Daphnis et Chloé— . . . Persée déliv. Andromède . . . etc." (published by Debauve in "Laforgue romancier. Une Tentative avortée: *Un Raté*", 135). The notes date from around 1880.

3. "Le Plus Heureux des Trois" was first performed at the Palais Royal in 1870, and restaged in 1875. Laforgue moved to Paris in 1876. He

knew Labiche's plays and devoted a long chronicle to them in *La Guêpe* (18 May 1877, *O.C.* 1986, I, 169f.), where he mentions the eight volumes of Labiche's *Oeuvres complètes* just published.

4. "Le Meunier, son fils et l'âne."

5. Cf. the opening of *Persée et Andromède* with the passages on the sea in *Stéphane Vassiliew* (1881).

6. Cf. *Hamlet*: "(qui n'a entendu parler de ses étonnants yeux d'hirondelle de mer?)" (11); and *Le Miracle des Roses:* ". . . ses yeux, tantôt aigus comme ceux des inapprivoisables oiseaux des Atlantiques" (75).

7. Laforgue read Spinoza's *Ethics* and mentions it frequently. See letter 22 to Henry, 30 December 1881, *O.C.* 1986, I, 732; 27 and 47 to Ephrussi, 13 January and 12 May 1882; *Ibid.*, 744, 780; and letter 20 to Kahn, 6 April 1885, *L. A.*, 96: "J'ai lâché mes nouvelles et je relis Spinoza."

8. *Exorciser* is a Laforguian expression for sexual union. Cf. "aller chez sa maîtresse, aller s'exorciser" (*Dragées*, 56); and *E.P.L.* IV, 26, May 1892, 198: "pourquoi suis-je fou d'elle et non d'une autre? . . . Pourquoi est celle qui doit m'exorciser"

9. *La Vérité sur le cas de Tout* originally figured as the title of the Tetrarch's Bible in *Salomé*, where it made sense not only as the Unconscious truth that governs the island, but also as the source of Salomé's postmortem experiments on the Baptist's head in part four. Laforgue seems to have considered using "Incidents de la vérité sur mon cas" as the title of *F.B.V.* (letter to Lindenlaub, ca. 17 April 1886, in Durry, *Jules Laforgue*, 240).

10. The poem may be compared, in language and theme, to Laforgue's own outline of this philosophy in *L'Art moderne en Allemagne* (*Revue blanche* IX, 56, 1 October 1895, 293).

11. Cf. Laforgue's own Romantic sunset in *Stéphane Vassiliew*, *O.C.* 1986, I, 469. (Ruchon also makes this connection in his introduction, 18).

12. The most famous usage of the parodic nature of the pumpkin is Seneca's satire on the deification of Claudius, the *Apocolocyntosis*, or "Pumpkinification."

13. Cf. the vulgarization of the sun from plenipotentiary monarch to dying animal in "L'Hiver qui vient":

Soleils plénipotentiaires des travaux en blonds Pactoles
Des spectacles agricoles,
Où êtes-vous ensevelis?
Ce soir un soleil fichu gît au haut du coteau
Gît sur le flanc, dans les genêts, sur son manteau,

Un soleil blanc comme un crachat d'estaminet
Sur une litière de jaunes genêts
De jaunes genêts d'automne.
. . .
Et il gît là, comme une glande arrachée dans un cou,
Et il frissonne, sans personne! . . .

The more spectacular bloody sunset of *D.V.* II, "Le Mystère des trois cors," is also described in terms of death and compared ironically to vitriol and poison. "L'Hiver qui vient" associates the "Adieu paniers" refrain with the barrenness of oncoming winter and the proximity of death. Cf. also *Le Miracle des Roses,* in which the phrase occurs just after the procession and before Ruth awakens to proclaim the "miracle."

14. In a note, Laforgue paraphrases Hartmann's discussion of mysticism as "la désagrégation, l'abandon, la dissolution, la dilution du moi dans l'Absolu ou de l'absolu dans le moi . . . Annihilation de la conscience dans l'inconscient, sauf un soupçon de quoi jouir de son annihilation—une agonie perpétuelle." Mystical pleasure can be had not in total annihilation, but in near annihilation which preserves enough consciousness to enjoy it. (Repr. ms. in Ruchon, *Jules Laforgue,* 49. Cf. *Philosophie de l'Inconscient,* I, 402f.)

15. Jean-Aubry (*M.L., O.C.* 1922, III, 314) likens Laforgue's epilogue to *Les Nuits espagnoles* of the popular Second Empire novelist Joseph Méry (1854, repr. 1881). In this work, a group of society people meet nightly to hear a story told by one of them; the stories generally have some relation to the stars. Besides this similarity, however, there is little other resemblance between the novel and Laforgue's epilogue, in theme, subject, detail, or even general technique. The narrator is usually conspicuous in Méry's story, unlike Laforgue's who appears unexpectedly at the end. The link between the stars and the individual tales in Méry's book is often so tenuous as to be meaningless, unlike the direct relation between the constellations of the epilogue and the *Moralité*. It is possible that Laforgue knew this work; Pia, though sceptical, observes that Méry's works were easily available on the quais, a favorite haunt of Laforgue's (*M.L.,* 243). Whether Laforgue knew the work or not, *Les Nuits espagnoles* play no role at all in the epilogue.

16. Cf. Laforgue's play on this word at the end of *Salomé* (see above, 167.)

Chapter 8

1. In 1882, Laforgue stated his intention of writing a "Complainte de Pan" (letter 67 to Henry, 2 December 1882, *O.C.* 1986, I, 810). The evi-

dence suggests that he wrote *Pan et la Syrinx* slightly earlier than is generally thought, probably in October and early November 1886. On an envelope addressed to him in Leah's handwriting and postmarked 5 October from London, he scribbled a line from its first page, along with some ideas for revisions of *Salomé*: "Immortel et jeune, Pan n'avait pas encore vraiment aimé comme je l'entends" (see Jean-Aubry's edition of the *M. L., O.C.* 1922, III, 306 and 309). Moreover, the story has many affinities of language and theme with the *Derniers Vers* written around October, "Simple Agonie" (VI) and "Solo de lune" (VII). In "Simple Agonie," one finds Pan's *sanglot d'amour,* his concern for expressing "la chose qu'est la chose," and the sustained association of love with art. With "Solo de lune," the story shares the themes of regret and nostalgia, the physical and emotional warmth of the summer season in which both are set (particularly the summer night of heightened sensation), the hero's concern for reconciling his soul to the Present, the image of the primitive deep forest, and even the "solo de lune" of the title ("la vallée inondée d'un mémorable *solo de lune,*" 283). The poems written in November—*D.V.* IX, X, and XI—also have echoes in the story but to a lesser extent.

2. But Laforgue complains of not knowing Mallarmé's poem well. See letter 28 to Kahn, 10 November 1885, *L. A.,* 127: "En somme, qu'est-ce que j'ai lu? Prose pour des Esseintes, l'Après-midi d'un Faune, *en passant seulement et pas à mon aise,* et jadis, tout jadis, les proses de la *République des lettres* et les vers du *Parnasse*" (emphasis mine).

3. Laforgue developed this theme in his later works, including his notes on art. "Il faut dire qu'une description porte la note de votre coeur—et le moment où vous avez votre coeur, c'est non pas devant la chose crue, encombrante, mais quand plus tard, songeant, seul, nostalgique, vous évoquez l'éphémère . . . Ce n'est que dans le souvenir qu'on a son coeur, et qu'on tamise la chose avec son coeur, c'est-à-dire avec art durable—sur place, vous êtes aveuglé, objectif, vous avez le pied dans le plat. Une chose n'a son existence d'art, sa poésie, son existence en somme (puisque la réalité passe) que dans la poésie du souvenir" ("Carnet 1884–1885," 430). His interest in the role of memory at this time was possibly inspired by his reading of Baudelaire, who expresses similar ideas, notably in "L'Art mnémonique" (*O.C.* II, 697ff.).

4. Laforgue used the figure of Ariel several times in his writings of 1886. Cf. *F.B.V.* II: "au-dessus du Présent en Ariel"; "Dragées grises," *E.P.L.* II, 10, January 1891, 8: "Je me sens comme un Ariel au-dessus du Présent"; and "Solo de lune": "Mon âme danse / Comme un Ariel."

5. All the heroines of the *Moralités* have large eyes and diminutive breasts. Cf. also the long legs of Andromède and Elsa, Kate's "moue" (37), and Ruth's "cheveux d'ambre roux massés sur le front" (69–71).

6. In his notes, Laforgue refers explicitly to "cet amour de l'Idéal qui

mène le monde," and describes the attainment of happiness as a contradiction in terms (*E.P.L.* II, 10, January 1891, 6f.). Cf. *Revue blanche* VII, 36, October 1894, 300: "Le bonheur—tous nous le voyons réellement dans l'avenir et nous en rappelons réellement des échappées dans le *passé*, on n'a jamais entendu personne, nul n'a jamais pu se dire—le voici, j'en ai, en ce moment, *dans le présent.*"

7. Laforgue used this metaphor in a jotting of verse of 1886: "Des jourdains de Champagne / Arrosaient la campagne" (unedited). See *Dessins d'écrivains français au XIXè siècle*, cat. Maison de Balzac, November 1983–February 1984, pl. 81.

8. The Grojnowski edition reads "le bonheur est *s*ans la poursuite de l'Idéal," clearly a mistake. The earlier editions all have *d*ans, the only reading which makes sense in the context.

9. Pia (*M.L.*, 241) argues that the poems sung by Pan are the last that Laforgue wrote. Jean-Aubry implies likewise by noting that they resemble some of the *F.B.V.*, but reworked according to Laforgue's new free-verse manner. This suggests that Pan's verses are the sort that Laforgue intended to include in his last volume, which he never completed but to which the *D.V.* belonged.

10. Cf. *D.V.* V: "Etalées et découvrant vos gencives comme un régal, / Et bâillant des aisselles au soleil / Dans l'assourdissement des cigales!" (ll.20–22). Cf. also *D.V.* III: "Mon corps, ô ma soeur, a bien mal à sa belle âme," with *Pan:* "Mon corps a mal à sa belle âme, / Ma belle âme a mal à son corps" (285); and "Et ce n'est pas sa chair qui me serait tout / Et je ne serais pas qu'un grand coeur pour elle, / Mais quoi s'en aller faire les fous / Dans des histoires fraternelles!," with *Pan:* "Ce n'est pas sa chair qui me serait tout, / Et je ne serais pas que le grand Pan pour elle, / Mais quoi aller faire les fous / Dans des histoires fraternelles!" (285).

11. See above n. 8.

12. Cf. Laforgue's notes in *Revue blanche* VII, 36, October 1894: "Le bonheur positif—catégorie des illusoires nécessaires comme fins intermédiaires pour l'Evolution universelle."

13. This is the traditional interpretation. See Panofsky's alternative in "Et in Arcadia Ego."

14. Cf. *Lohengrin* (127): "Je suis la Sulamite!"

15. *Salammbô, O.C.* I, 747.

16. At least Pan gets the character of the goddess right. Cf. *Salammbô:* "Les épouses hurlent ton nom dans la douleur des enfantements! Tu gonfles les coquillages! Tu fais bouillonner les vins! Tu putréfies les cadavres! Tu formes les perles au fond de la mer! Et tous les germes, ô Déesse! fermentent dans les obscures profondeurs de ton humidité" (*Ibid.*, 748).

Conclusion

1. Laforgue, *Textes de critique d'art*, 29.
2. F. Brouez, *La Société nouvelle*, 1888 (Debauve, 223); *L'Art moderne*, 8 January 1888 (Debauve, 221ff.); R. Godet, *Le Passant*, February 1888.
3. R. Godet, *Le Passant*, February 1888.
4. *L'Art moderne*, 8 January 1888 (Debauve, 221ff.).
5. *Mercure de France* XVII, 75, March 1896, 317ff.

Bibliography

The bibliography includes works cited, or otherwise relevant to this study. It does not contain the many nineteenth-century articles cited in chapter two, whose references are given fully in the notes. For a full bibliography on Decadence to 1976, see J. Pierrot. For complete bibliographies of works on Laforgue to 1955, see W. Ramsey. Entries marked by an asterisk are referred to in the text by author's name only. Unless otherwise indicated, numbers in parentheses in the text refer to D. Grojnowski's edition of the *Moralités* (Geneva. Droz, 1980). For Laforgue's other works, I have used the following abbreviations (see below for full references):

D.V.	*Dernier Vers*
E.P.L.	*Entretiens politiques et littéraires*
F.B.V.	*Des Fleurs de bonne volonté*
Imitation	*L'Imitation de Notre-Dame la Lune*
L.A.	*Lettres à un ami*
M.L.	*Moralités légendaires*
M.P.	*Mélanges posthumes*
O.C. 1986	*Oeuvres complètes*, ed. J. L. Debauve et al.
O.C. 1922	*Oeuvres complètes*, ed. G. Jean-Aubry

The first volume (of three) of the L'Age d'Homme edition of Laforgue's *O.C.*, containing works to 1883, appeared in 1986 after years of delay. One can only hope that the subsequent two volumes, which will contain most of the material relevant to this study, will follow shortly. I have referred to the new edition whenever possible, but in the absence of the later volumes have had to refer to older (and often more obscure) editions for material not presented in volume one.

Abastado, C., "Le Complexe de Lohengrin," *Europe* (q.v.), 65–71.
———, "'Préludes autobiographiques' de Laforgue. Anamorphose d'un mythe et dérive d'une écriture," *Romantisme* 39, 1983.

———, "Situation de la parodie," *Cahiers du vingtième siècle* 6, 1976, 9–37.
Annoni, Carlo, *Il Decadentismo*, Brescia, La Scuola, 1982.
Anton, B., *Romantische Parodieren. Ein spezifische erzählform der deutschen Romantik*, Abhandlungen zur Kunst-, Musik- und Literaturwissenschaft, 285, Bonn, 1979.
Aristotle, *Poetics*, ed. D. W. Lucas, Oxford, Clarendon Press, 1968.
Arkell, D., *Looking for Laforgue*, Manchester, Carcanet, 1979.
Baguley, D., "Parody and the Realist Novel," *University of Toronto Quarterly* 55, 1, Fall 1985, 94–108.
Bailey, H. P., *Hamlet in France from Voltaire to Laforgue*, Geneva, Droz, 1964.
Bajomée, D., "Hamlet, une moralité oubliée de Jules Laforgue," *Revue des langues vivantes* 33, 4, 1967, 386–405.
Baju, A., *L'Ecole décadente*, Paris, Vanier 1887.
Bakhtin, M., *The Dialogic Imagination*, trans. C. Emerson and M. Holquist, Austin, University of Texas Press, 1981.
———, *Problèmes de la poétique de Dostoïevski*, trans. G. Verret, L'Age d'homme, 1970.
Balzac, H. de, *Séraphita*, Paris, Calmann-Levy, 1950.
Bandy, W. T., *Baudelaire devant ses contemporains*, Monaco, Editions du Rocher, 1957.
Barrault, J. L., *Cahiers Renaud-Barrault* 38, April 1962.
Barrès, M., *Les Taches d'encre, Oeuvres Complètes* I, Paris, Club de l'Honnête Homme, 1965.
Barthes, R., *S/Z*, Paris, Seuil, 1970.
Baudelaire, C., *Oeuvres complètes*, ed. C. Pichois, Paris, Gallimard, 1975–76.
Beauclair, H. and Vicaire, G., *Les Déliquescences d'Adoré Floupette*, ed. S. Cigada, Milan, Cisalpino-Goliardica, 1972.
Belleli, M. L., "Laforgue e il Decadentismo," in *Il Decadentismo in Francia*, Turin, Edit. Tirrenia, 1977.
Benrekassa, G., "Jules Laforgue, Wagner et l'opéra," in *Regards sur l'opéra*, Paris, Presses Universitaires de France, 1976.
Bernard, G., "Peut-on dire d'une langue qu'elle tombe?" in *L'Esprit de décadence* 2 (q.v.), 245–51.
Bilous, D., "Intertexte/pastiche: l'intermimotexte," *Texte* 2, 1983, 135–60.
Birkett, J., *The Sins of the Fathers: Decadence in France 1870–1914*, London, Quartet, 1986.
Bonnefoy, Y., "Hamlet et la couleur," in *Laforgue aujourd'hui* (q.v.), 167–84.
Booth, W., *A Rhetoric of Irony*, University of Chicago Press, 1974.
Borgeaud, P., *Recherches sur le dieu Pan*, Rome, Bibliotheca Helvetica Romana 17, 1979.
Borges, J., "Magias parciales del *Quijote*," *Páginas de J. L. Borges*, Buenos Aires, Editorial Celtia, 1982, 98–100.

Bibliography

*Bourget, P., *Essais de psychologie contemporaine*, in *Oeuvres complètes* I, Paris, Plon, 1899.
Brower, R., *Mirror on Mirror: Translation, Imitation, Parody*, Cambridge, Harvard University Press, 1974.
Bullough, G., *Narrative and Dramatic Sources of Shakespeare*, London, Routledge and Kegan Paul, 1957–75.
Caesar, T., "Victorian Parody," *ELH* 51, 4, 1984, 795–818.
Cahiers de l'Association Internationale des Etudes Françaises 12, 1960. Issue on "Pastiche et parodie" and "Impressionnisme et symbolisme dans la littérature et les arts."
Carassus, E., *Le Snobisme et les lettres françaises de Paul Bourget à Marcel Proust*, Paris, Armand Colin, 1966.
Caro, E., *Le Pessimisme au dix-neuvième siècle*, Paris, Hachette, 1878.
Carter, A. E., *Baudelaire et la critique française 1868–1917*, Columbia, University of South Carolina Press, 1963.
———, *The Idea of Decadence in French Literature 1830–1900*, University of Toronto Press, 1958.
Cèbe, J. -P., *La Caricature et la parodie dans le monde romain antique des origines à Juvénal*, Paris, Boccard, 1966.
Cervantes, M. de, *Don Quijote de la Mancha*, ed. M. de Riquer, Barcelona, Editorial Juventud, 1979.
Challemel-Lacour, P., "Un Bouddhiste contemporain en Allemagne. Schopenhauer," *Revue des deux mondes*, 15 March 1870, 296–332.
Charbonnel, V., *Les Mystiques dans la littérature présente*, Paris, Mercure de France, 1897.
Chateaubriand, R., *Atala*, Geneva, Droz, 1973.
Charlton, D. G., *Positivist Thought in France during the Second Empire*, Oxford, Clarendon Press, 1959.
Colin, R.-P., "Les Décadents: nuanceurs ou barbares de l'idée," Romantisme (q.v.), 47–53.
———, *Schopenhauer en France: un mythe naturaliste*, Presses universitaires de Lyon, 1980.
Compagnon, A., *La Seconde Main ou le travail de la citation*, Paris, Seuil, 1979.
Conlon, M., "Parody and Swift's Example." *Genre* 16, 3, 1983.
Courville, X. de, "Le Pastiche et la parodie chez Jules Lemaître," *Cahiers de l'Association Internationale des Etudes Françaises* 12, 1960, 31–41.
Damerval, G., *Ubu Roi: la bombe comique de 1896*, Paris, Nizet, 1984.
Dane, J., "Parody and Satire. A Theoretical Model," *Genre* 13, 2, 1980, 149–59.
———, *Parody: Critical Concepts versus Literary Practices, Aristophanes to Sterne*, Norman, University of Oklahoma Press, 1988.
Darwin, C., *La Faculté motrice dans les plantes*, trans. E. Heckel, Paris, Reinwald, 1882.

———, *The Power of Movement in Plants,* London, John Murray, 1880.
*Debauve, J. L., *Laforgue en son temps,* Neuchâtel, La Baconnière, 1972.
———, "Laforgue romancier. une tentative avortée: *Un Rate,*" *Revue des sciences humaines* (q.v.), 130–38.
———, *Les Pages de la Guêpe,* Paris, Nizet, 1969.
———, "*Le Sanglot de la Terre* enfin restitué," *Revue des sciences humaines* (q.v.), 139–46.
Décaudin, M., "Définir la décadencé," in *L'Espirit de décadencé* 1 (q.v.), 5–11.
———, "Un Mythe 'fin de siècle': Salomé," *Comparative Literature Studies* 4, 1967, 109–27.
Deffoux, L., *Le Pastiche littéraire des origines à nos jours,* Paris, Delagrave, 1932.
Delepierre, O., *La Parodie chez les Grecs, chez les Romains et chez les Modernes,* London, Philobiblion Society, 1879.
Delsemme, P., *Teodor de Wyzewa et le cosmopolitanisme littéraire en France à l'époque du symbolisme,* Presses Universitaires de Bruxelles, 1967.
Dottin, M., "La Danseuse bavarde. A propos de la *Salomé* de Jules Laforgue," *Littératures,* Annales de l'Université de Toulouse-le-Mirail n.s. 14, 1979, 284–94.
———, "Hamlet aux iris noirs," *Littératures* 23, 1976, 93–114.
———, "Laforgue salonnier," *Europe* (q.v.).
———, "Oedipe et Salomé: recherches sur *Stéphane Vassiliew* de Jules Laforgue," *Littératures* 9–10, Spring 1974, 199–205.
Douchin, J. L., "Michelet inspirateur de Laforgue," *Revue d'histoire littéraire de la France,* 1981, 968–70.
Duisit, L., *Satire, parodie, calembour,* Stanford French and Italian Studies 11, 1978.
Dumonceaux, P., "Les 'Décadents' ont-ils renouvelé la langue?" in *L'Esprit de décadence* 2 (q.v.).
Durrière, G., "Jules Lemaître et le théâtre," diss., University of Paris, 1934.
Durry, M. -J., *Jules Laforgue,* Paris, Seghers, 1966.
L'Esprit de décadencé 1, Colloque de Nantes, 1976, Paris, Minard, 1980.
Ibid., 2, 1984.
Europe, no. 673, May 1985. Issue devoted to Laforgue.
Flaubert, G., *Correspondance,* Paris, Conard, 1926.
———, *Oeuvres complètes,* Paris, Gallimard, 1951–52.
Foucault, M., *Les Mots et les choses,* Paris, Gallimard, 1966.
Frappier-Mazur, L., "Parodie, imitation et circularité: les epigraphes dans les romans de Balzac," *Acta Baltica* 1, 1980, 169–80.
Freidenberg, O. M., "The Origin of Parody," in H. Baran, ed., *Semiotics and Structuralism. Readings from the Soviet Union,* New York, International Arts & Sciences Press, 1974.

Freud, S., *Jokes and their Relation to the Unconscious,* trans. J. Strachey, Penguin, 1976.
Frye, N., "The Nature of Satire," *University of Toronto Quarterly* 14, 1944, 75–90.
*Gautier, T., "Préface aux *Fleurs du mal* de Charles Baudelaire," in *Souvenirs romantiques,* Paris, Garnier, 1929, 268–341.
*Genette, G., *Palimpsestes: la littérature au second degré,* Paris, Seuil, 1982.
Giovine, E., *Bibliographie de Corbière, Lautréamont et Laforgue en Italie,* Florence, Edizioni Sansoni, 1962.
Giusto, J. -P., "Les *Moralités légendaires* de Jules Laforgue," *Revue des sciences humaines* (q.v.), 38–49.
Gollancz, I., *The Sources of Hamlet,* London, Frank Cass, repr. 1967.
Golopentia-Eretescu, S., "Grammaire de la parodie," *Cahiers de linguistique théorique et appliquée* 6, 1969, 167–81.
Grojnowski, D., "Un Inédit de Jules Laforgue: 'Paul Bourget,'" *Revue d'histoire littéraire de la France,* 1972, 688–702.
———, "Moralité légendaire", *Critique* 368, 1978, 63–71.
———, "La Poétique des Complaintes," *Revue des sciences humaines* (q.v.).
———, "Poétique du rien. *L'Imitation de Notre-Dame la Lune,*" *Europe* (q.v.), 48–64.
———, "Poétique du vers libre. les *Derniers vers de Laforgue,*" *Revue d'histoire littéraire de la France* 84, 3, 1984, 390–413.
Guaraldo, E., "Scrittura pregenitale nelle *Moralités* di Laforgue," *Scritti in onore di Giovanni Macchia,* Milan, Mondadori, 1983, 638–61. Repr., with slight alteration, from his *La Scena della poesia: Mallarmé, Laforgue, Apollinaire,* Turin, Albra, 1979.
Guillerm, J. -P., *Tombeau de Léonard de Vinci. Le Peintre et ses tableaux dans l'écriture symboliste et décadent,* Presses Universitaires de Lille, 1981.
Hannoosh, M., "The Early Laforgue. *Tessa,*" *French Forum* 8, 1, January 1983, 20–32.
———, "Jules Laforgue, lecteur de Delacroix. notes inédites," *Studi francesi* 93, 1987, 407–20.
———, "Laforgue's *Salomé* and the Poetics of Parody," *Romanic Review,* 85, January 1984, 51–69.
———, "The Poet as Art Critic. Laforgue's Aesthetic Theory," *Modern Language Review* 79, 3, July 1984, 553–69.
———, "The Reflexive Function of Parody: Self-Criticism and Creativity," *Comparative Literature* 41, 2, 1989.
Hansen, W. F., *Saxo Grammaticus and the Life of Hamlet,* Lincoln, University of Nebraska Press, 1983.
Hartmann, E. von, *La Philosophie de l'Inconscient,* trans. D. Nolen, Paris, Germer Baillière, 1877.
Hell, V., "Schopenhauer et le mouvement décadent en France," *L'Esprit de décadence* 2 (q.v.), 223–34.

Hempel, W., "Parodie, Travestie und Pastiche: Zur Geschichte von Wort und Sache," *Germanische-Romanische Monatsschrift* 46, 1965, 150–76.
Hiddleston, J., ed., *Laforgue aujourd'hui*, Paris, José Corti, 1988.
Highet, G., *The Anatomy of Satire*, Princeton University Press, 1962.
Holmes, E. A., "The Poetic Development of Jules Laforgue," Ph.D. diss., Cambridge University, 1955.
Householder, F., "*Parodia,*" *Classical Philology* 39, 1, 1944, 1–9.
Huret, J., *Enquête sur l'évolution littéraire*, Paris, Charpentier, 1891.
*Hutcheon, L., *A Theory of Parody. The Teachings of Twentieth-Century Art Forms*, London, Methuen, 1985.
———, "Parody without Ridicule," *Canadian Review of Comparative Literature* 5, 1978.
Huysmans, J. K., *A Rebours*, Paris, Garnier-Flammarion, 1978.
———, *En Ménage*, Paris, Charpentier, 1881.
Issacharoff, M., *Joris-Karl Huysmans devant la critique en France 1874–1960*, Paris, Klincksieck, 1970.
Jäckel, K., *Richard Wagner in der französischen Literatur*, Breslau, Priebatsch, 1931.
Janko, R., *Aristotle on Comedy*, Berkeley, University of California Press, 1984.
Jullian, P., *Esthètes et magiciens*, Paris, Perrin, 1969.
Kahn, G., *Symbolistes de décadents*, Paris, Vanier, 1902.
Kamberbeek, J., "Style et décadence," *Revue de littérature comparée* 39, 2, 1965, 268–86.
Karrer, W., *Parodie, Travestie, Pastiche*, Munich, Wilhelm Fink, 1977.
Kennedy, J. G., "Parody as Exorcism. 'The Raven' and 'The Jewbird,'" *Genre* 13, 2, 1980, 161–69.
Kiremidjian, G. D., "The Aesthetics of Parody," *Journal of Aesthetics and Art Criticism* 28, 1969, 231–42.
———, *A Study of Modern Parody*, New York, Garland Monographs in Comparative Literature, 1985.
Koller, H., 'Die Parodie," *Glotta* 35, 1956, 17–32.
Kristeva, J., "Bakhtine, le mot, le dialogue, le roman," *Critique*, April 1967, 438–65.
———, *Semiotiké: Recherches pour une sémanalyse*, Paris, Seuil, 1969.
Kufferath, M., *Le Théâtre de Richard Wagner. Lohengrin*, Leipzig, Junne, 1891.
Kuhn, H., "Was parodiert die Parodie?" *Die Neue Rundschau* 85, 4, 1974, 600–18.
Laforgue, J., "Carnet 1884–1885," *Mercure de France*, 1 October & 1 November 1953, 202–15 and 426–43.
———, *Choix de poésies. Hamlet*, ed. M. Dansel, Paris, Larousse, 1966.
———, *Dragées. Charles Baudelaire, Tristan Corbière*, ed. A. Malraux, Paris, La Connaissance, 1920.

——, *Entretiens politiques et littéraires* II, 10, 1 January 1891; II, 13, April 1891; III, 18, September 1891; III, 20, November 1891; IV, 22, January 1892; IV, 23, February 1892; IV, 26, May 1892.

——, *Feuilles volantes,* ed. D. Grojnowski, Paris, Le Sycomore, 1981.

——, *Lettres à un ami 1880–1886,* ed. G. Jean-Aubry, Paris, Mercure de France, 1941.

——, *Mélanges posthumes, Oeuvres complètes* III, ed. C. Mauclair, Paris, Mercure de France, 1903.

——, *Moralités légendaires,* ed. D. Grojnowski, Geneva, Droz, 1980.

——, *Moralités légendaires,* ed. P. Pia, Paris, Gallimard, 1977.

——, *Oeuvres complètes,* ed., J.-L. Debauve, D. Grojnowski, P. Pia, P. O. Walzer, I, Lausanne, L'Age d'Homme, 1986.

——, *Oeuvres complètes,* ed. G. Jean-Aubry, 6 volumes, Paris, Mercure de France, 1922–30.

——, *Poésies,* ed. P. Pia, Paris, Gallimard, 1970.

——, *Revue blanche* VII, 36, October 1894; VIII, 49, 15 June 1895; XI, 84, 1 December 1896; XI, 85, 15 December 1896; XII, 94, 1 May 1897.

——, *Stéphane Vassiliew,* ed. F. Ruchon, Geneva, Pierre Cailler, 1946.

——, *Textes de critique d'art,* ed. M. Dottin, Presses universitaires de Lille, 1988.

Laurette, P., "A l'Ombre du pastiche: la réécriture—automatisme et contingence," *Texte* 2, 1983, 113–34.

Lee, G., *Allusion, Parody and Imitation,* Hull, 1971.

Lehmann, A. G., *The Symbolist Aesthetic in France,* Oxford, Blackwell, 2nd ed., 1968.

Lelièvre, F. J., "The Basis of Ancient Parody," *Greece and Rome* ser. 2, 1, 1954, 66–81.

——, "Parody in Juvenal and T. S. Eliot," *Classical Philology* 53, 1958, 22–26.

Lemon, L. T. and Reiss, M. G., eds., *Russian Formalist Criticism: Four Essays,* Lincoln, University of Nebraska Press, 1965.

Lethève, J., *Impressionnistes et symbolistes devant la presse,* Paris, Colin, 1959.

——, "Un Mot témoin fin-de-siècle: esthète," *Revue d'histoire littéraire de la France,* 64, 3, 1964, 436–46.

——, "Le Thème de la décadence dans la littérature française à la fin du XIXè siècle," *Revue d'histoire littéraire de la France,* 63, 1, 1963, 46–61.

Levin, H., *Contexts of Criticism,* Cambridge, Harvard University Press, 1957.

L'Henry-Evans, O., "Le Thème de la mort dans l'oeuvre de Laforgue," in *La Mort en toutes lettres,* ed. G. Ernst, Presses Universitaires de Nancy, 1983.

Livi, F., *A Rebours et l'esprit décadent,* Paris, Nizet, 1972.

Madsen, D., "The Figure of Hamlet in Baudelaire, Mallarmé, and Laforgue," Ph.D. diss., Duke University, 1978.

Mallarmé, S., *Oeuvres complètes*, Paris, Gallimard, 1945.
Mansuy, M., *Un Moderne: Paul Bourget, de l'enfance au Disciple*, Annales littéraires de l'Université de Besançon, Paris, 1960.
Markiewicz, H., "On the Definitions of Literary Parody," *To Honor Roman Jakobson*, II, The Hague, Mouton, 1966, 1264–72.
McFadden, G., *Discovering the Comic*, Princeton University Press, 1982.
Meyer, H., *The Poetics of Quotation in the European Novel*, trans. T. & Y. Ziolkowski, Princeton University Press, 1968.
Michaud, G., *Message poétique du symbolisme*, Paris, Nizet, 1947.
Michel, A., "Tradition antique et philosophies de la décadence dans la littérature française autour de 1880," *Romantisme* (q.v.), 55–76.
Michel, F. -B., "Laforgue, le poète anti-camélias," *Le Souffle coupé. Respirer et écrire*, Paris, Gallimard, 1984, 131–36.
Moreau, P., "Les *Moralités légendaires* de Laforgue. Egotisme et symbolisme," *Studi in onore di Italo Siciliano* II, Florence, 1966, 863–73.
Mori, Shigetaro, "Poétique du silence ou le principe de la composition chez Laforgue," *Etudes de langue et littérature françaises* 42, March 1983, 66–86.
Mourier-Casile, P., "Modernités à rebours," *Romantisme* (q.v.), 151–65.
Nautet, F., *Notes sur la littérature moderne*, Brussels, 1885–89.
Nordmann, J. -T., "Taine et la décadence," *Romantisme* (q.v.), 35–40.
*Pakenham, M., ed., *Les Premières Armes du symbolisme*, University of Exeter, 1973.
Panofsky, E., "Et in Arcadia ego," *Meaning in the Visual Arts*, New York, Doubleday, 1955.
Peeters, L., "La Parodie du romantisme. Laforgue, Corbière, Cros," *La Roulette aux mots: la parodie et le jeu de mots dans la poésie française du symbolisme au surréalisme*, Paris, La Pensée Universelle, 1975.
Péladan, J., *Le Vice suprême. Etudes passionnelles de Décadence*, Paris, Librairie Moderne, 1884.
Petit, J., *Barbey d'Aurevilly critique*, Paris, Belles-Lettres, 1963.
Petitjean, A., "Pastiche et parodie. Enjeux théoriques et pédagogiques," *Pratiques* 42, June 1984, 3–33.
Pica, V., *Letteratura d'eccezione*, Milan, Casa Editrice Baldini, 1898.
*Pierrot, J., *L'Imaginaire décadent*, Presses Universitaires de France, 1977.
———, "Laforgue, décadent?," in *Laforgue aujourd'hui* (q.v.), 25–50.
Pouilliart, R., *Paul Bourget et l'esprit de Décadence*, *Les Lettres romanes*, August 1951.
Praz, M., *Romantic Agony*, 2nd ed., London, Oxford University Press, 1951.
Priestman, J., "The Age of Parody. Literary Parody and some Nineteenth-Century Perspectives," Ph.D. diss., University of Kent, 1980.
Ramsey, W., *Jules Laforgue and the Ironic Inheritance*, New York, Oxford University Press, 1953.
Raynaud, E., *La Mêlée symboliste*, Paris, Renaissance du livre, 1918–1922.

Reverseau, J. -P., "Pour une étude du thème de la tête coupée dans la littérature et la peinture dans la seconde partie du XIXè siècle," *Gazette des Beaux-Arts* 80, September 1972, 173–84.
Revue des sciences humaines 77, January–March 1955, "Autour du symbolisme."
Ibid., 153, January 1974, "Aspects du décadentisme européen."
Ibid., 178, June 1980, "Laforgue."
Ribot, T., *La Philosophie de Schopenhauer*, Paris, G. Baillière, 1874.
Richard, N., *A l'aube du symbolisme*, Paris, Nizet, 1961.
———, *Le Mouvement décadent*, Paris, Nizet, 1968.
———, *Profils symbolistes*, Paris, Nizet, 1972.
Riewald, J. G., "Parody as Criticism," *Neophilologus* 50, 1966, 125–48.
Riffaterre, M., *Essais de stylistique structurale*, Paris, Flammarion, 1971.
———, "Parodie et répétition," in Vernet, *Le Singe à la porte* (q.v.), 87–94.
———, "The Poetic Functions of Intertextual Humor," *Romanic Review* 65, 1974, 278–93.
———, *La Production du texte*, Paris, Seuil, 1979.
———, "Sémanalyse de l'intertexte," *Texte* 2, 1983.
———, *Semiotics of Poetry*, Bloomington, Indiana University Press, 1978.
Romantisme 42, 1983. Issue devoted to Decadence.
Rose, M., "Defining Parody," *Southern Review of Australia* 13, 1, 1981, 5–20.
*———, *Parody/Metafiction*, London, Croom Helm, 1979.
Rotelli, G. G., *Due Studi sul simbolismo: la metrica delle poesie di Rimbaud.*
Il tema liturgico nelle poesie di Laforgue, Bologna, Patron, 1979.
Ruchon, F., *Jules Laforgue, sa vie, son oeuvre*, Geneva, Albert Ciana, 1924.
Sagnes, G., *L'Ennui dans la littérature française de Flaubert à Laforgue*, Paris, Armand Colin, 1969.
Sakari, E., *L'Ecriture clownesque de Laforgue*, Jyväskylä Studies in the Arts 18, 1983.
Scaliger, J. C. *Poetics*, Stuttgart, F. Frommann Verlag, 1964 (facsimile of 1561 ed.).
Schaffner, R., "Die Salome-Dichtungen von Flaubert, Laforgue, Wilde und Mallarmé," diss. Würzburg, 1965.
Schopenhauer, A., *Le Monde comme volonté et comme représentation*, trans. A. Burdeau, Paris, G. Baillière, 1888.
Scofield, M., "Your only jig maker. Laforgue," *The Ghosts of Hamlet*, Cambridge University Press, 1980, 34–44.
Shlonsky, T., "Literary Parody: Remarks on its Method and Function," *Proceedings of the Fourth Congress of the International Comparative Literature Association* II, ed. F. Jost, The Hague, Mouton, 1966, 797–801.
Shklovsky, V., "Sterne's *Tristram Shandy*. Stylistic Commentary," in Lemon and Reiss, *Russian Formalist Criticism: Four Essays* (q.v.), 25–57.

Siohan, R., "Les formes musicalés de la parodie et du pastiche," *Cahiers de l'Association internationale des Etudes Françaises* (q.v.), 79–90.

Sonnenfeld, A., "Hamlet the German and Jules Laforgue," *Yale French Studies* 33, 1964, 92–100.

Stephan, P., *Paul Verlaine and the Decadence, 1882–90*, Manchester University Press, 1974.

Swart, K. W., *The Sense of Decadence in Nineteenth-Century France*, The Hague, Martinus Nijhoff, 1964.

Thornton, R. K. R., *The Decadent Dilemma*, London, Edward Arnold, 1983.

*Todorov, T., *Théorie de la littérature*, Paris, Seuil, 1965.

Travers, S., *Catalogue of French Nineteenth-Century Theatrical Parodies*, New York, King's Crown Press, 1941.

Tynjanov, J., "Destruction, parodie," *Change* 2, Paris, Seuil, 1968, 67–76.

Vadé, Y., "Mythe de la décadence et décadence du mythe," *L'Esprit de décadence* 2 (q.v.), 253–66.

Vernet, M., ed., *Le Singe à la porte*, New York and Berne, Peter Lang, 1984.

Waugh, P., *Metafiction. The Theory and Practice of Self-Conscious Fiction*, London, Methuen, 1984.

Weinbrot, H., "Parody as Imitation in the Eighteenth Century," *American Notes & Queries* 2, 1964, 131–34.

Weisstein, U., "Parody, Travesty, & Burlesque: Imitations with a Vengeance," *Proceedings of the Fourth International Comparative Literature Association* 2, ed. F. Jost, The Hague, Mouton, 1966, 802–11.

Wyzewa, T. de, *Nos Maîtres*, Paris, Perrin, 1895.

Zuili, M., "Etude d'un poème de Laforgue. 'Complainte d'un autre dimanche,'" *L'Information littéraire* 34, 1982, 123–26.

Index

Adam, Paul, 37
Aesthetic Movement, 60
Alexis, Paul, 45
Amadis of Gaul, 15
Amiel, Henri-Frédéric, 45
Amyot, Jacques, 190
Anachronism, 2, 3, 5, 26, 62, 63. *See also* Modernization: *Moralités légendaires:* as modernization; *Moralités légendaires:* stylistic features of
Aristophanes, 13
Aristotle, 11, 12, 13, 227n. 38, 228n. 52
Athenaeus, 11, 227n. 38
Austen, Jane: *Northanger Abbey,* 25
Autocitation. See *Moralités légendaires:* stylistic features of; Parody: autocitation in
Avant-garde: function of parody in, 2, 7, 72, 219; relation to Decadence, 37, 216
Avellaneda, A. Fernández, 19

Baguley, David, 14, 25
Baju, Anatole, 68
Bakhtin, Mikhail, 14, 17
Balzac, Honoré de: *Séraphita,* 40, 54, 110, 120–21
Barbe-bleue, parody of, 68
Barbey d'Aurevilly, Jules, 34, 38, 54
Barthes, Roland, 18
Battle of the Frogs and Mice, 11
Baudelaire, Charles, 37, 66, 142, 220, 246n. 14; Bourget on, 42–45, 51, 54, 55; as father of Decadence, 34, 38–41, 52, 216; *Les Fleurs du mal,* 6, 45, 118, 119, 155; Gautier on, 38–41, 44, 54; and Laforgue's aesthetics, 5, 254n. 3; Laforgue's notes on, 39, 53; and Poe, 39, 40, 44; on women, 50, 52, 118. *See also* Decadence: themes of
Beauclair, Henri, 69
Beaumarchais, Pierre Augustin Caron de: *Le Barbier de Séville,* 5
Beauty and the Beast, 173–75, 178, 179–80, 183, 185, 187, 192
Belleforest, 242n. 20
Bernard, Tristan, 66
Boileau, Nicolas, 63, 130
Borges, Jorge Luis, 28
Bossuet, Jacques Bénigne, 116
Boucher, François, 194
Bourde, Paul, 31, 52, 53, 55, 56
Bourges, Elémir, 52
Bourget, Paul, 51, 80; defense of Decadence, 43–45, 54, 55, 56; *Essais de psychologie contemporaine,* 41–47, 53; influence on Laforgue, 42; influence of Taine on, 43; and pessimism, 42–43; and the Unconscious, 46–47
Buddhism, 42, 43, 49, 150, 159, 237n. 76
Burlesque, 10, 150, 161, 226n. 26

Caricature, 10, 226n. 26
Carnivalesque literature, 14
Caro, Elme-Marie, 48
Cervantes, Miguel de. See *Don Quijote de la Mancha*
Challemel-Lacour, Paul, 48
Champsaur, Félicien, 63
Le Chasseur de Chevelures, 65–66

267

Le *Chat noir*, 61, 62–63, 69
Chateaubriand, François René de, 51, 246n. 15
Cicero, 12, 41
Comic, the: comic element of parody, 2, 8, 10–14, 65, 217–18, 226n. 29; 227n. 38, 228n. 52; and Decadence, 60–73; devices of, 26, 30, 62, 77, 105, 109 (*see also* Anachronism; *Moralités légendaires:* devices of parody in; Parody: deception of expectations in; Parody: distortion; forms of, 13–14; as signal of parody, 21, 26, 105, 153
Les Complaintes, 5, 55, 56, 57–58, 145; Laforgue's reviews of, 31, 32, 58, 71–72
Coolus, Roman, 66
Corbière, Tristan, 31, 58, 59
Corneille, Pierre, 64
Coypel, Antoine, 173
Crapoussin, Mitrophane, 68

Dante Alighieri, 5, 63
Darwin, Charles, 153; *The Power of Movement in Plants*, 111
Decadence: ancient models for, 25, 40–41, 43, 46, 51, 53, 69
—anti-bourgeois, 40, 44, 52, 97, 124, 136, 156–57
—anti-materialist, 40
—anti-progress, 40, 114, 156
—anti-socialist, 97, 155–56, 161
—aristocratic nature of, 44
—and etching, 242n. 14
—fictionality of, 23, 33
—hero, physical characteristics of, 53
—historical place of, 34–35
—humor in, 32, 59–60
—ideal of self-detachment, 32, 49
—imagery of: autumn, 37, 44, 53, 84; city, the, 37, 114; flowers, 37, 39, 52–53, 69, 71, 111–27 *passim*, 142; fragrances, 37, 39, 44, 52, 69, 71, 118; gems, 37, 39, 52, 69, 71, 105, 118, 155; liturgical, in erotic context, 43, 55, 69, 136–38, 141–42; moon, the 6, 37, 55, 130, 134, 136–38, 142, 149, 150, 154, 163, 165, 196, 200–201, 202, 213, 247n. 23; peacock-feather eye, 105, 106, 117, 119, 121–22, 139, 163; stagnant pond, 84, 142, 155, 180; sunset, 39, 183–84, 252n. 13; twilight, 37, 45, 53; under-water, 55, 142, 143 (see also *Salomé*: aquarium image)
—and Impressionism, 35, 37–38
—and individualism, 43–44, 47, 55–56, 217
—language of, 26, 33, 47
—life as art in, 23, 45, 56, 89, 118, 183, 218–19
—as modern art, 35, 39, 64, 216
—and Naturalism, 35, 37, 233n. 22
—nature of movement, 33–60, 113, 132, 216–17
—parodies of, 66–72
—parody in, 60–73, 217
—Salomé figure, 148–49
—self-parody in, 59, 60
—style of, 37, 40–41, 44, 47, 56–59, 69, 71, 217. See also *Moralités légendaires:* stylistic features of
—and Symbolism, interchangeability of terms, 34–37
—themes of: aestheticism, 52, 75, 97, 109, 155, 157; anemia, 45, 51, 53, 75, 154; artifice, 23, 33, 39–40, 44, 52, 114, 149, 150, 217; aversion to crowd, 44, 52, 76, 153; the bizarre, 39, 52; dandyism, 39, 53, 75, 85; degeneracy, 46, 113–14; desire for infinite, 54, 76, 97, 136, 172, 194–215 *passim*, 220; dilettantism, 39, 42, 43, 45, 74–103 *passim*, 110, 155; dream, 23, 71; egoism, 56, 67, 77, 132, 136, 138, 147; ennui, 37, 39, 41, 42, 51, 67, 76, 77, 87, 136, 154, 155, 171, 194–215 *passim*, 220; environment, 67, 76, 83, 92; evasion, 23, 51–52, 77, 134, 146, 217; exoticism, 33, 39, 52, 151; hamletism, 51, 75, 217; heredity, 33, 37, 43, 52, 67, 75, 76, 85, 93, 119, 153; hypochondria, 51, 135–36; illness, 33, 37, 40, 51, 52, 71, 105–27 *passim*; imitation, 23, 218; intoxicants, 34, 71; love, 15, 45, 46, 48, 129, 132, 147 (see also *Pan et la Syrinx:* themes of; *Persée et Andromède:* themes of); metaphysics, 15, 45, 76, 147, 162, 172, 196, 199, 210, 220; misanthropy, 42, 51, 66; moral relativism, 76, 95, 131, 155; morbidity, 44, 69, 76, 114, 131, 154; mysticism, 37, 39–42 *passim*, 53–54, 69, 71, 110, 138, 150, 154, 155; narcissism, 56, 76, 85, 138, 158, 160; neurosis, nerves, 33, 37, 39, 40, 42, 46, 51, 76, 105, 110, 113;

Index

nihilism, 42, 47, 54, 69, 76, 95, 96; nirvana, 43, 49, 159; Orientalism, 39, 52, 149, 151, 154; pantheism, 55, 69, 178, 202, 210; perversion, 33–34, 37, 39–40, 46, 52, 71, 94–96, 161; pessimism, *see* Pessimism, and Decadence; *poète-voyant*, 71; purity, 128–47 *passim*, 200, 202, 213; revolt against nature, 23, 34, 39, 46, 52, 71, 76; scepticism, 45, 67, 155; self-analysis, 45, 51, 54, 56, 75, 76, 82–83, 129, 164, 165; sensuality, 39, 43, 52, 54, 69; unconscious, the, 41, 84, 142, 217 (*see also* Unconscious, the); will, weakness of, 45–46, 51 (see also *Hamlet:* themes of); women in, 30, 39, 40, 44, 46, 50, 217 (*see also* individual *Moralités légendaires;* Laforgue: attitude to women). See also individual *Moralités légendaires*
—use of legend in, 6, 109, 161, 217
—and Wagnerism, 35, 129. See also Wagner, Richard
Le Décadent, 68
Décaudin, Michel, 60
Les Déliquescences d'Adoré Floupette, 24, 31, 47, 51, 53, 55–60 *passim*, 69, 70–72
Demetrins: *On Style*, 12
Derniers Vers. See Laforgue: works of
Don Quijote de la Mancha, 29; displaced authorship in, 28; and evolution of literary forms, 25; reference to *Galatea*, 28; and romances of chivalry, 15, 21, 22, 25; self-critical techniques in, 19; signals of parody in, 21; theme of imitation in, 22, 23–24
Dottin, Mireille, 217
Dubufe, E., 107
Dujardin, Edouard, 129
Dumas, Alexandre, *fils*, 45, 46, 48

Epic, 11–12, 226n. 33, 227n. 38
Epigraph, 29–30, 111, 151. See also individual *Moralités légendaires*
Etching, 241n. 14
Eternal feminine, 30, 39, 40, 46, 50, 62, 66, 129, 143, 163, 171, 202, 205
Evolution of literary forms, theory of, 17, 24–25

Femme fatale, 30, 40, 50, 123, 149, 150, 161, 217

Fielding, Henry, 25
Flaubert, Gustave, 15, 52, 63, 212–13
—Bourget on, 45, 46
—*Un Coeur simple*, model for *Le Miracle des Roses*, 105, 116–17, 124–26
—*Hérodias*, model for *Salomé*. See *Salomé*
—*La Légende de Saint Julien L'Hospitalier*, 95, 131
—*Salammbô*, model for *Salomé*. See *Salomé*
—*La Tentation de Saint-Antoine*, 54, 55, 149, 160; *Moralités* epigraph drawn from, 29–30
Forgery, 10, 68, 226n. 26
Fourest, Georges, 64, 68
Freud, Sigmund, 228n. 52

Gautier, Théophile, 35, 38–41, 44, 53, 69
Genette, Gérard, 10, 12, 226n. 27
Genre, Bakhtin's concept of, 17
Ghil, René, 36
Gide, André, 64
Gluck, Christoph, 64
Goethe, Johann Wolfgang von, 146
Goncourt, Edmond et Jules de, 37, 45, 47
Gospels, parodies of, 62, 65, 66, 133–34
Goudeau, Emile, 63
Gounod, Charles, 146
Guercino (Giovanni Franceso Barbieri), 173
Guizot, François, 97

Hamlet, 51, 217
Hamlet (Shakespeare), 15, 16, 74–103 *passim*, 138, 220
Hamlet, ou les suites de la piété filiale, 16, 18, 53, 59, 66–67, 74–103, 109, 131, 142, 153, 155, 171, 172, 177, 194, 197, 217, 218, 220. See also *Moralités légendaires:* devices of parody in
—themes of: acting, 82, 87, 101; art, 27, 67, 74, 77, 89–90, 98; death, 74, 76, 93, 97; ennui, 77, 87; evasion, 52, 97; fame, 74, 77, 78, 79, 89, 93; freedom, 74, 77; hyperactive imagination, 77, 81, 83; moral relativism, 81, 95, 97, 100; will, 75, 81, 83, 93, 98; women, 46, 74, 76–77, 87–88, 94–95, 96, 98–99
Hartmann, Eduard von, 47, 49, 50, 95,

Hartmann *(cont.)*
  95, 97, 162, 178, 210, 253n. 14. *See also* Unconscious, the
Hegemon of Thasos, 11, 227n. 38
Heine, Heinrich, 5
Heliodorus: *Ethiopica*, 190
Hennequin, Emile, 51
Hobbes, Thomas, 88
Homer, 12, 15, 65, 227n. 38
Householder, Fred W., Jr., 226n. 29
Hugo, Victor, 60, 63, 66
Hutcheon, Linda, 10, 13–14, 16
Huysmans, Joris-Karl, 31, 43, 45, 53, 58, 60, 75, 149
—*A Rebours*, 33–34, 47, 48, 53, 56, 70, 149, 161, 167, 194; des Esseintes, 31, 32, 33, 41, 48, 51–52, 54, 58, 75, 77, 78, 96, 121, 149, 194
L'Hydropathe, 61
Hydropathes, Club des, 63

Imitation, 9, 11, 12–13, 26, 70; as theme of parody, 22–24, 27–28, 218. *See also* Decadence: life as art in; Parody: imitation, challenge to
L'Imitation de Notre Seigneur Jésus-Christ, 5, 54
Impressionism: relation to Decadence, 35, 37–38
Intertextuality, 3, 26, 175; as principle of parody, 2, 3, 14, 20–21, 180, 216, 219. *See also* Riffaterre, Michael
Irony, 13, 218

Janet, Paul, 48
Jarry, Alfred, 60, 72
Jordaens, Jacob, 194

Kahn, Gustave, 1, 31, 36, 105
Koller, H., 227n. 38
Kristeva, Julia, 230n. 67

Labiche, Eugène, 174
La Fontaine, Jean de, 175
Laforgue, Jules:
—aesthetic of, 4–8; conception of modern art, 224n. 8; and evolution, 219, 224n. 8; of modernity, 32, 64, 65, 219; of modernization, 219, 224n. 8, 224n. 11 (*see also* Modernization); originality in, 32, 221, 224n. 8; role of memory in, 254n. 3; tradition in, 219
—attitude to Decadence, 31–33
—on Baudelaire, 39, 53
—considered a Decadent, 31, 36, 57
—on *Les Déliquescences*, 71–72
—influences on, 42, 50
—metaphysical beliefs of, 50
—pessimism of, 50, 220. *See also* Pessimism, and Decadence
—reviews of, 56, 57–58, 219–21
—self-irony of, 32. *See also* Parody, self-parody in; Parody, self-mockery in
—style of, 26, 27, 47, 57–59
—attitude to women, 46, 50, 247n. 25. *See also* individual *Moralités légendaires*
—works of: *A propos de Hamlet*, 75, 80; *L'Art moderne en Allemagne*, 4, 252n. 10; "Bobo," 247n. 25–26; *Chronique stygianopolitaine*, 5; *Les Complaintes* (see *Les Complaintes*); *Derniers Vers*, 5, 184, 252n. 13, 253n. 1, 255n. 10; *Les Deux Pigeons*, 224n. 20; 1883 Agenda, 107; essay on Impressionism, 4, 38; *Des Fleurs de bonne volonté*, 6; *L'Imitation de Notre-Dame la Lune*, 5–6; *Stéphane Vassiliew*, 246n. 12, 252n. 11; *Tessa*, 5. *See also* individual works

Lange, Antoni, 37
Lanson, Gustave, 104
Leconte de Lisle, 45
Lelièvre, F. J., 14–15
Lemaître, Jules, 65, 240n. 117
Liszt, Franz: *Die Legende von der heiligen Elisabeth*, 106–9, 217
Lohengrin (Wagner), 15. *See also* Wagner, Richard
Lohengrin, fils de Parsifal, 107, 109, 128–47, 148, 154, 171, 192, 202, 217, 218
—flashback structure of, 28, 134, 143
—imagery of: liturgical, 43, 55, 136–38, 141–42; swan, 129, 132, 135, 140–41, 146
—themes of: egoism, 132, 136, 138, 147; evasion, 52, 133, 134, 142, 146; music, 130, 131, 145, 146; purity, 129–32 *passim*, 134, 136, 138, 146; sexuality, 134–37 *passim*, 144–45, 147; women, 46, 129–32, 134, 139–40, 141, 143–44
Lombard, Jean, 33
Lorrain, Jean, 52
Louÿs, Pierre, 64

Index

Lucian, *Dialogues of the Dead*, 5
Lucretius, *De Rerum Natura*, 79–80
Lutèce, 61, 68, 70

Maeterlinck, Maurice, 66
Mallarmé, Stéphane, 58, 148, 149, 216; "L'Après-midi d'un faune," 194–97 *passim*, 214; and Decadence, 36–37, 55; "Hérodiade," 248n. 7; parodied, 68, 69, 71
Markiewicz, Henryk, 15
Mauclair, Camille, 220
Maupassant, Guy de, 8, 45
Mechanization, 12, 15, 24, 33
Merrill, Stuart, 36
Méry, Joseph, 253n. 15
Metafiction, 2, 17, 115, 170, 188–93. See also *Moralités légendaires*: devices of parody in; Parody: metalinguistic character of
Michaud, Guy, 35
Michelangelo Buonarroti, 91
Les Mille et Une Nuits, 214, 215
Le Miracle des Roses, 59, 104–27, 139, 171, 177, 218. See also Liszt, Franz
—flashback structure of, 28, 112, 115, 121
—identification of model of, 21–22, 104–10, 219
—identity of narrator, 114–16, 120–21
—imagery of: floral, 106–27 *passim*; liturgical, 116–17, 124–26
—parodic miracle in, 105–6, 110, 125–26
—signals of parody in, 22, 105, 107–8
—themes of: hallucination, 105, 110, 117, 121, 123, 126; illness, 105, 110; neurosis, 51, 110, 113, 171; sexuality, 119, 121–22, 123
Mirror, image of, 23–24
Mock epic, 11–12, 15, 226n. 29, 227n. 33
Model of parody, 2, 14–17, 19, 20–22, 24–25, 107, 190, 217, 218; allusions to, 66, 107–10; contained within parody, 20–22, 33, 104, 107, 127, 188, 219. See also *Moralités légendaires*: devices of parody in
Modernism, 35, 64; parody and, 73, 216
Modernization, 1, 5–7, 26, 62–65 *passim*, 105, 110, 153, 196, 198–99, 203, 216, 220. See also Anachronism; Laforgue: aesthetic of
Molière (Jean-Baptiste Poquelin), 66–67, 72, 165

Montalembert, Charles Forbes, comte de, 106
Moralités légendaires: and aesthetic of the modern, 72, 219, 220
—chronology of, 8–9, 225n. 20
—and Decadence, 15, 23, 32–33, 58, 216–17
—devices of parody in: false etymology, 153, 204–5; incomplete narration, 139, 154, 157; metaphors referring to parody, 105, 108, 113, 118, 128, 148, 175, 183, 184, 187, 192, 193, 203, 215; model, author of, as character in parody, 86; model, author of, other works alluded to in parody, 86–87, 89, 97; model, distortion of episodes of, in parody, 93, 95, 100, 156, 160, 163, 167–68, 181, 183, 184–85, 203; model, genre of, in parody, 66, 82, 109–10, 142; model, language or imagery of, in parody, 82, 83, 87, 90, 93, 94, 97, 100, 101, 140, 176; model, model of, in parody, 86, 135, 162; model, names of characters of, deformed in parody, 155; model, omission of episodes of, in parody, 79, 81, 83, 150, 174, 185; model, secondary characters of foregrounded, in parody, 148, 175; model, transformed into metaphor in parody, 181, 215; models, fusion of, in parody, 86, 89, 95, 106, 116, 123–26, 149, 160–63, 166–68, 170–93 *passim*, 209, 210, 212, 215; narrator, as character in parody, 116, 120–21, 147, 170–71, 188; narrator, intervention of (see *Moralités légendaires:* stylistic features of); other versions, anticipation of, 102–3, 120, 126–27, 134, 147, 162, 168–69, 189, 192, 196, 214–15, 218, 219; parody within parody, 27, 91–92, 93, 110, 117, 124, 133, 137, 145, 146, 160–62, 174, 179, 183–84, 186, 207–8; reader's reaction provided in parody, 30, 145, 157, 162, 165, 186
—epigraph to, 29–30
—imagery of: moon, the, 130–34, 136–38, 142, 150, 154, 163, 165, 196, 200–201, 202, 213; sea, the, 87, 142, 155, 171
—models, relation to, 15, 217, 218 (*see also* Model of parody; *Moralités légendaires:* devices of parody in)
—as modernization, 1, 3–4, 7, 10, 26,

Moralités légendaires (cont.)
64, 105, 110, 153, 196, 198–99, 203, 216, 220
—as *nouvelles*, 4, 8
—order of stories in, 8–9, 225n. 21
—reputation of, 8, 219–20
—as self-parody, 139, 146, 150, 162, 202, 206, 217, 218
—stylistic features of, 9, 58–59, 251n. 1; anachronism, 3, 84–85, 91, 105, 138, 153, 220; apostrophe, 178, 181; autocitation, 28, 92, 96, 139, 145–46, 155, 162, 205–6; clichés, 87, 127, 130, 131, 139–40, 154, 157, 174, 177, 188, 218; double-entendres, 138, 140; mixed levels of diction, 168; narrator's interventions, 114–15, 143; puns, 82, 87, 101, 102, 115–16, 124, 125, 137, 140–41, 145, 164, 167, 192, 201; repetition, 58, 158; sound-play, 145, 158, 164; subjective narrative, 59, 84, 176, 204; synaesthesia, 214
—target, relation to, 15, 58, 216–17, 218. See also Model of parody
—themes of: acting, 82, 87, 101, 118, 161, 163, 164; art and illusion, 9, 196; revolution, 85, 97, 101, 152–53, 156, 164
—title of, 6, 224n. 13
Moréas, Jean, 31, 34, 36, 48, 52
Moreau, Gustave, 24, 106, 149, 161, 163, 217; "L'Apparition," 149, 160, 167; "La Jeune Fille thrace portant la tête d'Orphée," 166, 251n. 37
Moreau, Pierre, 45, 56, 59
Morice, Charles, 51
Music, allusions to, 109, 110, 112–13, 124, 137. See also Liszt, Franz; Offenbach, Jacques; *Opéra-comique*; Wagner, Richard
Musset, Alfred de, 66, 208, 240n. 119
Mystification. See Pastiche

Narcissus, 180, 209
Naturalism, relation to Decadence, 35, 37, 233n. 22
Nautet, F., 58
Nero, 46, 53, 81, 101
Nicochares, 11
Nisard, Désiré, 38
Nouvelle, 4, 8
Nouvelle Rive Gauche, 62

Offenbach, Jacques, 7, 105, 109, 113, 114; *La Belle Hélène*, 64, 98, 101
Opéra-comique, 64, 174, 187; as model for parody, 7; as theme in the *Moralités*, 7, 64, 98, 105, 109–10, 112–13
Originality, aesthetic of, 2, 4, 6, 8
Orpheus, 64, 163, 166, 168, 251n. 37
Overbeck, Johann Friedrich, 106
Ovid, 7, 25, 161
—*Metamorphoses*: as model for *Pan et la Syrinx*, 194, 195; as model for *Persée et Andromède*, 173–74, 178, 179, 184, 186, 187–88, 194

Pan et la Syrinx, 59, 109, 171, 172, 194–215, 217, 218
—autocitation in, 28, 205–6
—fusion of myths in, 209, 210, 212, 215
—Ovid as model, 7, 194, 195
—relation to Mallarmé's "L'Après-midi d'un faune," 194–97 *passim*, 214
—themes of: art, 27, 194, 195–96, 198, 199, 206, 210, 211, 214; fantasy, 195, 197, 206–7, 210–14 *passim*; love, 195–99 *passim*, 204, 212; modernity, 198–99, 206; music, 195–98 *passim*, 206, 207–8, 214–15, 231n. 93; unattainability of the ideal, 194, 195–96, 200–201, 202, 204–5, 206, 210, 254n. 6, 255n. 12; women, 202, 207, 208, 213
Le Parnassiculet contemporain, 69, 71
Parodic narrative, features of, 26–29. See also *Moralités légendaires*: devices of parody in
La Parodie, 62
Parodist: as author and reader, 16, 17–18, 189, 218; as character in parody, 116, 120–21, 147, 170–71, 188–93 *passim*; in epigraph, 30; intervention by, 27, 28, 143, 188; as model for reader, 17–18, 26, 28–29, 157; reference to own work by, 28 (see also *Moralités légendaires*: stylistic features of; Parody: autocitation in); unreliability of, 19, 102, 115, 153, 154, 157, 190, 192
Parody: and aesthetic of modernity, 61, 65, 73, 217, 219; and aesthetic of originality, 2, 4, 8, 61, 221; ambivalence of, 14, 16, 17, 25–26, 150–

51, 179, 217; autocitation in, 28, 63, 92, 96, 139, 145–46, 155, 162, 205–6; and censorship, 25; change and continuity in, 24–25, 29, 72, 78, 80, 85, 127, 128, 147, 153–54, 168, 171, 188, 219; comedy, relation to, 11; conservatism, theoretically inconsistent with, 7, 16, 219; creativity of, creative and regenerative possibilities of, 2, 3, 20, 24, 29, 78, 171, 202, 221 (see also *Moralités légendaires:* devices of parody in; *Moralités légendaires:* other versions, anticipation of); critical purposes of, 12–13, 16, 17; in Decadent movement, 60–73, 217; deception of expectations in, 13, 26, 105, 175, 217–18; definition of, 9, 10, 12, 13, 14, 18; not derivative or parasitic, 20–21, 28–29, 219; devices of, 62 (*see also* Anachronism; Comic, the; Modernization; *Moralités légendaires:* devices of parody in); displaced authorship in, 27–28; distortion, 12–15 *passim*, 20, 26, 70, 72, 81, 82, 107–8, 148, 175, 186, 190, 203, 217, 218, 219 (see also *Moralités légendaires:* devices of parody in); etymology of, 11; as fulfillment of Laforgue's aesthetic, 4, 6, 8; generic status, 10; helps fix conventions, 24–25, 70, 72, 216; history of, 9–13; imitation as theme of, 22–24, 27–28, 218 (*see also* Imitation); imitation, challenge to, 23–24, 175, 179, 218 (*see also* Imitation); incongruity in, 3, 14, 63, 109; intelligibility of, in absence of model, 2, 21–22, 104, 107, 219; and interpretation, 23–24, 27–28, 175; in Laforgue's *oeuvre*, 3; message of, 19–20, 170, 188, 191–92, 196, 207, 218; metalinguistic character of, 16, 28 (*see also* Metafiction); and mock epic, 11–12, 15, 226n. 29, 227n. 33; narrative features, 26–28 (see also *Moralités légendaires:* devices of parody in); not elitist, 20; parody within parody, 27, 70 (see also *Moralités légendaires:* devices of parody in); potential to be parodied, 18–19, 86, 92, 102–3, 146, 162, 168–69, 202, 218, 219; puns, 3, 70 (see also *Moralités légendaires:* stylistic features of); as quotation, 9, 13, 29, 231n. 91; quotation out of context in, 62, 63, 70, 82; reader, involvement of, 27–28, 67, 145, 157, 165, 189, 192, 204, 206, 218; and repetition, 12, 157–58; and ridicule, 14, 217; scepticism of, 19–20, 24, 170, 192–93; self-criticism of, 2, 17–19, 92, 168–69, 189, 192–93, 218; self-mockery in, 15, 30, 32, 70–71, 134; self-parody in, 15, 19, 30, 92, 139, 146, 150, 155, 162, 202, 206, 218; self-reflexivity, 2, 7, 17, 18–20, 27–28, 67, 86, 93, 102, 120, 147, 162, 168–69, 170, 189–93, 214–15, 218; self-sufficiency of, 2, 21–22, 104, 107, 219; signals of, 9, 105, 150 (see also *Moralités légendaires:* devices of parody in; *Moralités légendaires:* stylistic features of); subtitles, function of, 74–75, 109, 174–75, 195; tripartite structure of, 15, 64, 217. See also Anachronism; Avant-garde; Intertextuality; Metafiction; Model; Modernization; *Moralités légendaires:* devices of parody in; Parodist; Target

Pastiche, 10, 12, 68, 226n. 26
Péladan, Joseph: *Etudes passionnelles de décadence. Le Vice suprême*, 33, 34
Pellegrini, Giovanni Antonio, 194
Perrault, Charles, 62
Persée et Andromède, ou le plus heureux des trois, 170–93, 194–95, 200, 217, 219
—as apologia for parody, 175–93 *passim*
—epilogue to, 28, 170–71, 188–93, 218; as challenge to parodic scepticism, 19–20, 170, 192–93; as self-critical technique, 18, 170, 189–93; theme of interpretation in, 27, 175, 190–92
—fusion of myths in, 173–75, 176, 179, 180, 181, 183, 186, 187, 192 (see also *Beauty and the Beast*)
—imagery of sea, 171, 176, 178
—Ovid as model, 7, 173–74, 178
—status of heroine, 171–72
—subtitle, 109, 174–75, 180, 185, 192
—themes of: adolescence, 171, 172, 174, 177–78, 180, 181; egoism, 179, 180, 187, 192; ennui, 171–72; freedom, 178, 180; hyperactive imagination, 176, 183; the ideal, 172–73, 182; love, 171, 174, 182–83, 184

Pessimism, and Decadence, 5, 23, 37, 41, 42, 45–51 *passim*, 69, 71, 77, 84, 147, 150, 172, 182, 195, 213, 217, 220
Le Petit Chaperon Rouge, 62
Philosophy of the Unconscious. See Hartmann, Eduard von
Pia, Pascal, 60, 62
Pica, Vittorio, 54
Pierrot, Jean, 35, 60
Pigeon, Amédée, 58
Plato, 228n. 52
La Plume, 69
Plutarch: *Moralia*, 190
Poe, Edgar Allan, 39, 40, 96, 158, 166, 181
Pope, Alexander: *Dunciad*, 15
Poussin, Nicolas, 194, 211
Priestman, Judith, 15, 25
Proverb, theory of, 151
Puget, Pierre, 173

Quintilian, 12

Rachilde, 33
Racine, Jean, 63, 64, 72
Ramsey, Warren, 150
Reader: competence of, 20–22; parodist as, 16, 17–18, 189, 218; represented in parody, 157, 165, 185, 186, 189, 192
Redon, Odilon, 121, 149
La Revue blanche, 65–66
La Revue wagnérienne, 129
Ribot, Théodule, 48
Richard, Noël, 69
Richardson, Samuel, 25
Riffaterre, Michael, 3, 20, 26, 227n. 37, 231n. 92
Rimbaud, Arthur, 34, 37, 58, 68, 80, 133–34
Robinson Crusoe, 66
Romanticism, relation to Decadence, 39, 42, 50–51, 53, 54, 56, 109–10, 112–14, 136
Ronsard, Pierre de, 63
Rose, Margaret, 10, 16, 17–18, 23, 25, 226n. 27
Rubens, Peter Paul, 173
Ruchon, François, 150
Russian formalists, 15, 16, 21; evolution of literary forms, theory of, 17, 24–25, 219, 230n. 83

Sade, Marquis de, 33, 38
Saint Elizabeth of Hungary. See Liszt, Franz
Salomé, 59, 107, 139, 142, 148–69, 171, 172, 212, 217, 218
—aquarium image, 150, 159–60, 237n. 76, 249nn. 26–28
—and *Hérodias*, 15, 24, 148, 149, 150, 152, 154–55, 157, 160, 161
—and Huysmans, 24, 149, 167
—and Moreau, 24, 149, 160–61, 163, 166, 167, 251n. 37
—as parody of Salomé genre, 149, 160, 248n. 7
—and *Salammbô*, 149, 150, 152, 154, 155, 161, 163, 168
—Salomé in: as astronomer, 158, 165, 166; as Decadent poet, 150, 161, 163, 171; as mad scientist, 158, 166
—themes: narcissism, 158, 160; revolution, 152–53, 156, 164; self-analysis, 164, 165; sexuality, 149, 151, 158, 160, 161, 166; the Unconscious, 150, 155, 158, 160, 161, 166
Sarcey, Francisque, 68–69
Satire, 10, 15, 17, 22, 61, 64
Saxo Grammaticus, 86, 242nn. 15, 20
Scaliger, Julius Caesar, 227n. 33
Le Scapin, 61
Schopenhauer, Arthur, 5, 147, 178, 202; on art, 49, 144; influence on Decadence, 47–49, 54; on love and women, 5, 46, 48, 130, 131, 132, 144, 147; pessimism of, 5, 47–49; popularization in France, 48, 235n. 47; the Will, 6, 48–49, 162, 202
Schwind, Moritz von, 107, 243n. 7
Self-critical techniques of parody, 18–20. See also *Moralités légendaires*: devices of parody in; Parody: scepticism of; Parody: self-criticism of
Seneca, L. Annaeus, 252n. 12
Shakespeare, William, 15, 16, 86, 220 (see also *Hamlet* [Shakespeare]); *Macbeth*, 72, 97, 105, 106, 118, 123–24, 125; *The Tempest*, 200, 209
Shlonsky, Tuvia, 10, 23
Sophocles, 72, 91
Spinoza, Baruch, 178, 202; and pessimism, 45–46
Stendhal (Henri Beyle), 45, 166

Index

Stephan, P., 60
Sterne, Laurence: *Tristram Shandy*, 25
Subjective narrative, 9, 27
Swedenborg, Emmanuel, 40, 54, 110
Symbolism, and Decadence, interchangeability of terms, 34–36. *See also* Decadence

Tailhade, Laurent, 68
Taine, Hippolyte, 43–44, 46–47
Target, 19, 21, 24–25, 33, 70, 134, 179, 183, 188, 216–18 *passim;* relation to model, 2, 13, 14–17, 64, 217
Theory, nature of, 2–3
Thornton, R. K. R., 60
Thorvaldsen, Bertel, 91
Tiepolo, Giambattista, 194
Titian (Tiziano Vecelli), 173
Tomachevski, B., 231n. 91
Toulet, Paul-Jean, 65
Transformation, 16, 22–26 *passim,* 104, 110, 127, 175, 179, 221. *See also* Parody: distortion in
Travesty, 10, 14, 226n. 26
Trézenik, Léo, 57–58, 68, 70
Tynjanov, Juri, 16–17, 21, 230n. 83

Unconscious, the, 56, 184, 201–2; in *Hamlet,* 76, 80, 96; as metaphysical Absolute, 49, 50, 138, 178, 181–82; in *Salomé,* 150, 155, 159, 160, 161, 164, 165

Vanier, Léon, 69
Veber, Pierre, 66–68
Verlaine, Paul, 31, 34, 37, 43, 52–55 *passim,* 58, 216; *Les Poètes maudits,* 47, 70; parodied, 66, 68, 69, 71
Veronese, Paolo, 173
Vicaire, Gabriel, 69
Viélé-Griffin, Francis, 55
Villiers de l'Isle-Adam, Auguste, comte de, 8, 31, 34, 52, 54, 55–56, 158
Villon, François, 63
Virgil, 41, 65, 204

Wagner, Richard, 15, 63, 64, 200, 245n. 3; model for *Lohengrin,* 128–29, 134–35, 141–42, 145, 148
Wagnerism, and Decadence, 35, 37, 58, 129
Wolfram von Eschenbach, 135
Wyzewa, Téodor de, 32, 37, 58, 104, 129

Zola, Emile, 37, 62, 63

www.ingramcontent.com/pod-product-compliance
Lightning Source LLC
Chambersburg PA
CBHW020944230426
43666CB00005B/153